Midnight Secretary

Volume 2

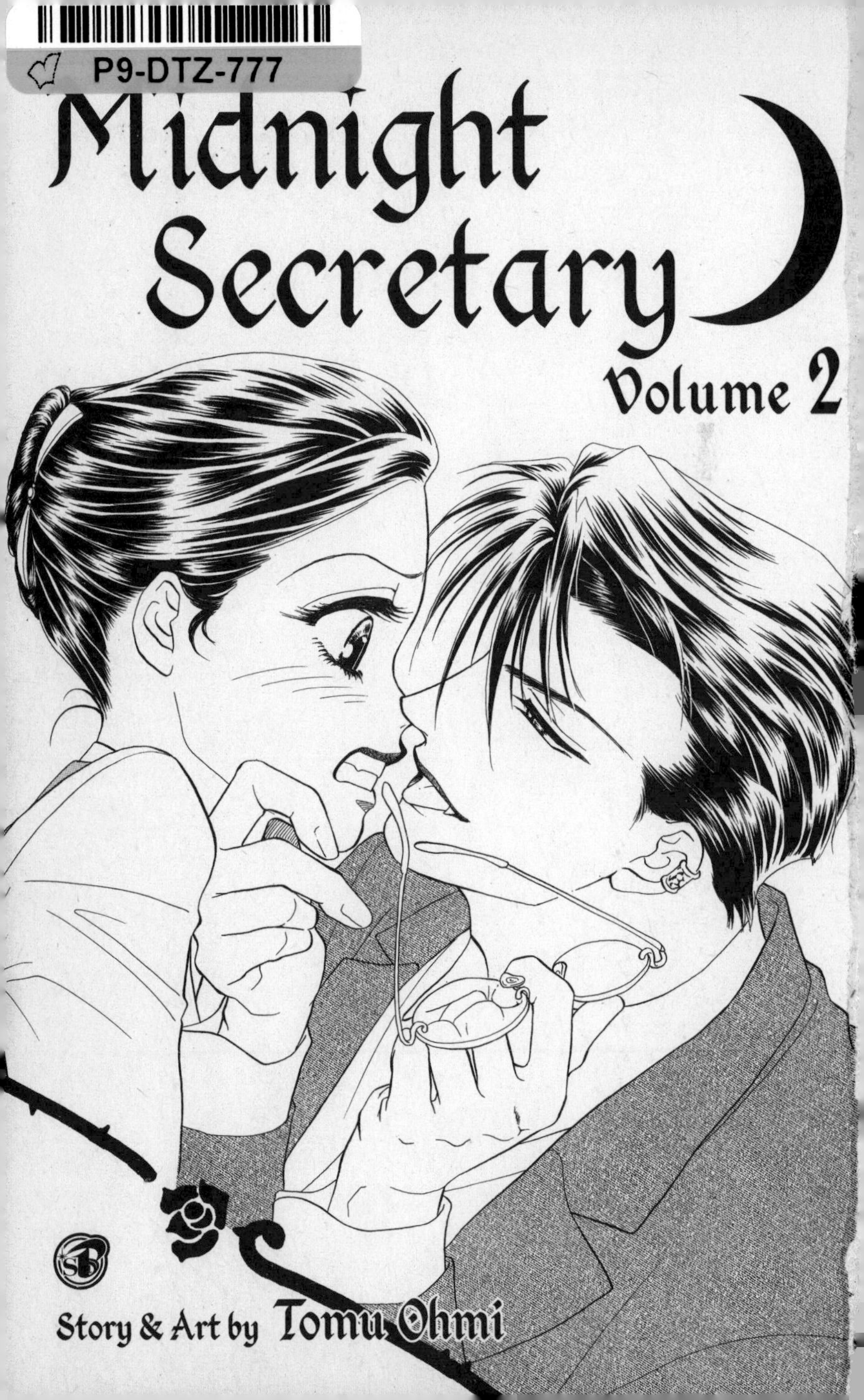

Story & Art by Tomu Ohmi

Midnight Secretary Volume 2

—Character—

Kaya Satozuka (22)
Kaya is a talented woman who has been working at Tohma Corp. for two years. Because of her exceptional skills, she's been selected as the new executive secretary for the demanding managing director, Kyohei Tohma. Her father passed away six years ago and she lives with her mother. Kaya is uptight, serious, and quite stubborn. She has a complex about her baby face.

Kyohei Tohma (26)
Managing director of Tohma Corp., a major tableware manufacturer. He is the younger son of the company president. His older brother Masaki is the senior director. Kyohei is good at his job, but he's demanding and arrogant and has a reputation as a womanizer. He is also a vampire.

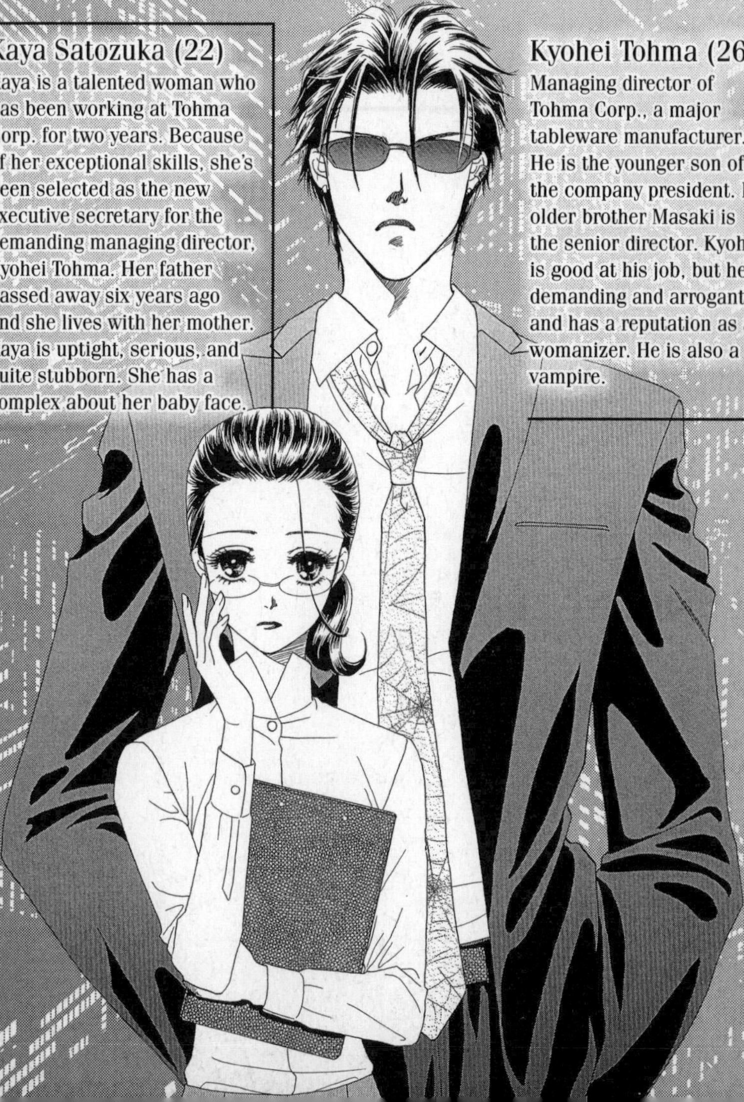

–Story–

Kaya started her new position as Kyohei's secretary, and while he reviled her for being unattractive and having no sex appeal, her exceptional abilities soon gained her his professional respect. But one night Kaya becomes an accidental voyeur to one of Kyohei's late-night trysts in his office and sees way more than she bargained for. In the midst of a passionate embrace, Kyohei unveils a pair of fangs and feeds off his orgasmic partner!

As it turns out, Kyohei is a vampire from a prestigious clan and subsists on the blood of beautiful women. Every night he strokes a woman to ecstasy and feasts on her pleasure-spiced blood. He can't bear strong sunlight or the expressions of Christian faith, but in all other ways he can pass as human even though he despises them.

Kyohei's contempt for humanity angers Kaya, but she continues to work as his secretary due to her innate sense of responsibility. She's even willing to give up some blood in the line of duty. But she soon realizes that she hopes he wants more than just her blood!

Midnight Secretary

Volume 2

Contents

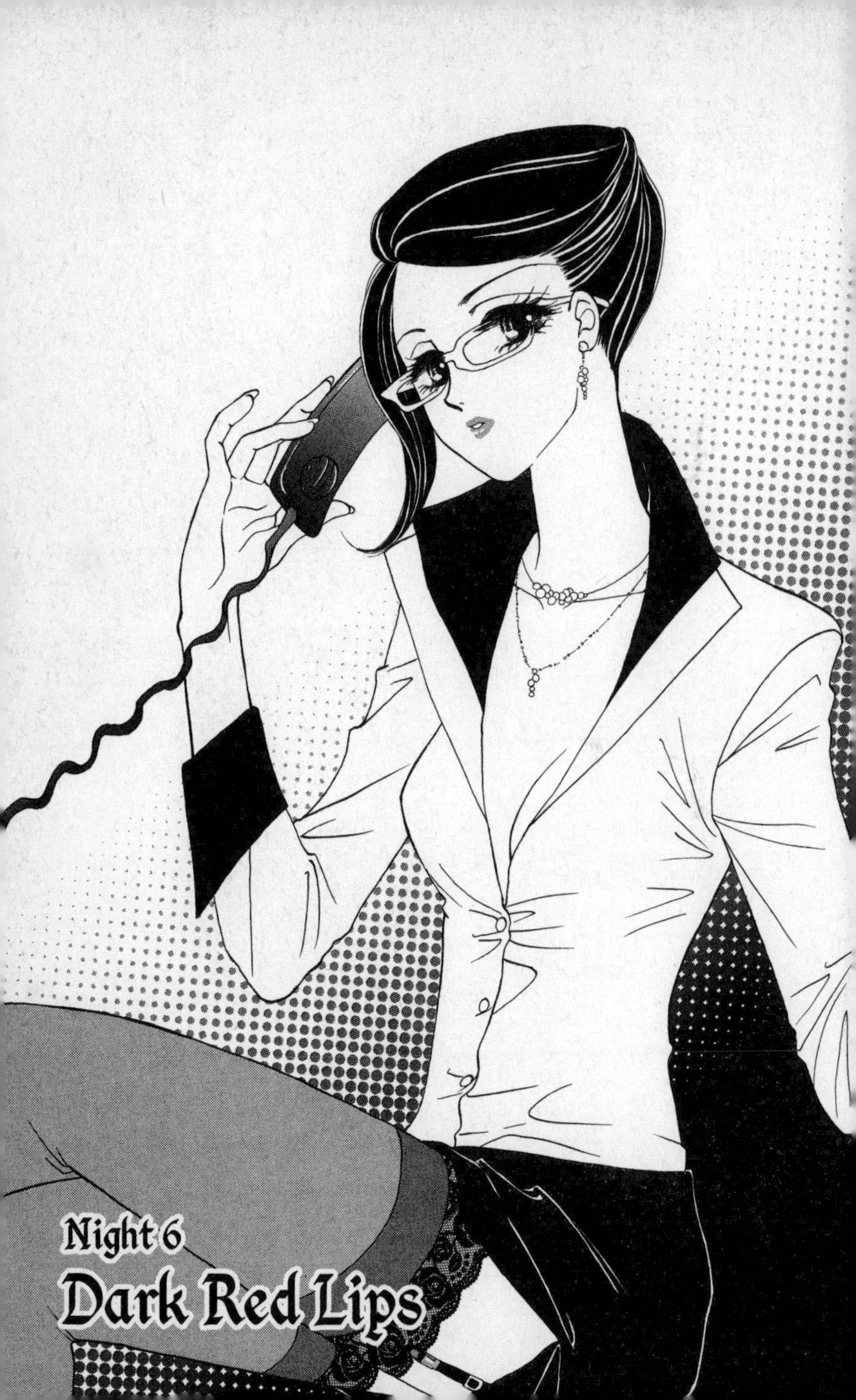
Night 6
Dark Red Lips

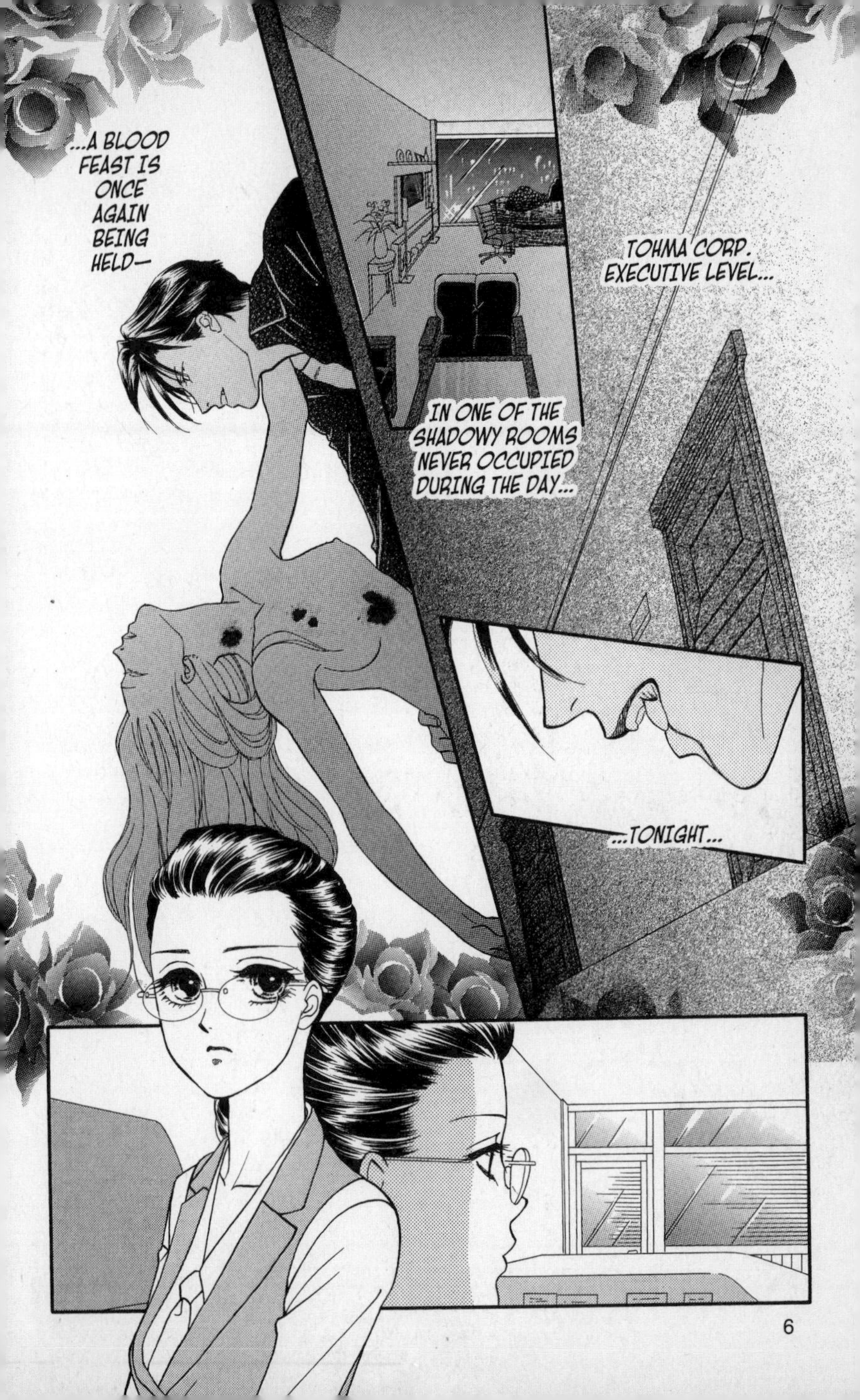
TOHMA CORP. EXECUTIVE LEVEL...
IN ONE OF THE SHADOWY ROOMS NEVER OCCUPIED DURING THE DAY...
...TONIGHT...
...A BLOOD FEAST IS ONCE AGAIN BEING HELD—

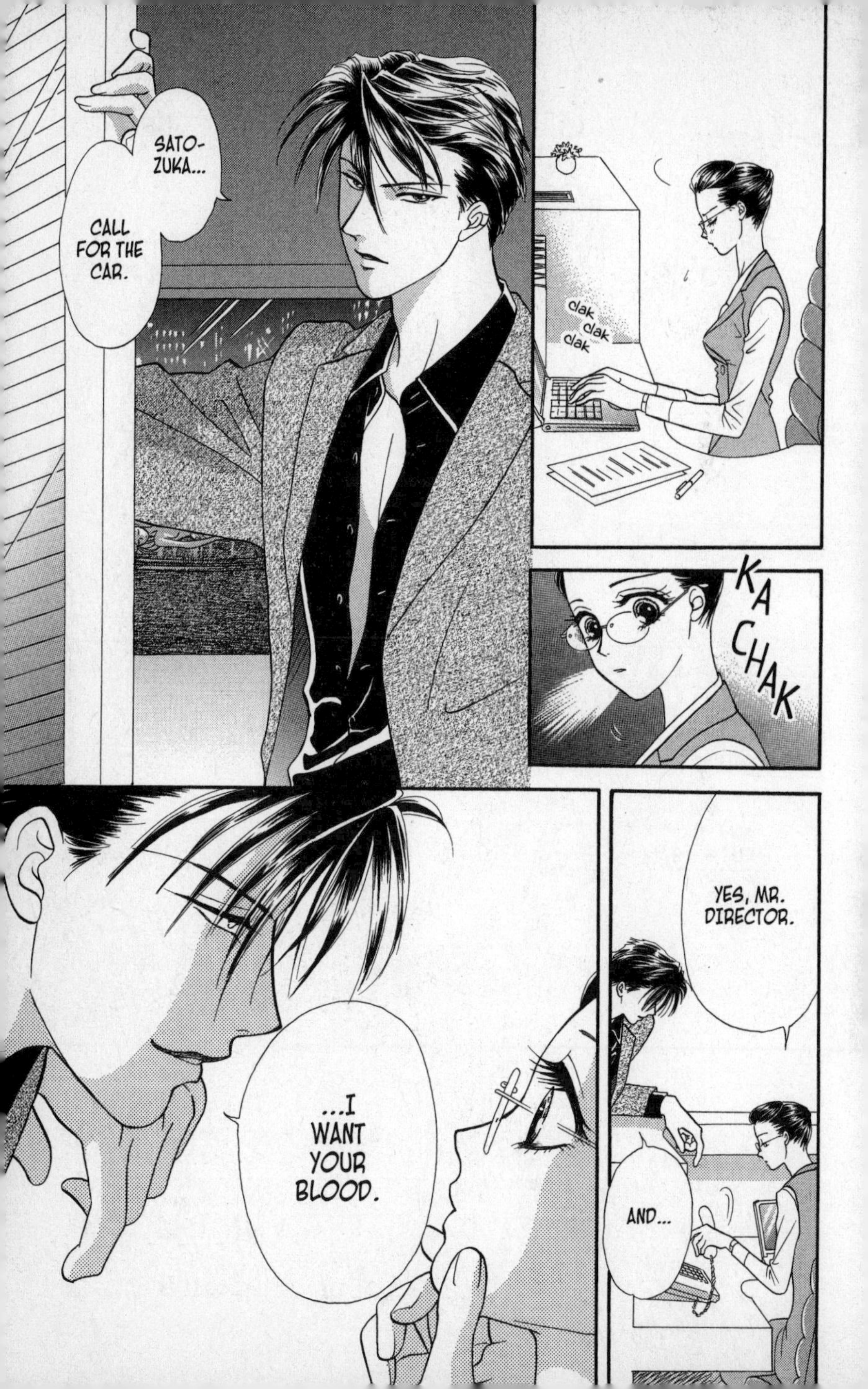
clak clak clak
KA CHAK
SATO-ZUKA...
CALL FOR THE CAR.
YES, MR. DIRECTOR.
AND...
...I WANT YOUR BLOOD.

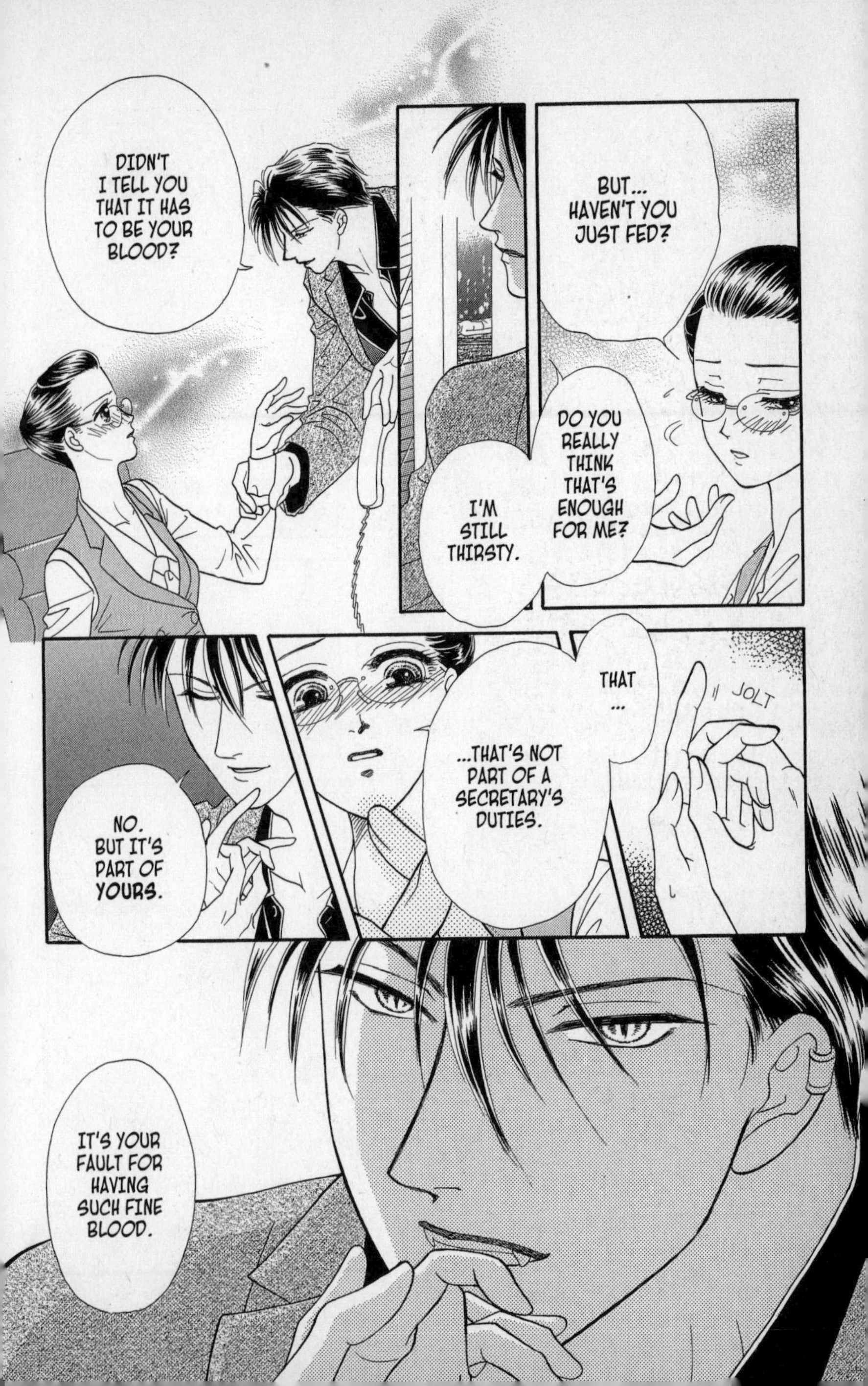
BUT... HAVEN'T YOU JUST FED?
DO YOU REALLY THINK THAT'S ENOUGH FOR ME?
I'M STILL THIRSTY.
DIDN'T I TELL YOU THAT IT HAS TO BE YOUR BLOOD?
JOLT
THAT ...
...THAT'S NOT PART OF A SECRETARY'S DUTIES.
NO. BUT IT'S PART OF YOURS.
IT'S YOUR FAULT FOR HAVING SUCH FINE BLOOD.

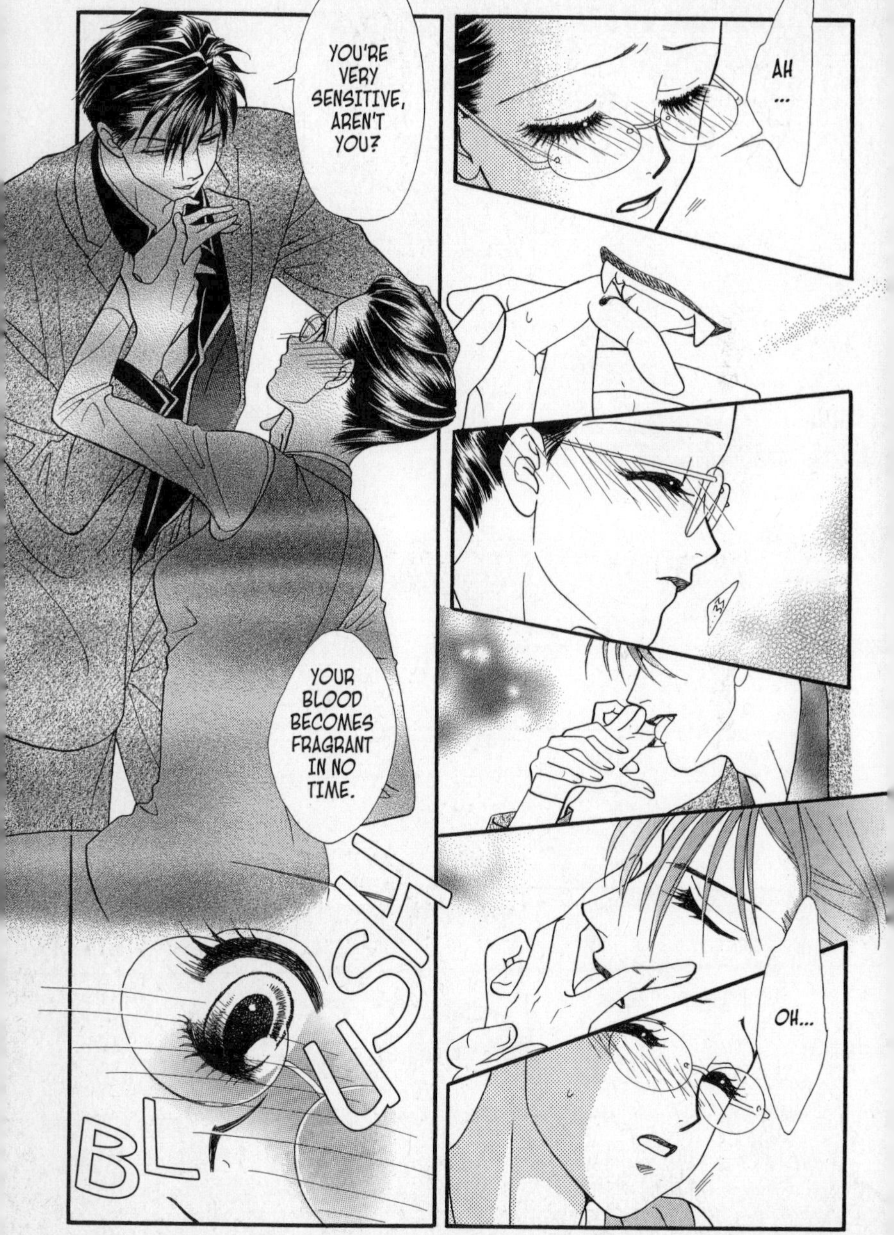
AH ...
OH...
YOU'RE VERY SENSITIVE, AREN'T YOU?
YOUR BLOOD BECOMES FRAGRANT IN NO TIME.
BLUSH

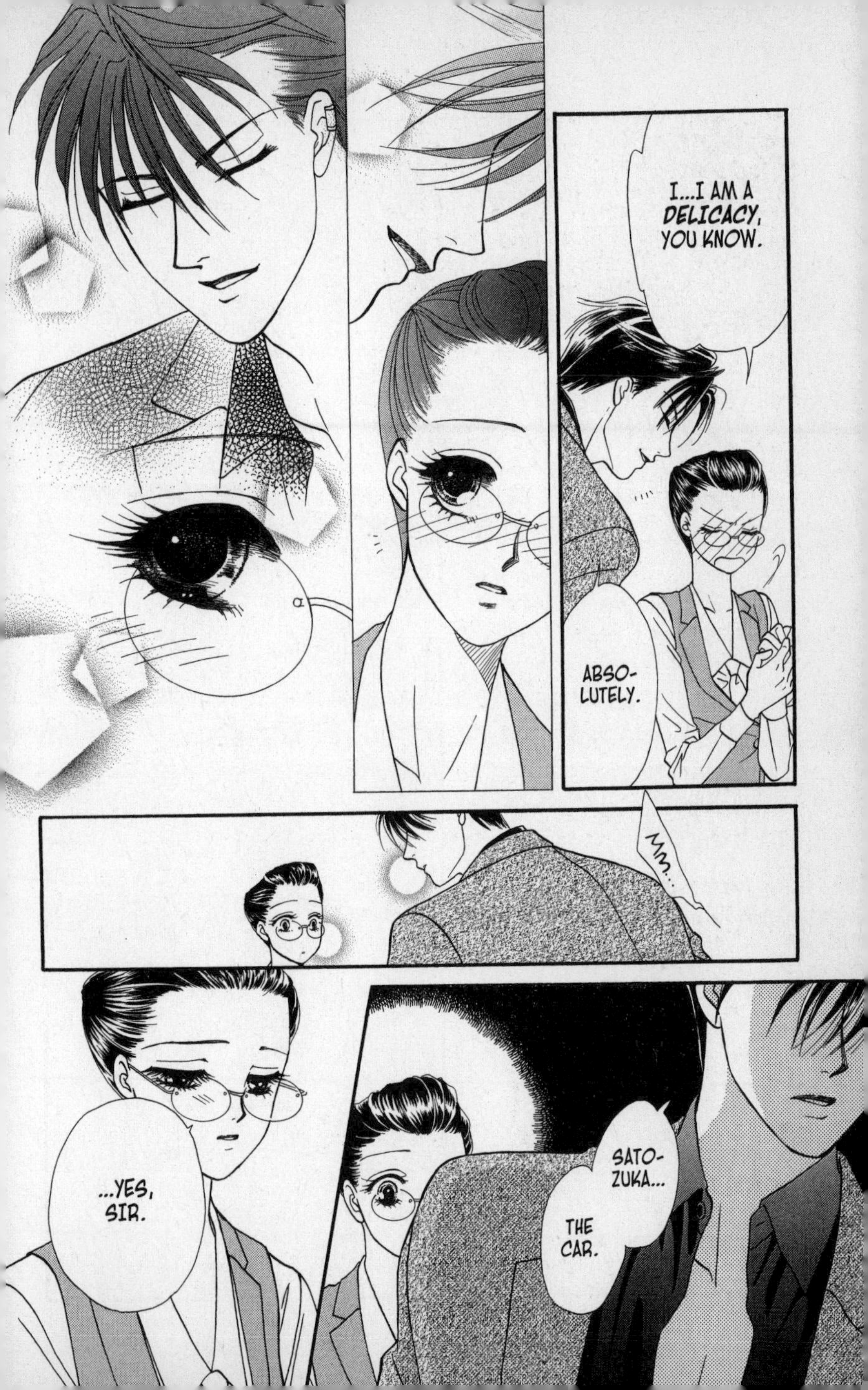
I...I AM A DELICACY, YOU KNOW.
ABSO-LUTELY.
MM...
SATO-ZUKA...
THE CAR.
...YES, SIR.

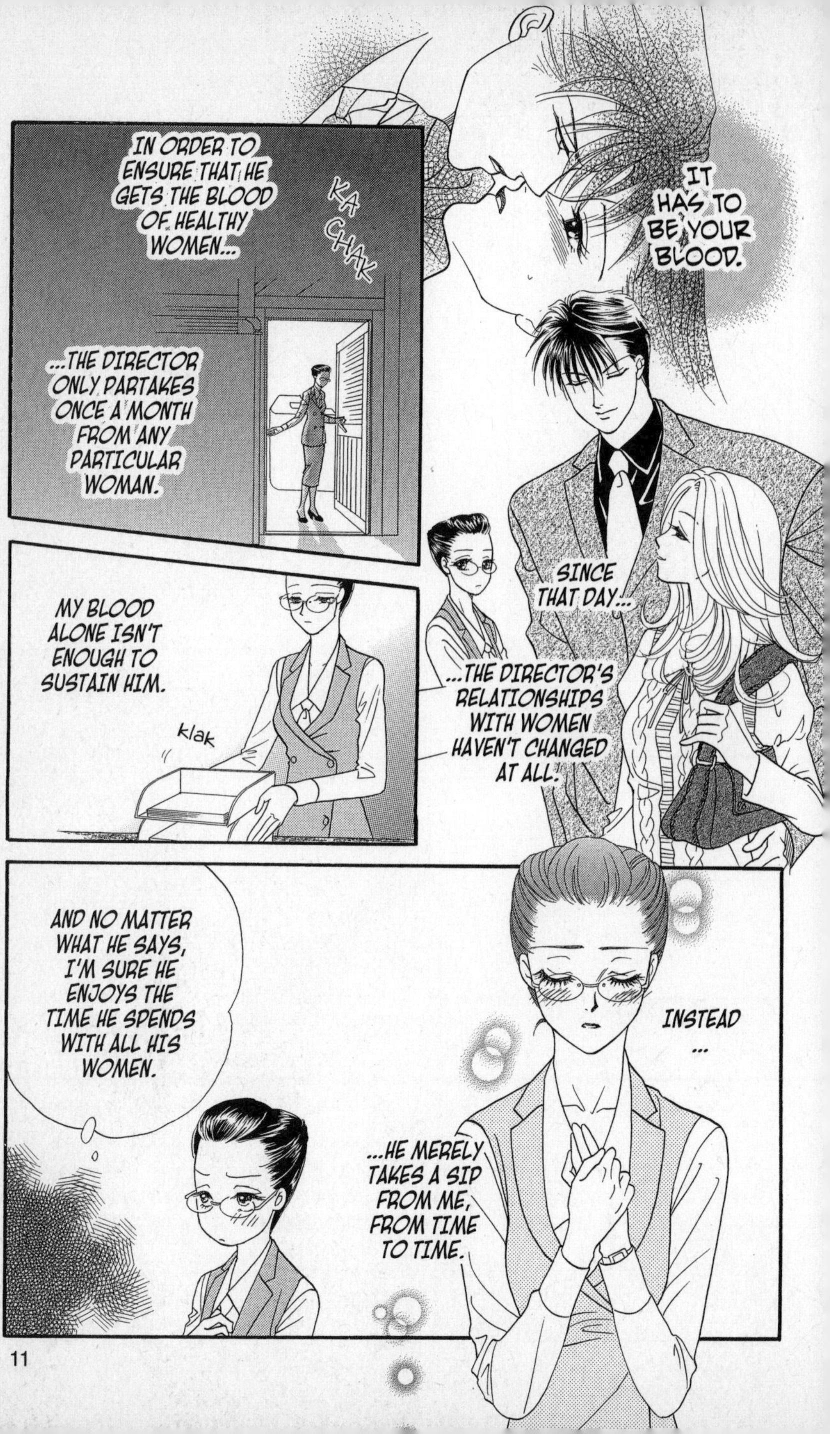
IT HAS TO BE YOUR BLOOD.
SINCE THAT DAY...
...THE DIRECTOR'S RELATIONSHIPS WITH WOMEN HAVEN'T CHANGED AT ALL.
IN ORDER TO ENSURE THAT HE GETS THE BLOOD OF HEALTHY WOMEN...
KA CHAK
...THE DIRECTOR ONLY PARTAKES ONCE A MONTH FROM ANY PARTICULAR WOMAN.
MY BLOOD ALONE ISN'T ENOUGH TO SUSTAIN HIM.
klak
INSTEAD...
...HE MERELY TAKES A SIP FROM ME, FROM TIME TO TIME.
AND NO MATTER WHAT HE SAYS, I'M SURE HE ENJOYS THE TIME HE SPENDS WITH ALL HIS WOMEN.

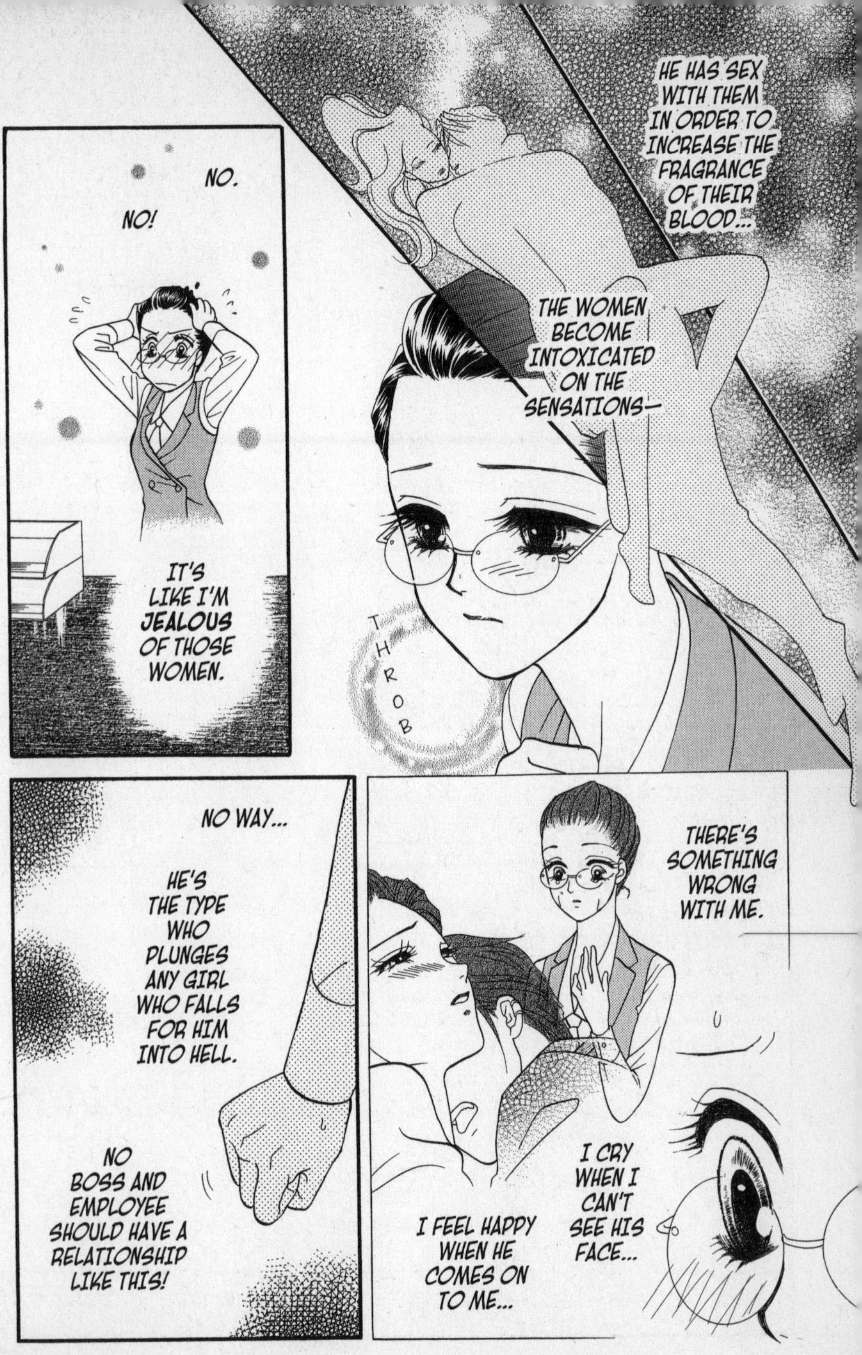
HE HAS SEX WITH THEM IN ORDER TO INCREASE THE FRAGRANCE OF THEIR BLOOD...
THE WOMEN BECOME INTOXICATED ON THE SENSATIONS—
THROB
NO.
NO!
IT'S LIKE I'M **JEALOUS** OF THOSE WOMEN.
THERE'S SOMETHING WRONG WITH ME.
I CRY WHEN I CAN'T SEE HIS FACE...
I FEEL HAPPY WHEN HE COMES ON TO ME...
NO WAY...
HE'S THE TYPE WHO PLUNGES ANY GIRL WHO FALLS FOR HIM INTO HELL.
NO BOSS AND EMPLOYEE SHOULD HAVE A RELATIONSHIP LIKE THIS!

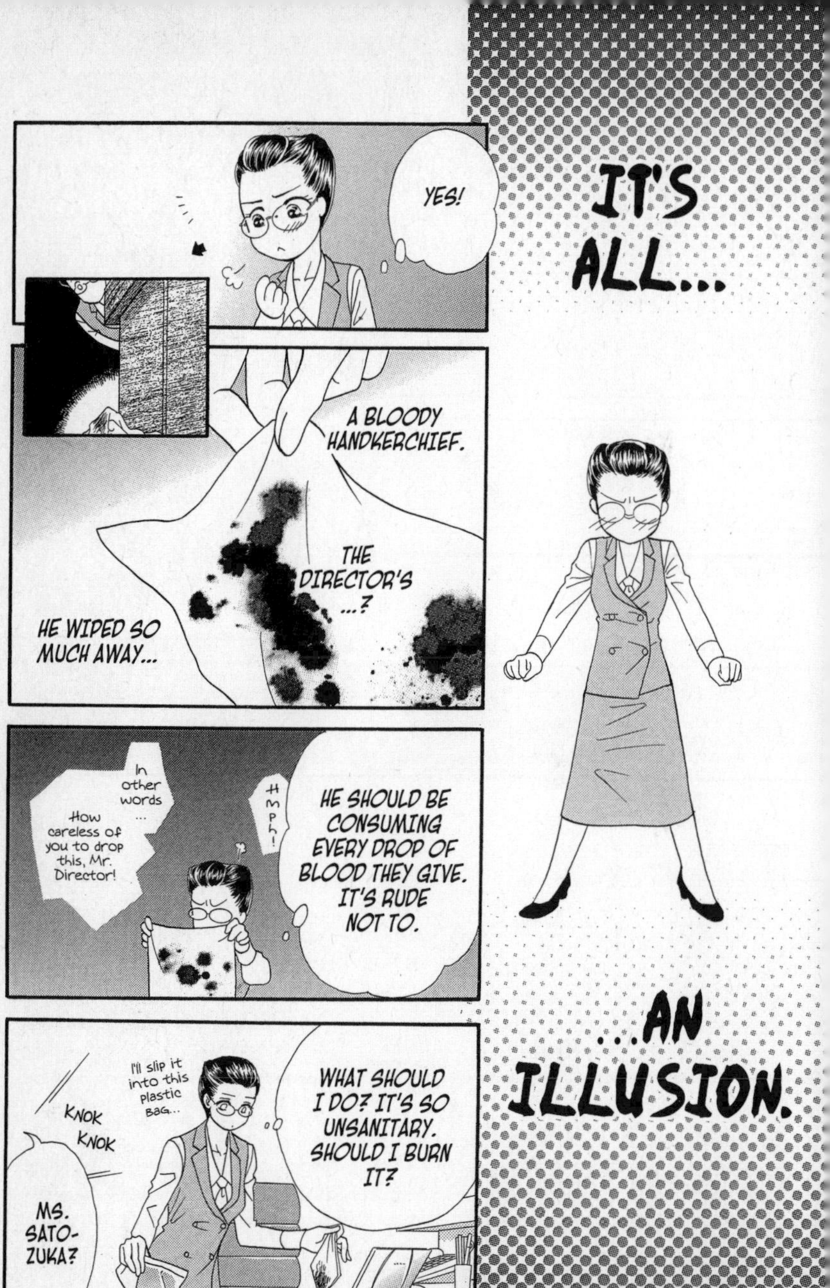

IT'S ALL...
...AN ILLUSION.
YES!
A BLOODY HANDKERCHIEF.
THE DIRECTOR'S ...?
HE WIPED SO MUCH AWAY...
HE SHOULD BE CONSUMING EVERY DROP OF BLOOD THEY GIVE. IT'S RUDE NOT TO.
Hmph!
In other words...
How careless of you to drop this, Mr. Director!
WHAT SHOULD I DO? IT'S SO UNSANITARY. SHOULD I BURN IT?
I'll slip it into this plastic bag...
KNOK KNOK
MS. SATO-ZUKA?

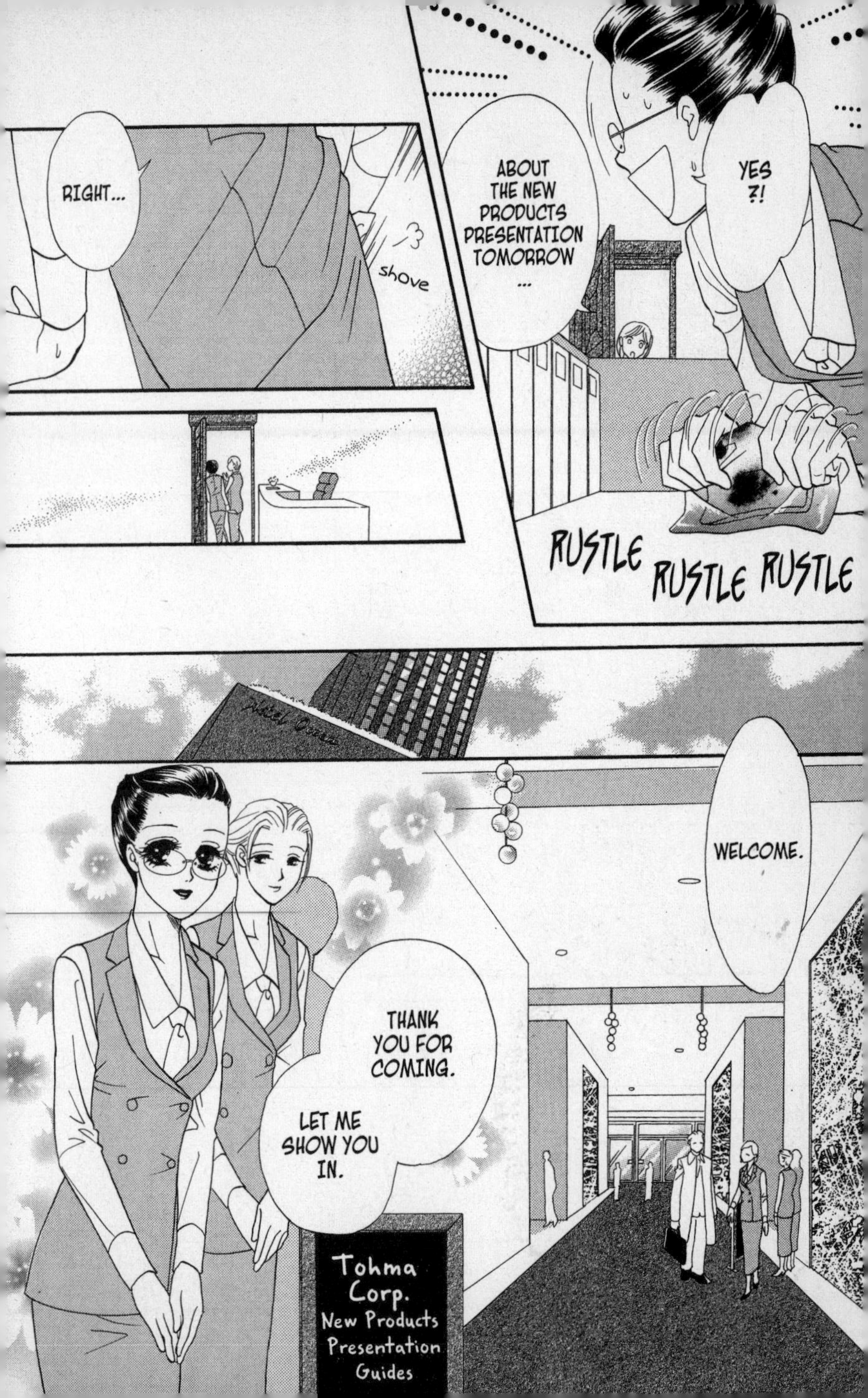
YES ?!
ABOUT THE NEW PRODUCTS PRESENTATION TOMORROW ...
RUSTLE RUSTLE RUSTLE
RIGHT...
shove
WELCOME.
THANK YOU FOR COMING.
LET ME SHOW YOU IN.
Tohma Corp. New Products Presentation Guides

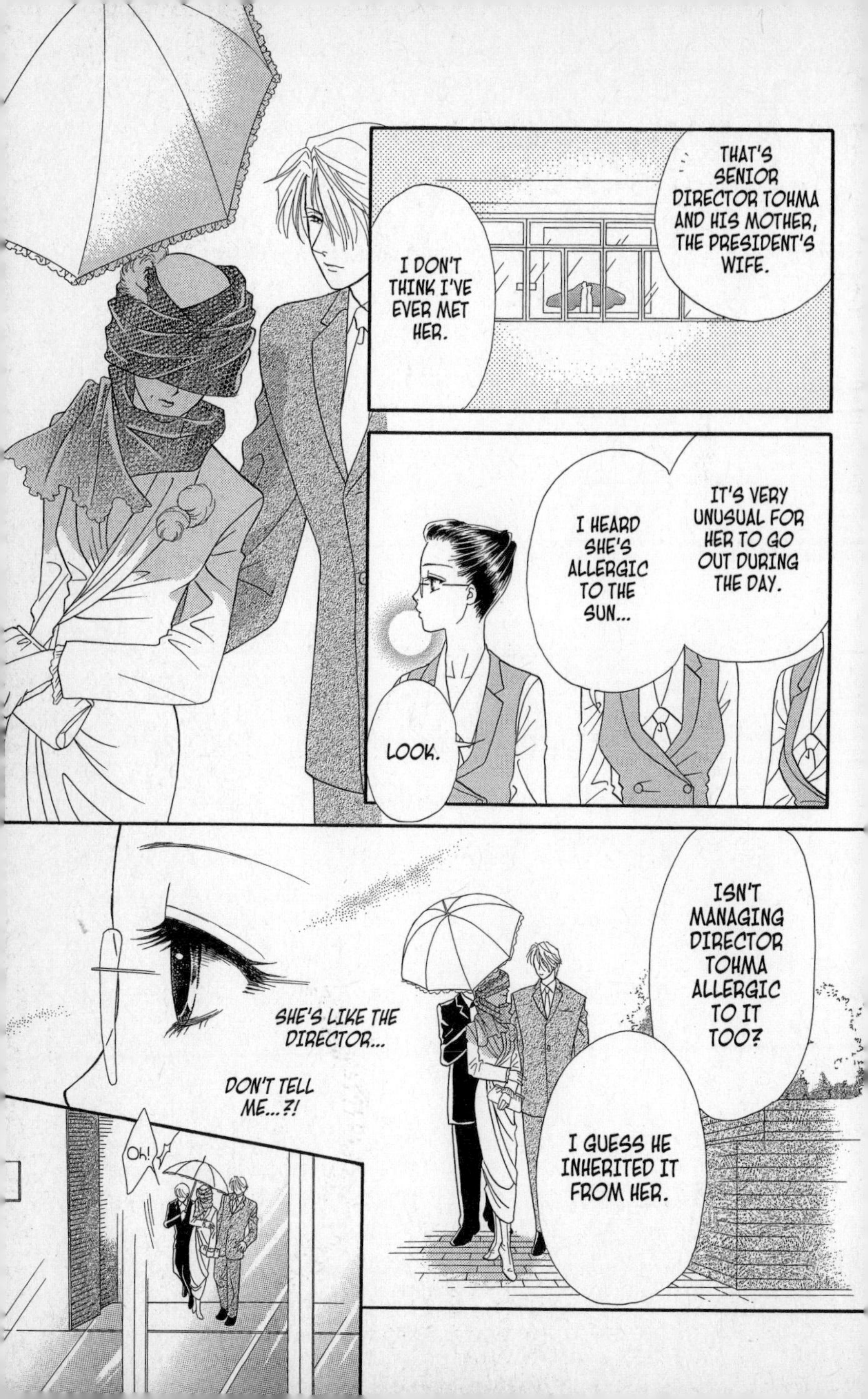
THAT'S SENIOR DIRECTOR TOHMA AND HIS MOTHER, THE PRESIDENT'S WIFE.
I DON'T THINK I'VE EVER MET HER.
IT'S VERY UNUSUAL FOR HER TO GO OUT DURING THE DAY.
I HEARD SHE'S ALLERGIC TO THE SUN...
LOOK.
ISN'T MANAGING DIRECTOR TOHMA ALLERGIC TO IT TOO?
I GUESS HE INHERITED IT FROM HER.
SHE'S LIKE THE DIRECTOR...
DON'T TELL ME...?!
Oh!

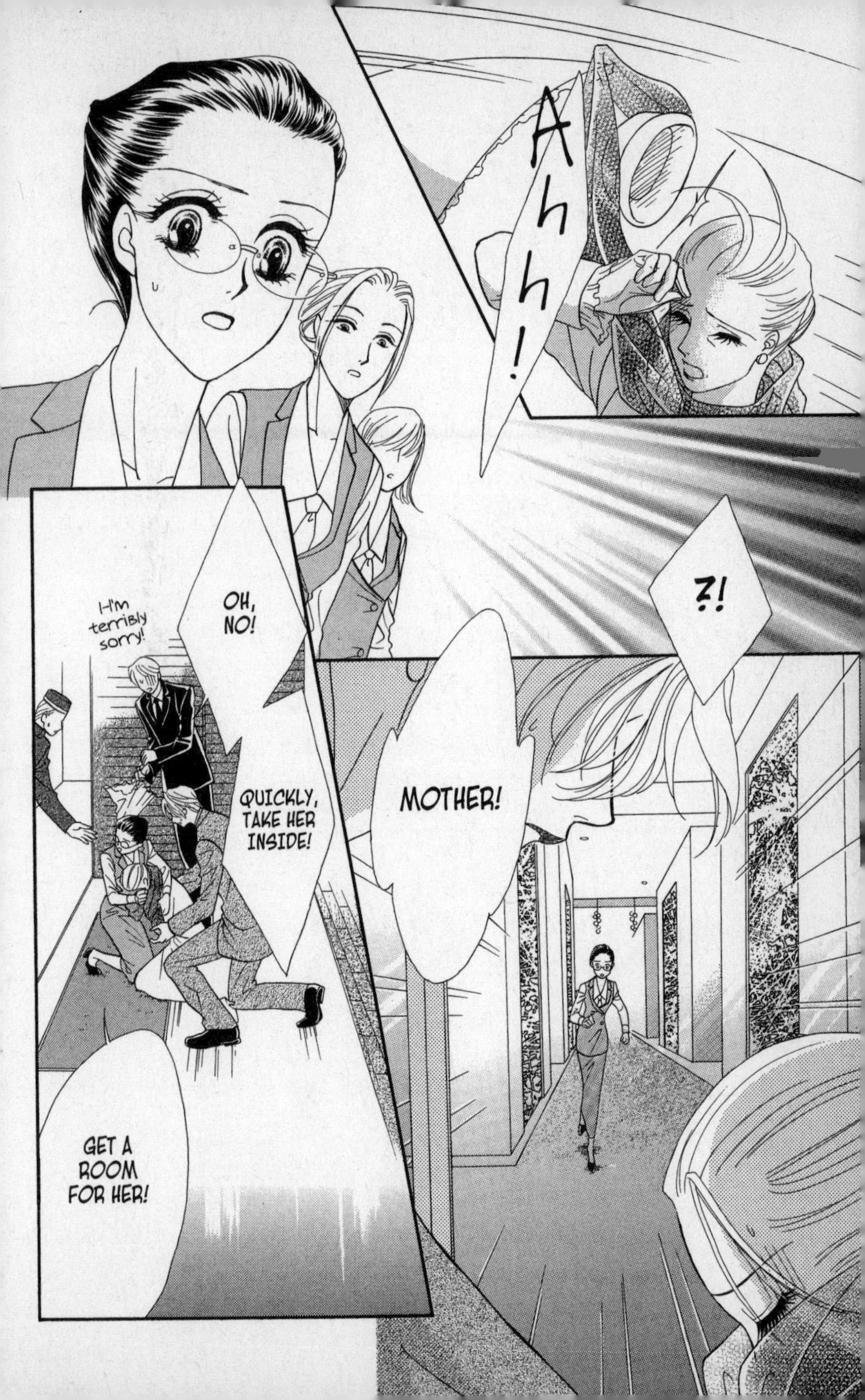
Ahh!
?!
MOTHER!
OH, NO!
I-I'm terribly sorry!
QUICKLY, TAKE HER INSIDE!
GET A ROOM FOR HER!

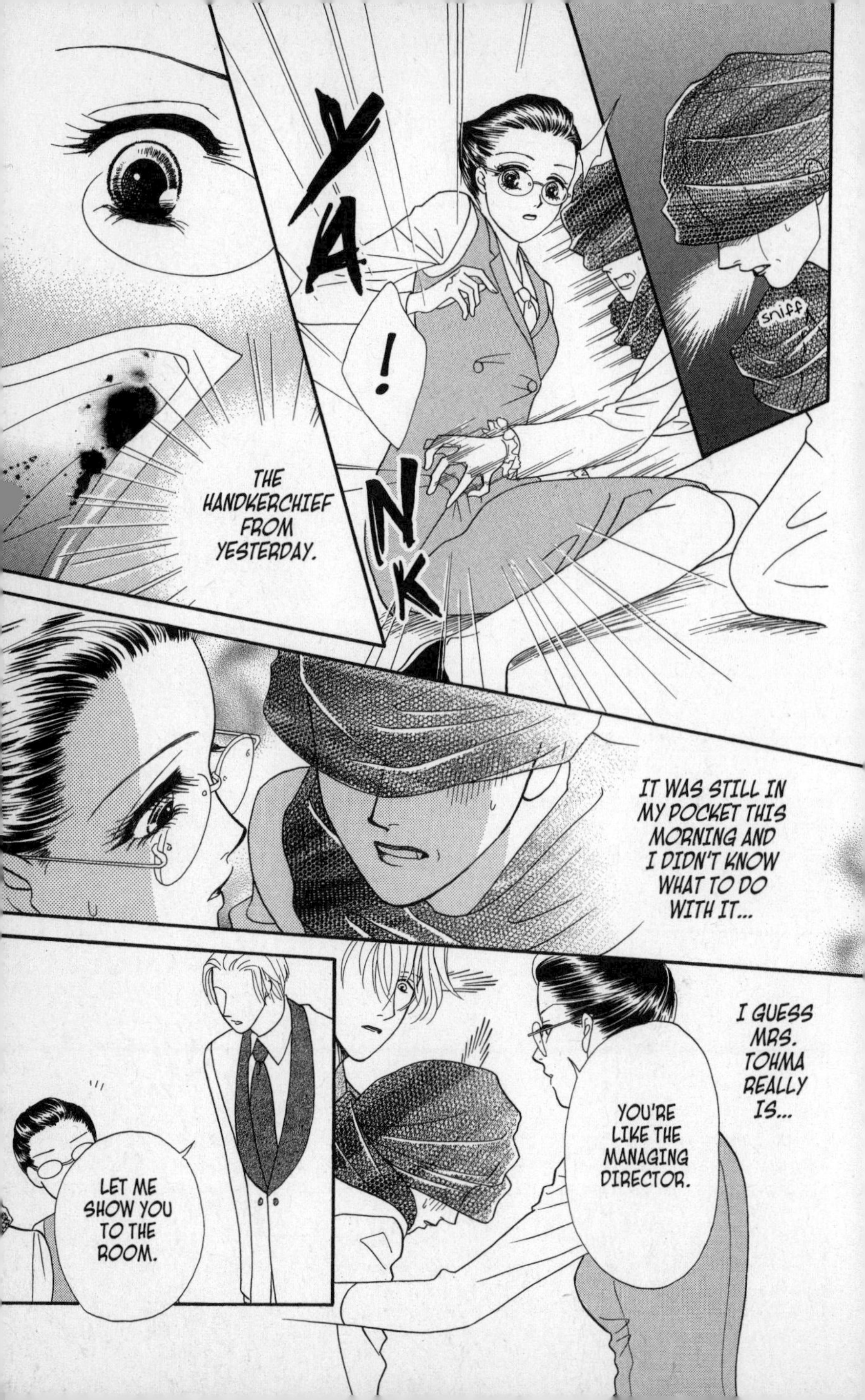
sniff
YANK!
THE HANDKERCHIEF FROM YESTERDAY.
IT WAS STILL IN MY POCKET THIS MORNING AND I DIDN'T KNOW WHAT TO DO WITH IT...
I GUESS MRS. TOHMA REALLY IS...
YOU'RE LIKE THE MANAGING DIRECTOR.
LET ME SHOW YOU TO THE ROOM.

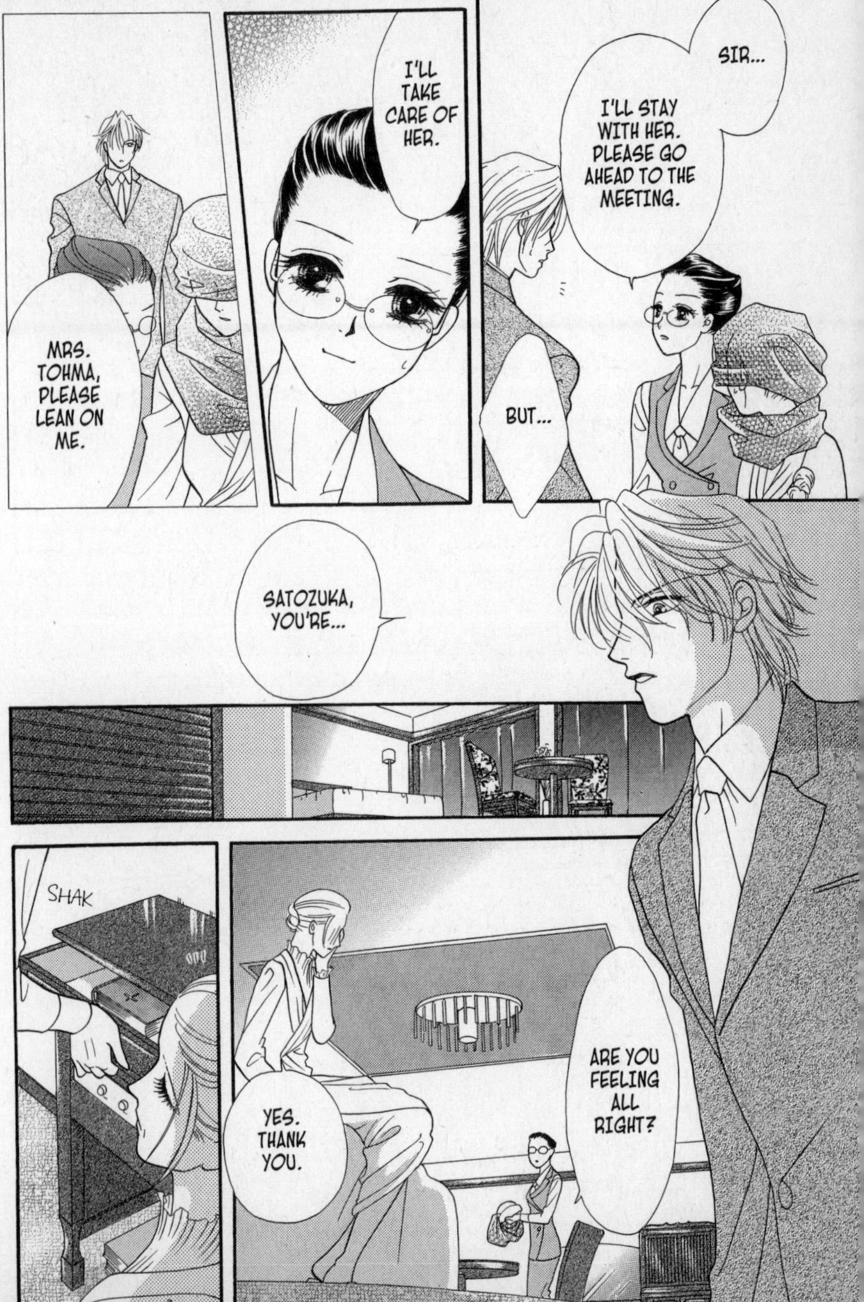
SIR...
I'LL STAY WITH HER. PLEASE GO AHEAD TO THE MEETING.
BUT...
I'LL TAKE CARE OF HER.
MRS. TOHMA, PLEASE LEAN ON ME.
SATOZUKA, YOU'RE...
ARE YOU FEELING ALL RIGHT?
YES. THANK YOU.
SHAK

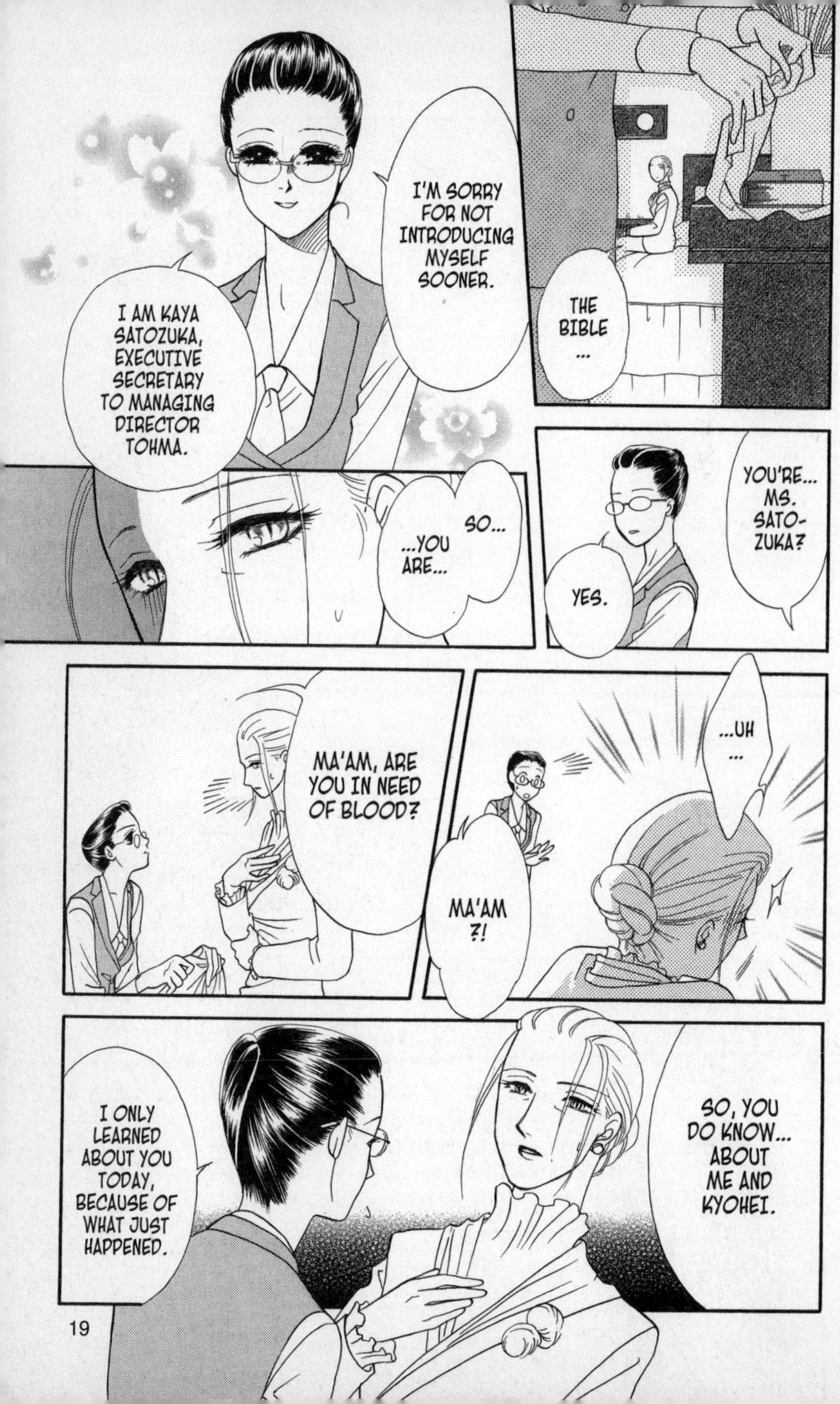
THE BIBLE ...
I'M SORRY FOR NOT INTRODUCING MYSELF SOONER.
I AM KAYA SATOZUKA, EXECUTIVE SECRETARY TO MANAGING DIRECTOR TOHMA.
YOU'RE... MS. SATO-ZUKA?
YES.
SO...
...YOU ARE...
...UH ...
MA'AM ?!
MA'AM, ARE YOU IN NEED OF BLOOD?
SO, YOU DO KNOW... ABOUT ME AND KYOHEI.
I ONLY LEARNED ABOUT YOU TODAY, BECAUSE OF WHAT JUST HAPPENED.

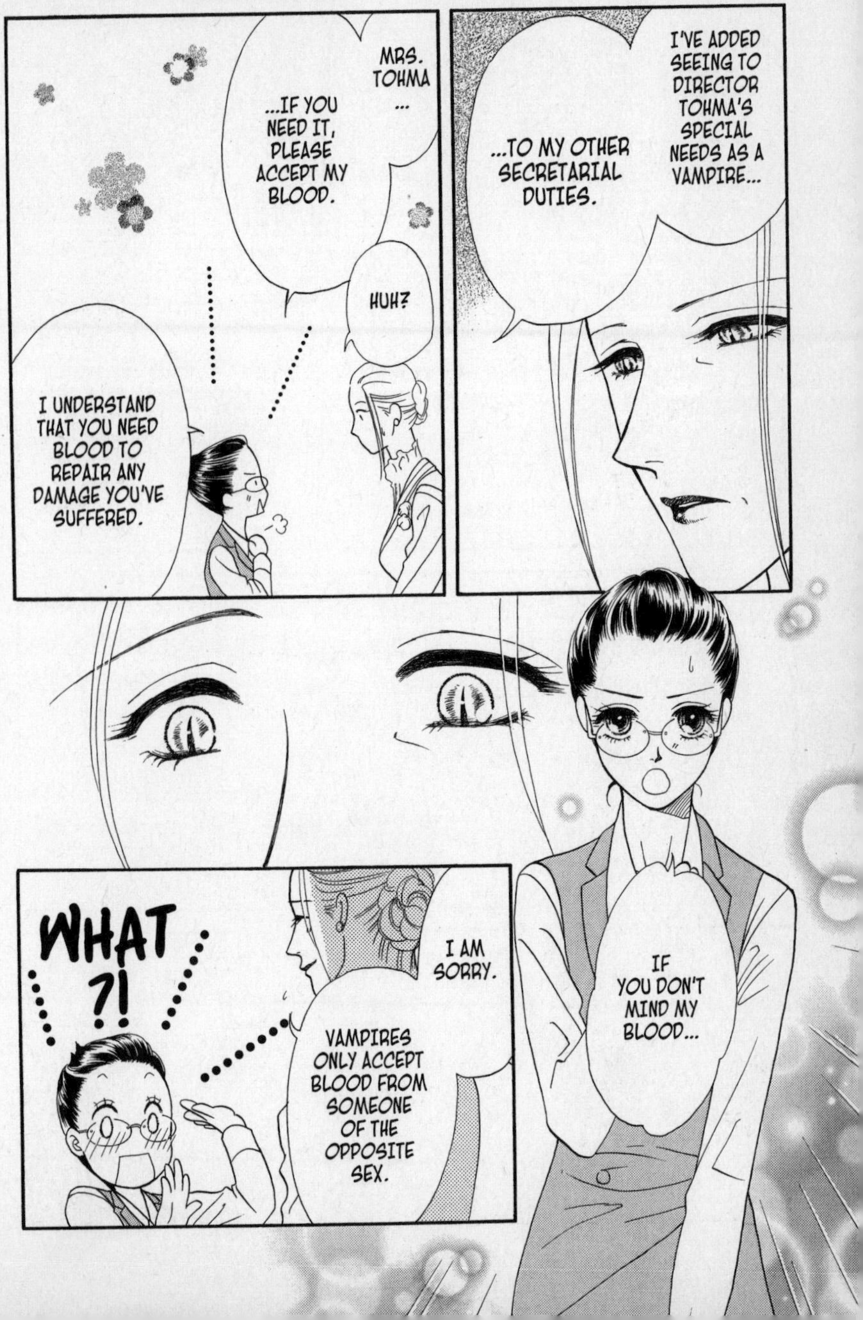
I'VE ADDED SEEING TO DIRECTOR TOHMA'S SPECIAL NEEDS AS A VAMPIRE...
...TO MY OTHER SECRETARIAL DUTIES.
MRS. TOHMA ...
...IF YOU NEED IT, PLEASE ACCEPT MY BLOOD.
HUH?
I UNDERSTAND THAT YOU NEED BLOOD TO REPAIR ANY DAMAGE YOU'VE SUFFERED.
IF YOU DON'T MIND MY BLOOD...
I AM SORRY.
VAMPIRES ONLY ACCEPT BLOOD FROM SOMEONE OF THE OPPOSITE SEX.
WHAT ?!

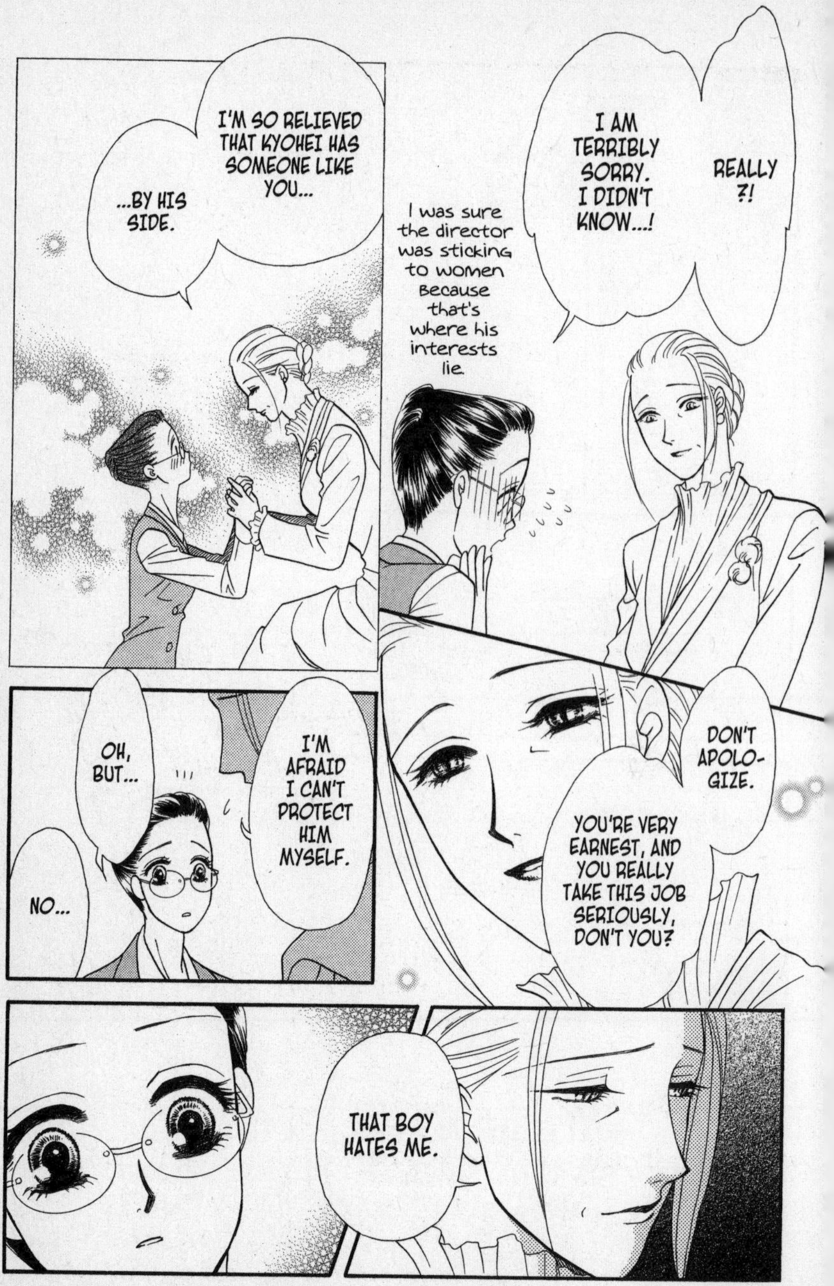
REALLY ?!
I AM TERRIBLY SORRY. I DIDN'T KNOW...!
I was sure the director was sticking to women because that's where his interests lie.
I'M SO RELIEVED THAT KYOHEI HAS SOMEONE LIKE YOU...
...BY HIS SIDE.
DON'T APOLO-GIZE.
YOU'RE VERY EARNEST, AND YOU REALLY TAKE THIS JOB SERIOUSLY, DON'T YOU?
I'M AFRAID I CAN'T PROTECT HIM MYSELF.
OH, BUT...
NO...
THAT BOY HATES ME.

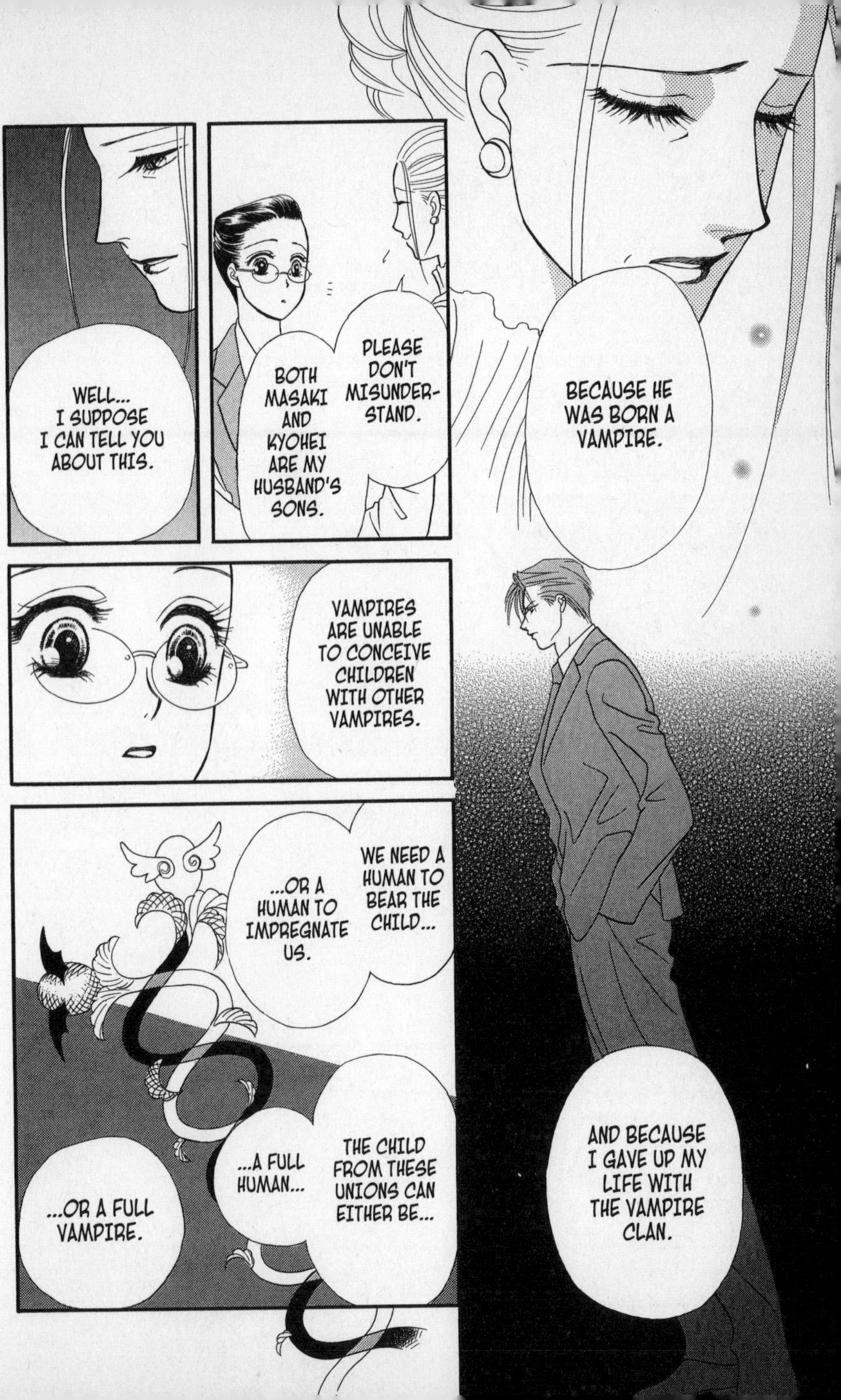
PLEASE DON'T MISUNDERSTAND.
BOTH MASAKI AND KYOHEI ARE MY HUSBAND'S SONS.
WELL... I SUPPOSE I CAN TELL YOU ABOUT THIS.
BECAUSE HE WAS BORN A VAMPIRE.
VAMPIRES ARE UNABLE TO CONCEIVE CHILDREN WITH OTHER VAMPIRES.
WE NEED A HUMAN TO BEAR THE CHILD...
...OR A HUMAN TO IMPREGNATE US.
THE CHILD FROM THESE UNIONS CAN EITHER BE...
...A FULL HUMAN...
...OR A FULL VAMPIRE.
AND BECAUSE I GAVE UP MY LIFE WITH THE VAMPIRE CLAN.

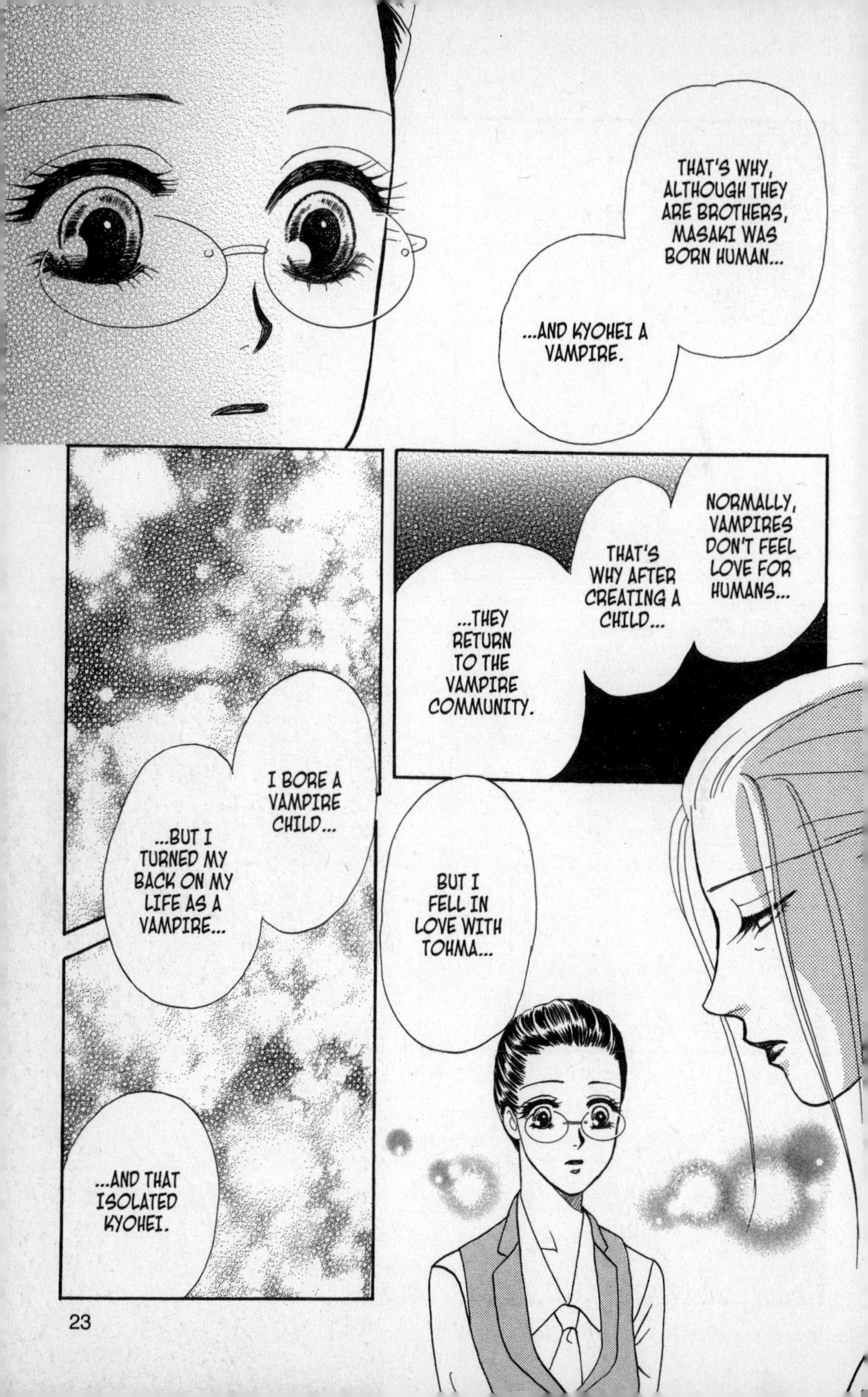
THAT'S WHY, ALTHOUGH THEY ARE BROTHERS, MASAKI WAS BORN HUMAN...
...AND KYOHEI A VAMPIRE.
NORMALLY, VAMPIRES DON'T FEEL LOVE FOR HUMANS...
THAT'S WHY AFTER CREATING A CHILD...
...THEY RETURN TO THE VAMPIRE COMMUNITY.
BUT I FELL IN LOVE WITH TOHMA...
I BORE A VAMPIRE CHILD...
...BUT I TURNED MY BACK ON MY LIFE AS A VAMPIRE...
...AND THAT ISOLATED KYOHEI.

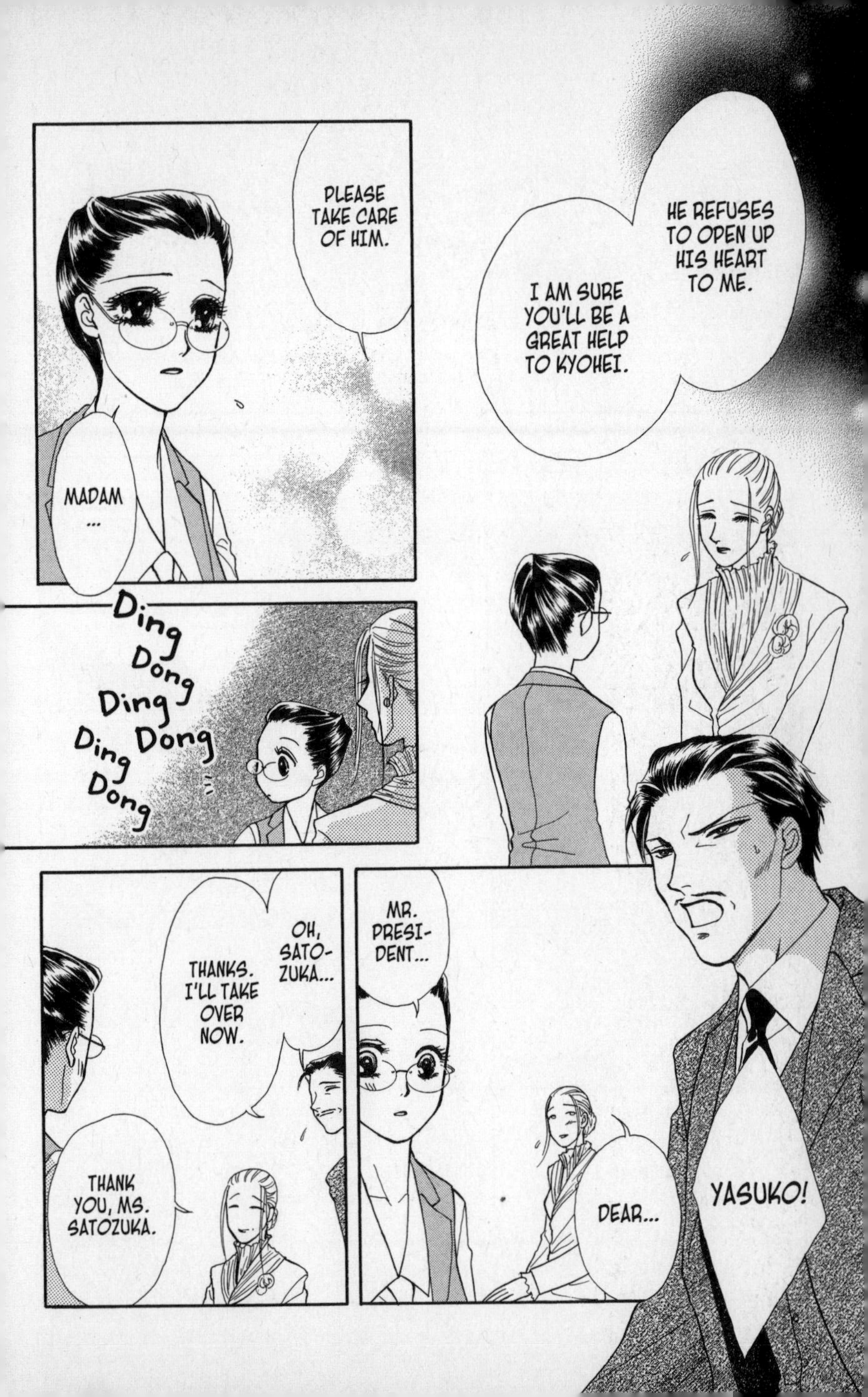
HE REFUSES TO OPEN UP HIS HEART TO ME.
I AM SURE YOU'LL BE A GREAT HELP TO KYOHEI.
PLEASE TAKE CARE OF HIM.
MADAM ...
Ding Dong Ding Dong Ding Dong
YASUKO!
DEAR...
MR. PRESIDENT...
OH, SATOZUKA...
THANKS. I'LL TAKE OVER NOW.
THANK YOU, MS. SATOZUKA.

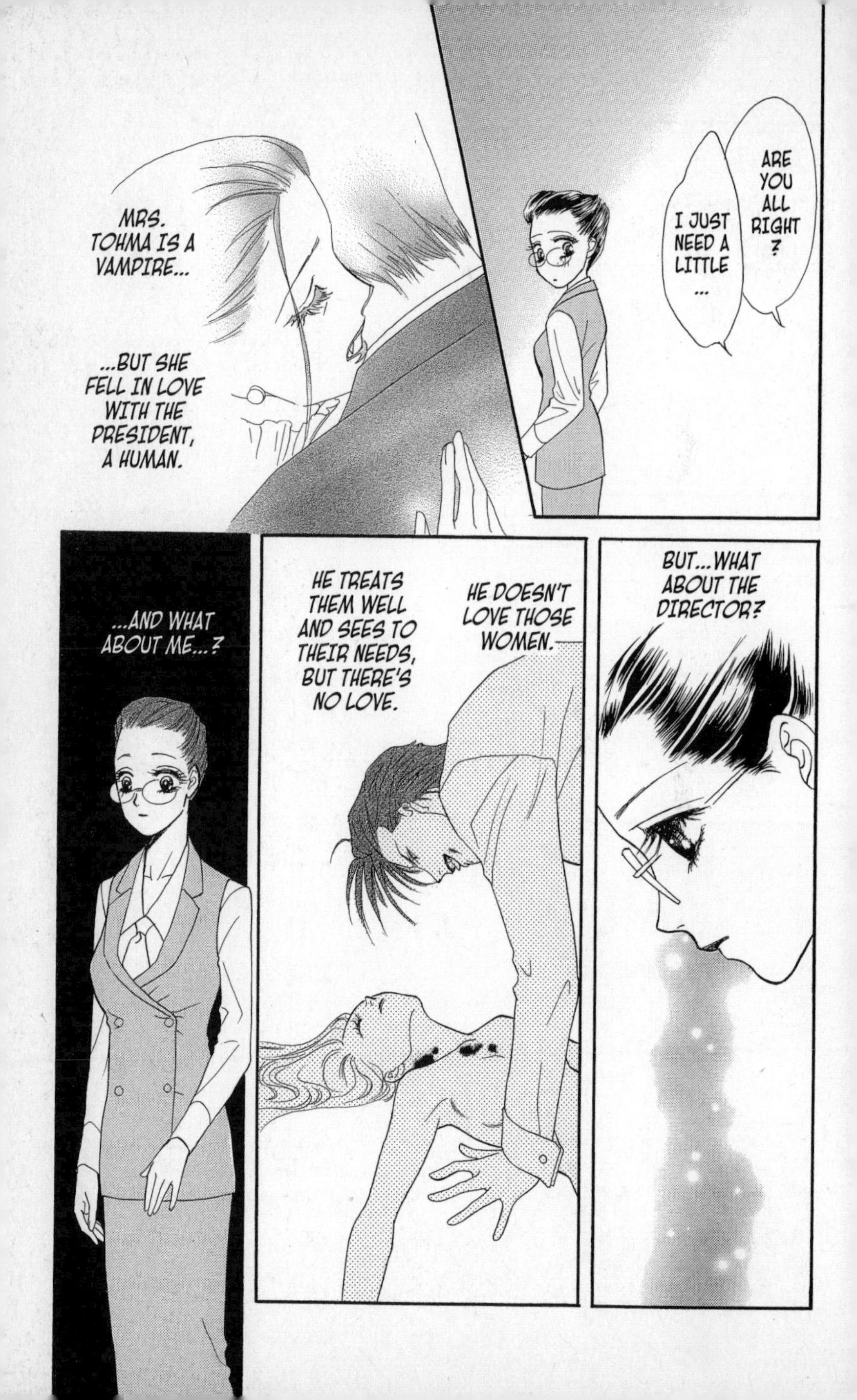
ARE YOU ALL RIGHT?
I JUST NEED A LITTLE...
MRS. TOHMA IS A VAMPIRE...
...BUT SHE FELL IN LOVE WITH THE PRESIDENT, A HUMAN.
BUT...WHAT ABOUT THE DIRECTOR?
HE DOESN'T LOVE THOSE WOMEN.
HE TREATS THEM WELL AND SEES TO THEIR NEEDS, BUT THERE'S NO LOVE.
...AND WHAT ABOUT ME...?

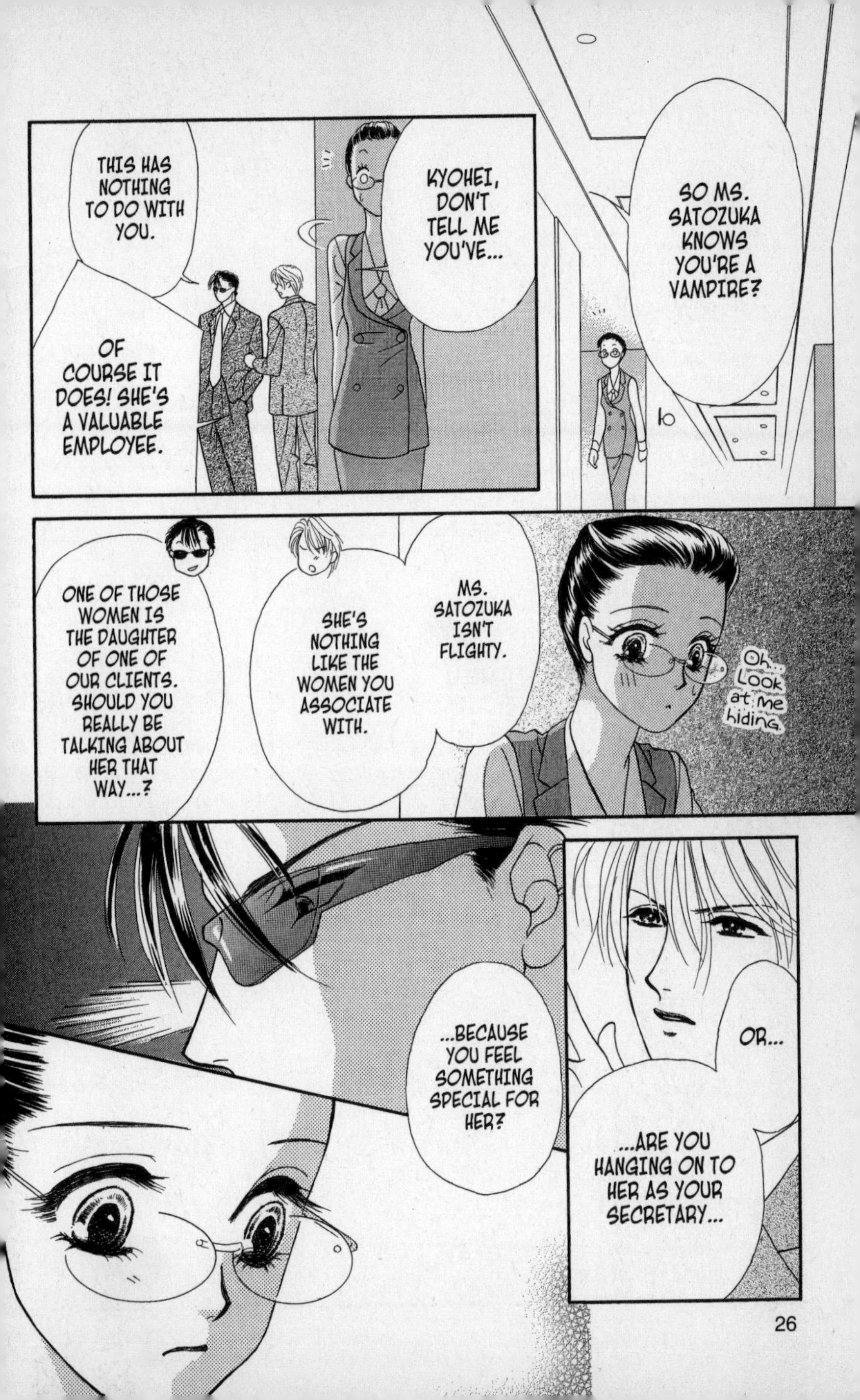
SO MS. SATOZUKA KNOWS YOU'RE A VAMPIRE?
KYOHEI, DON'T TELL ME YOU'VE...
THIS HAS NOTHING TO DO WITH YOU.
OF COURSE IT DOES! SHE'S A VALUABLE EMPLOYEE.
Oh... Look at me hiding.
MS. SATOZUKA ISN'T FLIGHTY.
SHE'S NOTHING LIKE THE WOMEN YOU ASSOCIATE WITH.
ONE OF THOSE WOMEN IS THE DAUGHTER OF ONE OF OUR CLIENTS. SHOULD YOU REALLY BE TALKING ABOUT HER THAT WAY...?
OR...
...ARE YOU HANGING ON TO HER AS YOUR SECRETARY...
...BECAUSE YOU FEEL SOMETHING SPECIAL FOR HER?

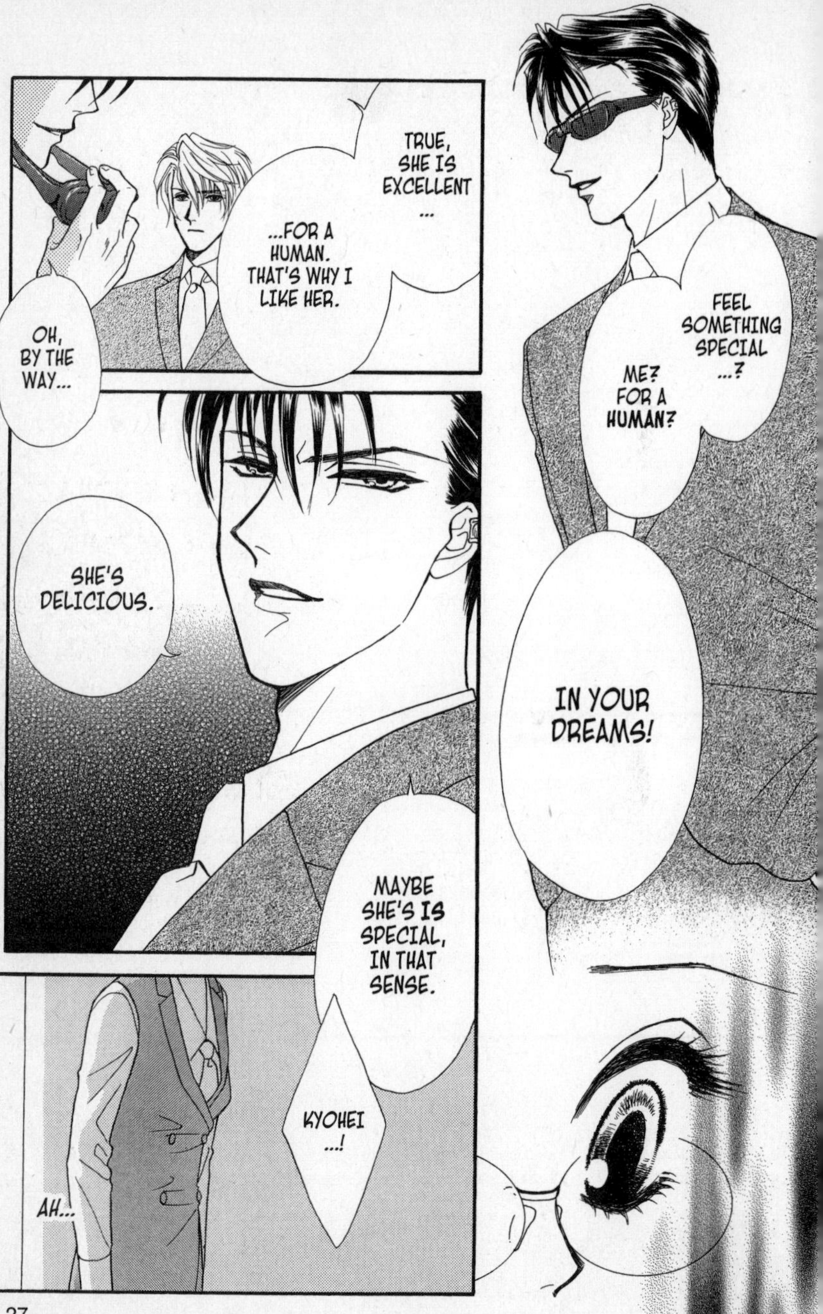
FEEL SOMETHING SPECIAL ...?
ME? FOR A HUMAN?
IN YOUR DREAMS!
TRUE, SHE IS EXCELLENT ...
...FOR A HUMAN. THAT'S WHY I LIKE HER.
OH, BY THE WAY...
SHE'S DELICIOUS.
MAYBE SHE'S IS SPECIAL, IN THAT SENSE.
KYOHEI ...!
AH...

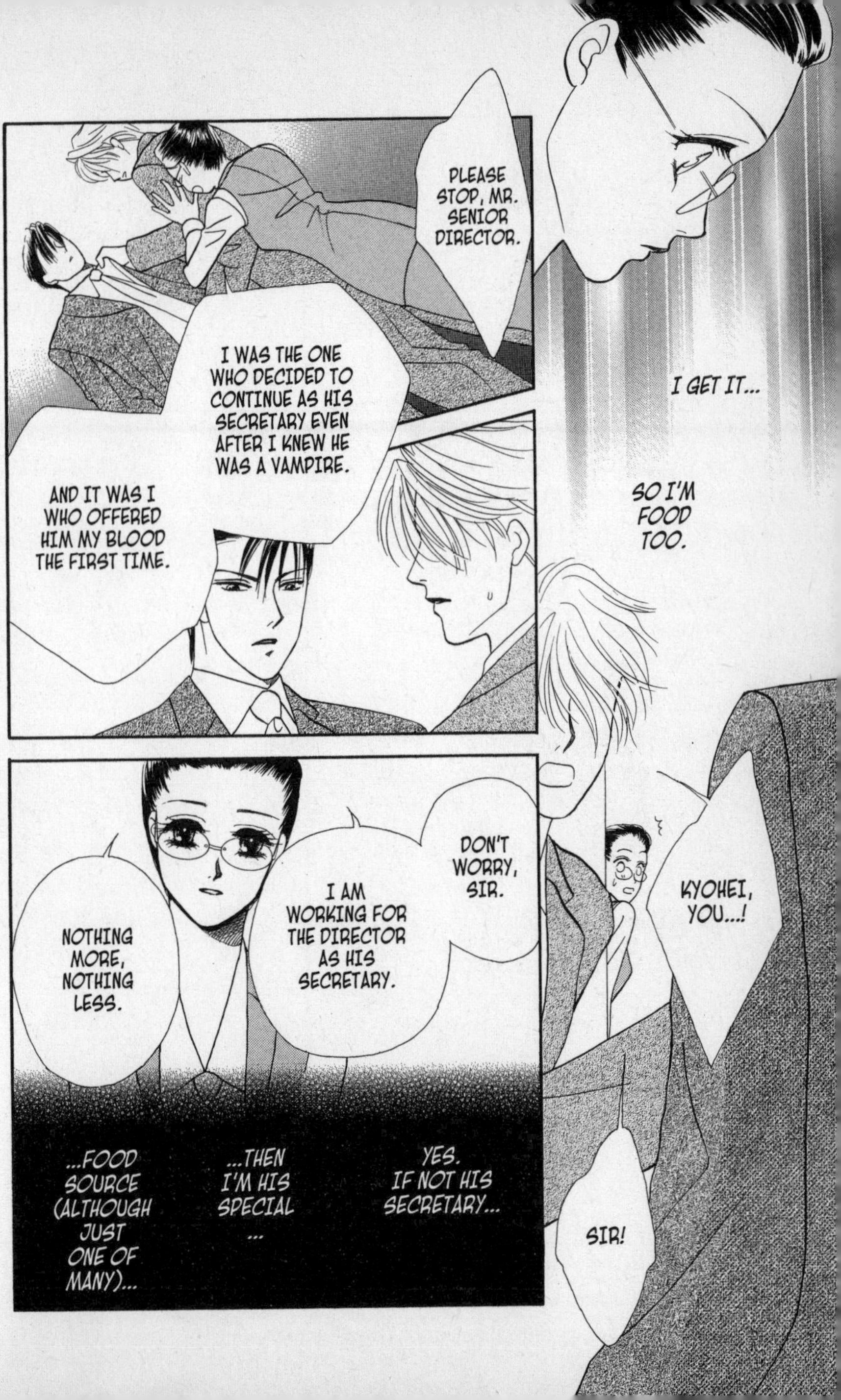
PLEASE STOP, MR. SENIOR DIRECTOR.
I WAS THE ONE WHO DECIDED TO CONTINUE AS HIS SECRETARY EVEN AFTER I KNEW HE WAS A VAMPIRE.
AND IT WAS I WHO OFFERED HIM MY BLOOD THE FIRST TIME.
I GET IT...
SO I'M FOOD TOO.
DON'T WORRY, SIR.
I AM WORKING FOR THE DIRECTOR AS HIS SECRETARY.
NOTHING MORE, NOTHING LESS.
YES. IF NOT HIS SECRETARY...
...THEN I'M HIS SPECIAL ...
...FOOD SOURCE (ALTHOUGH JUST ONE OF MANY)...
KYOHEI, YOU...!
SIR!

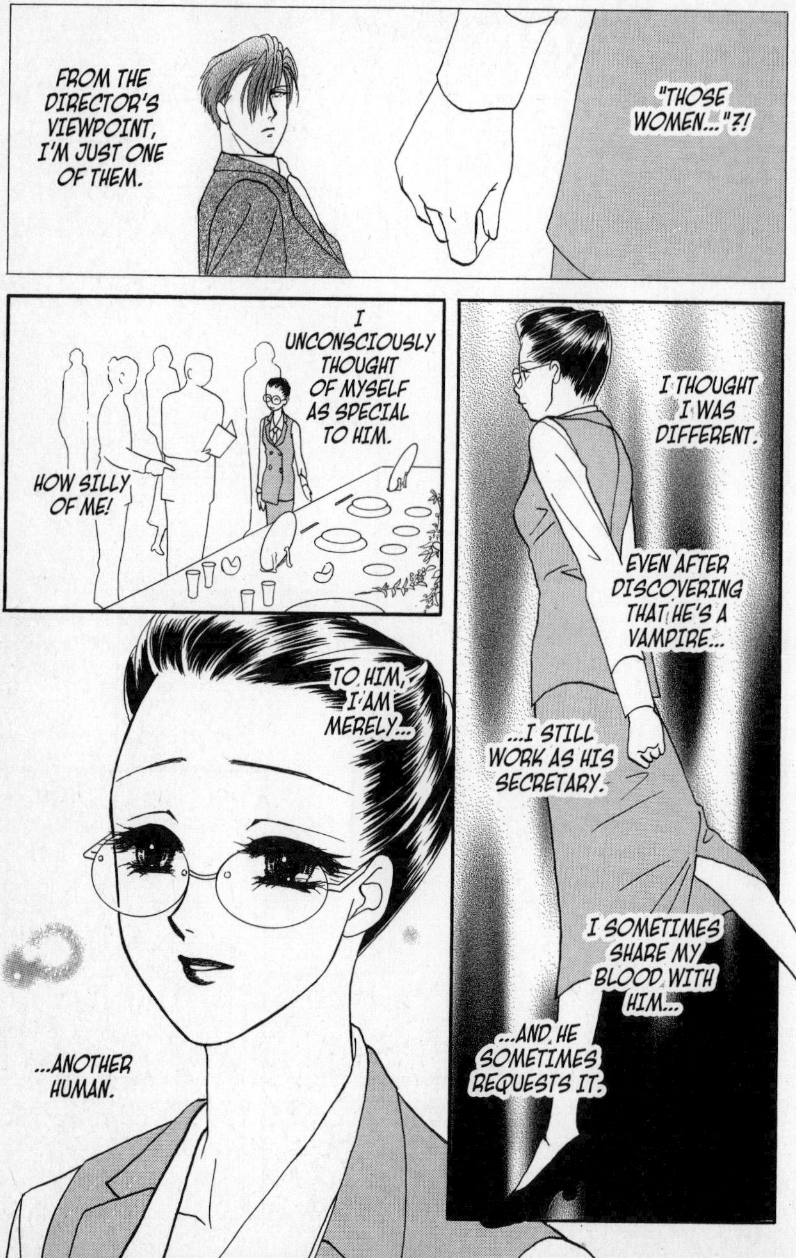
"THOSE WOMEN..."?!
FROM THE DIRECTOR'S VIEWPOINT, I'M JUST ONE OF THEM.
I THOUGHT I WAS DIFFERENT.
EVEN AFTER DISCOVERING THAT HE'S A VAMPIRE...
...I STILL WORK AS HIS SECRETARY.
I SOMETIMES SHARE MY BLOOD WITH HIM...
...AND HE SOMETIMES REQUESTS IT.
I UNCONSCIOUSLY THOUGHT OF MYSELF AS SPECIAL TO HIM.
HOW SILLY OF ME!
TO HIM, I AM MERELY...
...ANOTHER HUMAN.

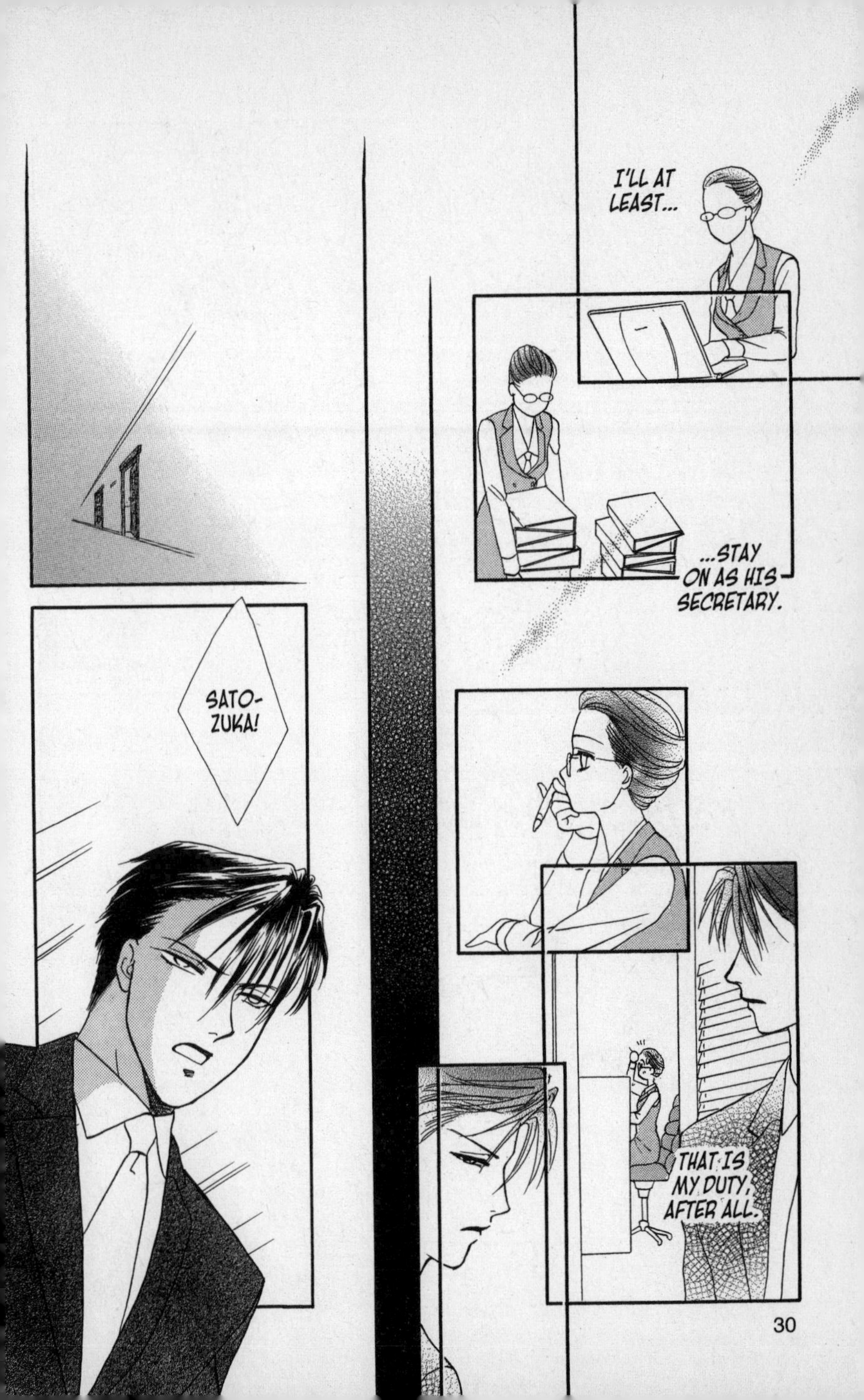
I'LL AT LEAST...
...STAY ON AS HIS SECRETARY.
THAT IS MY DUTY, AFTER ALL.
SATO-ZUKA!

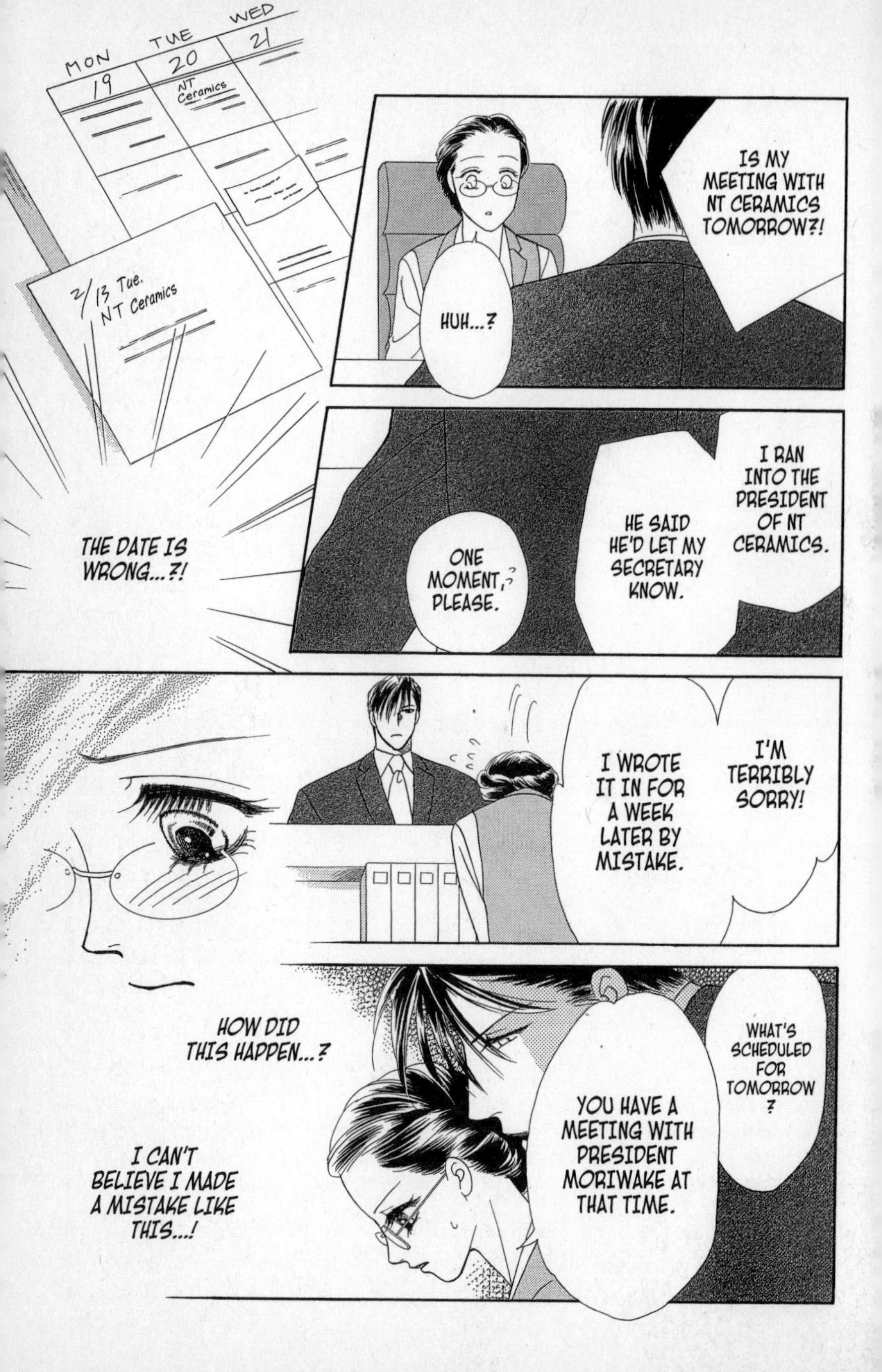
IS MY MEETING WITH NT CERAMICS TOMORROW?!
HUH...?
I RAN INTO THE PRESIDENT OF NT CERAMICS.
HE SAID HE'D LET MY SECRETARY KNOW.
ONE MOMENT, PLEASE.
MON
TUE
WED
19
20
21
NT Ceramics
2/13 Tue.
NT Ceramics
THE DATE IS WRONG...?!
I'M TERRIBLY SORRY!
I WROTE IT IN FOR A WEEK LATER BY MISTAKE.
WHAT'S SCHEDULED FOR TOMORROW?
YOU HAVE A MEETING WITH PRESIDENT MORIWAKE AT THAT TIME.
HOW DID THIS HAPPEN...?
I CAN'T BELIEVE I MADE A MISTAKE LIKE THIS...!

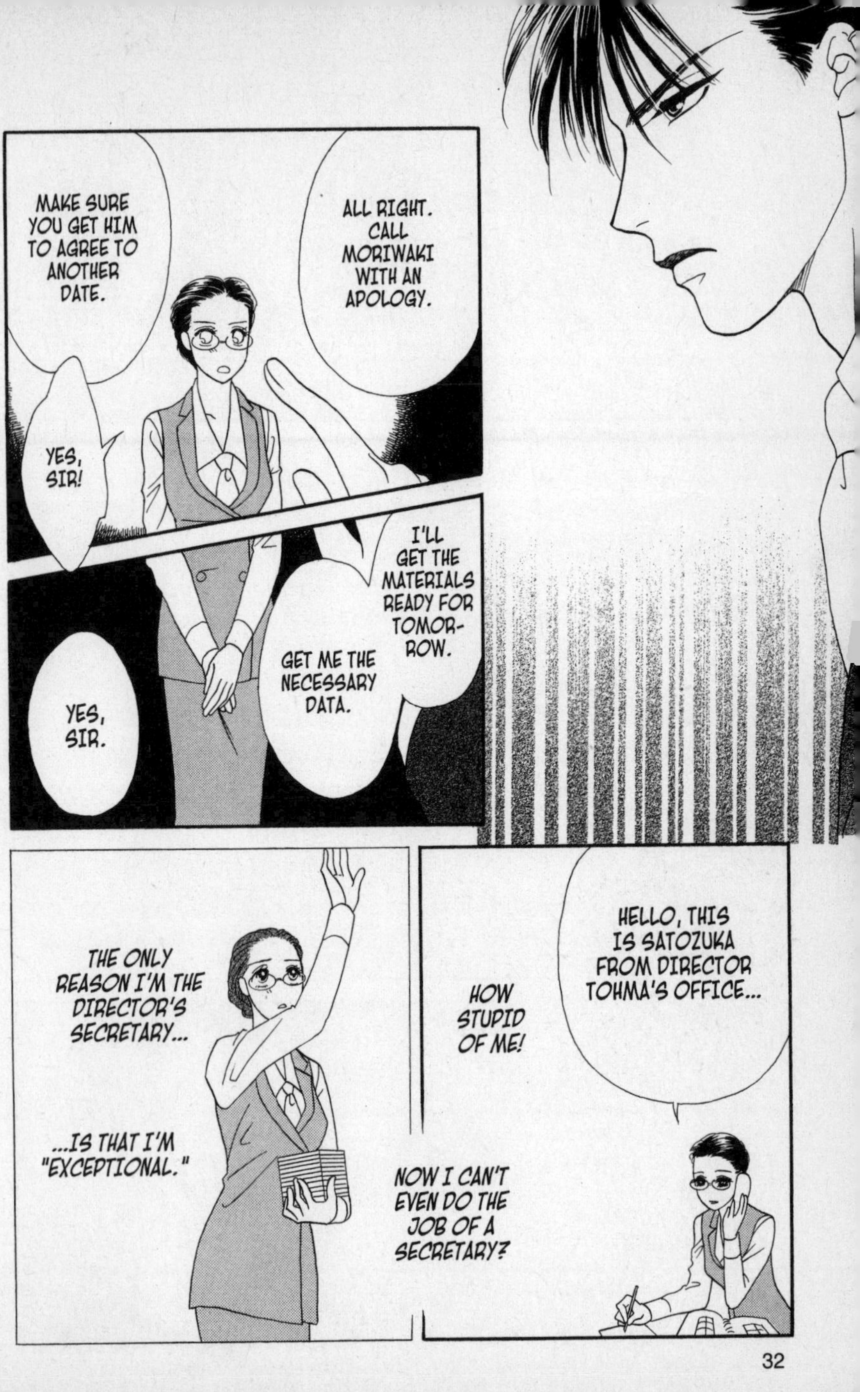
ALL RIGHT. CALL MORIWAKI WITH AN APOLOGY.
MAKE SURE YOU GET HIM TO AGREE TO ANOTHER DATE.
YES, SIR!
I'LL GET THE MATERIALS READY FOR TOMORROW.
GET ME THE NECESSARY DATA.
YES, SIR.
HELLO, THIS IS SATOZUKA FROM DIRECTOR TOHMA'S OFFICE...
HOW STUPID OF ME!
NOW I CAN'T EVEN DO THE JOB OF A SECRETARY?
THE ONLY REASON I'M THE DIRECTOR'S SECRETARY...
...IS THAT I'M "EXCEPTIONAL."

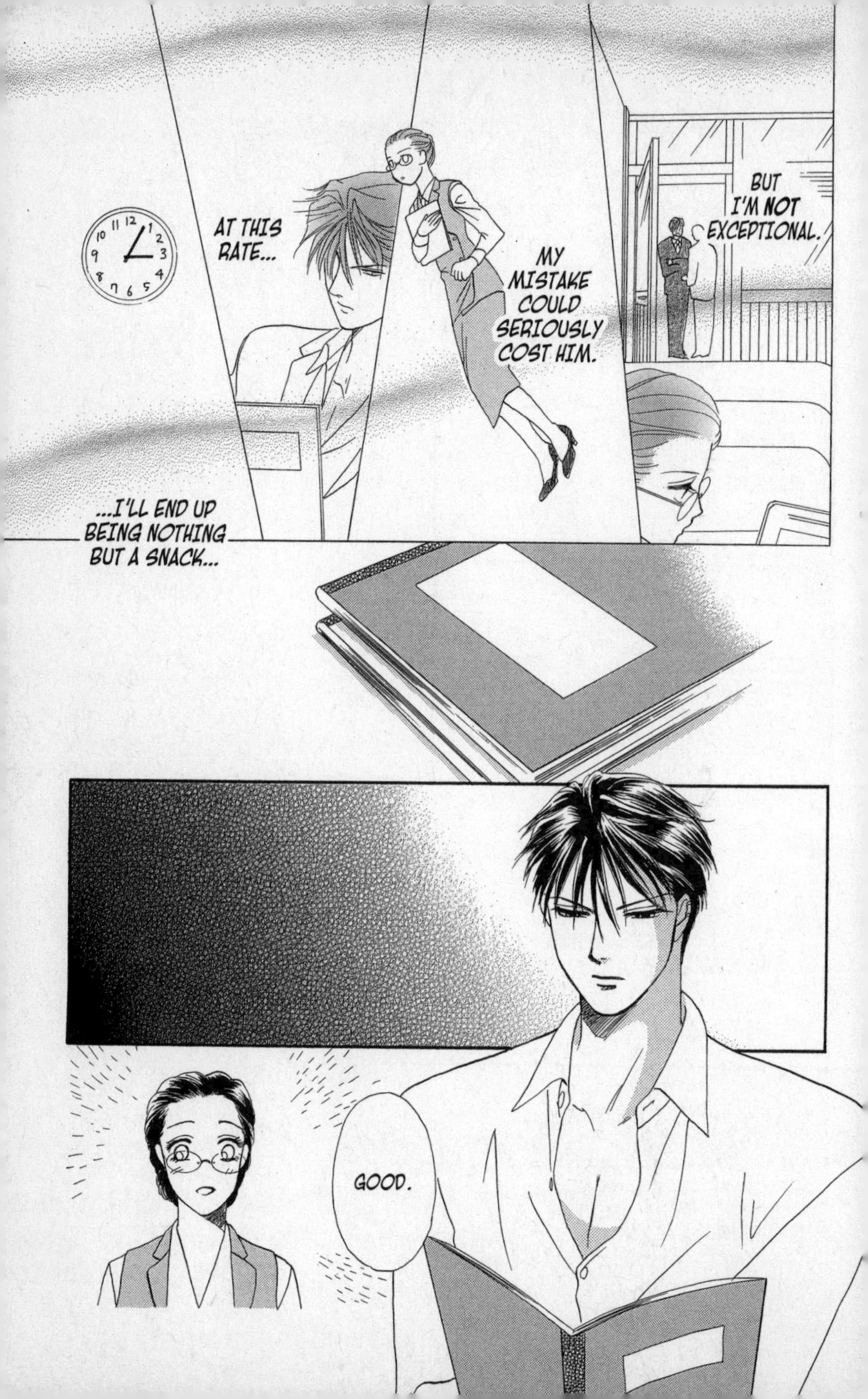
BUT I'M NOT EXCEPTIONAL.
MY MISTAKE COULD SERIOUSLY COST HIM.
AT THIS RATE...
...I'LL END UP BEING NOTHING BUT A SNACK...
GOOD.

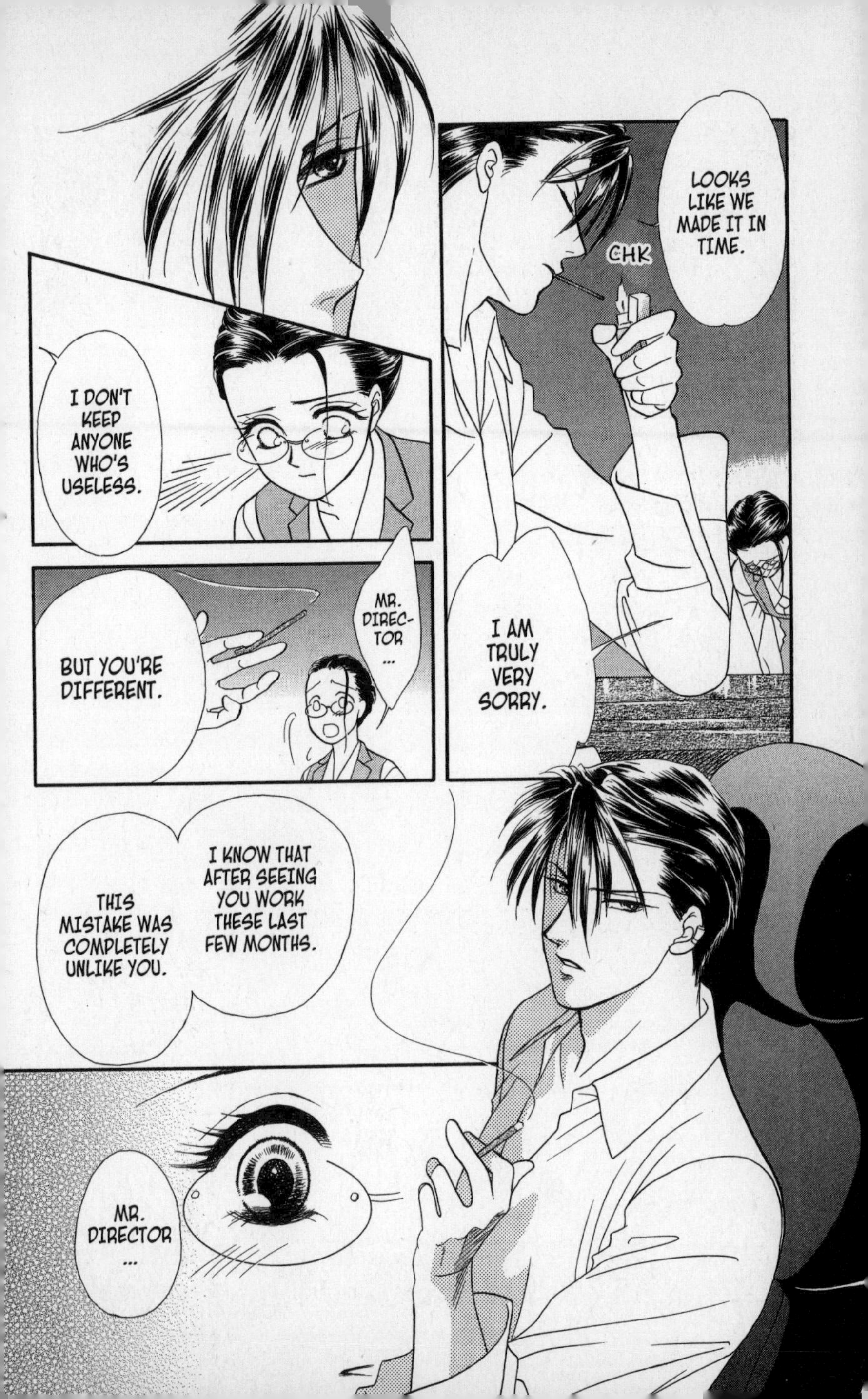
LOOKS LIKE WE MADE IT IN TIME.
CHK
I AM TRULY VERY SORRY.
I DON'T KEEP ANYONE WHO'S USELESS.
MR. DIREC-TOR...
BUT YOU'RE DIFFERENT.
I KNOW THAT AFTER SEEING YOU WORK THESE LAST FEW MONTHS.
THIS MISTAKE WAS COMPLETELY UNLIKE YOU.
MR. DIRECTOR...

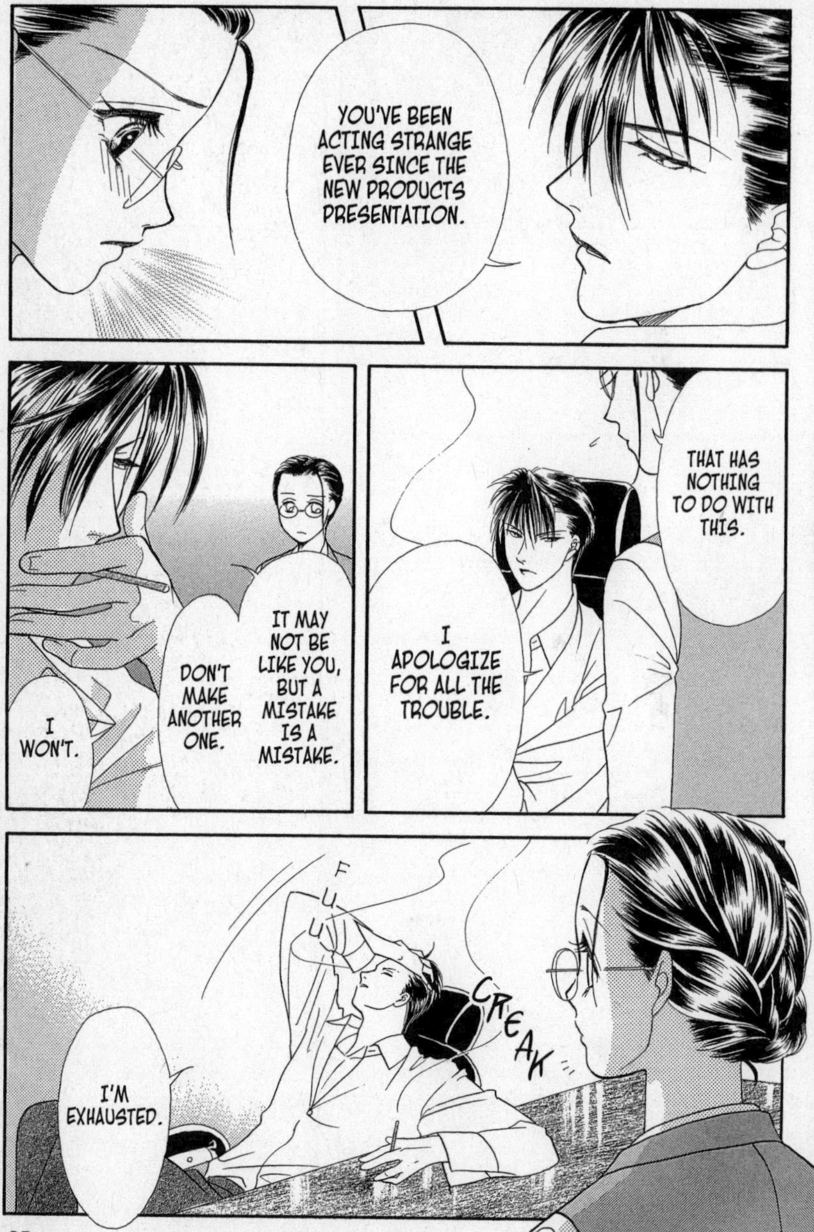
YOU'VE BEEN ACTING STRANGE EVER SINCE THE NEW PRODUCTS PRESENTATION.
THAT HAS NOTHING TO DO WITH THIS.
I APOLOGIZE FOR ALL THE TROUBLE.
IT MAY NOT BE LIKE YOU, BUT A MISTAKE IS A MISTAKE.
DON'T MAKE ANOTHER ONE.
I WON'T.
CREAK
FUUU
I'M EXHAUSTED.

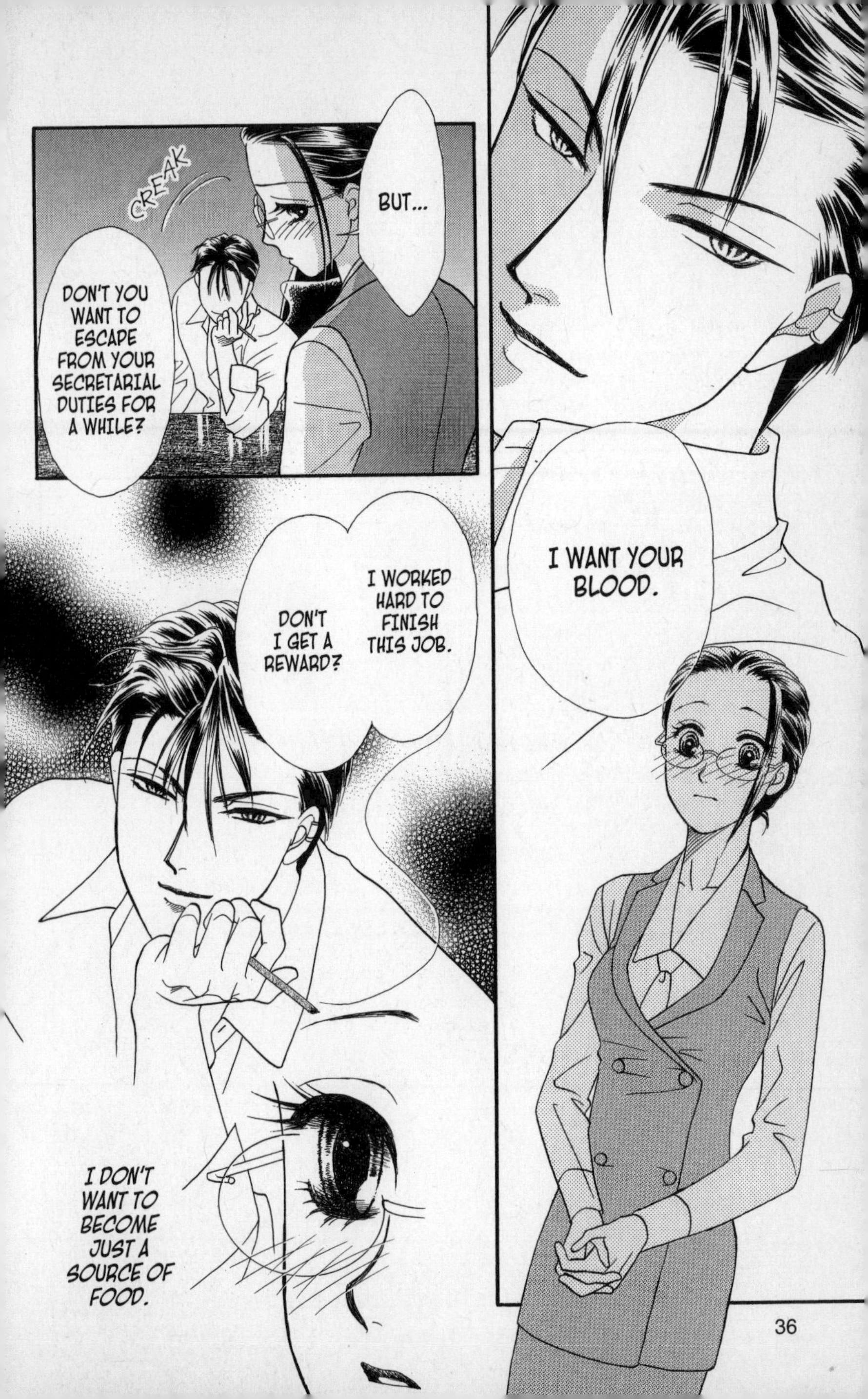
I WANT YOUR BLOOD.
BUT...
CREAK
DON'T YOU WANT TO ESCAPE FROM YOUR SECRETARIAL DUTIES FOR A WHILE?
I WORKED HARD TO FINISH THIS JOB.
DON'T I GET A REWARD?
I DON'T WANT TO BECOME JUST A SOURCE OF FOOD.

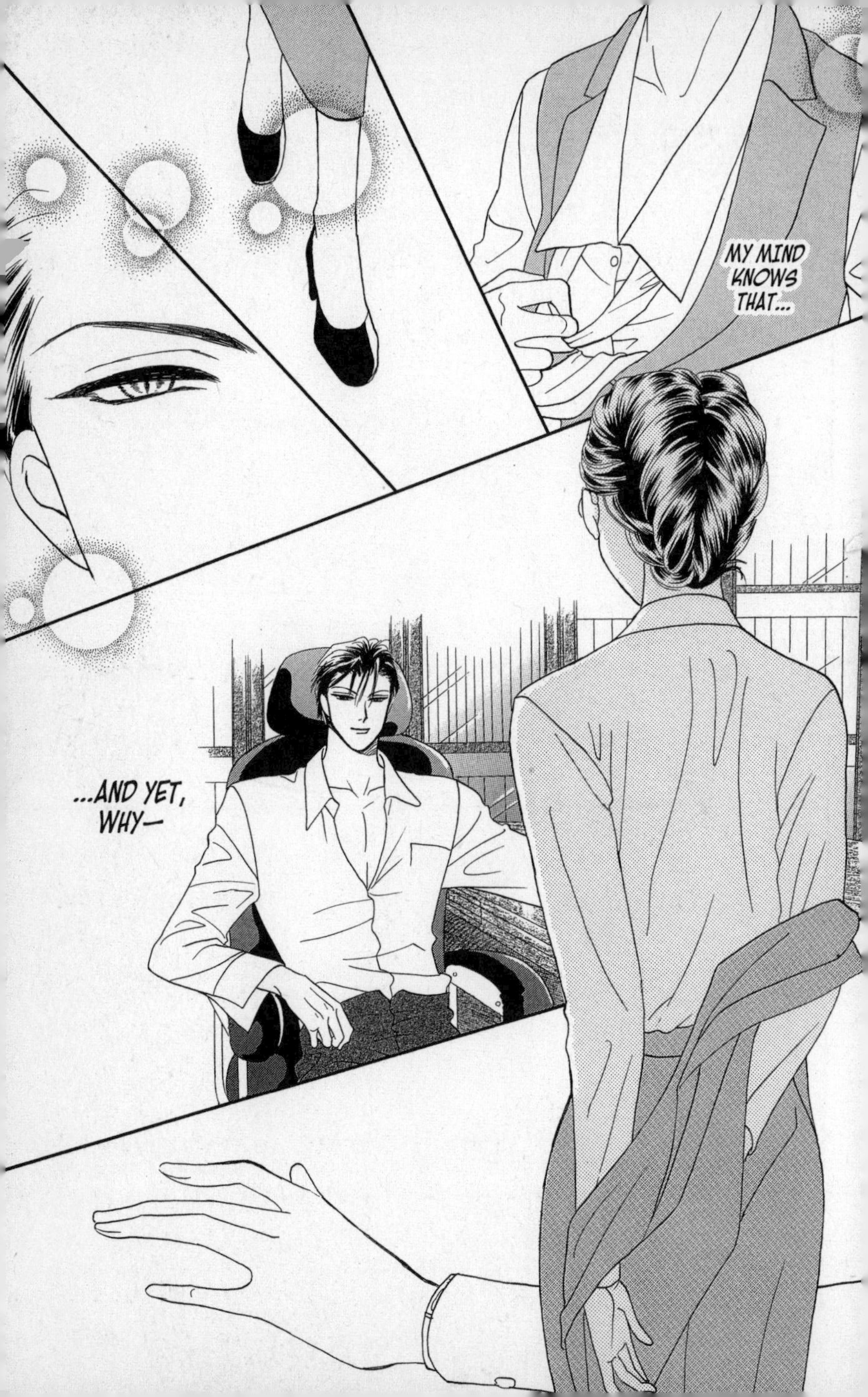
MY MIND KNOWS THAT...
...AND YET, WHY—

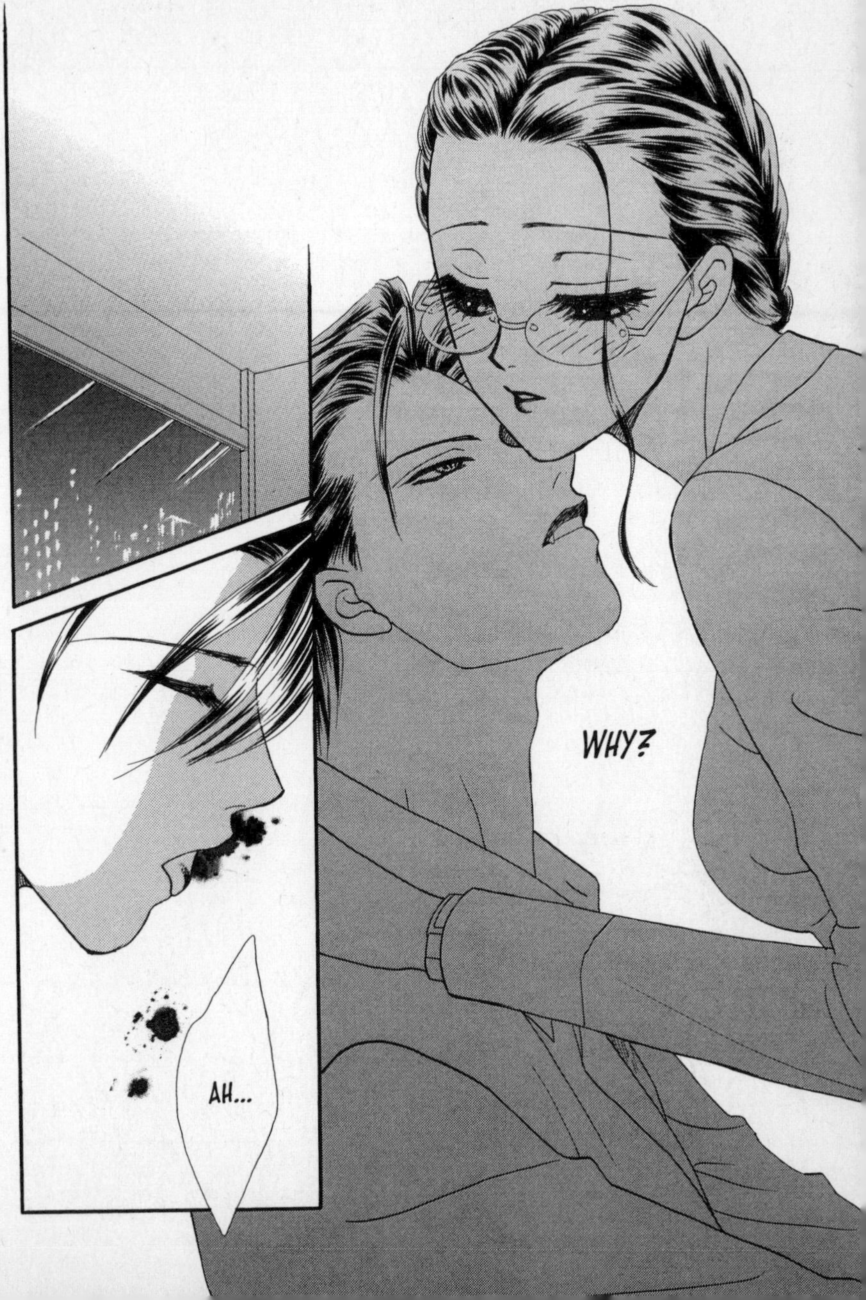
WHY?
AH...

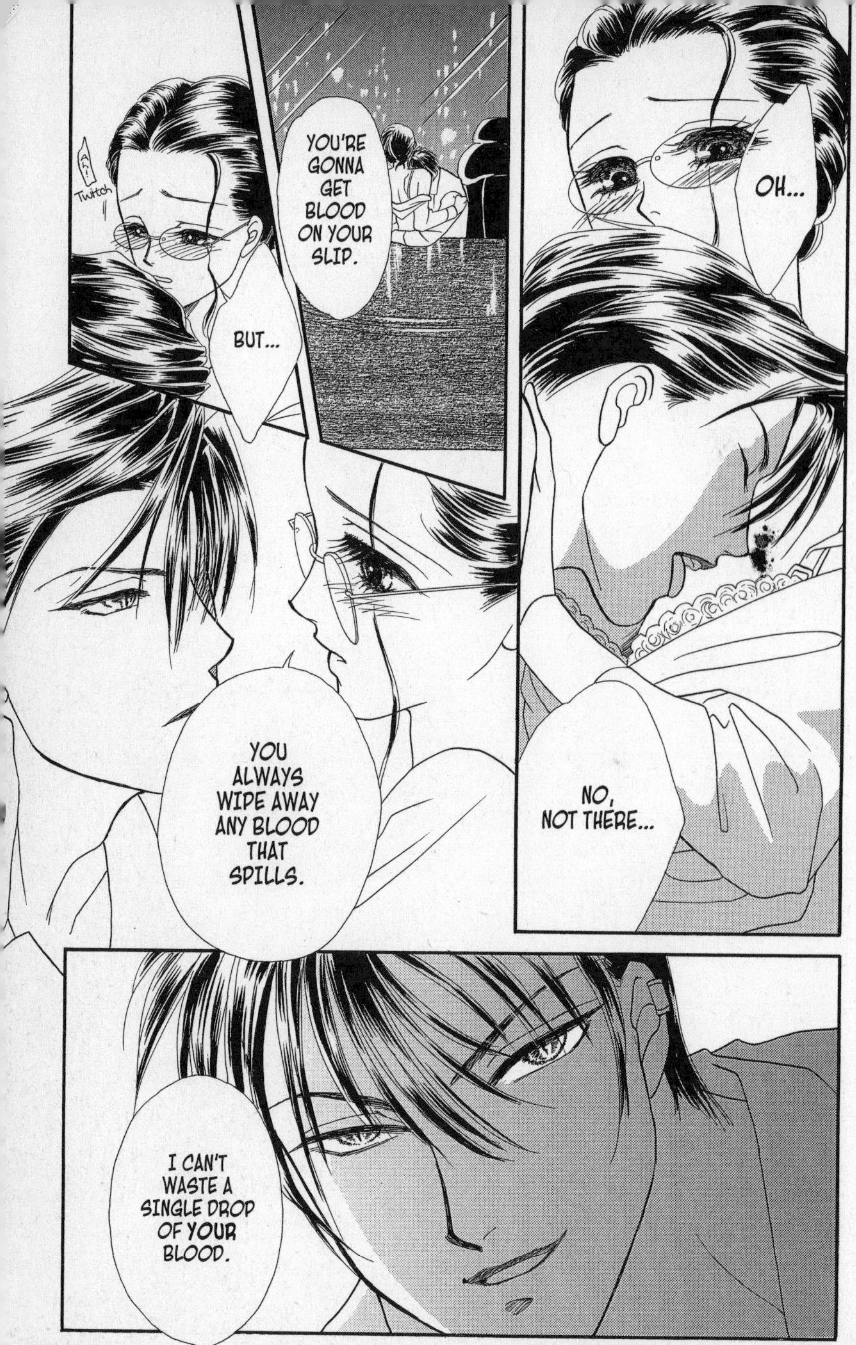
OH...
NO, NOT THERE...
YOU'RE GONNA GET BLOOD ON YOUR SLIP.
Ah!
Twitch
BUT...
YOU ALWAYS WIPE AWAY ANY BLOOD THAT SPILLS.
I CAN'T WASTE A SINGLE DROP OF YOUR BLOOD.

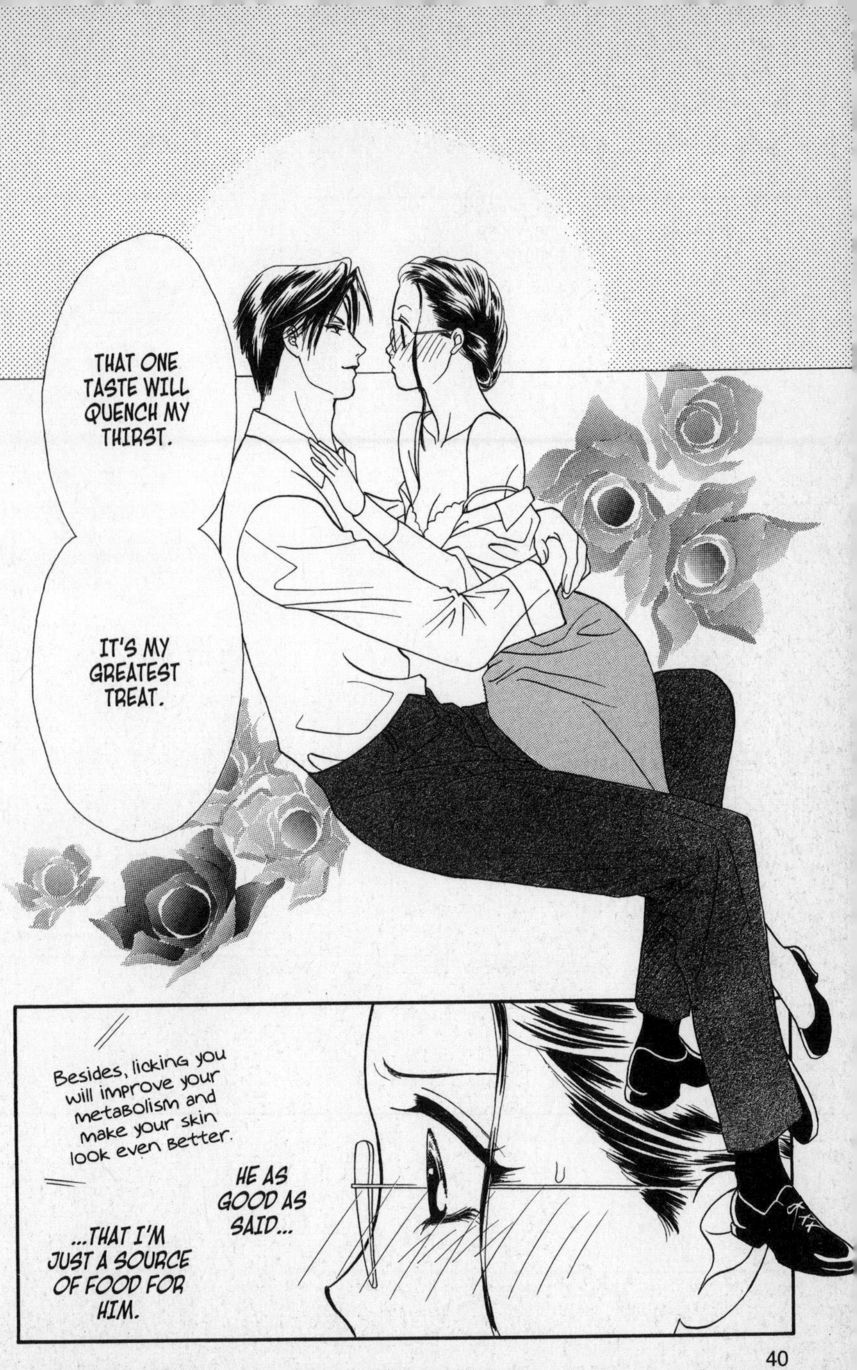
THAT ONE TASTE WILL QUENCH MY THIRST.
IT'S MY GREATEST TREAT.
Besides, licking you will improve your metabolism and make your skin look even better.
HE AS GOOD AS SAID...
...THAT I'M JUST A SOURCE OF FOOD FOR HIM.

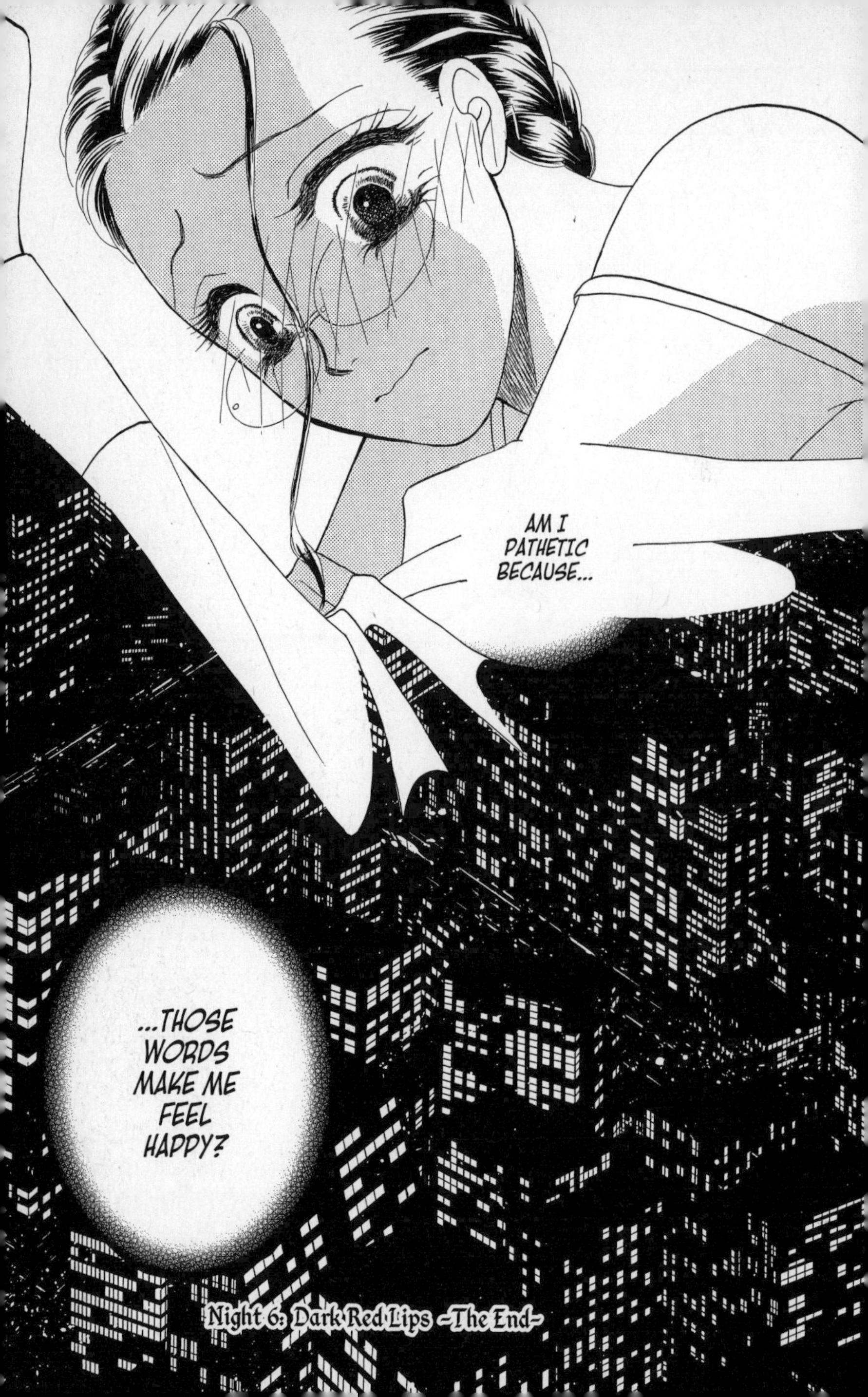
AM I PATHETIC BECAUSE...
...THOSE WORDS MAKE ME FEEL HAPPY?
Night 6: Dark Red Lips -The End-

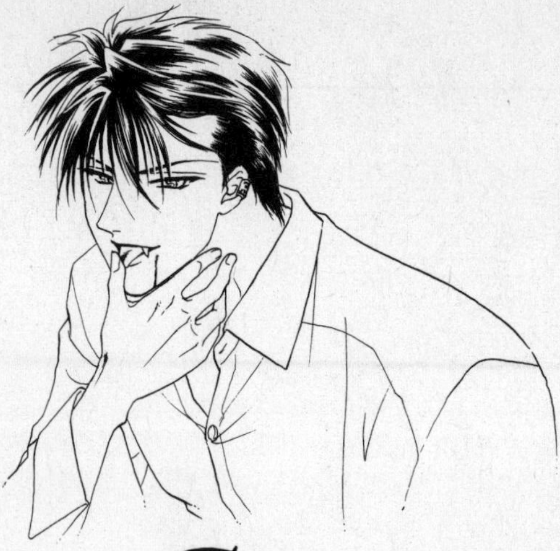

▲ Night Six: Dark Red Lips preview

- Dark Red Lips -

It is time for the Tohma's brothers' mother to make her appearance. Vampires utilize the wombs and sperm of humans to create babies. The babies are born either full human, or full vampire. This premise was set up in my very first vampire work (the first one after my debut, "Vampire ni Onegai" /Flower Comics "Kindan no Koi wo Shiyo" /recording). However, in those days, vampires didn't have such an obstinate image.

- For Whom Is This Night Long? -

I was allowed a color drawing for this title page. I remember spending hours drawing the lace on Kaya's bra on New Year's Day. I love doing the lace on underwear. When Kaya is about to give blood, she opens up her blouse, so the chances of her bra showing are high. I drew several other scenes after this one, showing off her bra.

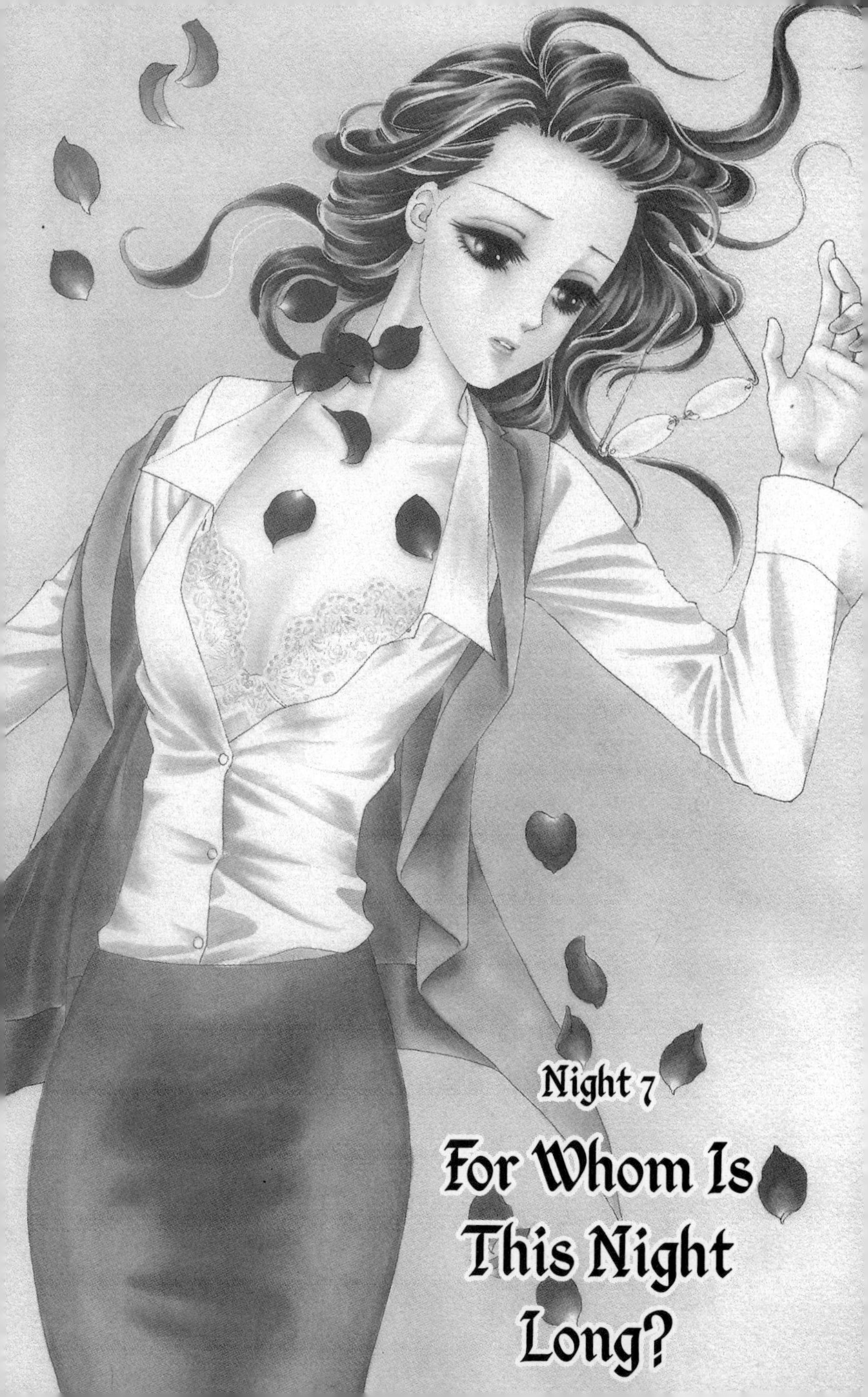
Night 7
For Whom Is
This Night
Long?

Thank you for all your letters and emails. Each message I receive helps me go forward.

I feel bad that I'm unable to answer your messages. I know it doesn't suffice, but I do send New Year's greeting cards to all those who sent me letters during the previous year.

In many cases, if you have emailed me through the Petit Comic website, I am unable to access your address. For this reason, unfortunately, I'm unable to send you a New Year's greeting card. I would appreciate it if you would include your address in your message, if you can.

Tomu Ohmi
c/o Shojo Beat
P.O. Box 77010
San Francisco, CA 94107

Petit Comic Website

http://www.petitcomic.com
"Fan Mail" section

I hope you will continue to support me and my work!

▼ Night 8: Between You and Me preview

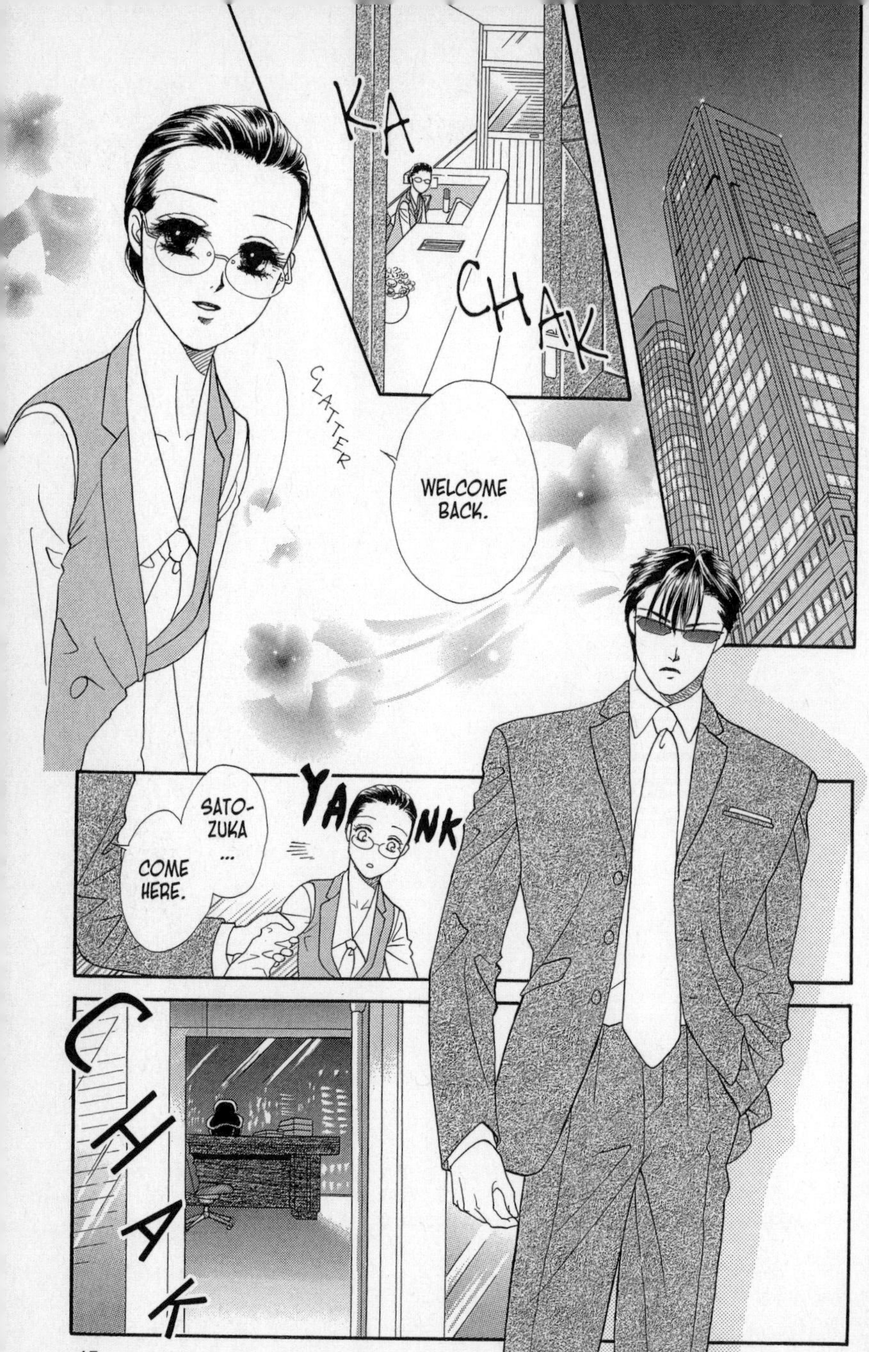
KA
CHAK
WELCOME BACK.
CLATTER
YANK
SATO-ZUKA ...
COME HERE.
CHAK

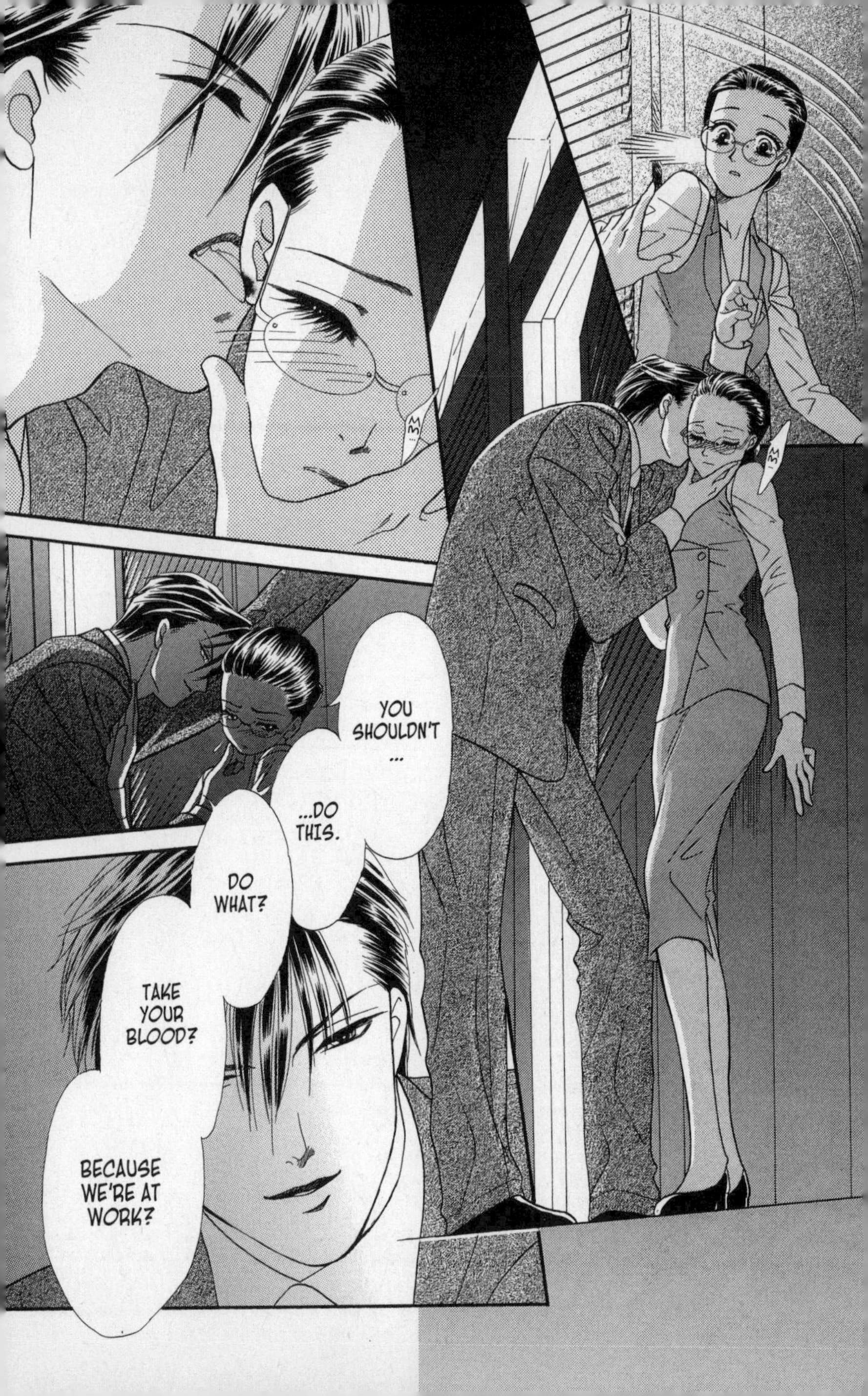
YOU SHOULDN'T ...
...DO THIS.
DO WHAT?
TAKE YOUR BLOOD?
BECAUSE WE'RE AT WORK?

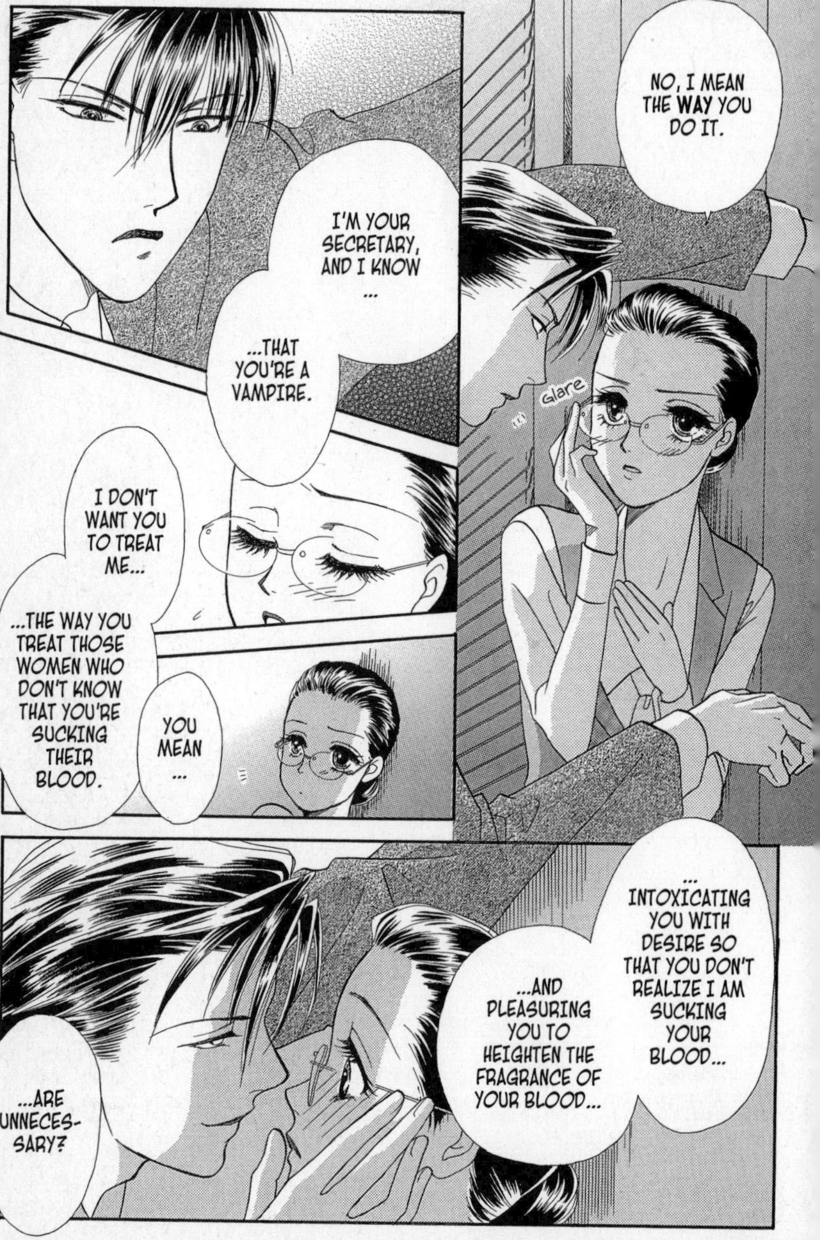
NO, I MEAN THE WAY YOU DO IT.
Glare
I'M YOUR SECRETARY, AND I KNOW ...
...THAT YOU'RE A VAMPIRE.
I DON'T WANT YOU TO TREAT ME...
...THE WAY YOU TREAT THOSE WOMEN WHO DON'T KNOW THAT YOU'RE SUCKING THEIR BLOOD.
YOU MEAN ...
... INTOXICATING YOU WITH DESIRE SO THAT YOU DON'T REALIZE I AM SUCKING YOUR BLOOD...
...AND PLEASURING YOU TO HEIGHTEN THE FRAGRANCE OF YOUR BLOOD...
...ARE UNNECES-SARY?

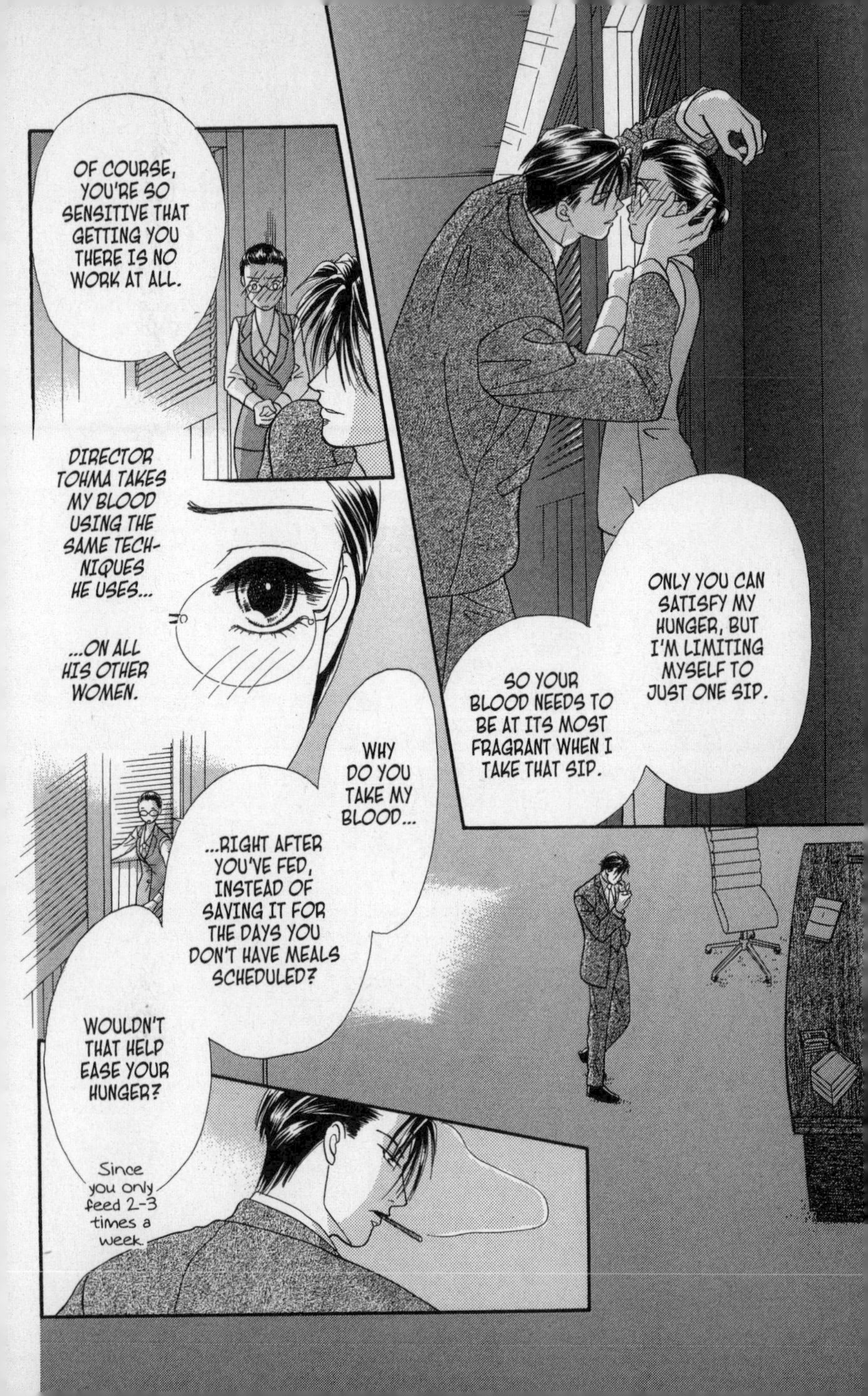
ONLY YOU CAN SATISFY MY HUNGER, BUT I'M LIMITING MYSELF TO JUST ONE SIP.
SO YOUR BLOOD NEEDS TO BE AT ITS MOST FRAGRANT WHEN I TAKE THAT SIP.
OF COURSE, YOU'RE SO SENSITIVE THAT GETTING YOU THERE IS NO WORK AT ALL.
DIRECTOR TOHMA TAKES MY BLOOD USING THE SAME TECH-NIQUES HE USES...
...ON ALL HIS OTHER WOMEN.
WHY DO YOU TAKE MY BLOOD...
...RIGHT AFTER YOU'VE FED, INSTEAD OF SAVING IT FOR THE DAYS YOU DON'T HAVE MEALS SCHEDULED?
WOULDN'T THAT HELP EASE YOUR HUNGER?
Since you only feed 2-3 times a week.

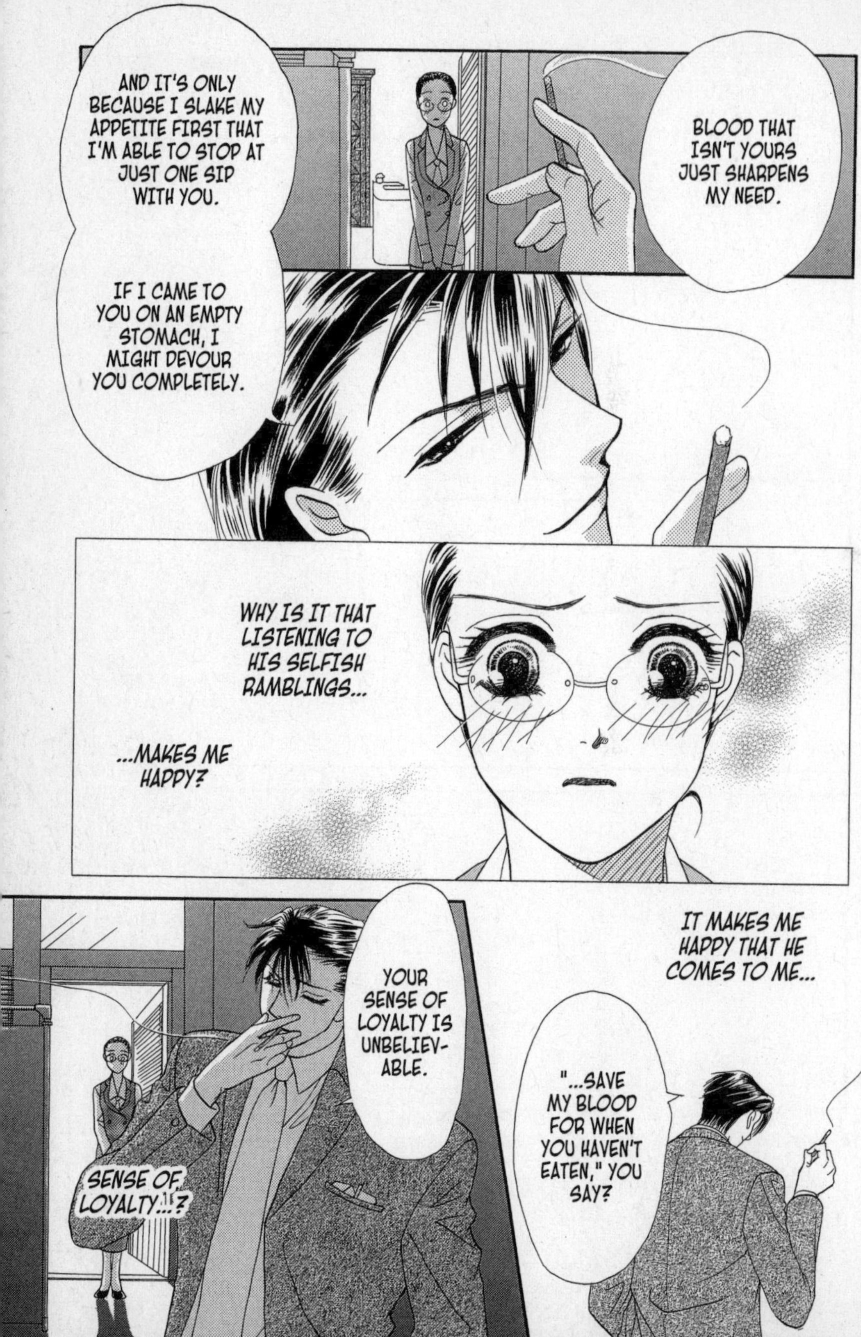
BLOOD THAT ISN'T YOURS JUST SHARPENS MY NEED.
AND IT'S ONLY BECAUSE I SLAKE MY APPETITE FIRST THAT I'M ABLE TO STOP AT JUST ONE SIP WITH YOU.
IF I CAME TO YOU ON AN EMPTY STOMACH, I MIGHT DEVOUR YOU COMPLETELY.
WHY IS IT THAT LISTENING TO HIS SELFISH RAMBLINGS...
...MAKES ME HAPPY?
IT MAKES ME HAPPY THAT HE COMES TO ME...
"...SAVE MY BLOOD FOR WHEN YOU HAVEN'T EATEN," YOU SAY?
YOUR SENSE OF LOYALTY IS UNBELIEV-ABLE.
SENSE OF LOYALTY...?

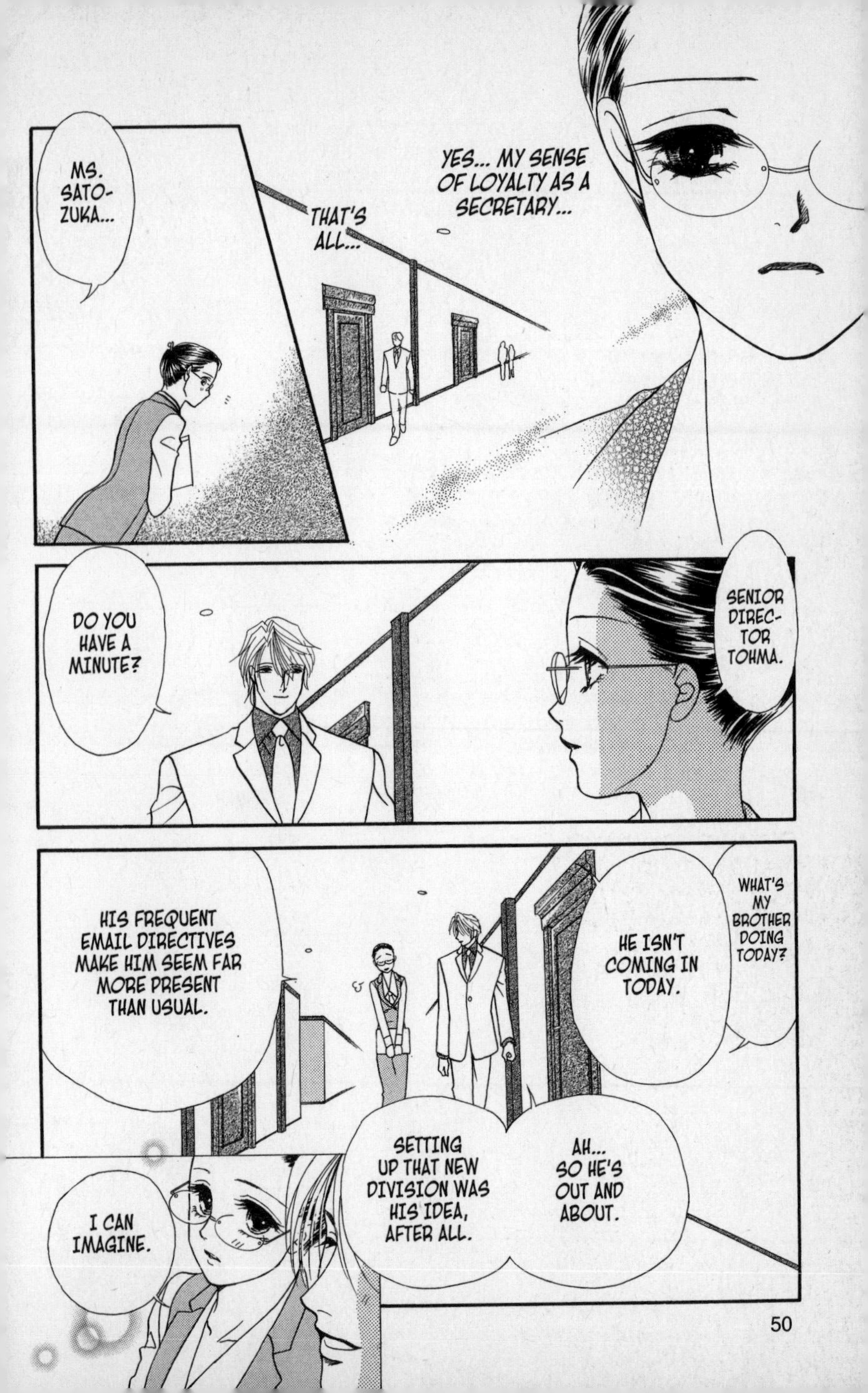
YES... MY SENSE OF LOYALTY AS A SECRETARY...
THAT'S ALL...
MS. SATO-ZUKA...
SENIOR DIREC-TOR TOHMA.
DO YOU HAVE A MINUTE?
WHAT'S MY BROTHER DOING TODAY?
HE ISN'T COMING IN TODAY.
HIS FREQUENT EMAIL DIRECTIVES MAKE HIM SEEM FAR MORE PRESENT THAN USUAL.
AH... SO HE'S OUT AND ABOUT.
SETTING UP THAT NEW DIVISION WAS HIS IDEA, AFTER ALL.
I CAN IMAGINE.

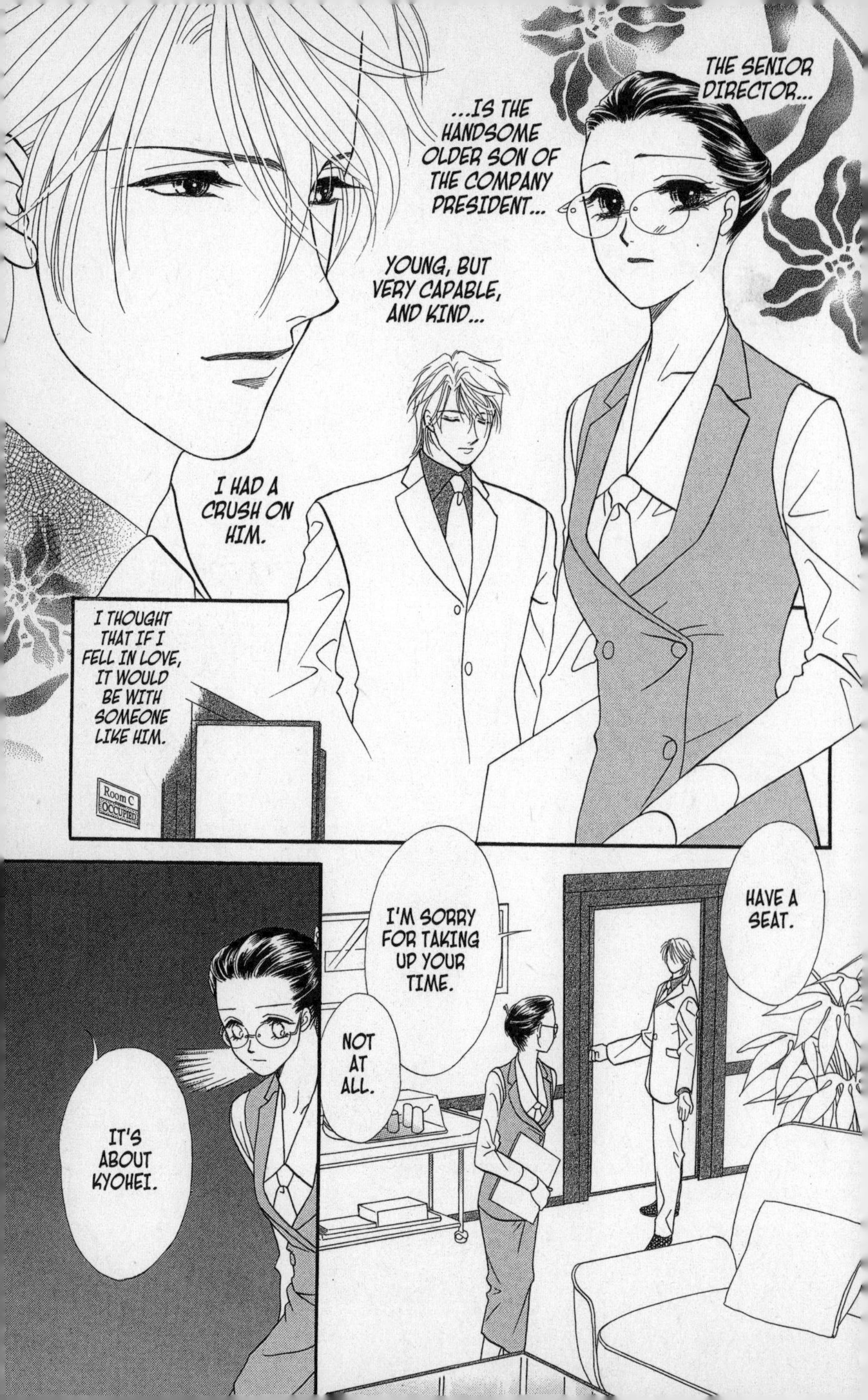
THE SENIOR DIRECTOR...
...IS THE HANDSOME OLDER SON OF THE COMPANY PRESIDENT...
YOUNG, BUT VERY CAPABLE, AND KIND...
I HAD A CRUSH ON HIM.
I THOUGHT THAT IF I FELL IN LOVE, IT WOULD BE WITH SOMEONE LIKE HIM.
Room C
OCCUPIED
HAVE A SEAT.
I'M SORRY FOR TAKING UP YOUR TIME.
NOT AT ALL.
IT'S ABOUT KYOHEI.

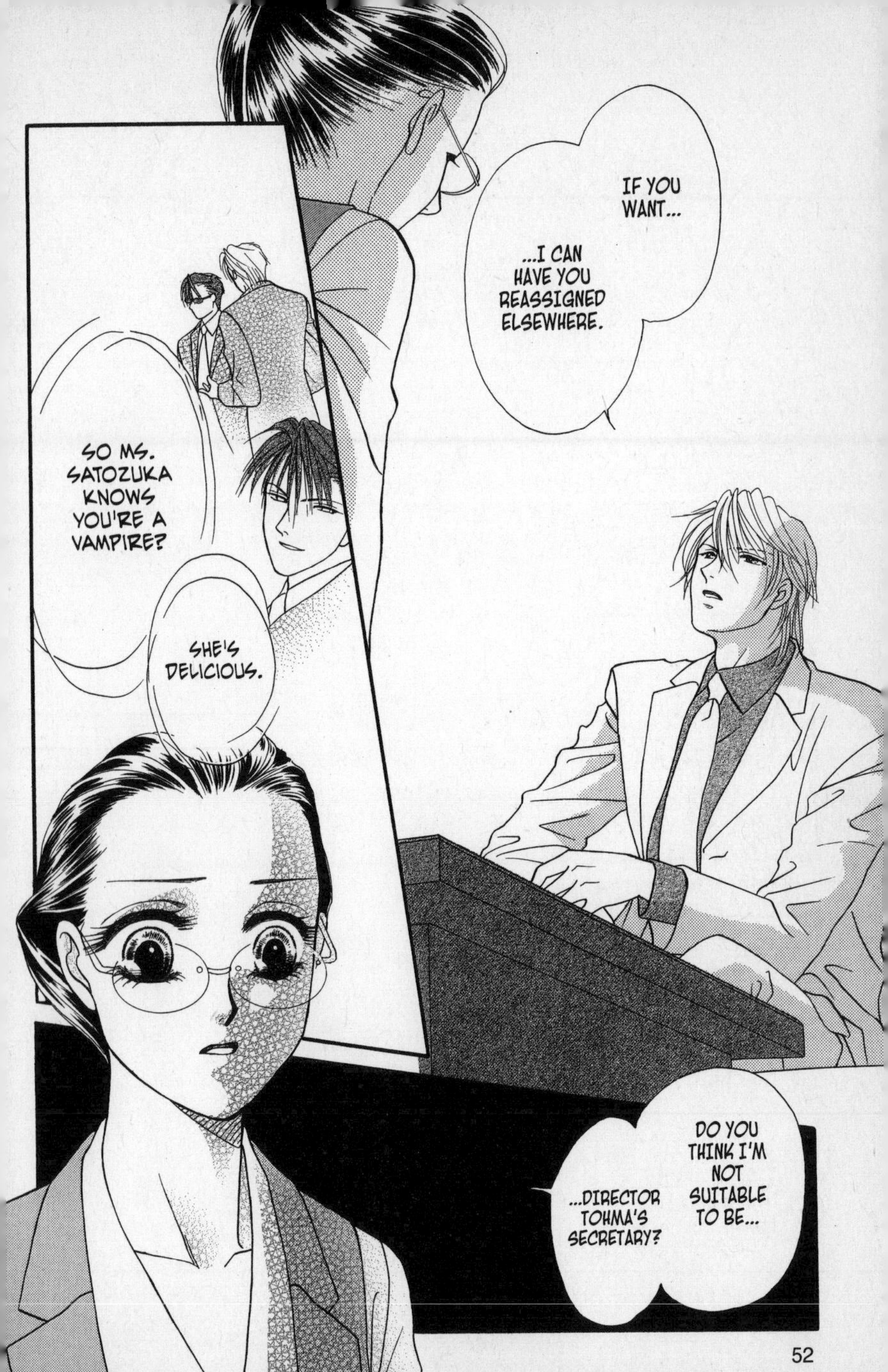
IF YOU WANT...
...I CAN HAVE YOU REASSIGNED ELSEWHERE.
SO MS. SATOZUKA KNOWS YOU'RE A VAMPIRE?
SHE'S DELICIOUS.
DO YOU THINK I'M NOT SUITABLE TO BE...
...DIRECTOR TOHMA'S SECRETARY?

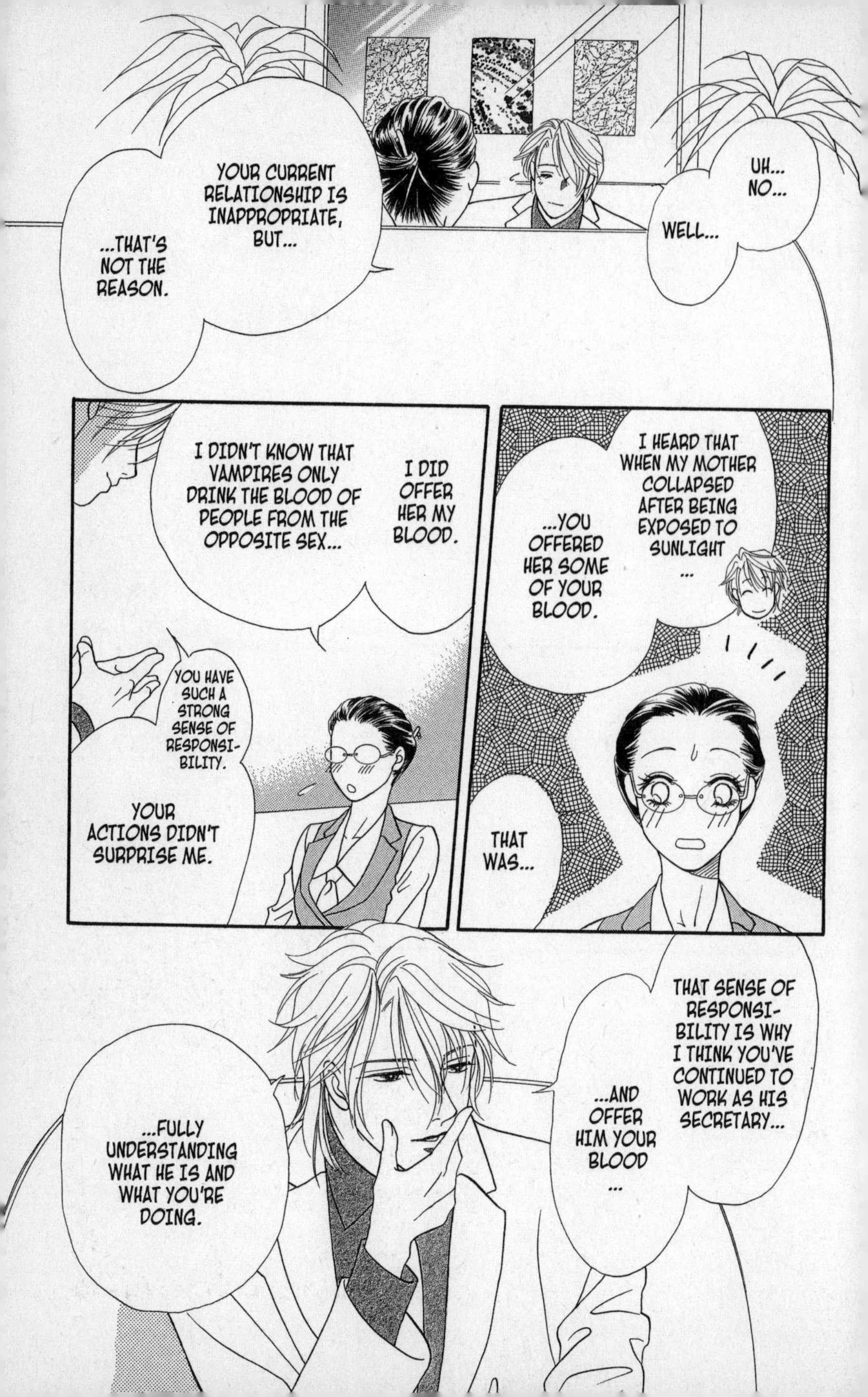
UH... NO...
WELL...
YOUR CURRENT RELATIONSHIP IS INAPPROPRIATE, BUT...
...THAT'S NOT THE REASON.
I HEARD THAT WHEN MY MOTHER COLLAPSED AFTER BEING EXPOSED TO SUNLIGHT ...
...YOU OFFERED HER SOME OF YOUR BLOOD.
THAT WAS...
I DID OFFER HER MY BLOOD.
I DIDN'T KNOW THAT VAMPIRES ONLY DRINK THE BLOOD OF PEOPLE FROM THE OPPOSITE SEX...
YOU HAVE SUCH A STRONG SENSE OF RESPONSIBILITY.
YOUR ACTIONS DIDN'T SURPRISE ME.
THAT SENSE OF RESPONSIBILITY IS WHY I THINK YOU'VE CONTINUED TO WORK AS HIS SECRETARY...
...AND OFFER HIM YOUR BLOOD ...
...FULLY UNDERSTANDING WHAT HE IS AND WHAT YOU'RE DOING.

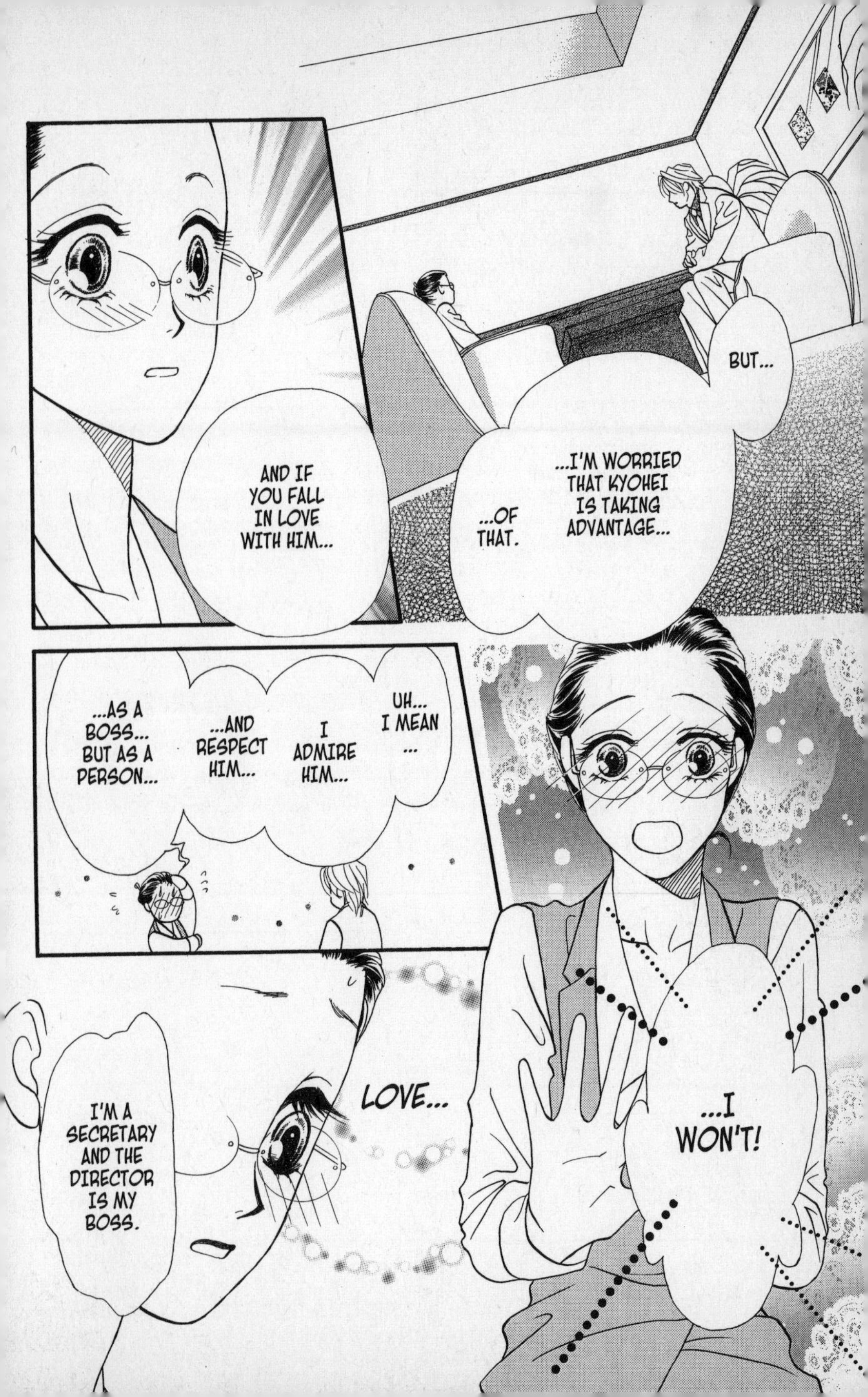
BUT...
...I'M WORRIED THAT KYOHEI IS TAKING ADVANTAGE...
...OF THAT.
AND IF YOU FALL IN LOVE WITH HIM...
...I WON'T!
UH... I MEAN ...
I ADMIRE HIM...
...AND RESPECT HIM...
...AS A BOSS... BUT AS A PERSON...
LOVE...
I'M A SECRETARY AND THE DIRECTOR IS MY BOSS.

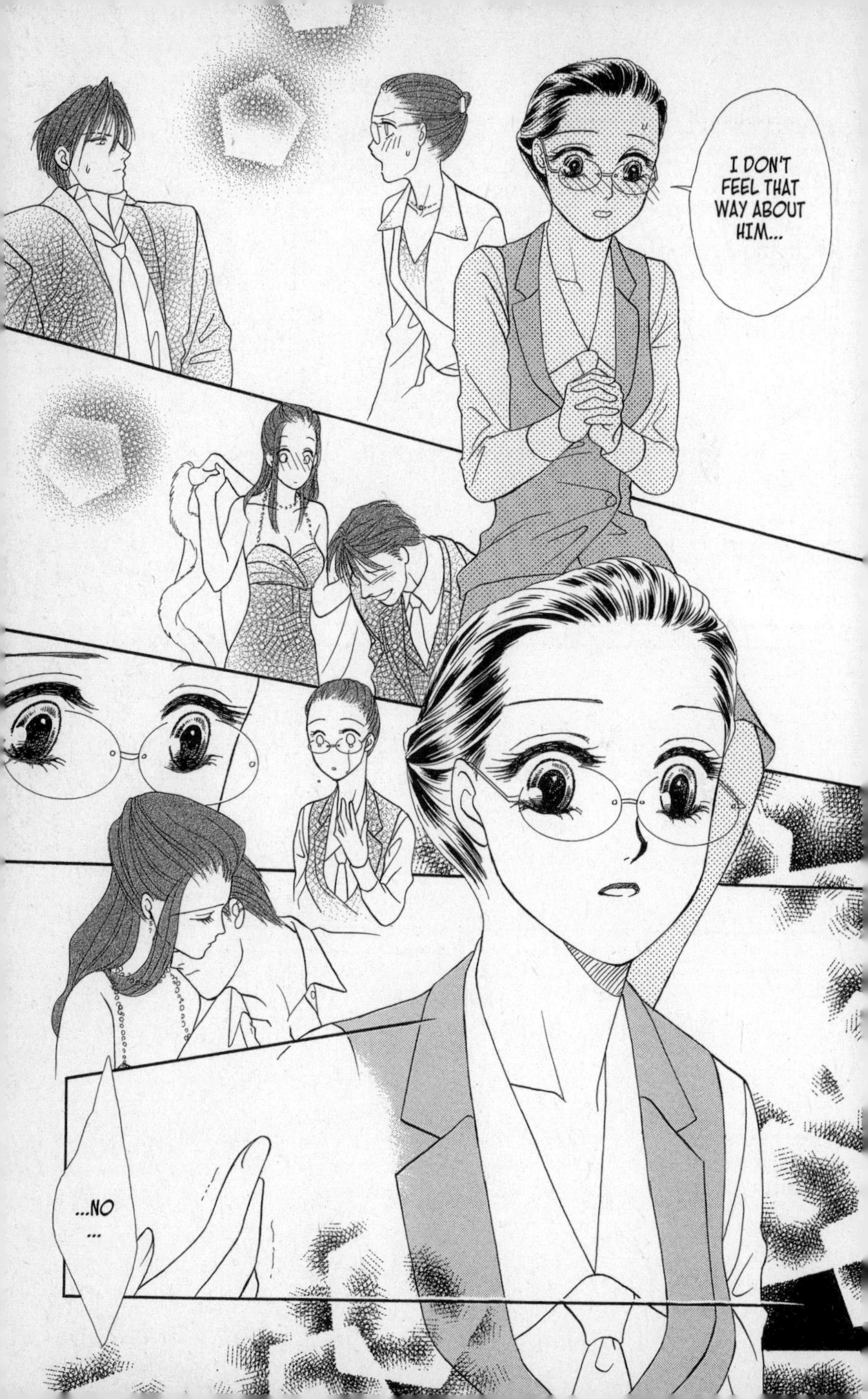
I DON'T FEEL THAT WAY ABOUT HIM...
...NO ...

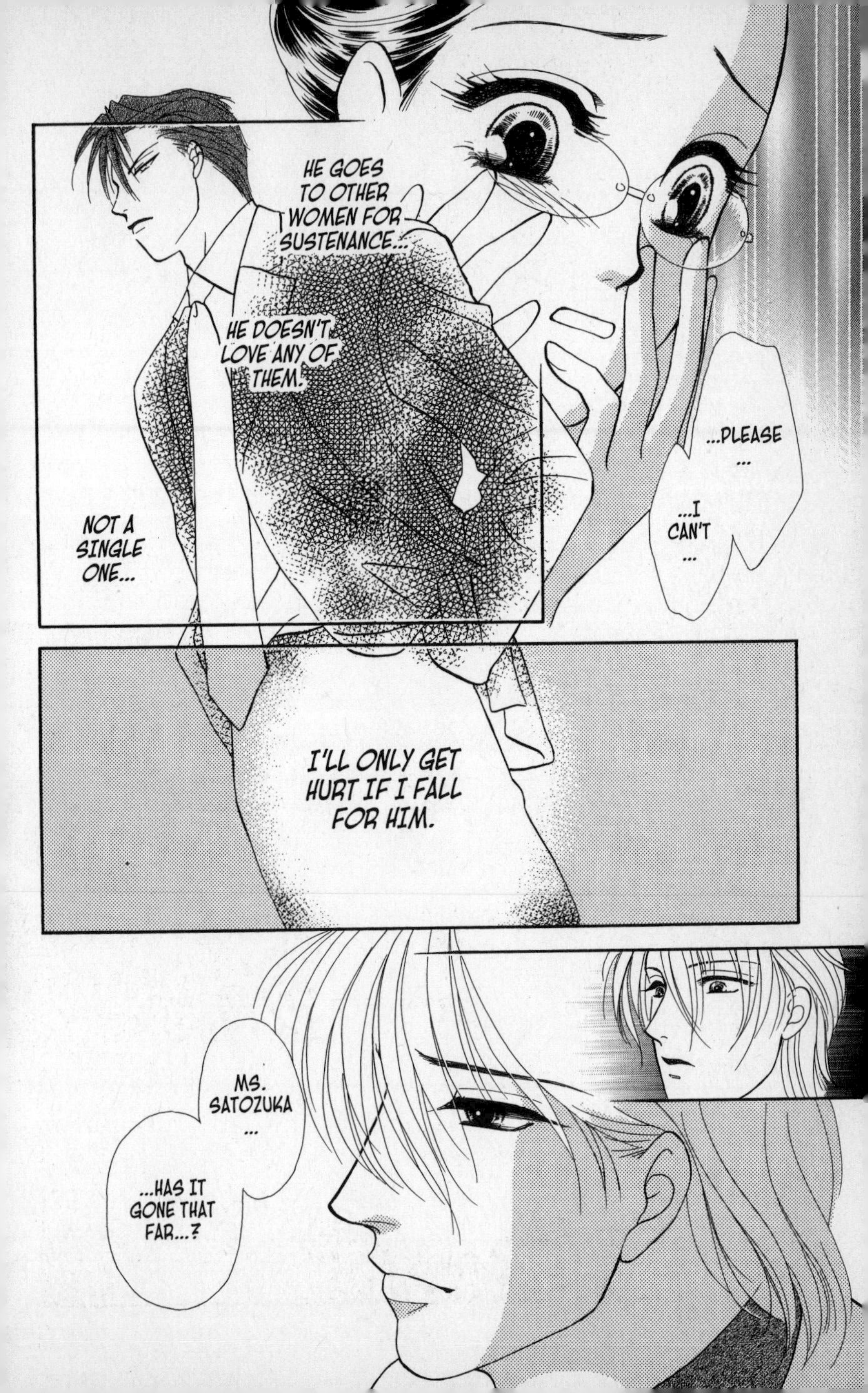
...PLEASE ...
...I CAN'T ...
HE GOES TO OTHER WOMEN FOR SUSTENANCE...
HE DOESN'T LOVE ANY OF THEM.
NOT A SINGLE ONE...
I'LL ONLY GET HURT IF I FALL FOR HIM.
MS. SATOZUKA ...
...HAS IT GONE THAT FAR...?

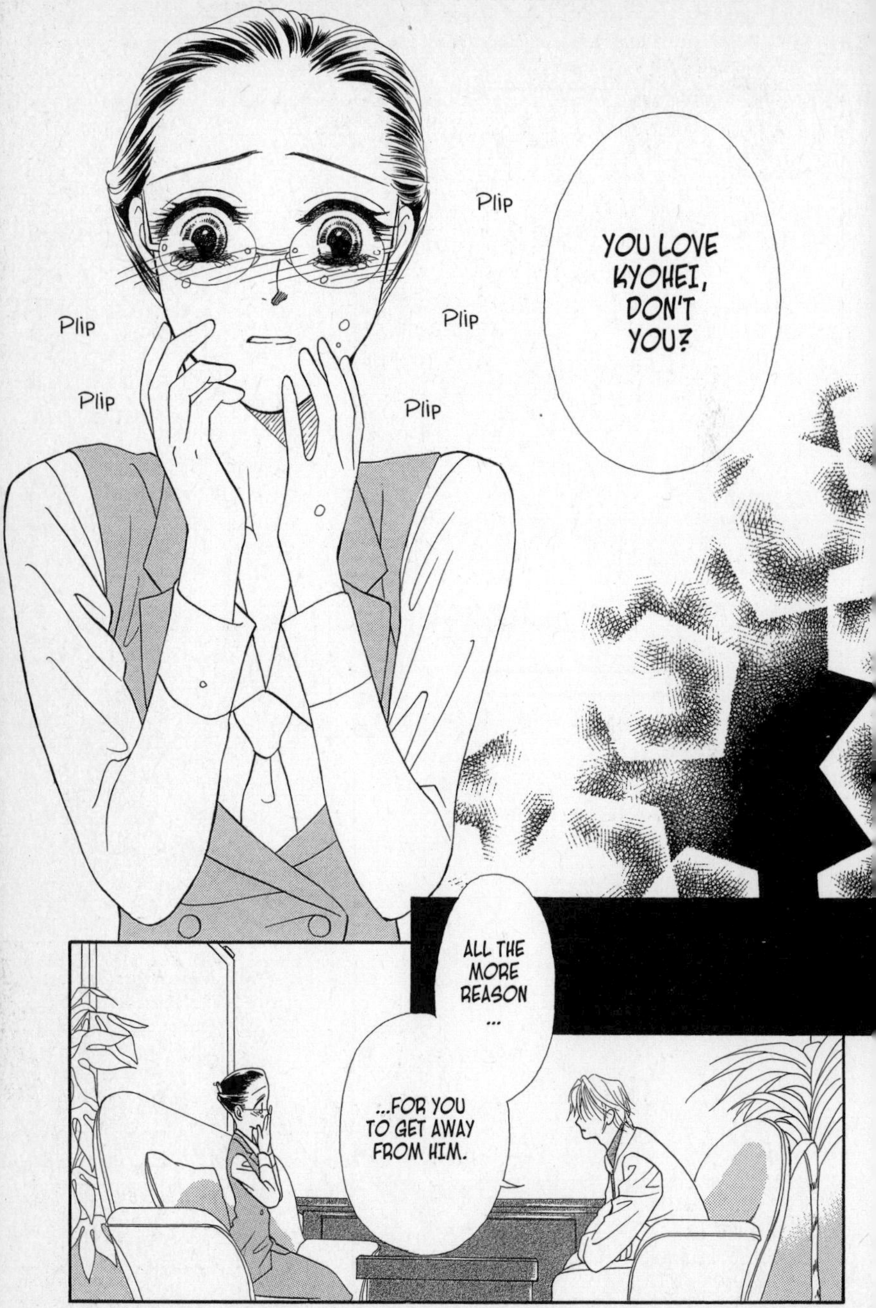
YOU LOVE KYOHEI, DON'T YOU?
Plip
Plip
Plip
Plip
Plip
ALL THE MORE REASON ...
...FOR YOU TO GET AWAY FROM HIM.

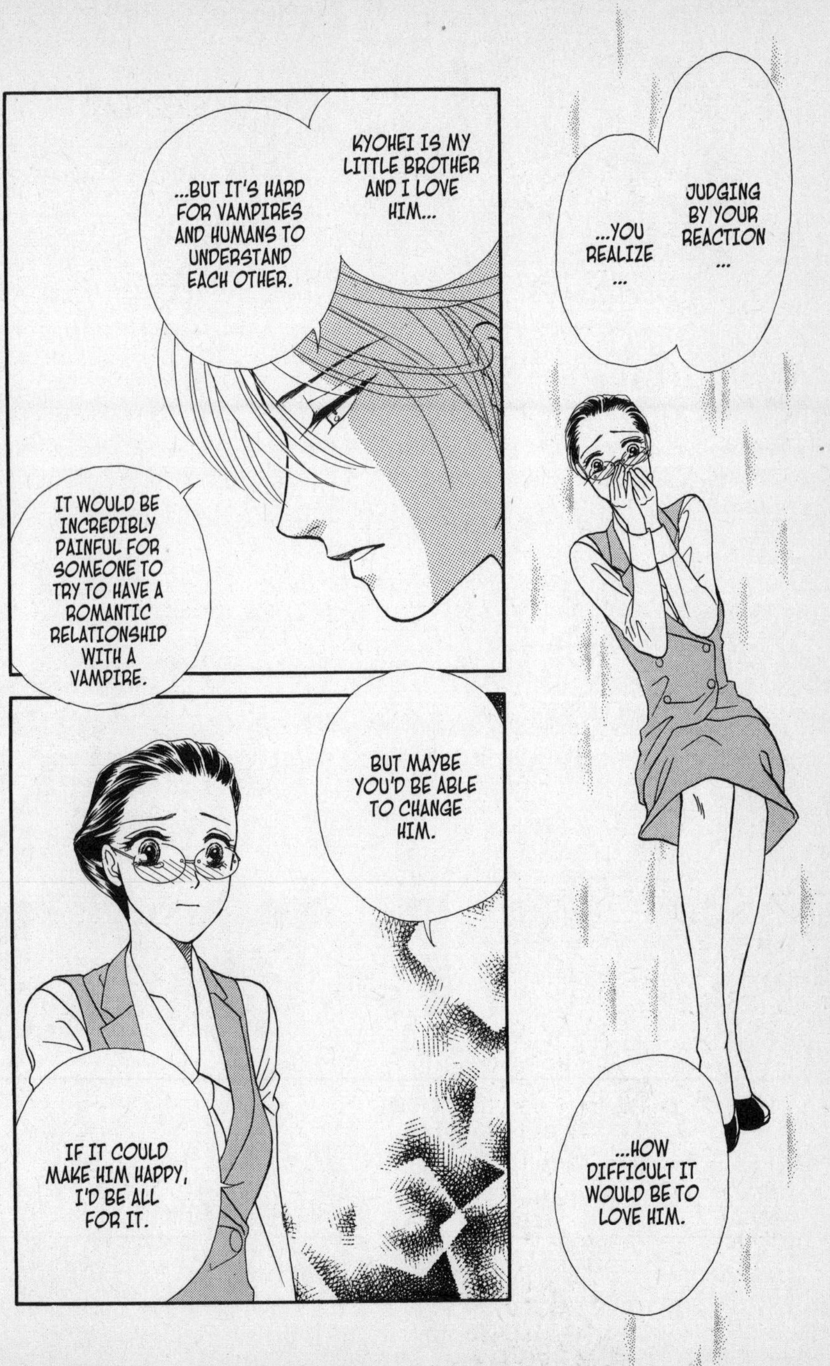
JUDGING BY YOUR REACTION ...
...YOU REALIZE ...
...HOW DIFFICULT IT WOULD BE TO LOVE HIM.
KYOHEI IS MY LITTLE BROTHER AND I LOVE HIM...
...BUT IT'S HARD FOR VAMPIRES AND HUMANS TO UNDERSTAND EACH OTHER.
IT WOULD BE INCREDIBLY PAINFUL FOR SOMEONE TO TRY TO HAVE A ROMANTIC RELATIONSHIP WITH A VAMPIRE.
BUT MAYBE YOU'D BE ABLE TO CHANGE HIM.
IF IT COULD MAKE HIM HAPPY, I'D BE ALL FOR IT.

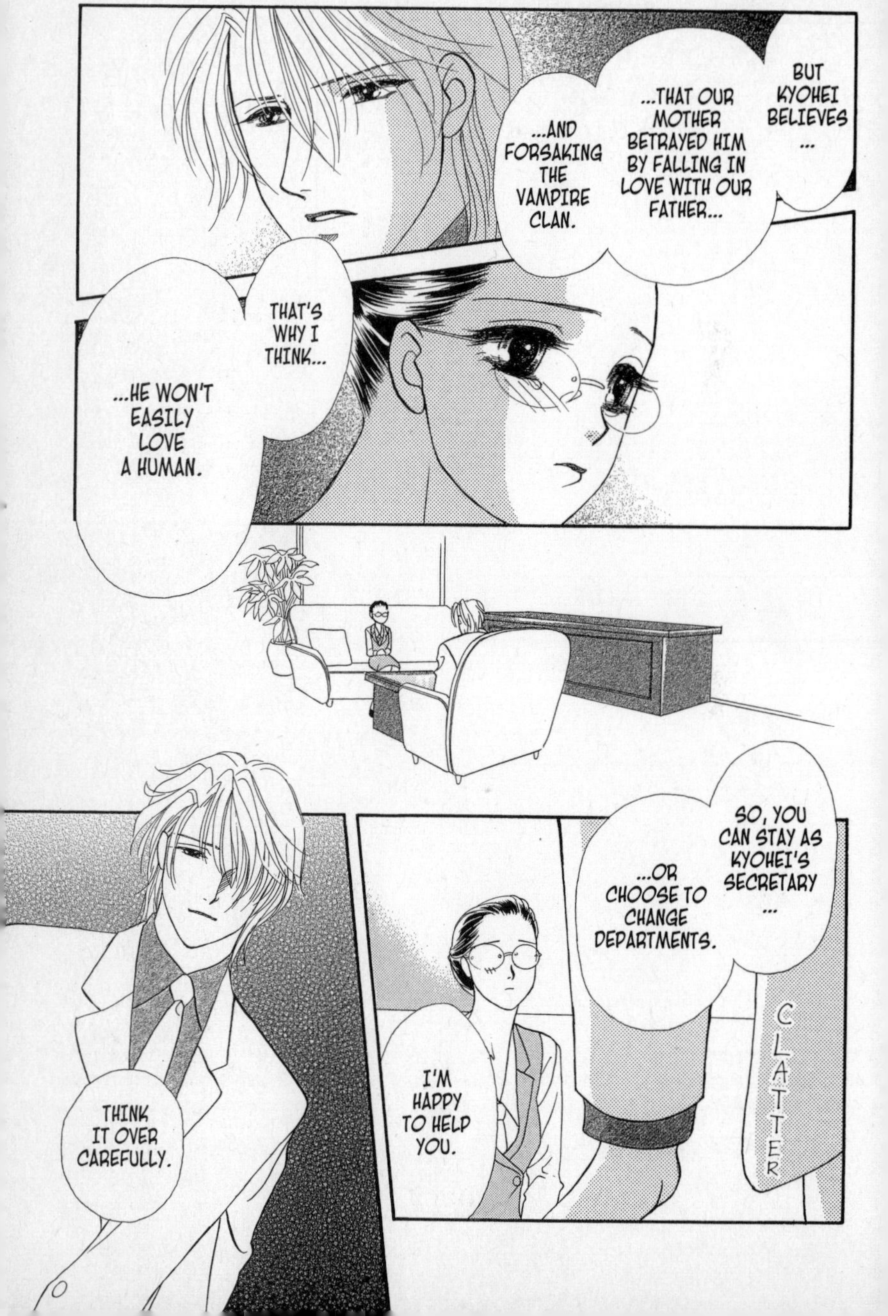
BUT KYOHEI BELIEVES ...
...THAT OUR MOTHER BETRAYED HIM BY FALLING IN LOVE WITH OUR FATHER...
...AND FORSAKING THE VAMPIRE CLAN.
THAT'S WHY I THINK...
...HE WON'T EASILY LOVE A HUMAN.
SO, YOU CAN STAY AS KYOHEI'S SECRETARY ...
...OR CHOOSE TO CHANGE DEPARTMENTS.
CLATTER
I'M HAPPY TO HELP YOU.
THINK IT OVER CAREFULLY.

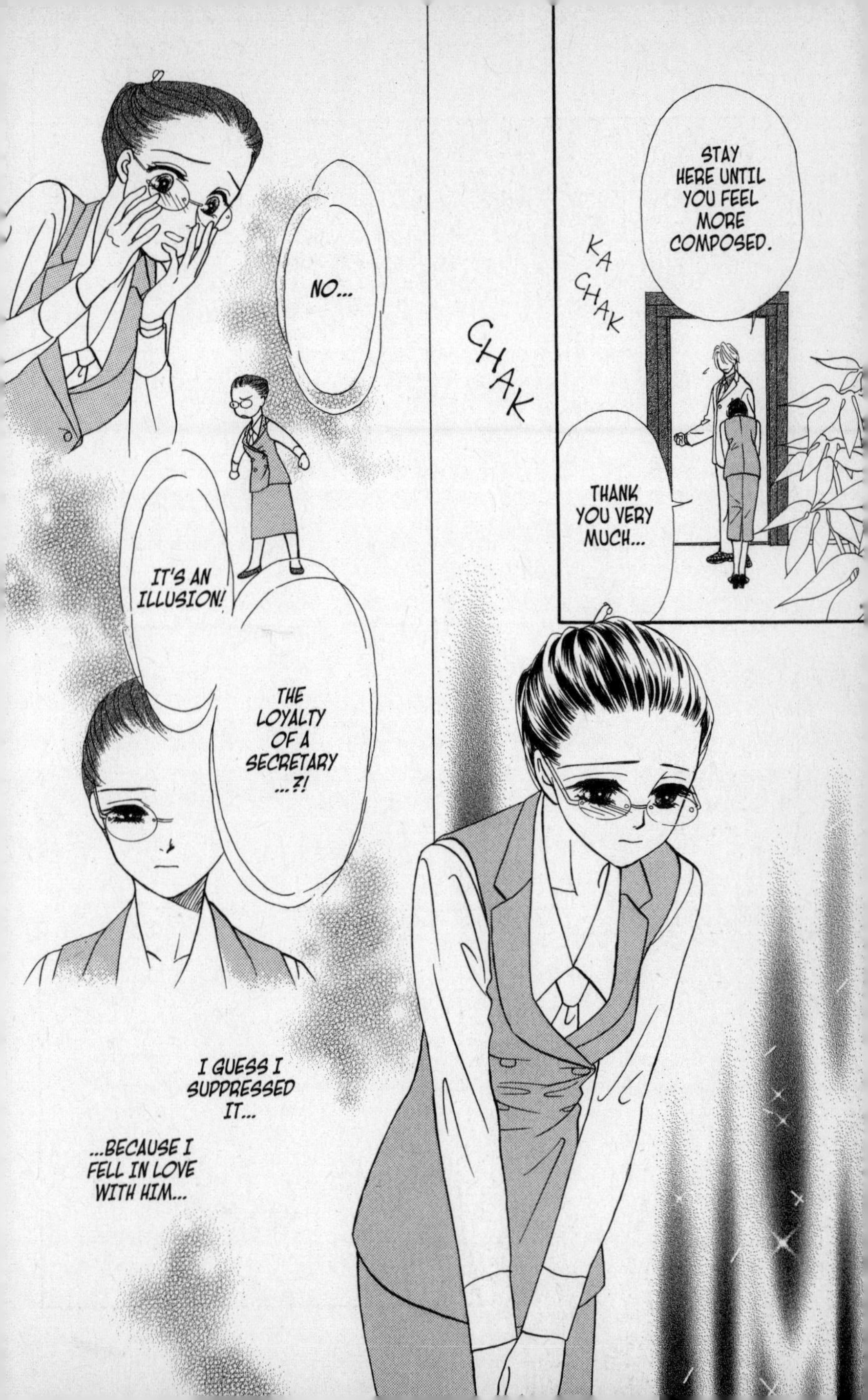
STAY HERE UNTIL YOU FEEL MORE COMPOSED.
KA CHAK
CHAK
THANK YOU VERY MUCH...
NO...
IT'S AN ILLUSION!
THE LOYALTY OF A SECRETARY ...?!
I GUESS I SUPPRESSED IT...
...BECAUSE I FELL IN LOVE WITH HIM...

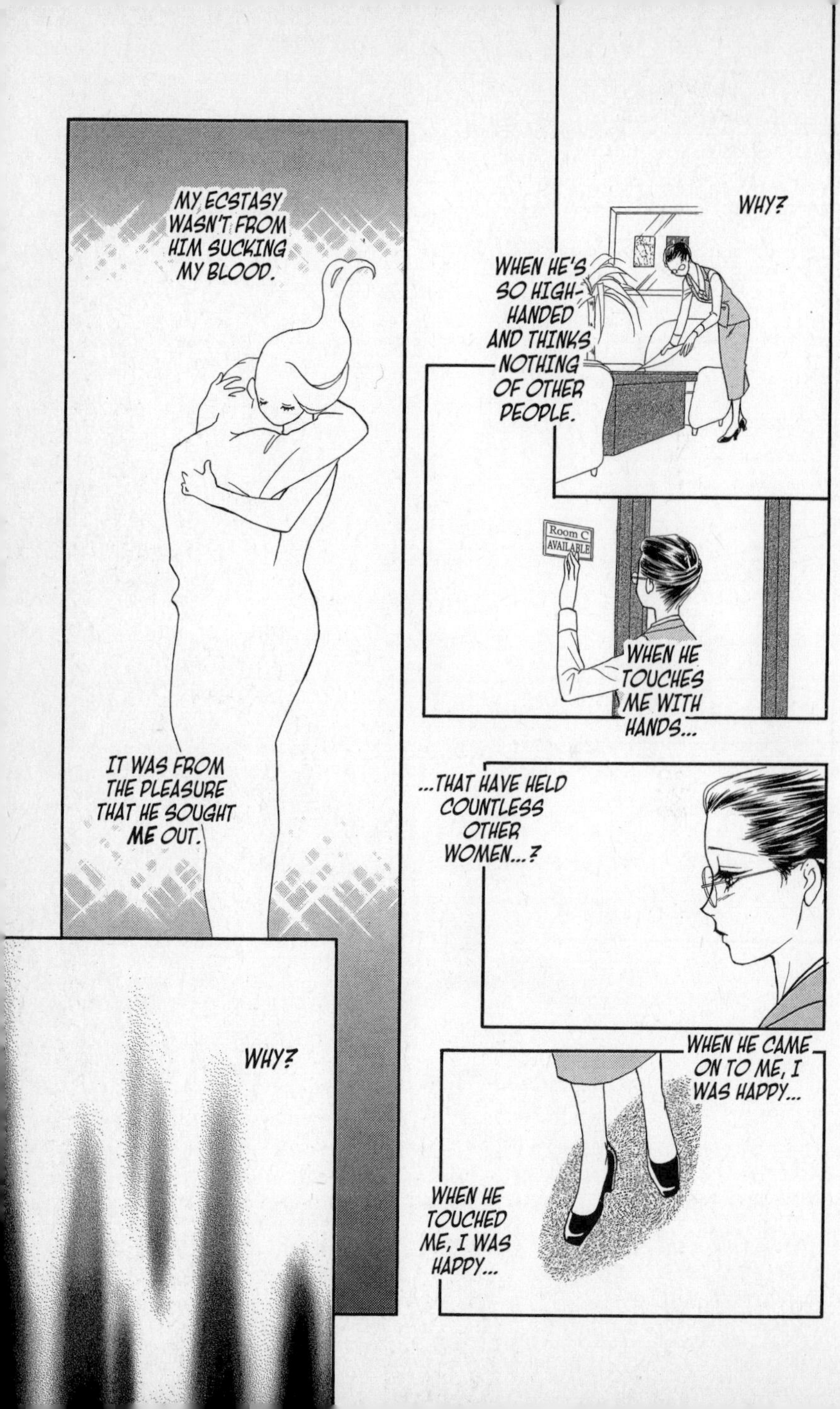
WHY?
WHEN HE'S SO HIGH-HANDED AND THINKS NOTHING OF OTHER PEOPLE.
Room C AVAILABLE
WHEN HE TOUCHES ME WITH HANDS...
...THAT HAVE HELD COUNTLESS OTHER WOMEN...?
WHEN HE CAME ON TO ME, I WAS HAPPY...
WHEN HE TOUCHED ME, I WAS HAPPY...
MY ECSTASY WASN'T FROM HIM SUCKING MY BLOOD.
IT WAS FROM THE PLEASURE THAT HE SOUGHT ME OUT.
WHY?

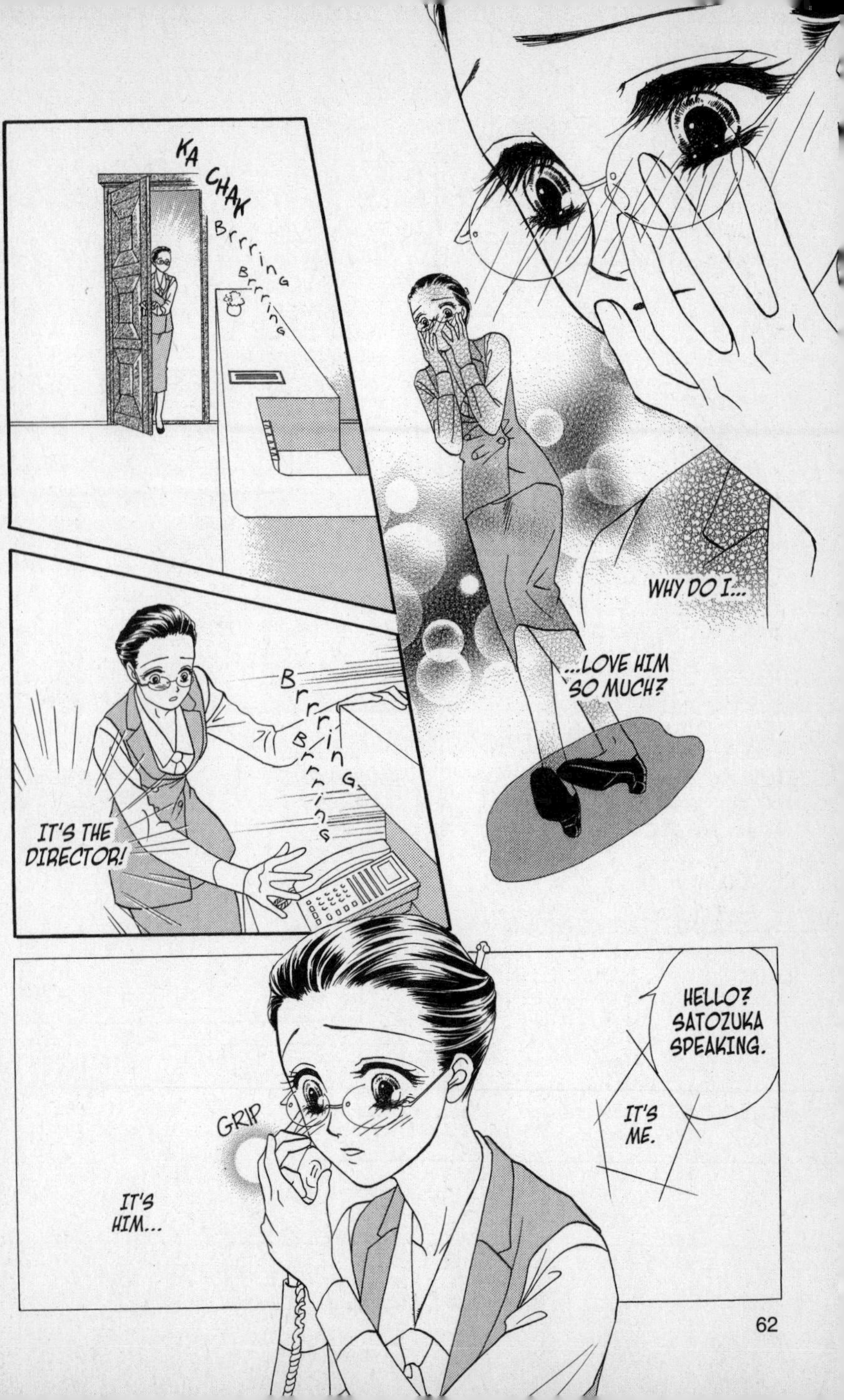
WHY DO I...
...LOVE HIM SO MUCH?
KA CHAK
Brrring
Brrrring
IT'S THE DIRECTOR!
Brrring
Brrrring
HELLO? SATOZUKA SPEAKING.
IT'S ME.
GRIP
IT'S HIM...

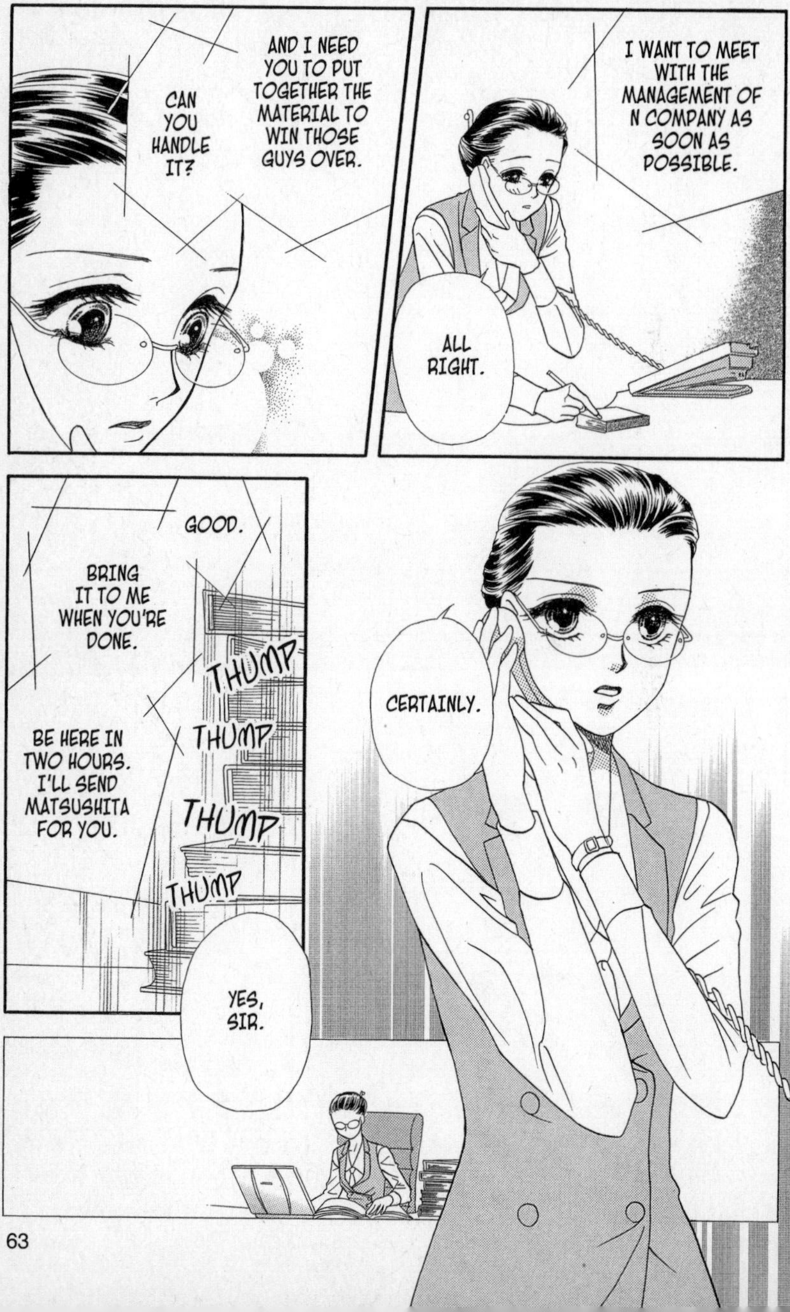
I WANT TO MEET WITH THE MANAGEMENT OF N COMPANY AS SOON AS POSSIBLE.
ALL RIGHT.
AND I NEED YOU TO PUT TOGETHER THE MATERIAL TO WIN THOSE GUYS OVER.
CAN YOU HANDLE IT?
CERTAINLY.
GOOD.
BRING IT TO ME WHEN YOU'RE DONE.
THUMP
THUMP
THUMP
THUMP
BE HERE IN TWO HOURS. I'LL SEND MATSUSHITA FOR YOU.
YES, SIR.

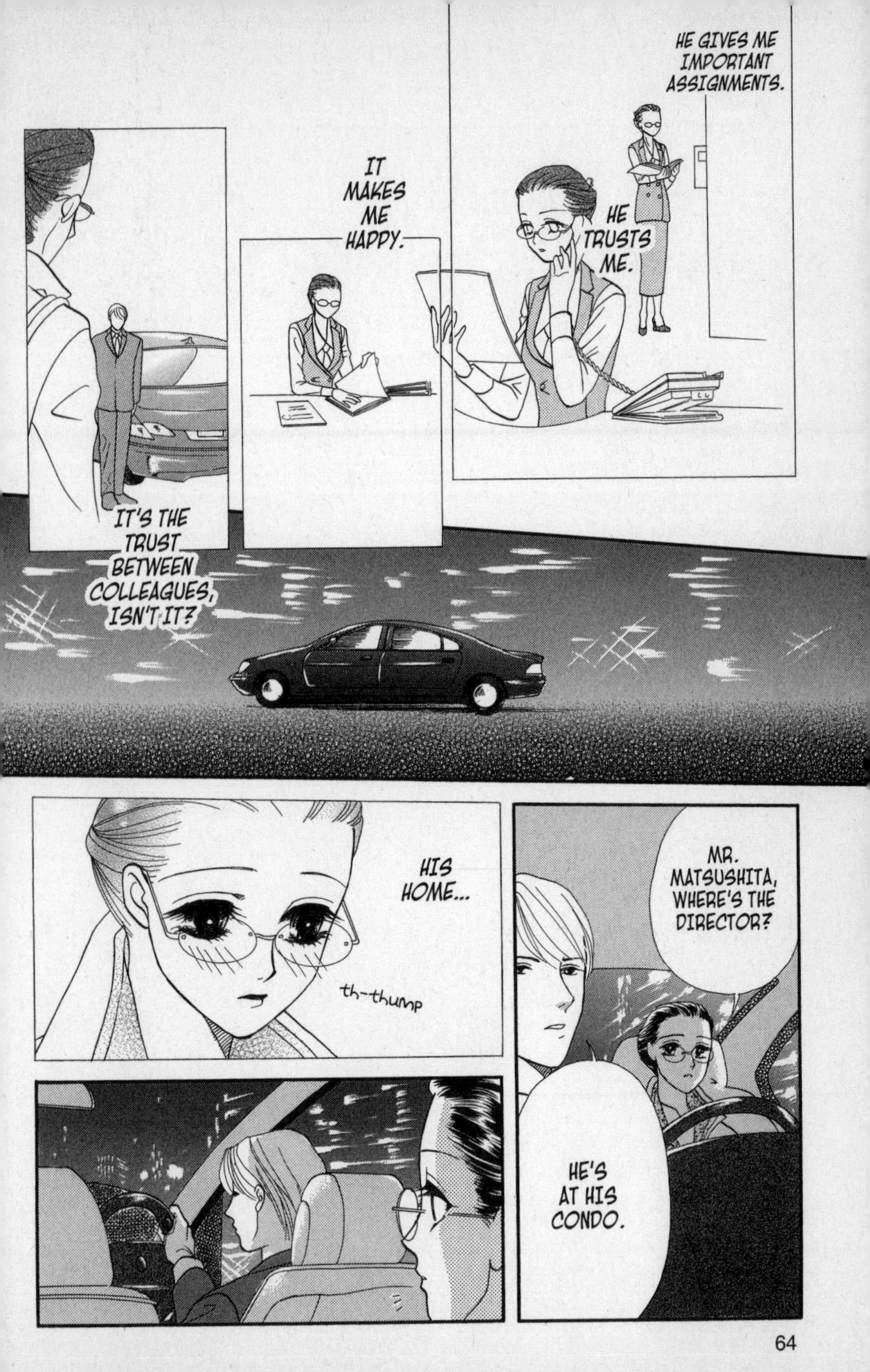
HE GIVES ME IMPORTANT ASSIGNMENTS.
HE TRUSTS ME.
IT MAKES ME HAPPY.
IT'S THE TRUST BETWEEN COLLEAGUES, ISN'T IT?
MR. MATSUSHITA, WHERE'S THE DIRECTOR?
HE'S AT HIS CONDO.
HIS HOME...
th-thump

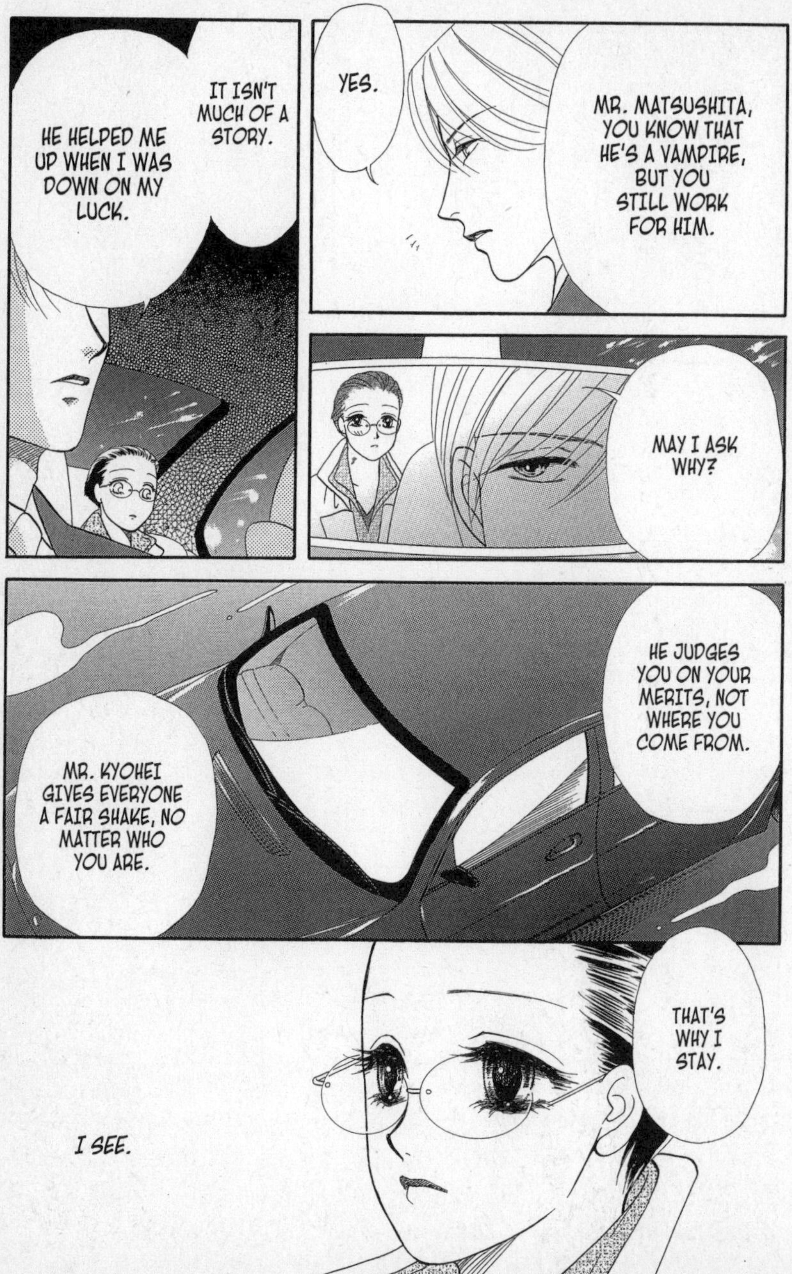
MR. MATSUSHITA, YOU KNOW THAT HE'S A VAMPIRE, BUT YOU STILL WORK FOR HIM.
YES.
MAY I ASK WHY?
IT ISN'T MUCH OF A STORY.
HE HELPED ME UP WHEN I WAS DOWN ON MY LUCK.
HE JUDGES YOU ON YOUR MERITS, NOT WHERE YOU COME FROM.
MR. KYOHEI GIVES EVERYONE A FAIR SHAKE, NO MATTER WHO YOU ARE.
THAT'S WHY I STAY.
I SEE.

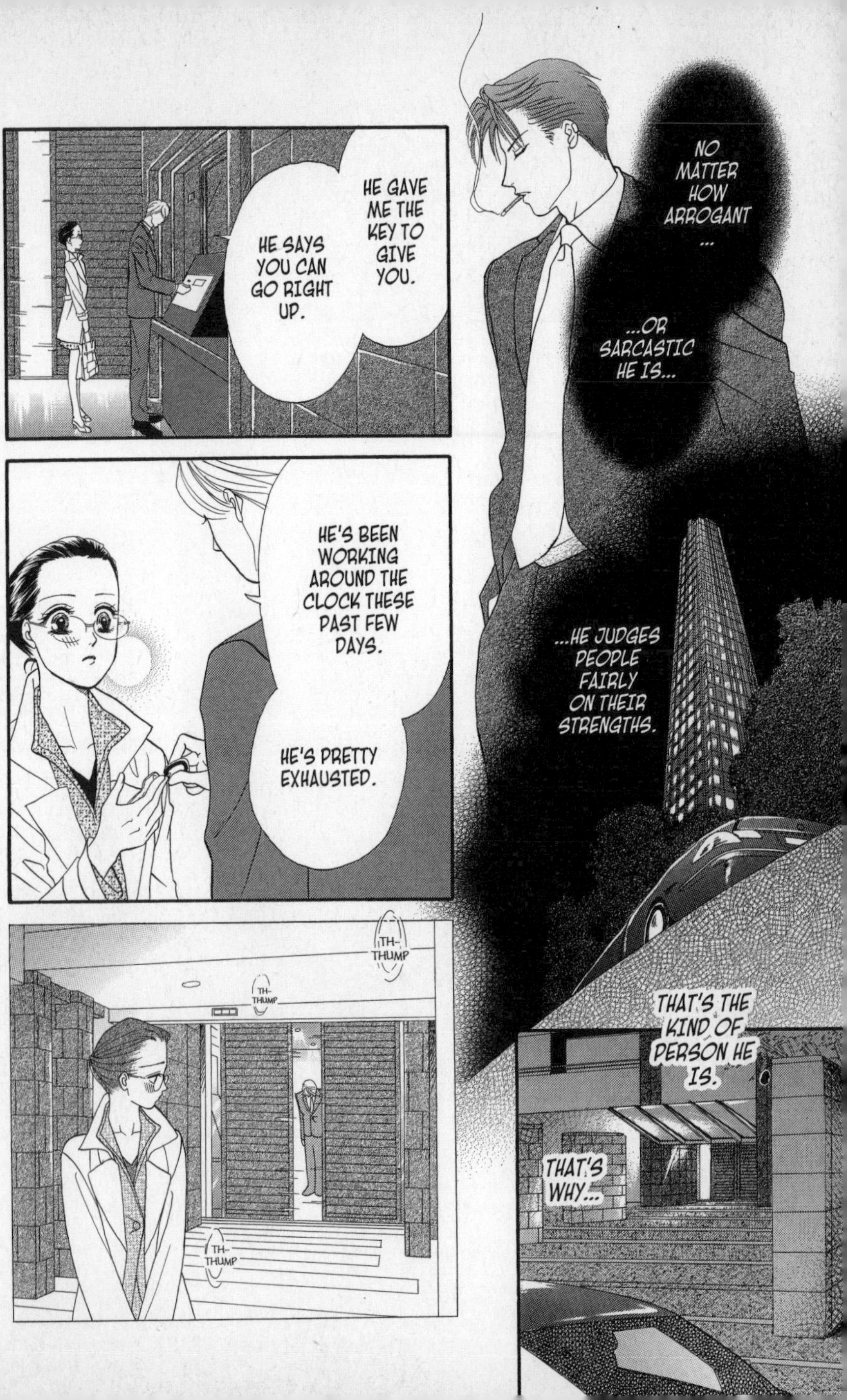
NO MATTER HOW ARROGANT...
...OR SARCASTIC HE IS...
...HE JUDGES PEOPLE FAIRLY ON THEIR STRENGTHS.
THAT'S THE KIND OF PERSON HE IS.
THAT'S WHY...
HE GAVE ME THE KEY TO GIVE YOU.
HE SAYS YOU CAN GO RIGHT UP.
HE'S BEEN WORKING AROUND THE CLOCK THESE PAST FEW DAYS.
HE'S PRETTY EXHAUSTED.
TH-THUMP
TH-THUMP
TH-THUMP

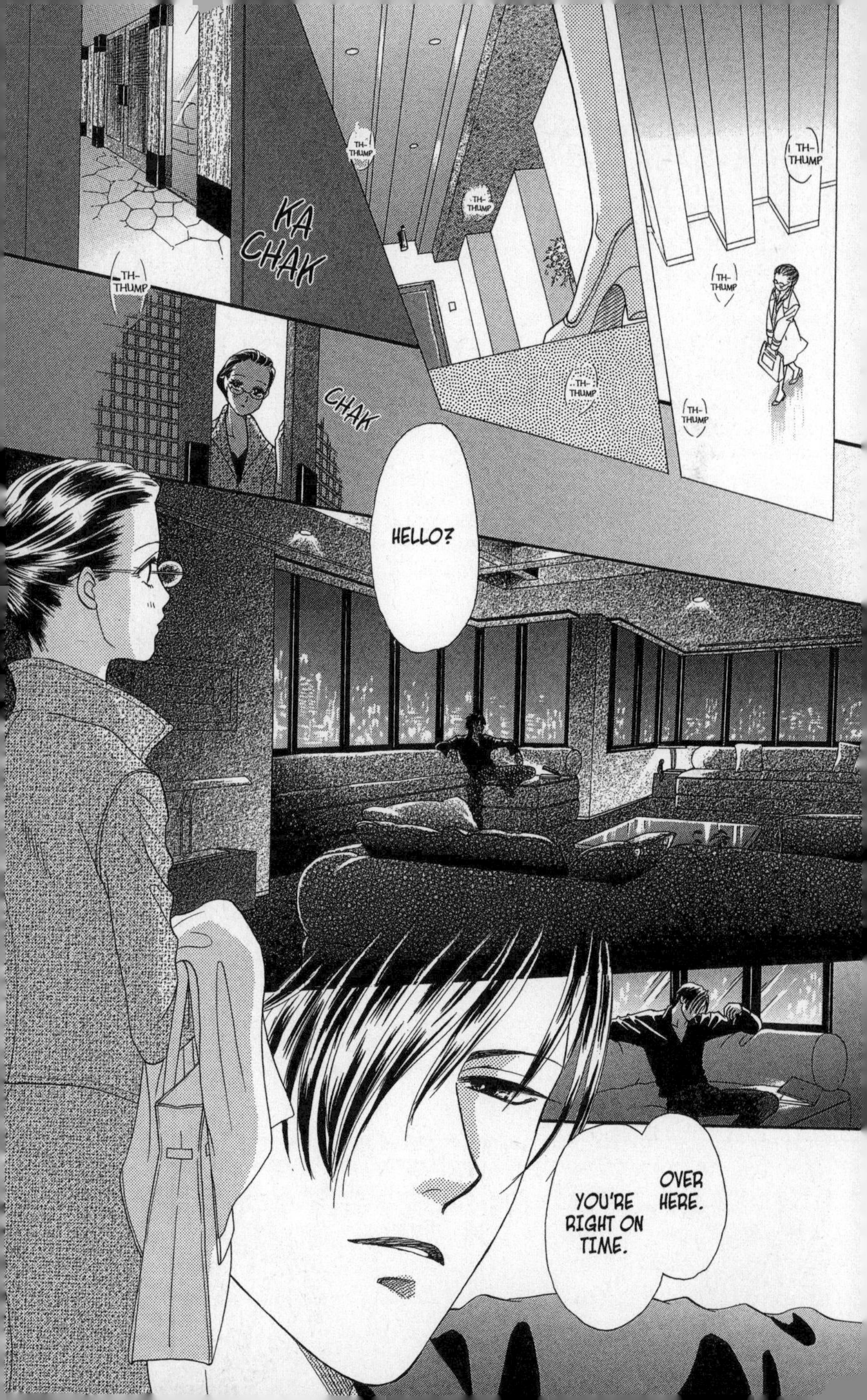

TH-THUMP
TH-THUMP
TH-THUMP
TH-THUMP
TH-THUMP
TH-THUMP
KA CHAK
TH-THUMP
CHAK
HELLO?
YOU'RE RIGHT ON TIME.
OVER HERE.

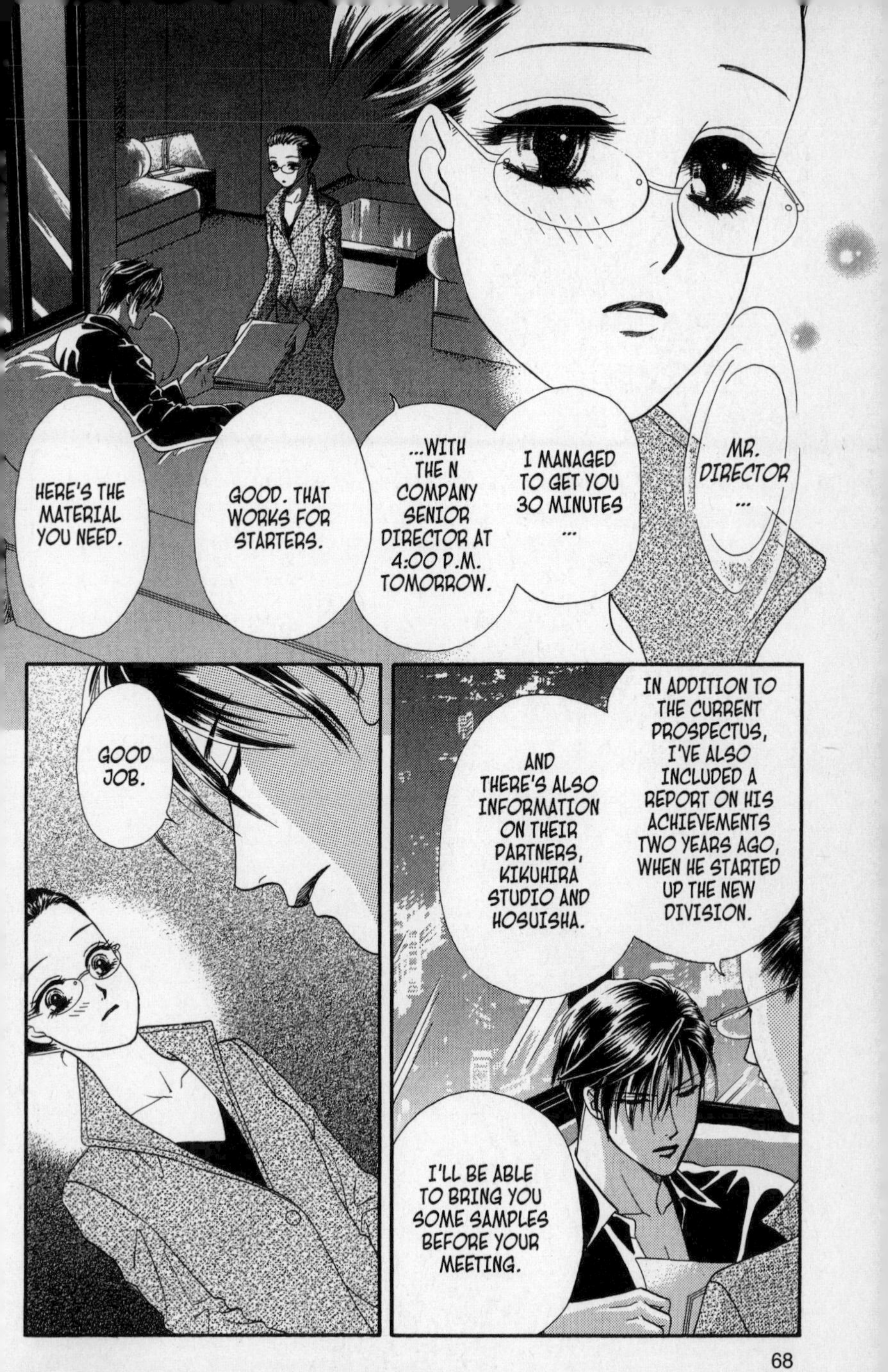
MR. DIRECTOR ...
I MANAGED TO GET YOU 30 MINUTES ...
...WITH THE N COMPANY SENIOR DIRECTOR AT 4:00 P.M. TOMORROW.
GOOD. THAT WORKS FOR STARTERS.
HERE'S THE MATERIAL YOU NEED.
IN ADDITION TO THE CURRENT PROSPECTUS, I'VE ALSO INCLUDED A REPORT ON HIS ACHIEVEMENTS TWO YEARS AGO, WHEN HE STARTED UP THE NEW DIVISION.
AND THERE'S ALSO INFORMATION ON THEIR PARTNERS, KIKUHIRA STUDIO AND HOSUISHA.
I'LL BE ABLE TO BRING YOU SOME SAMPLES BEFORE YOUR MEETING.
GOOD JOB.

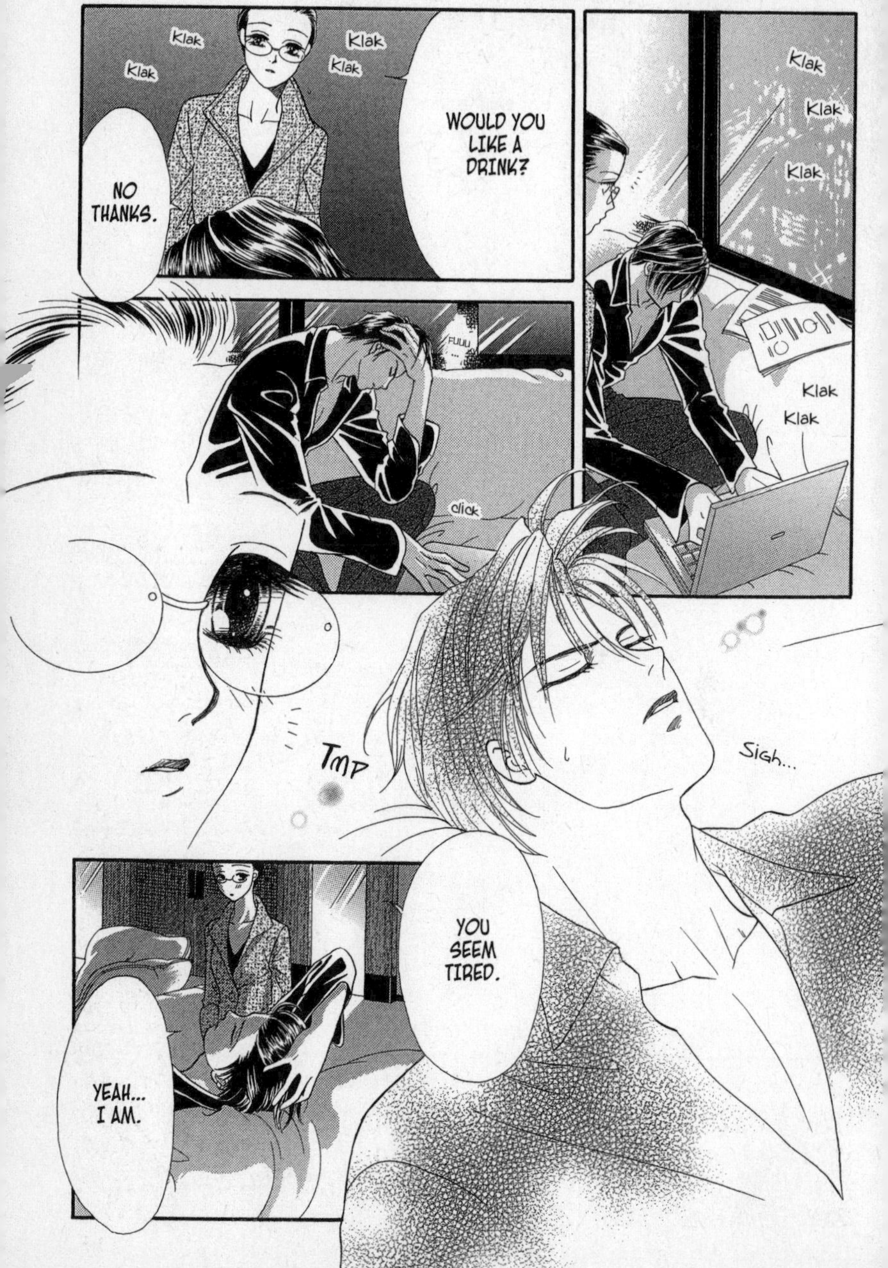
Klak
Klak
Klak
Klak
Klak
Klak
Klak
WOULD YOU LIKE A DRINK?
Klak
Klak
NO THANKS.
FUUU...
click
Sigh...
TMP
YOU SEEM TIRED.
YEAH... I AM.

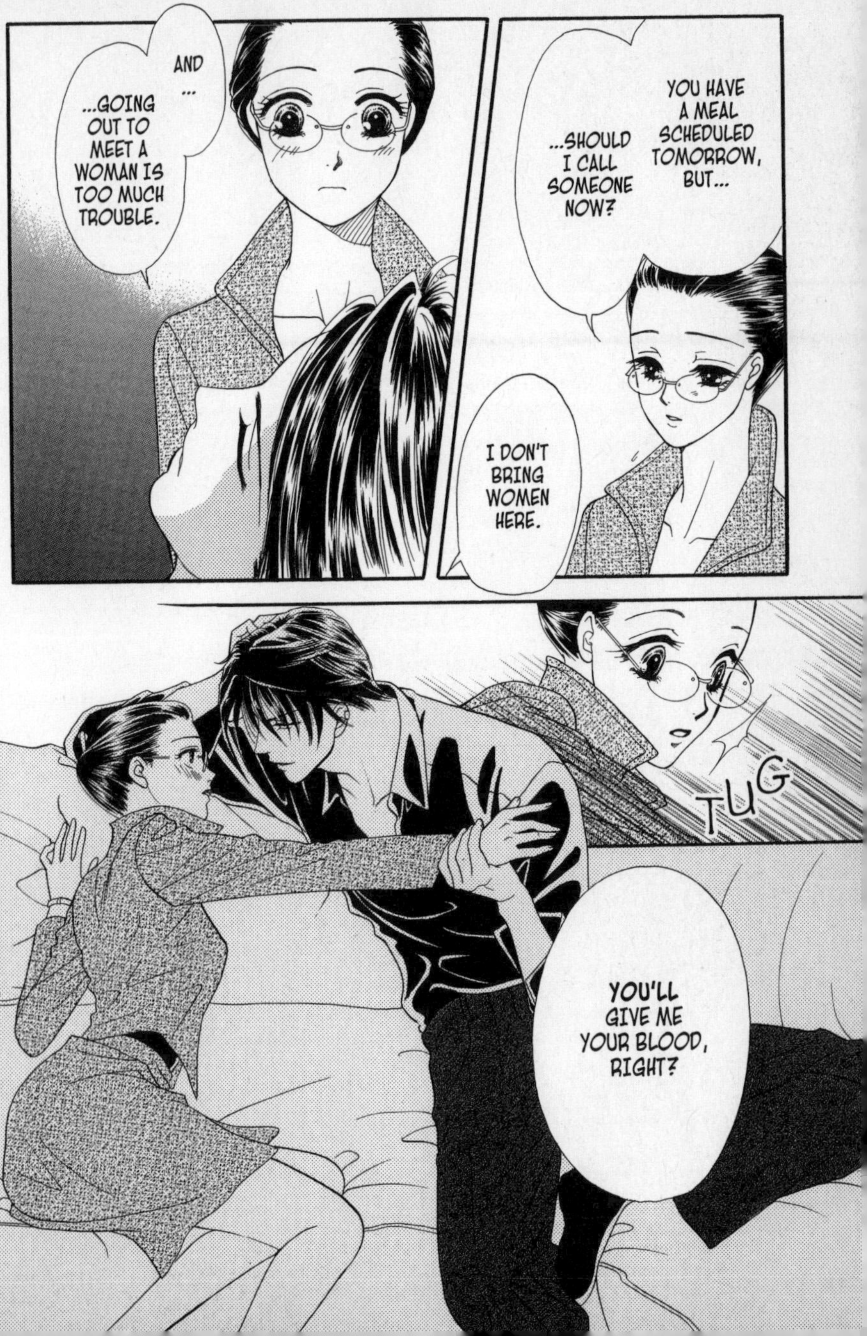
YOU HAVE A MEAL SCHEDULED TOMORROW, BUT...
...SHOULD I CALL SOMEONE NOW?
I DON'T BRING WOMEN HERE.
AND ...
...GOING OUT TO MEET A WOMAN IS TOO MUCH TROUBLE.
TUG
YOU'LL GIVE ME YOUR BLOOD, RIGHT?

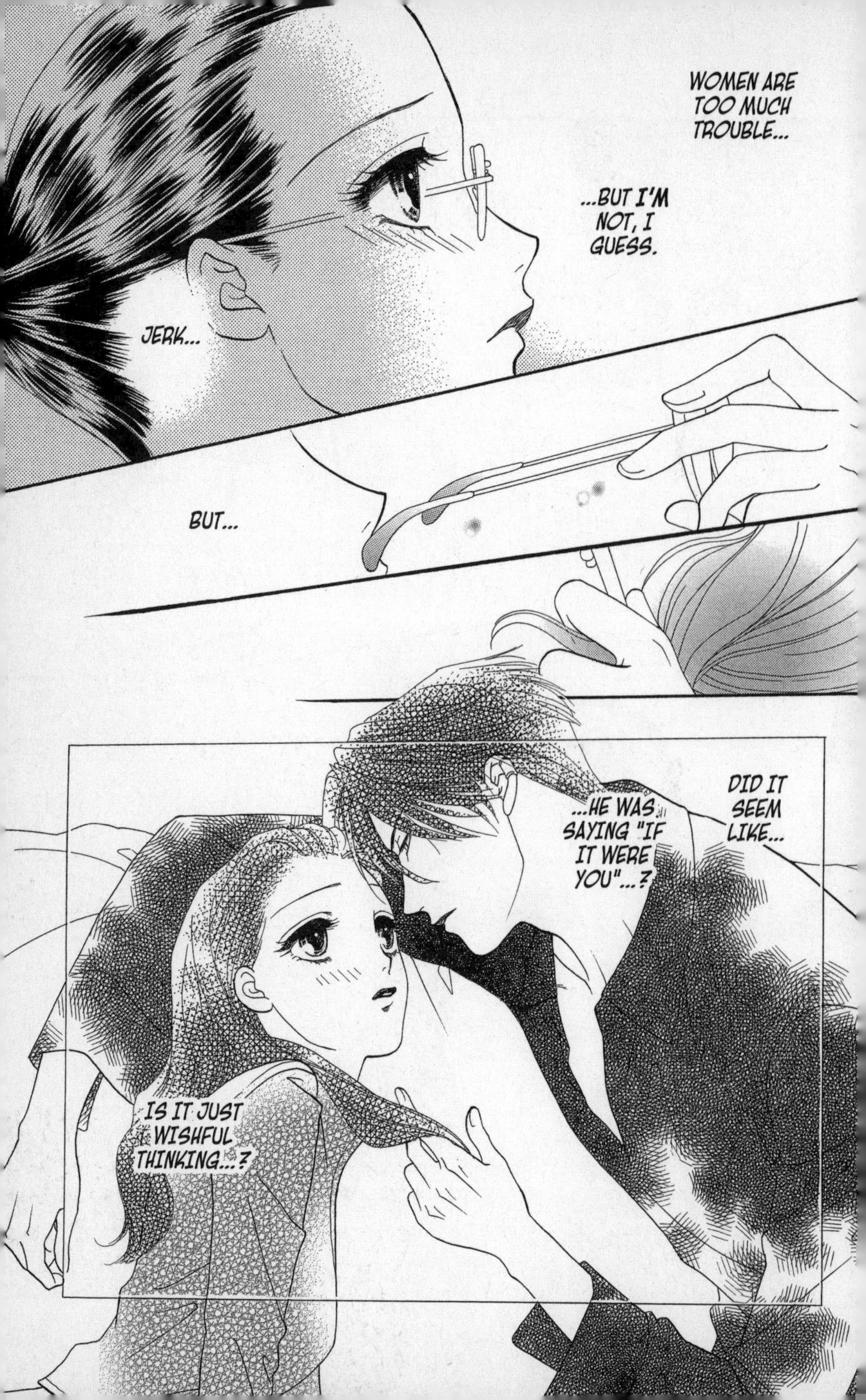
WOMEN ARE TOO MUCH TROUBLE...
...BUT I'M NOT, I GUESS.
JERK...
BUT...
DID IT SEEM LIKE...
...HE WAS SAYING "IF IT WERE YOU"...?
IS IT JUST WISHFUL THINKING...?

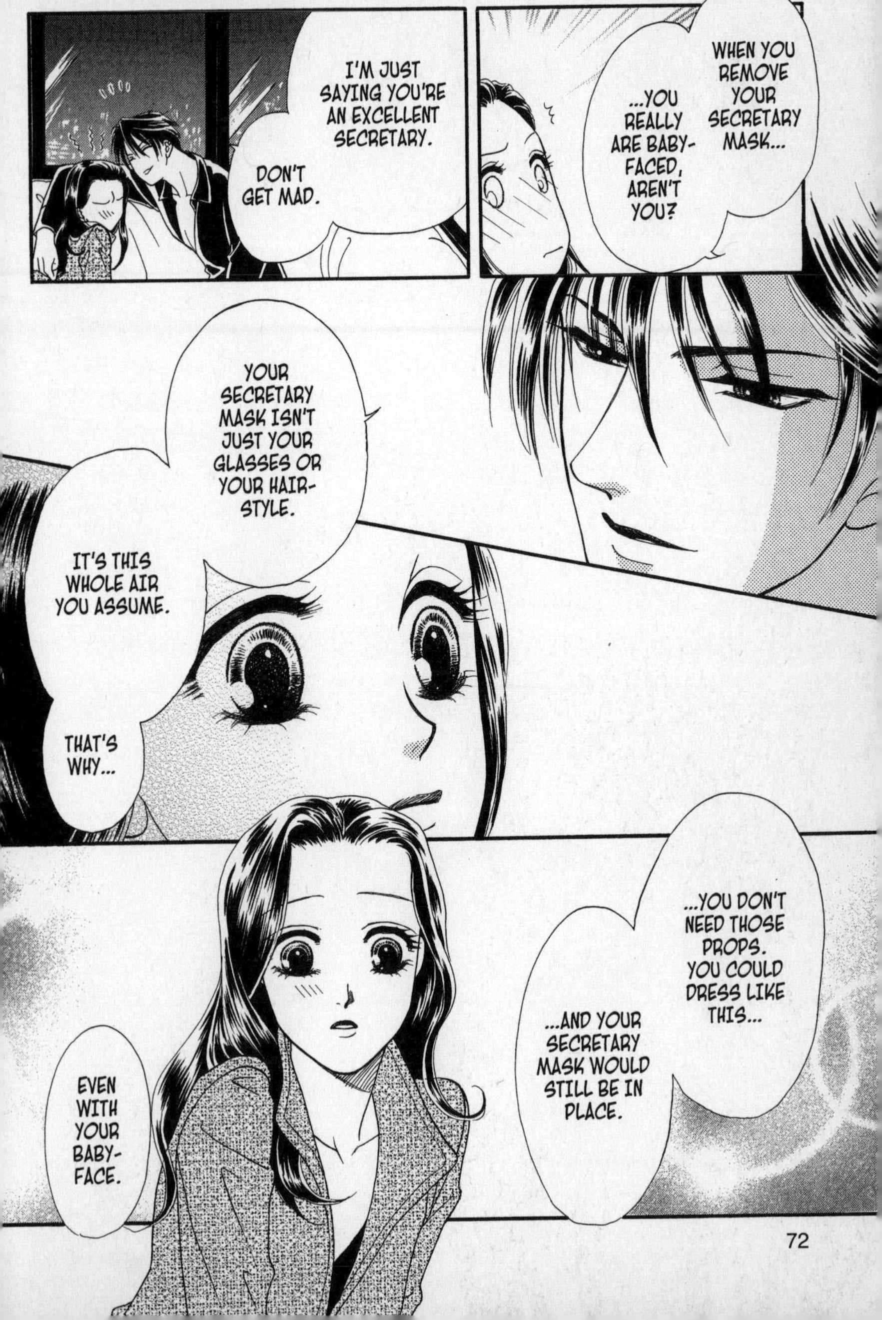
WHEN YOU REMOVE YOUR SECRETARY MASK...
...YOU REALLY ARE BABY-FACED, AREN'T YOU?
I'M JUST SAYING YOU'RE AN EXCELLENT SECRETARY.
DON'T GET MAD.
YOUR SECRETARY MASK ISN'T JUST YOUR GLASSES OR YOUR HAIR-STYLE.
IT'S THIS WHOLE AIR YOU ASSUME.
THAT'S WHY...
...YOU DON'T NEED THOSE PROPS. YOU COULD DRESS LIKE THIS...
...AND YOUR SECRETARY MASK WOULD STILL BE IN PLACE.
EVEN WITH YOUR BABY-FACE.

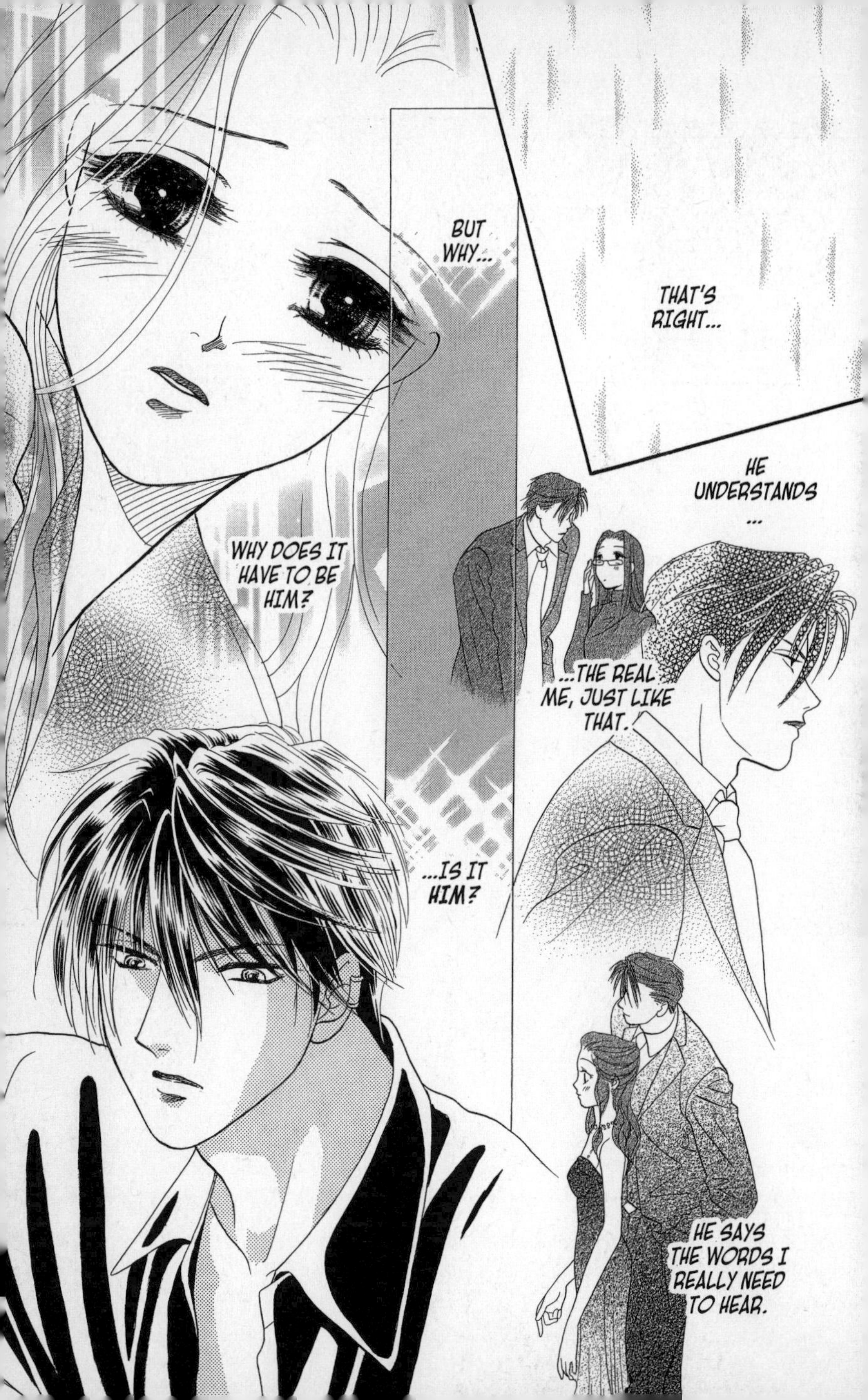
THAT'S RIGHT...
HE UNDERSTANDS...
...THE REAL ME, JUST LIKE THAT.
HE SAYS THE WORDS I REALLY NEED TO HEAR.
BUT WHY...
...IS IT HIM?
WHY DOES IT HAVE TO BE HIM?

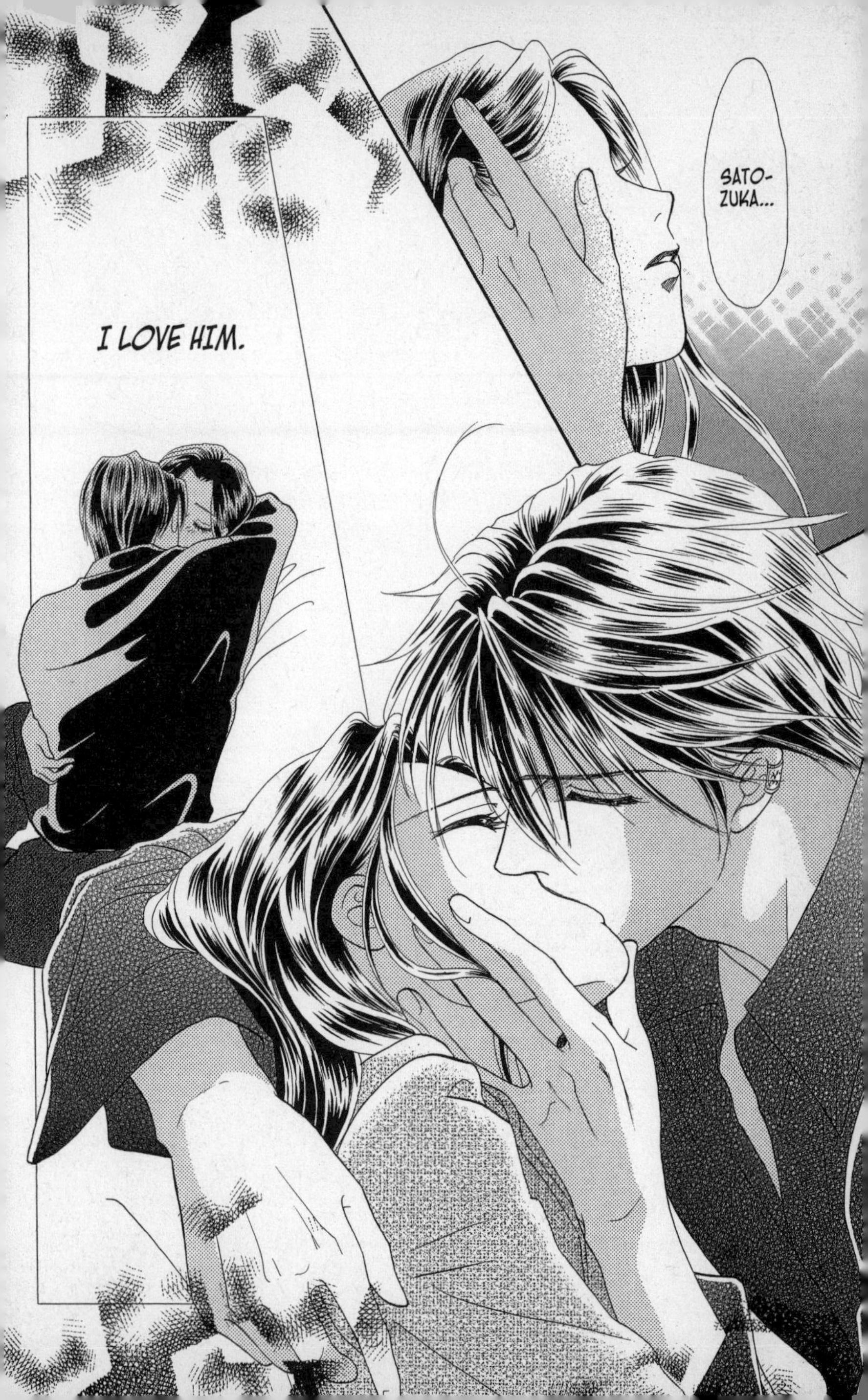
SATO-ZUKA...
I LOVE HIM.

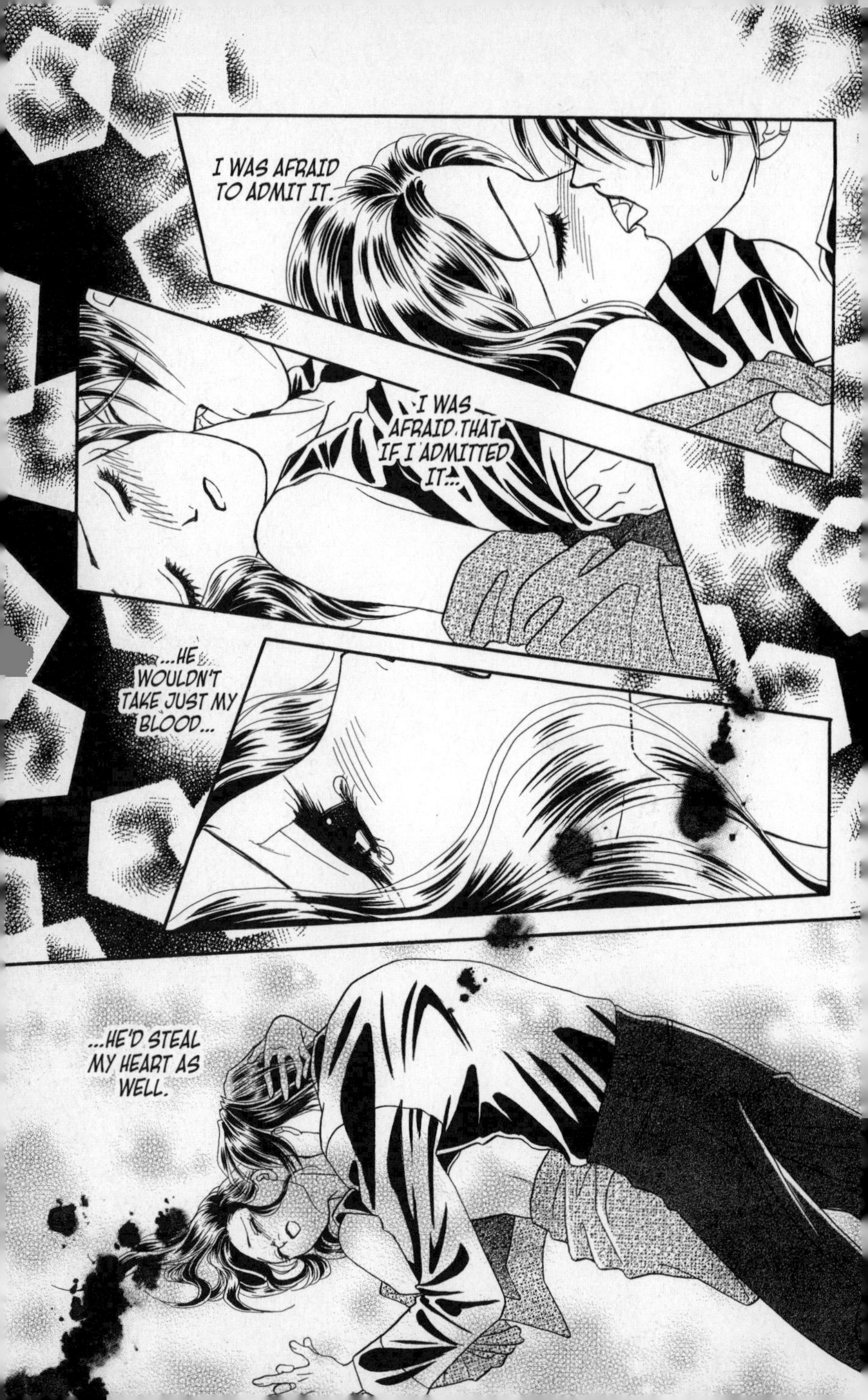
I WAS AFRAID TO ADMIT IT.
I WAS AFRAID THAT IF I ADMITTED IT...
...HE WOULDN'T TAKE JUST MY BLOOD...
...HE'D STEAL MY HEART AS WELL.

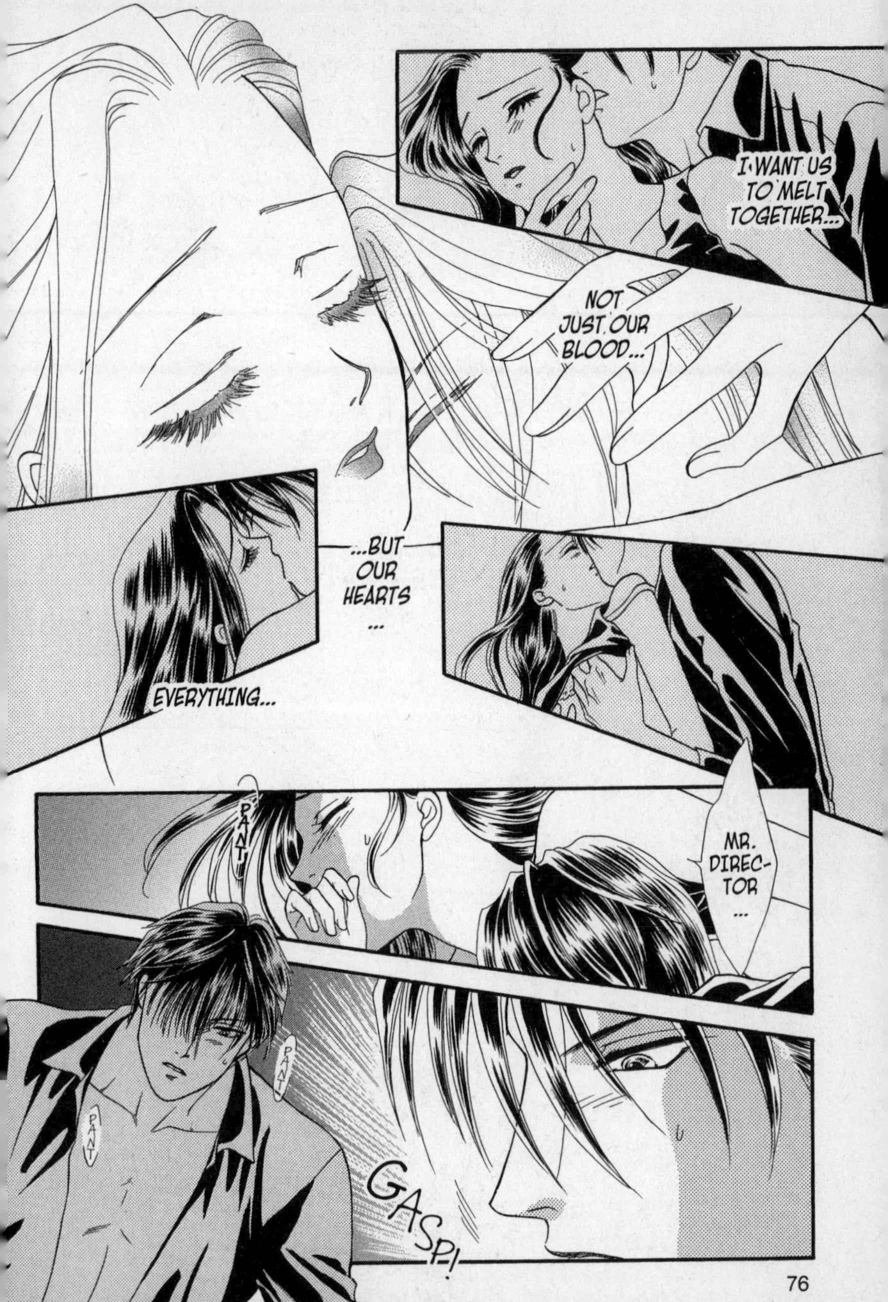
I WANT US TO MELT TOGETHER...
NOT JUST OUR BLOOD...
...BUT OUR HEARTS ...
EVERYTHING...
MR. DIRECTOR ...
PANT
GASP!
PANT
PANT

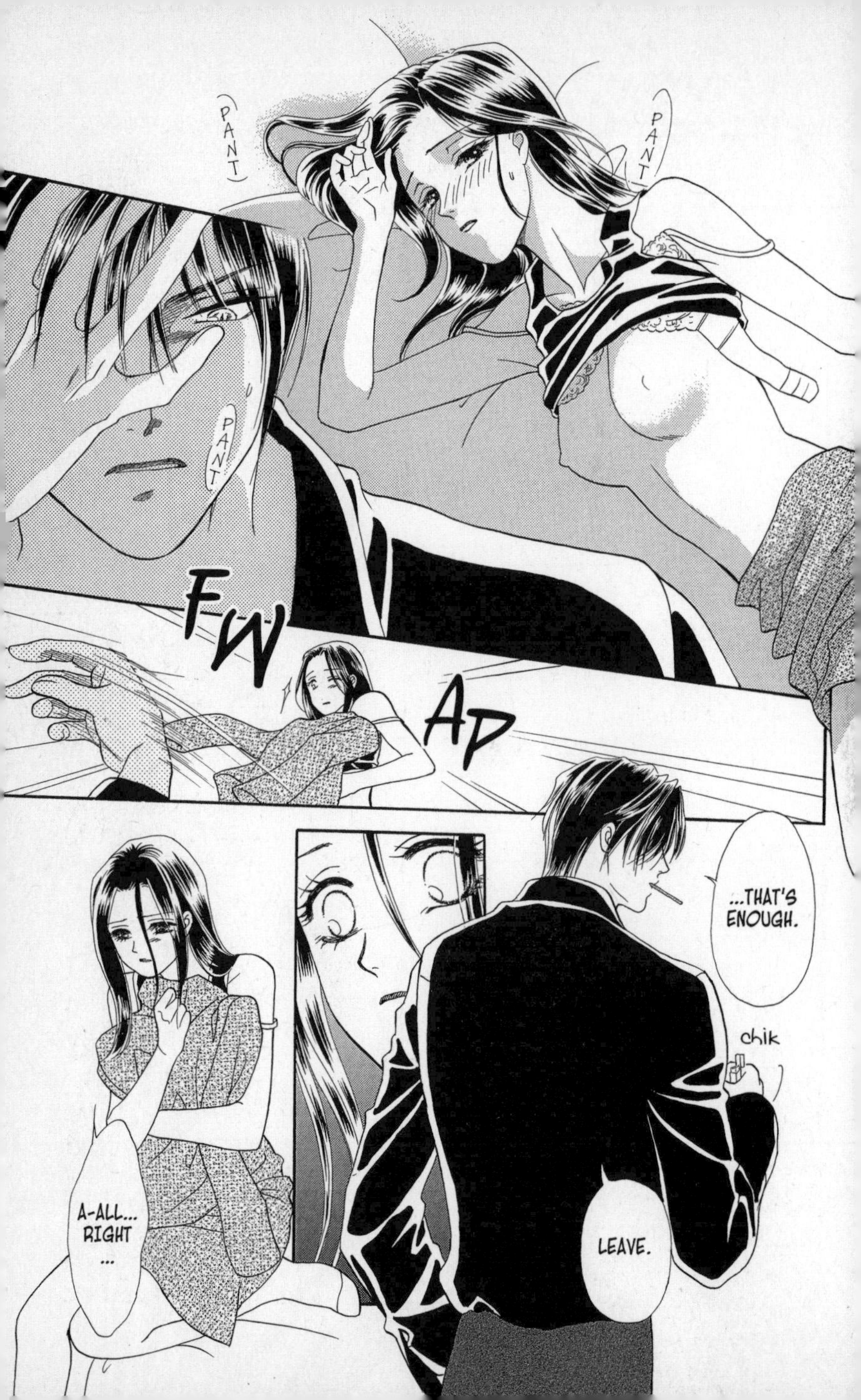
PANT
PANT
PANT
FWAP
...THAT'S ENOUGH.
chik
LEAVE.
A-ALL... RIGHT ...

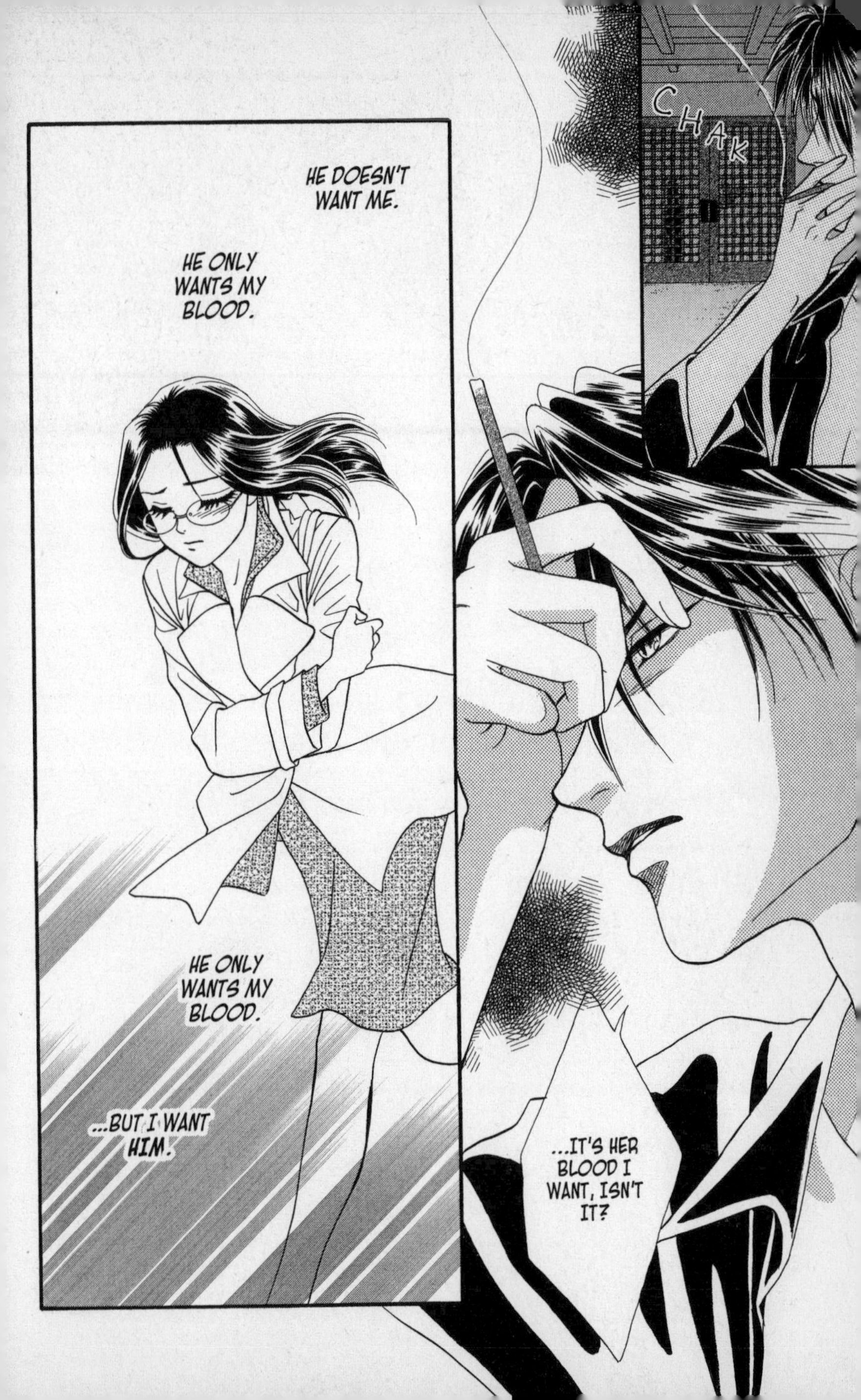
CHAK
...IT'S HER BLOOD I WANT, ISN'T IT?
HE DOESN'T WANT ME.
HE ONLY WANTS MY BLOOD.
HE ONLY WANTS MY BLOOD.
...BUT I WANT HIM.

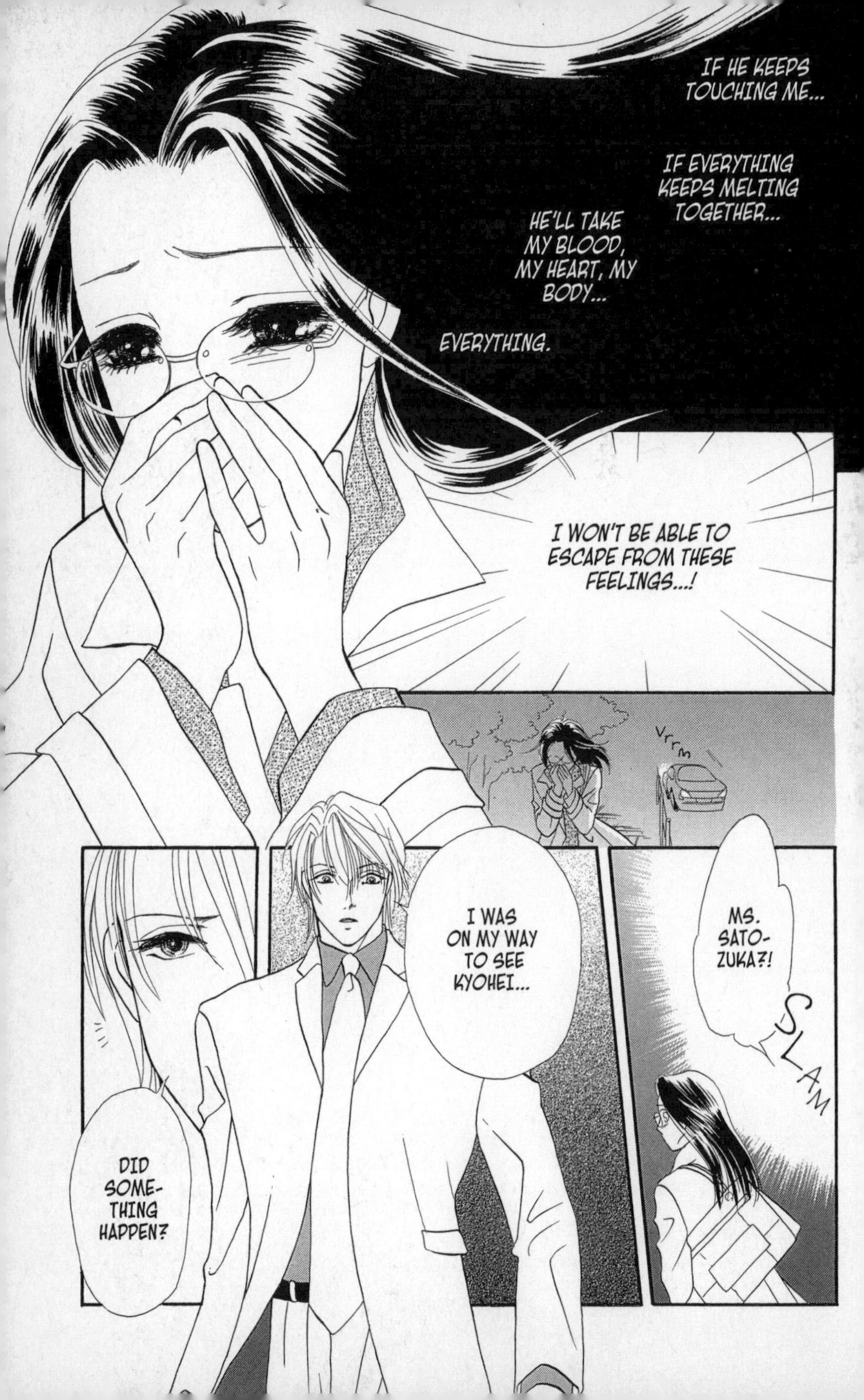
IF HE KEEPS TOUCHING ME...
IF EVERYTHING KEEPS MELTING TOGETHER...
HE'LL TAKE MY BLOOD, MY HEART, MY BODY...
EVERYTHING.
I WON'T BE ABLE TO ESCAPE FROM THESE FEELINGS...!
Vrrm
MS. SATO-ZUKA?!
SLAM
I WAS ON MY WAY TO SEE KYOHEI...
DID SOMETHING HAPPEN?

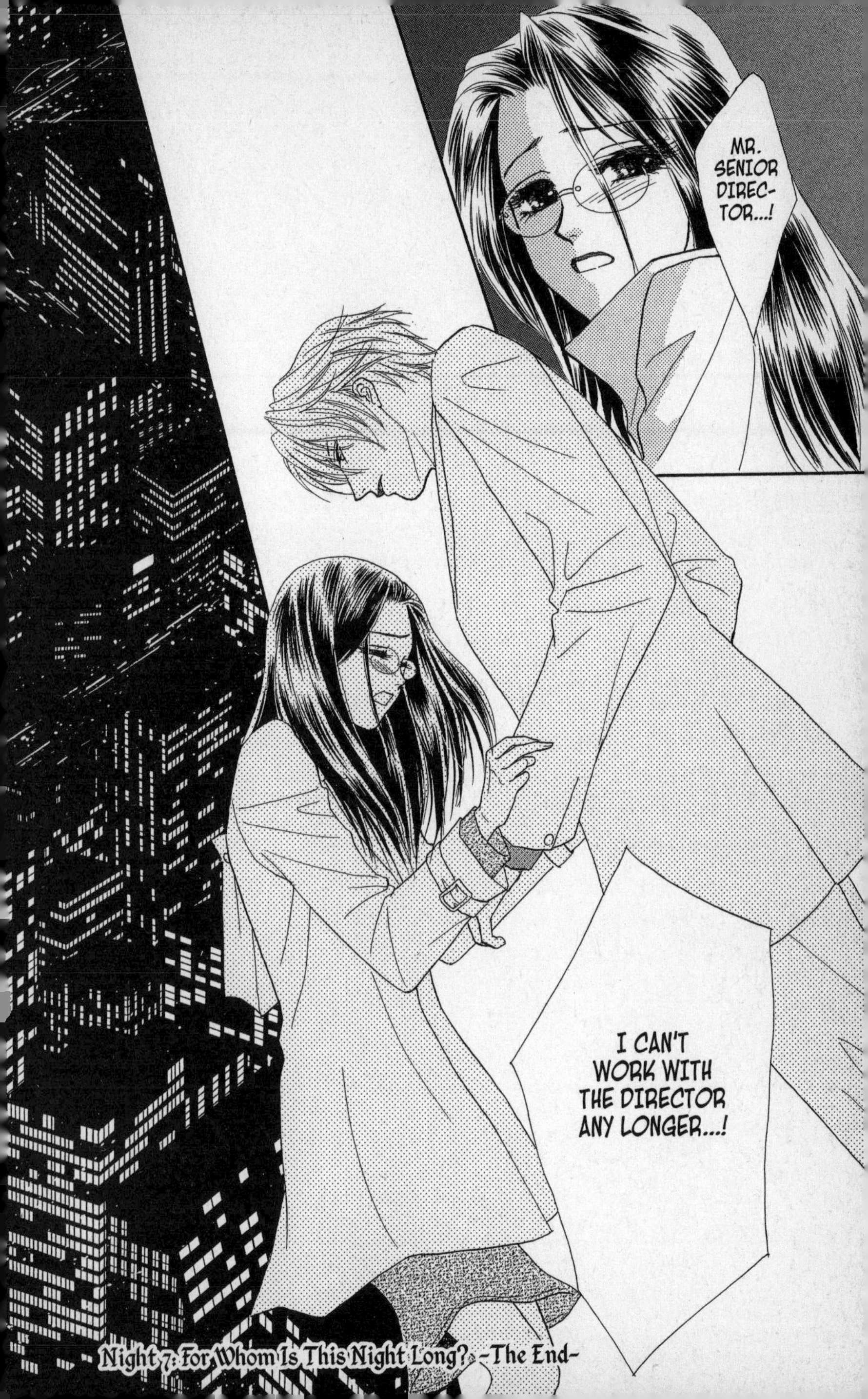
MR. SENIOR DIRECTOR...!
I CAN'T WORK WITH THE DIRECTOR ANY LONGER...!
Night 7: For Whom Is This Night Long? ~The End~

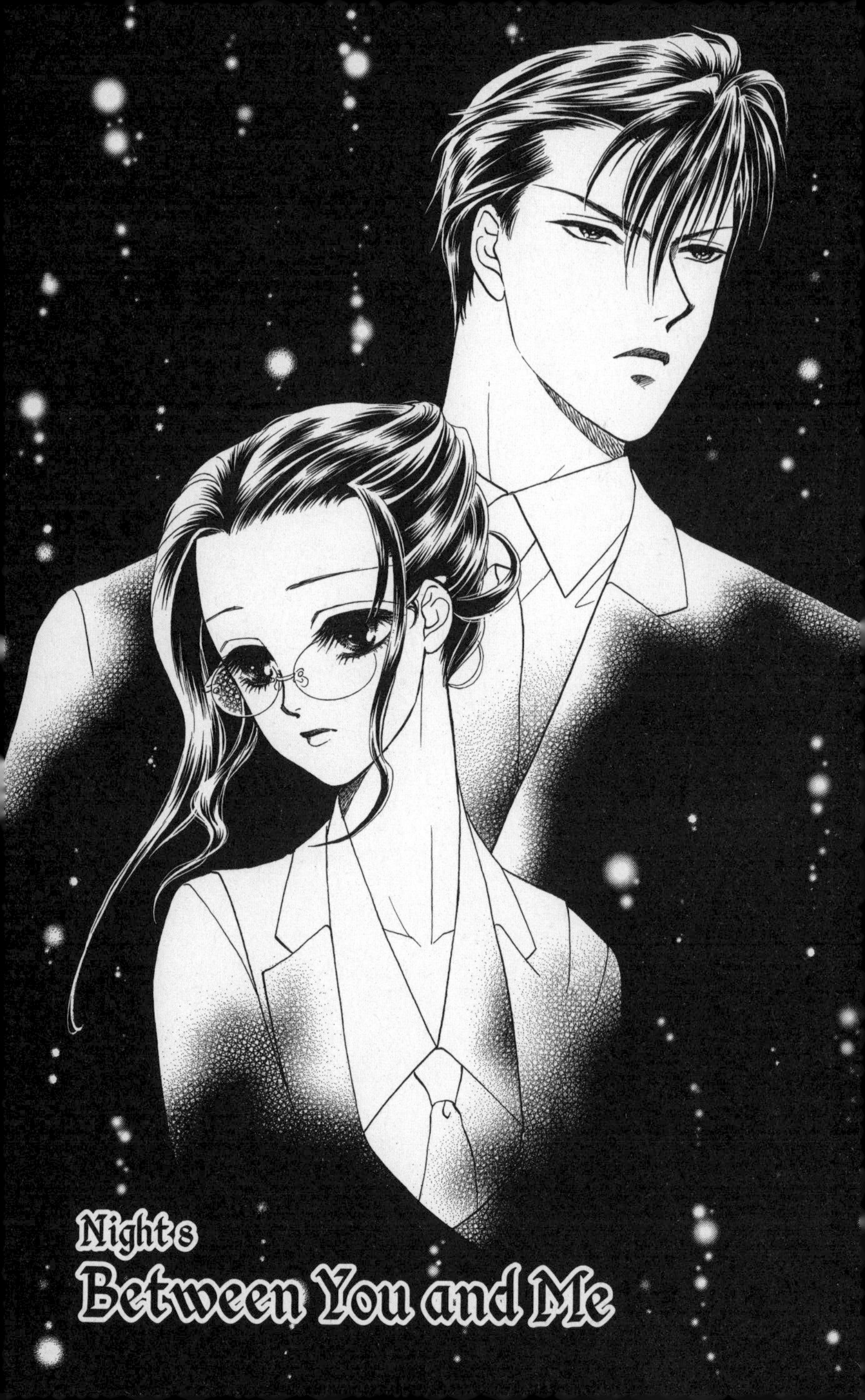

Night 8
Between You and Me

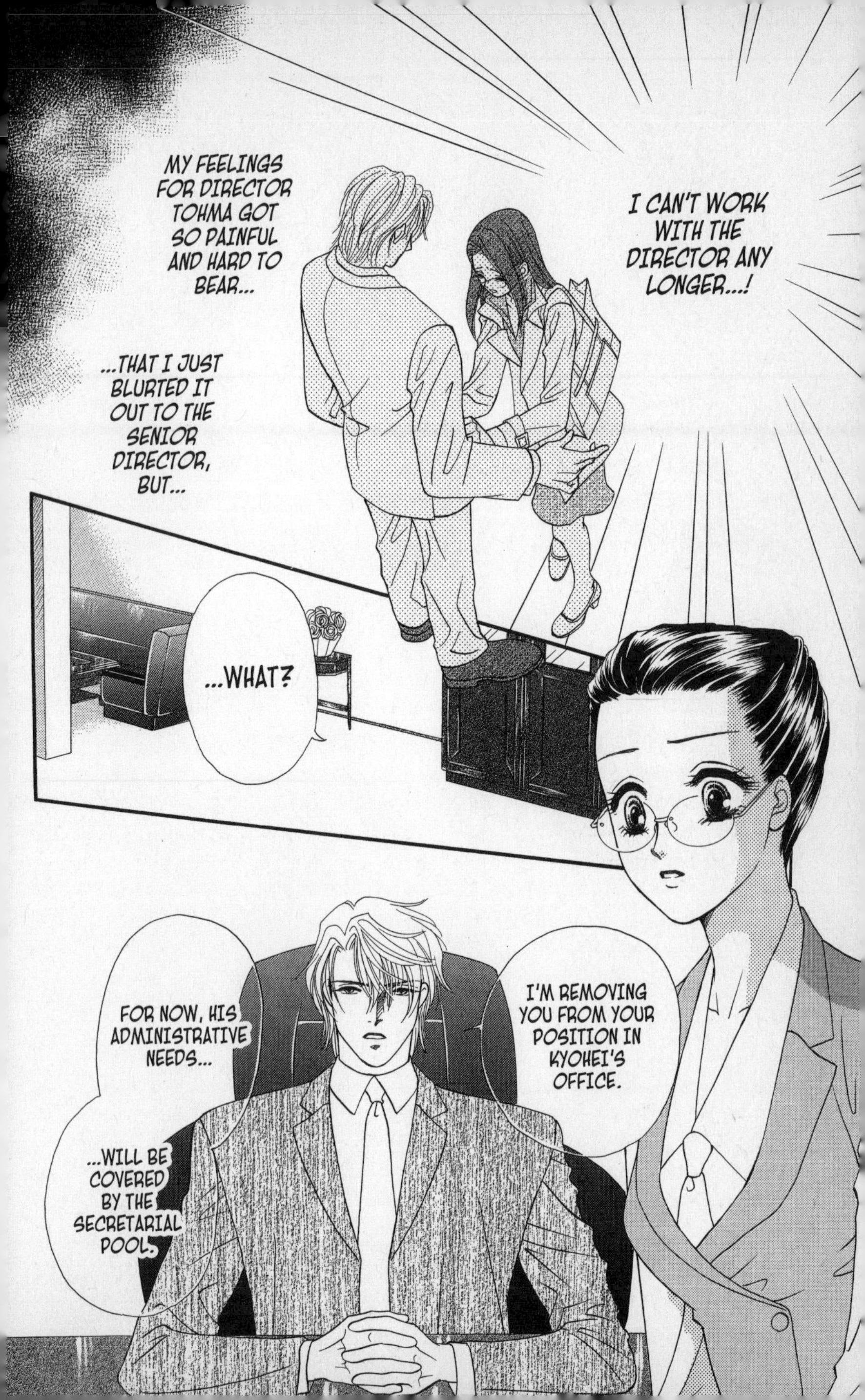
I CAN'T WORK WITH THE DIRECTOR ANY LONGER...!
MY FEELINGS FOR DIRECTOR TOHMA GOT SO PAINFUL AND HARD TO BEAR...
...THAT I JUST BLURTED IT OUT TO THE SENIOR DIRECTOR, BUT...
...WHAT?
I'M REMOVING YOU FROM YOUR POSITION IN KYOHEI'S OFFICE.
FOR NOW, HIS ADMINISTRATIVE NEEDS...
...WILL BE COVERED BY THE SECRETARIAL POOL.

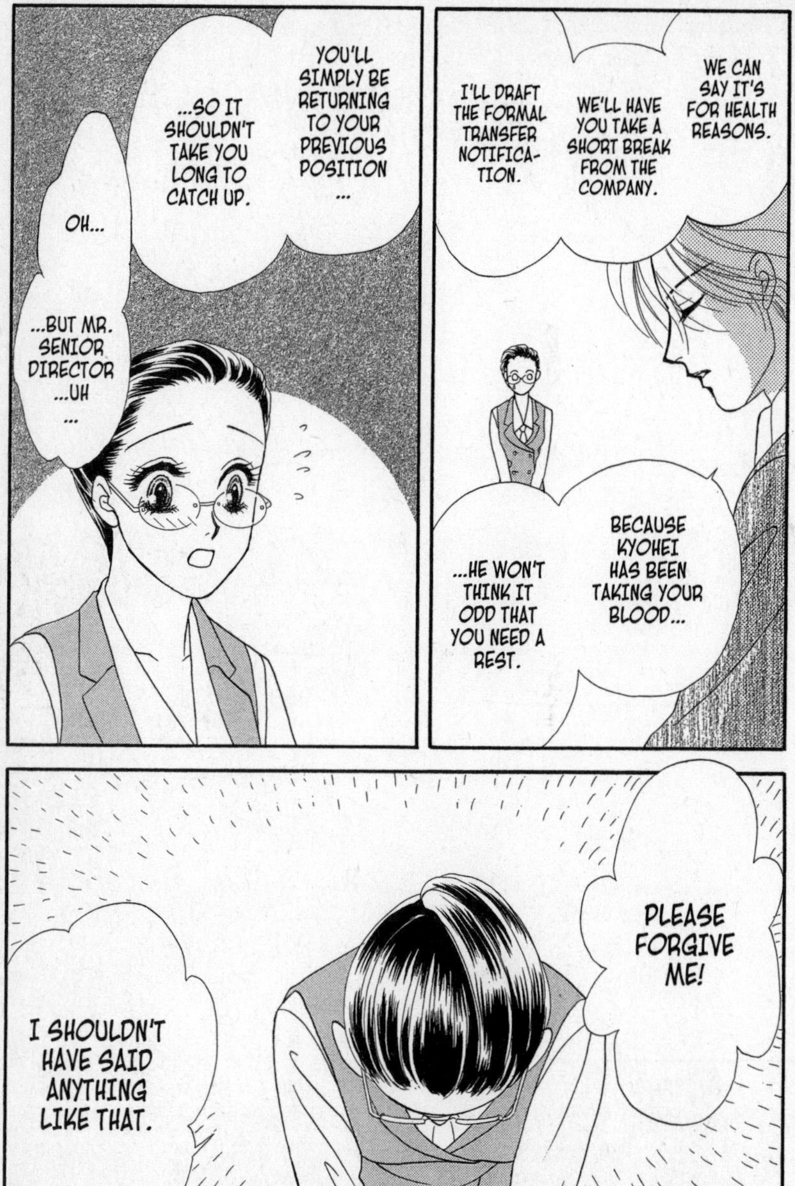
WE CAN SAY IT'S FOR HEALTH REASONS.
WE'LL HAVE YOU TAKE A SHORT BREAK FROM THE COMPANY.
I'LL DRAFT THE FORMAL TRANSFER NOTIFICA-TION.
BECAUSE KYOHEI HAS BEEN TAKING YOUR BLOOD...
...HE WON'T THINK IT ODD THAT YOU NEED A REST.
YOU'LL SIMPLY BE RETURNING TO YOUR PREVIOUS POSITION...
...SO IT SHOULDN'T TAKE YOU LONG TO CATCH UP.
OH...
...BUT MR. SENIOR DIRECTOR ...UH ...
PLEASE FORGIVE ME!
I SHOULDN'T HAVE SAID ANYTHING LIKE THAT.

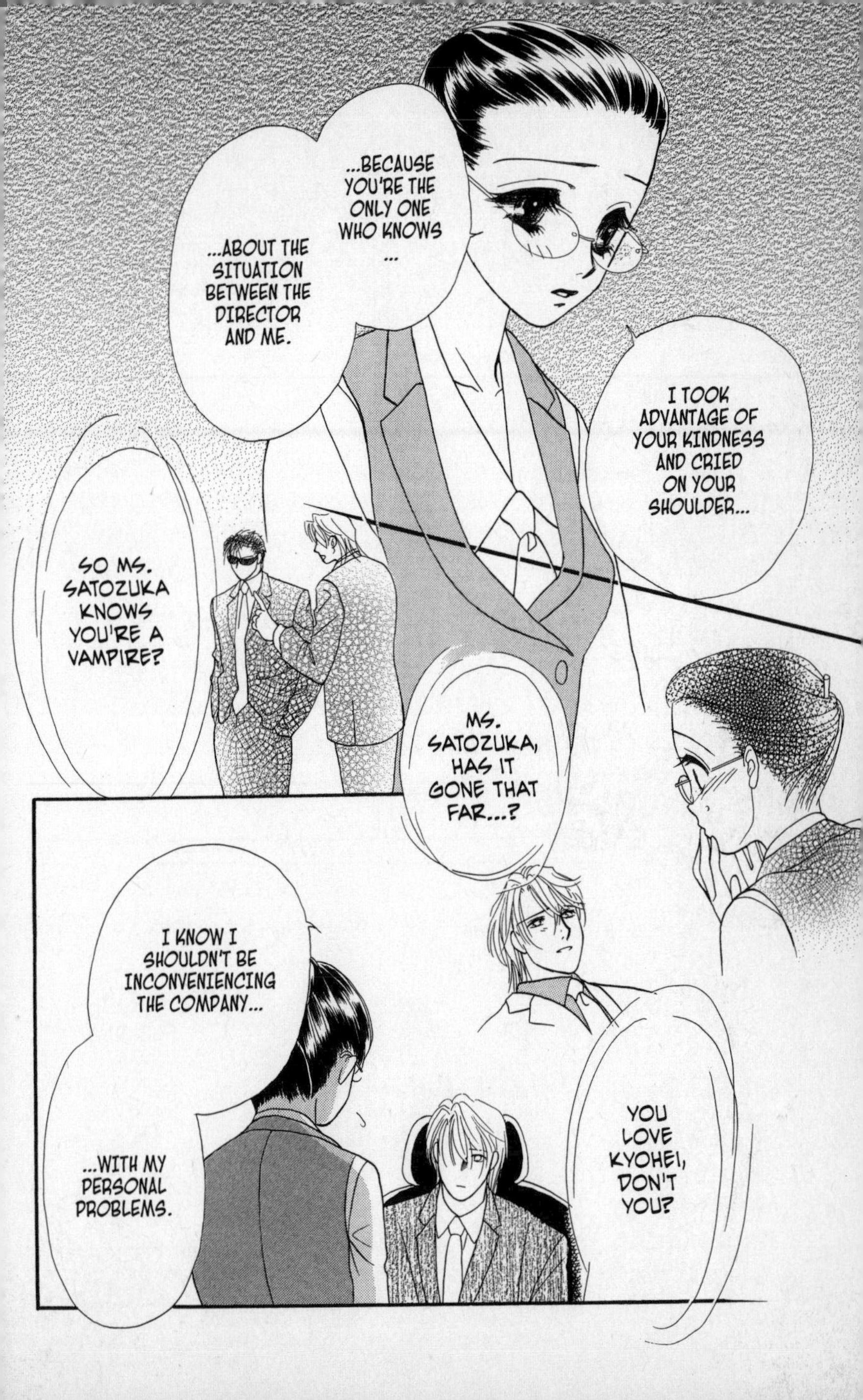
...BECAUSE YOU'RE THE ONLY ONE WHO KNOWS ...
...ABOUT THE SITUATION BETWEEN THE DIRECTOR AND ME.
I TOOK ADVANTAGE OF YOUR KINDNESS AND CRIED ON YOUR SHOULDER...
SO MS. SATOZUKA KNOWS YOU'RE A VAMPIRE?
MS. SATOZUKA, HAS IT GONE THAT FAR...?
YOU LOVE KYOHEI, DON'T YOU?
I KNOW I SHOULDN'T BE INCONVENIENCING THE COMPANY...
...WITH MY PERSONAL PROBLEMS.

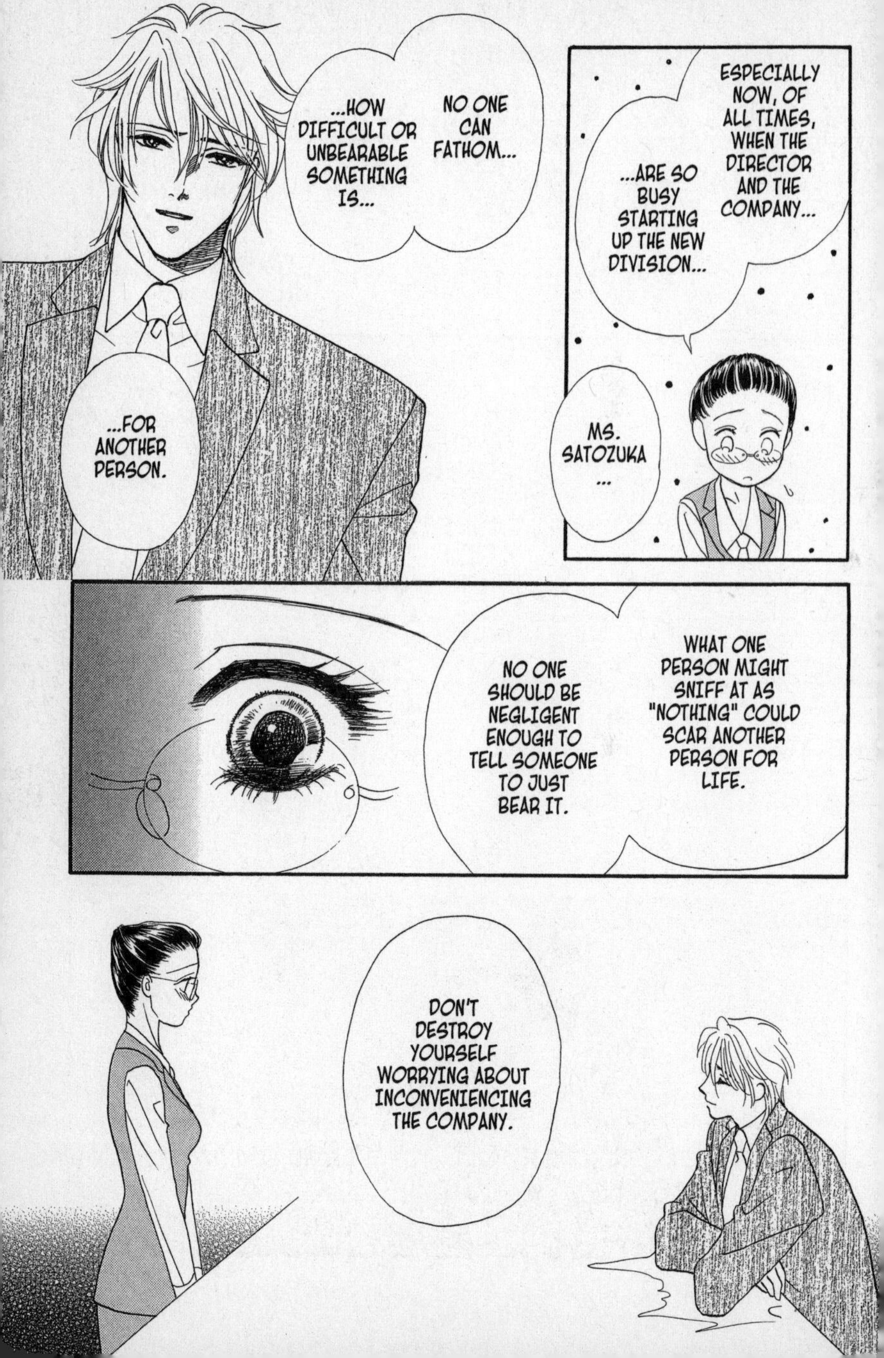
ESPECIALLY NOW, OF ALL TIMES, WHEN THE DIRECTOR AND THE COMPANY...
...ARE SO BUSY STARTING UP THE NEW DIVISION...
MS. SATOZUKA ...
NO ONE CAN FATHOM...
...HOW DIFFICULT OR UNBEARABLE SOMETHING IS...
...FOR ANOTHER PERSON.
WHAT ONE PERSON MIGHT SNIFF AT AS "NOTHING" COULD SCAR ANOTHER PERSON FOR LIFE.
NO ONE SHOULD BE NEGLIGENT ENOUGH TO TELL SOMEONE TO JUST BEAR IT.
DON'T DESTROY YOURSELF WORRYING ABOUT INCONVENIENCING THE COMPANY.

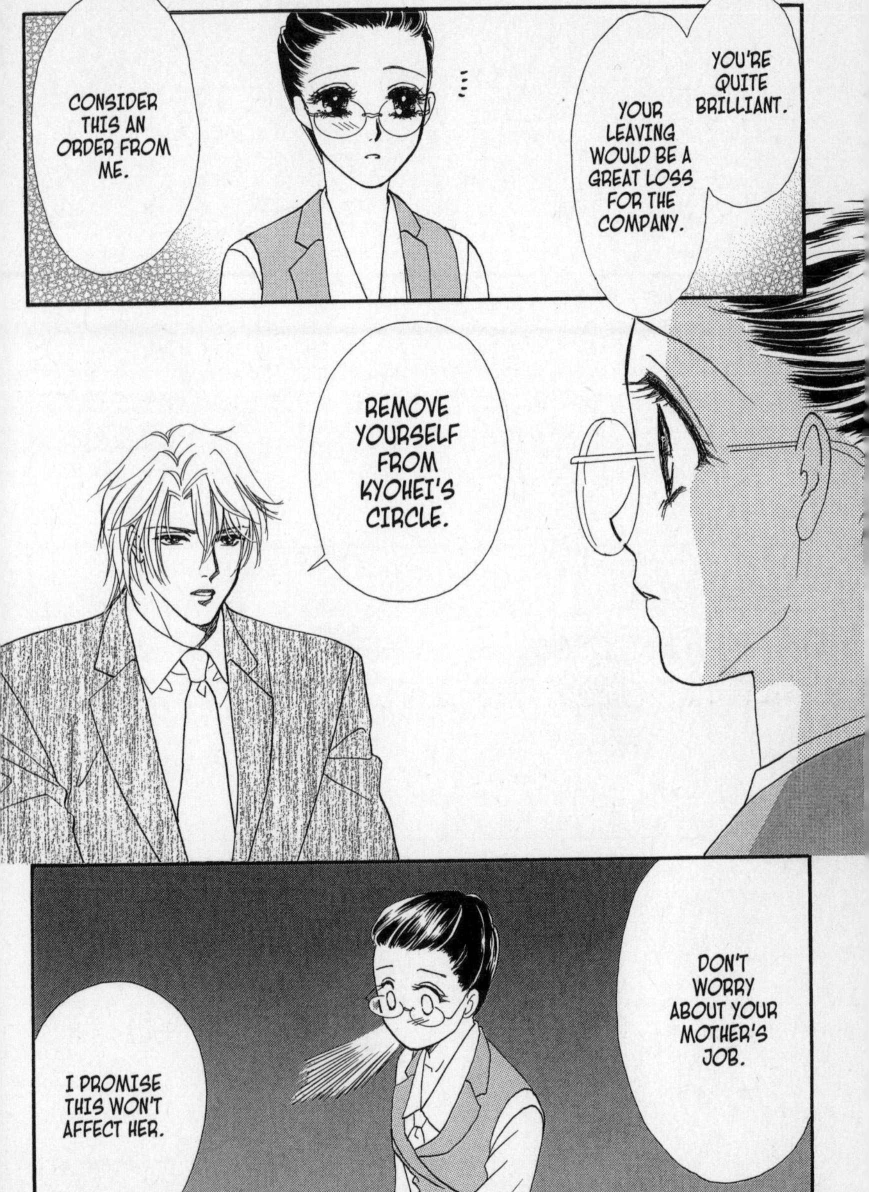
YOU'RE QUITE BRILLIANT.
YOUR LEAVING WOULD BE A GREAT LOSS FOR THE COMPANY.
...
CONSIDER THIS AN ORDER FROM ME.
REMOVE YOURSELF FROM KYOHEI'S CIRCLE.
DON'T WORRY ABOUT YOUR MOTHER'S JOB.
I PROMISE THIS WON'T AFFECT HER.

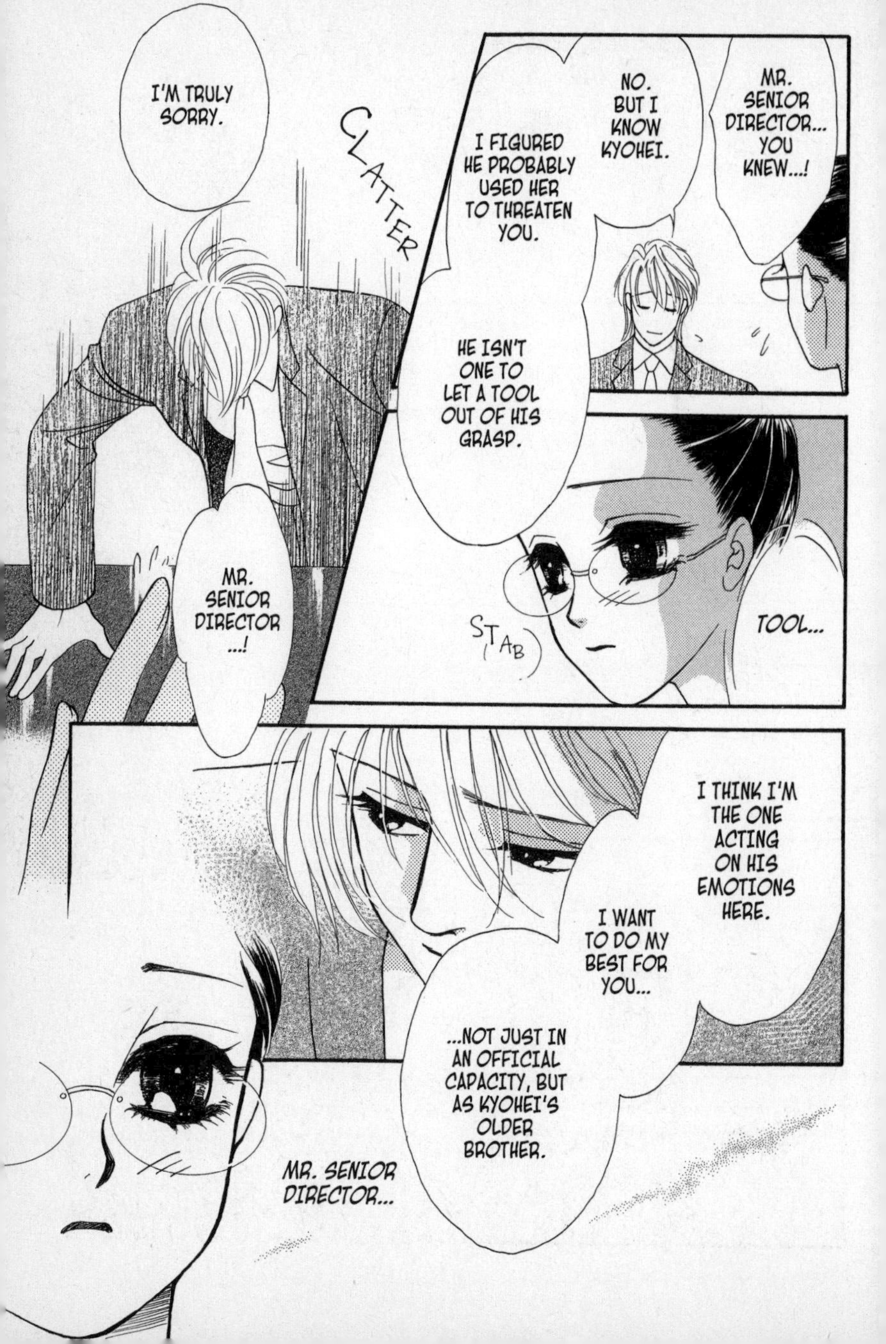
MR. SENIOR DIRECTOR... YOU KNEW...!
NO. BUT I KNOW KYOHEI.
I FIGURED HE PROBABLY USED HER TO THREATEN YOU.
HE ISN'T ONE TO LET A TOOL OUT OF HIS GRASP.
TOOL...
STAB
CLATTER
I'M TRULY SORRY.
MR. SENIOR DIRECTOR ...!
I THINK I'M THE ONE ACTING ON HIS EMOTIONS HERE.
I WANT TO DO MY BEST FOR YOU...
...NOT JUST IN AN OFFICIAL CAPACITY, BUT AS KYOHEI'S OLDER BROTHER.
MR. SENIOR DIRECTOR...

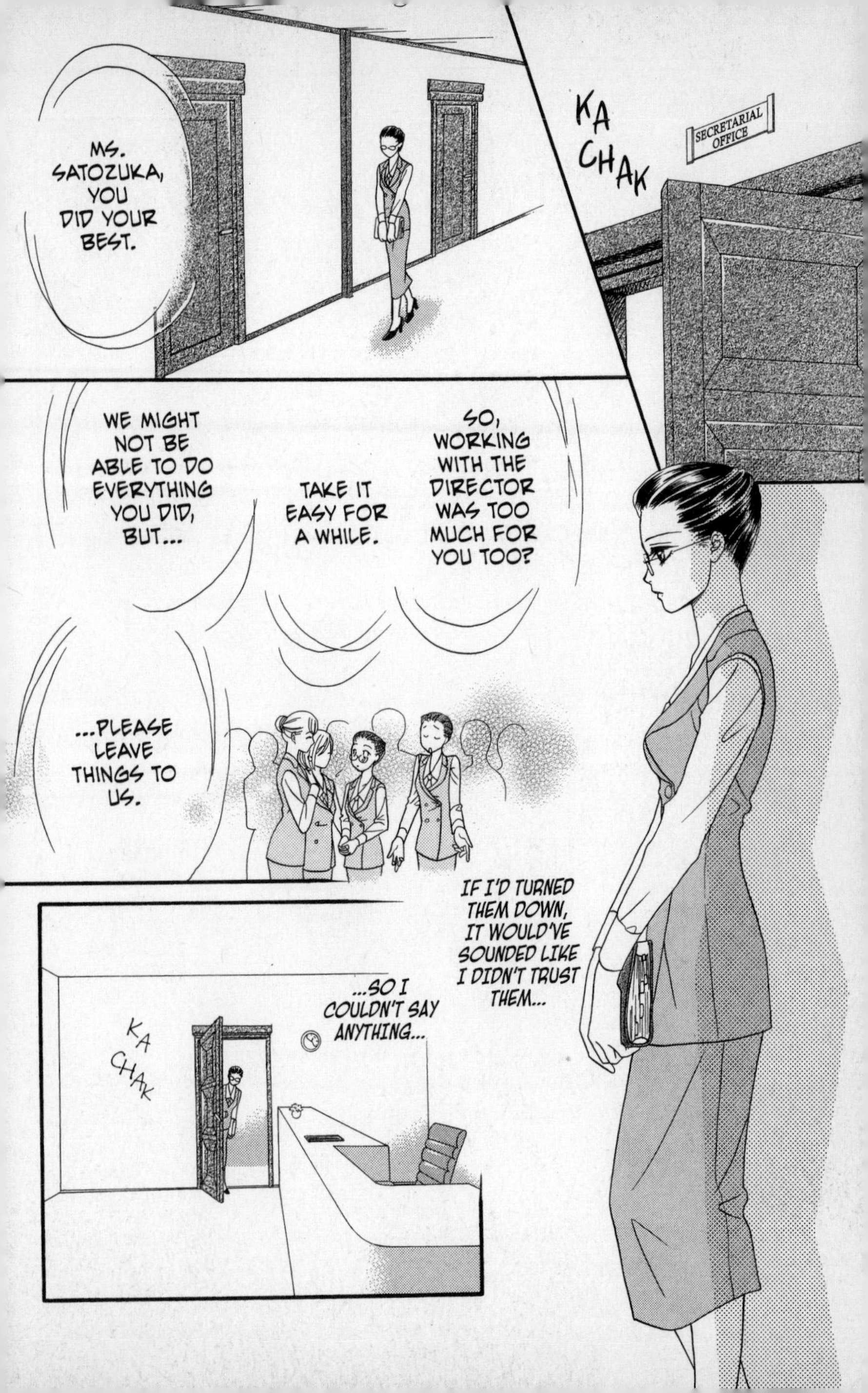
KA CHAK
SECRETARIAL OFFICE
IF I'D TURNED THEM DOWN, IT WOULD'VE SOUNDED LIKE I DIDN'T TRUST THEM...
MS. SATOZUKA, YOU DID YOUR BEST.
SO, WORKING WITH THE DIRECTOR WAS TOO MUCH FOR YOU TOO?
TAKE IT EASY FOR A WHILE.
WE MIGHT NOT BE ABLE TO DO EVERYTHING YOU DID, BUT...
...PLEASE LEAVE THINGS TO US.
...SO I COULDN'T SAY ANYTHING...
KA CHAK

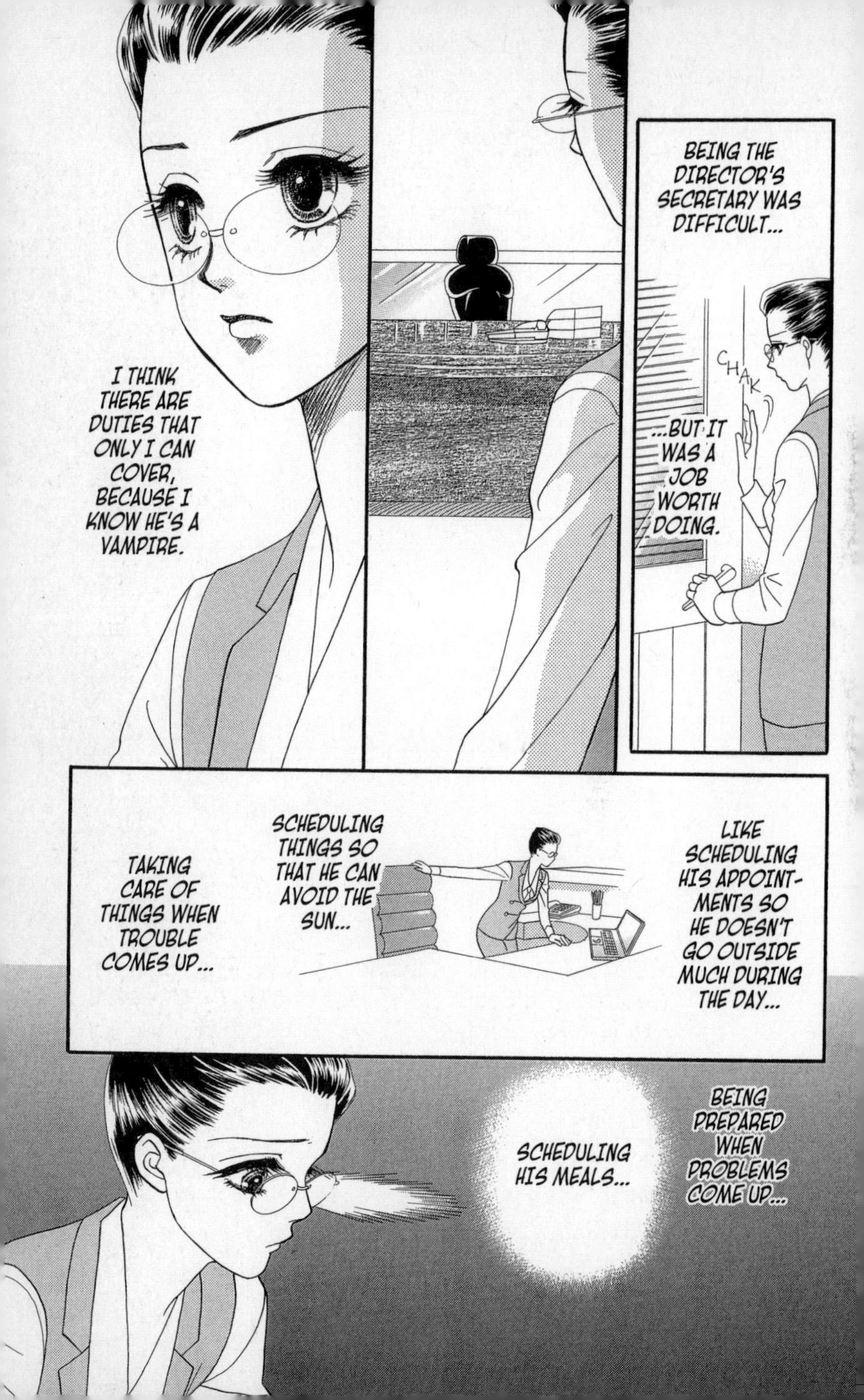
BEING THE DIRECTOR'S SECRETARY WAS DIFFICULT...
CHAK
...BUT IT WAS A JOB WORTH DOING.
I THINK THERE ARE DUTIES THAT ONLY I CAN COVER, BECAUSE I KNOW HE'S A VAMPIRE.
LIKE SCHEDULING HIS APPOINT-MENTS SO HE DOESN'T GO OUTSIDE MUCH DURING THE DAY...
SCHEDULING THINGS SO THAT HE CAN AVOID THE SUN...
TAKING CARE OF THINGS WHEN TROUBLE COMES UP...
BEING PREPARED WHEN PROBLEMS COME UP...
SCHEDULING HIS MEALS...

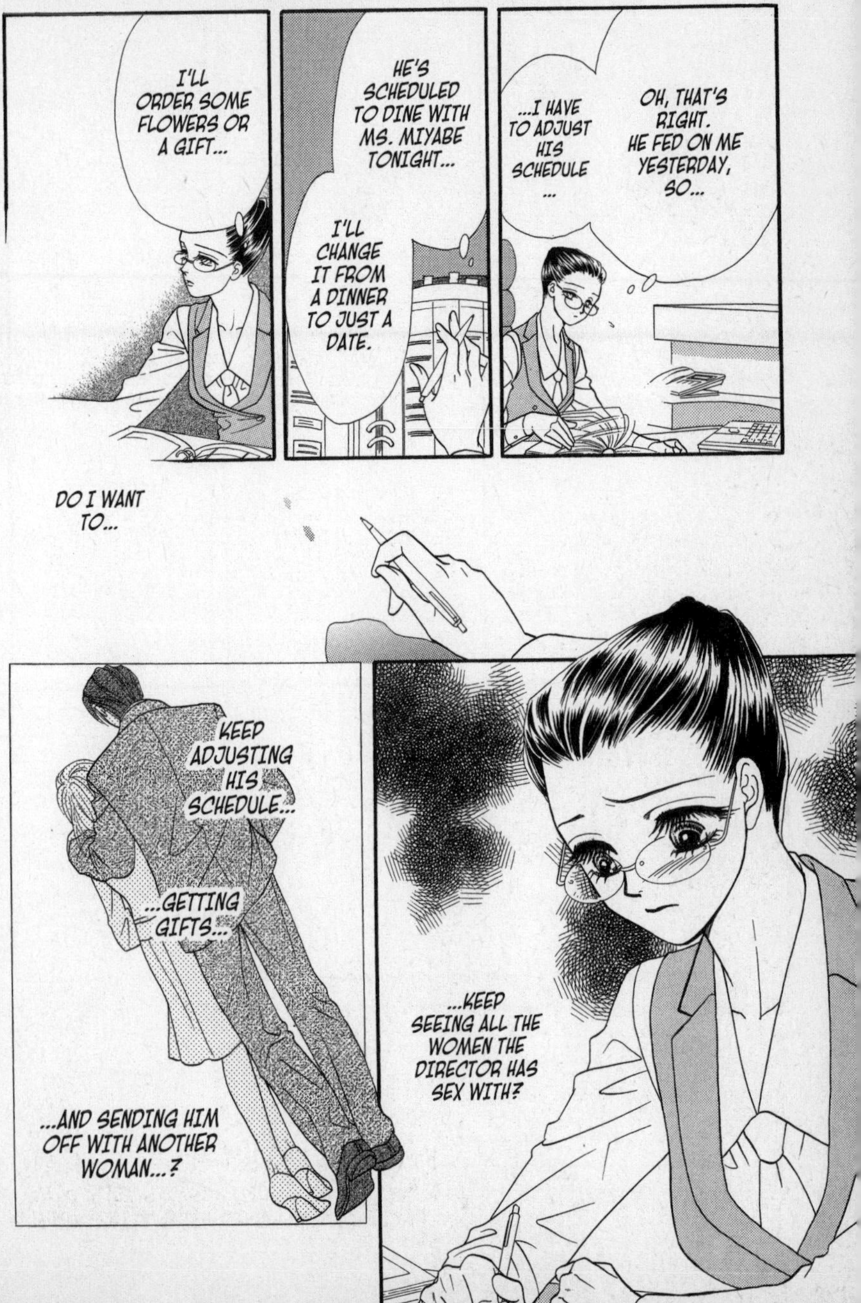
OH, THAT'S RIGHT. HE FED ON ME YESTERDAY, SO...
...I HAVE TO ADJUST HIS SCHEDULE...
HE'S SCHEDULED TO DINE WITH MS. MIYABE TONIGHT...
I'LL CHANGE IT FROM A DINNER TO JUST A DATE.
I'LL ORDER SOME FLOWERS OR A GIFT...
DO I WANT TO...
...KEEP SEEING ALL THE WOMEN THE DIRECTOR HAS SEX WITH?
KEEP ADJUSTING HIS SCHEDULE...
...GETTING GIFTS...
...AND SENDING HIM OFF WITH ANOTHER WOMAN...?

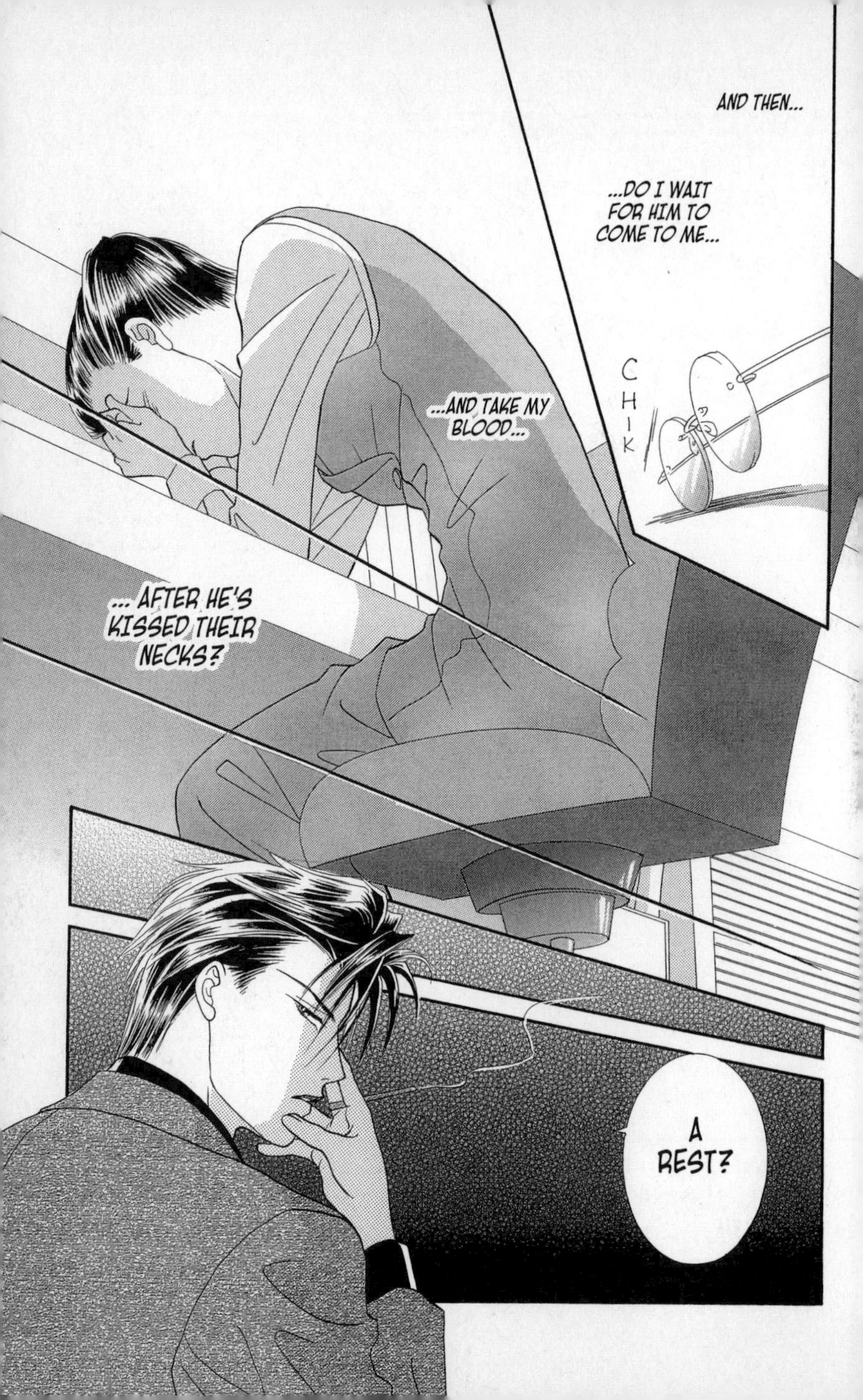
AND THEN...
...DO I WAIT FOR HIM TO COME TO ME...
CHIK
...AND TAKE MY BLOOD...
... AFTER HE'S KISSED THEIR NECKS?
A REST?

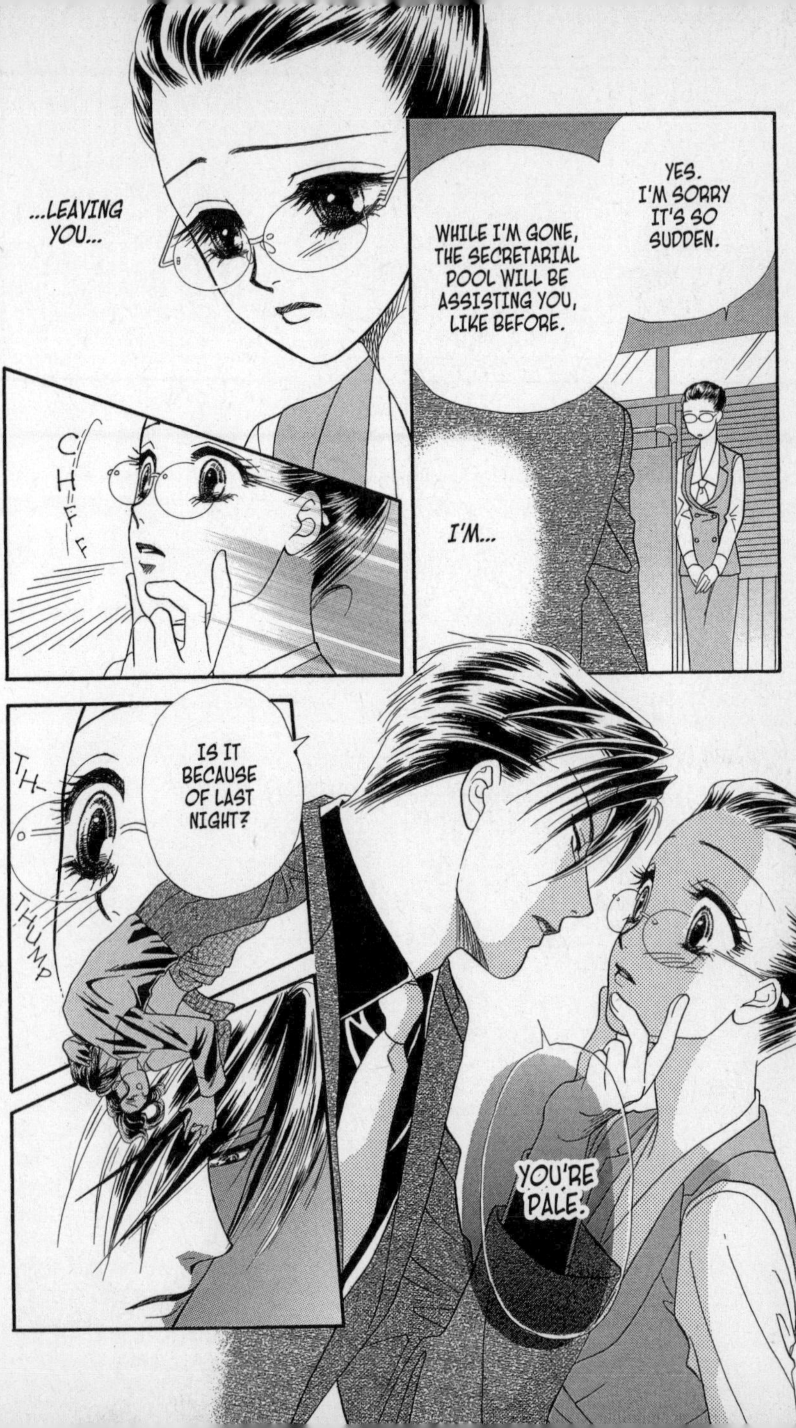
YES. I'M SORRY IT'S SO SUDDEN.
WHILE I'M GONE, THE SECRETARIAL POOL WILL BE ASSISTING YOU, LIKE BEFORE.
I'M...
...LEAVING YOU...
CHFF
YOU'RE PALE.
IS IT BECAUSE OF LAST NIGHT?
TH-THUMP

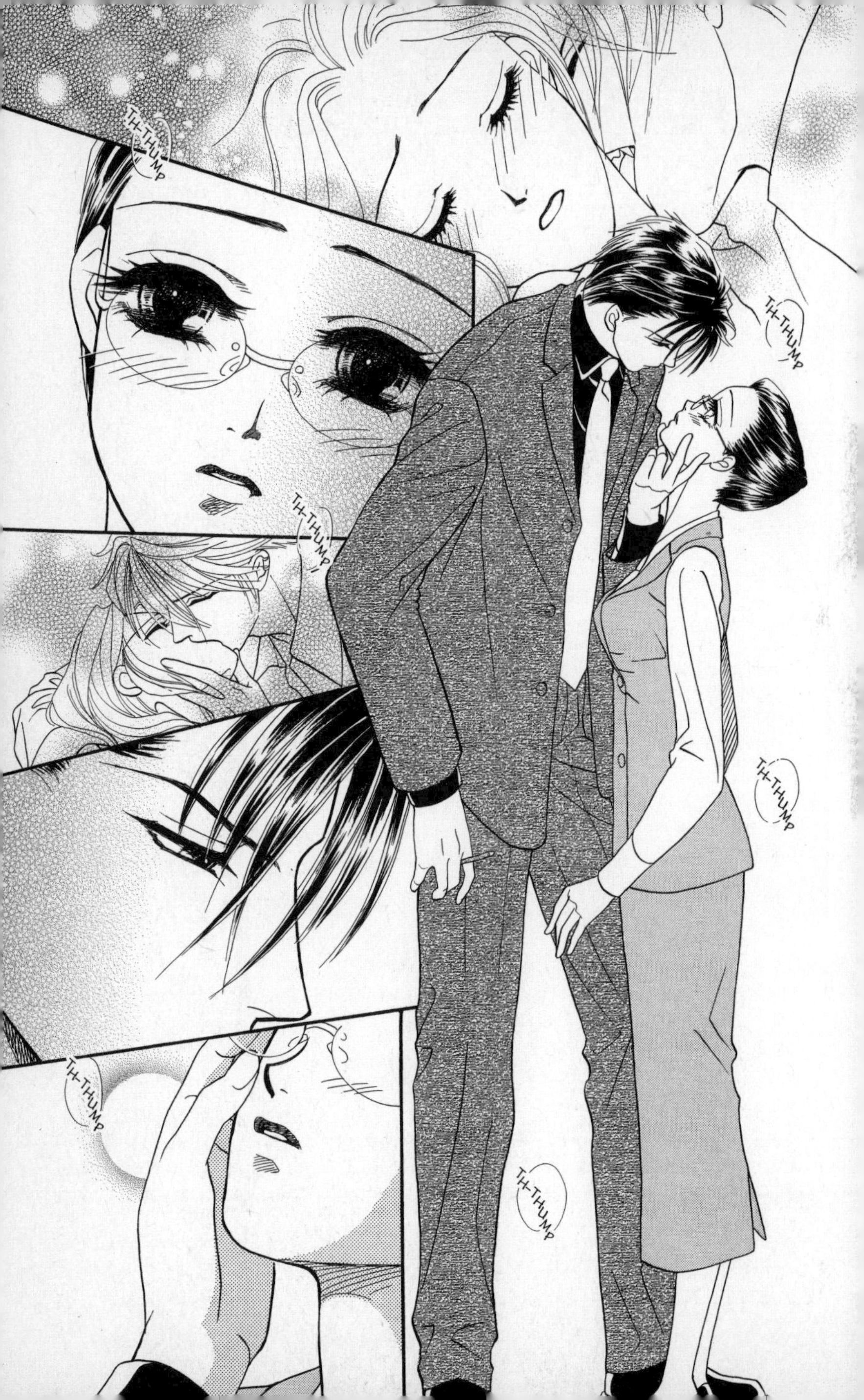
TH-THUMP
TH-THUMP
TH-THUMP
TH-THUMP
TH-THUMP
TH-THUMP

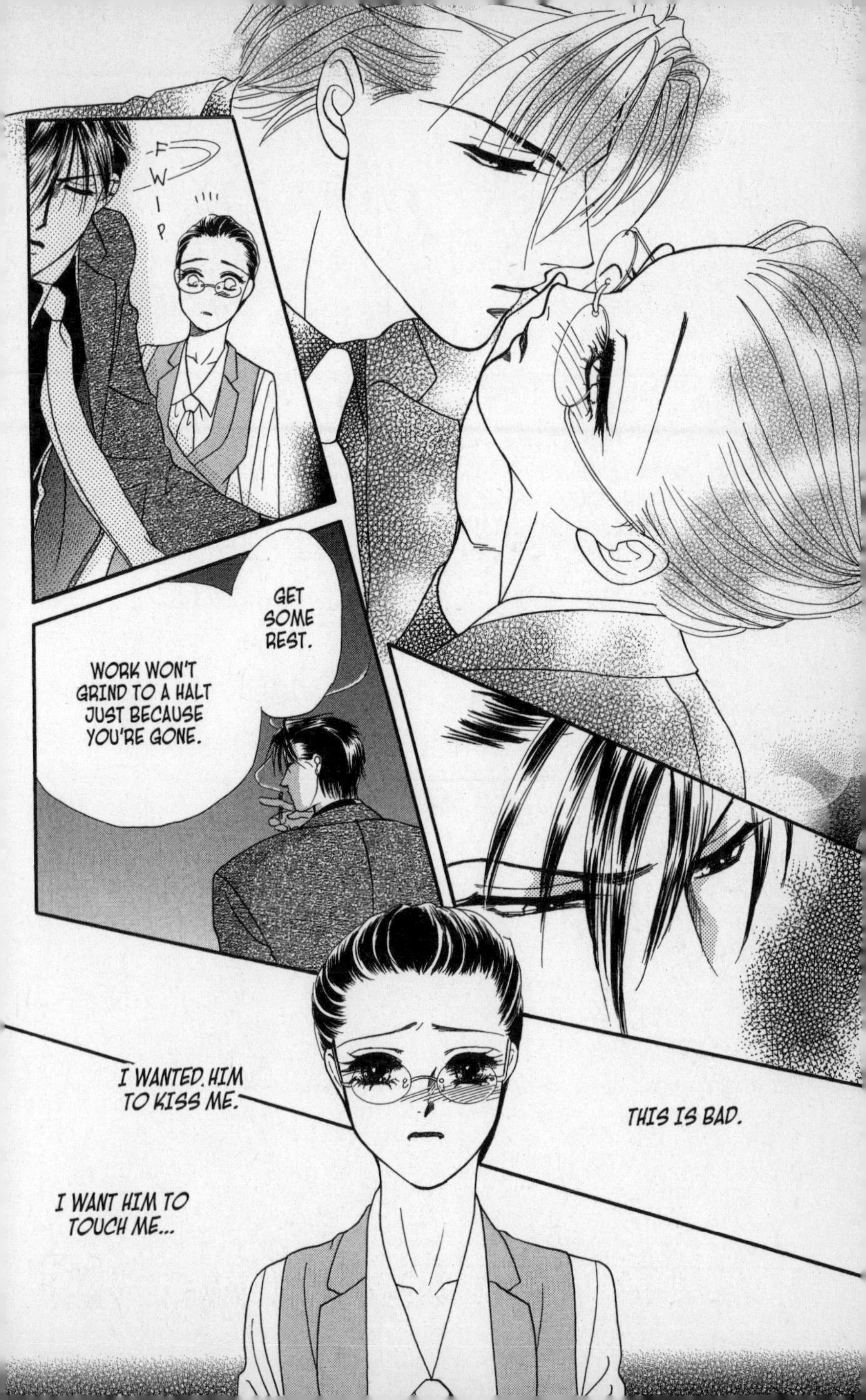

FWIP
GET SOME REST.
WORK WON'T GRIND TO A HALT JUST BECAUSE YOU'RE GONE.
THIS IS BAD.
I WANTED HIM TO KISS ME.
I WANT HIM TO TOUCH ME...

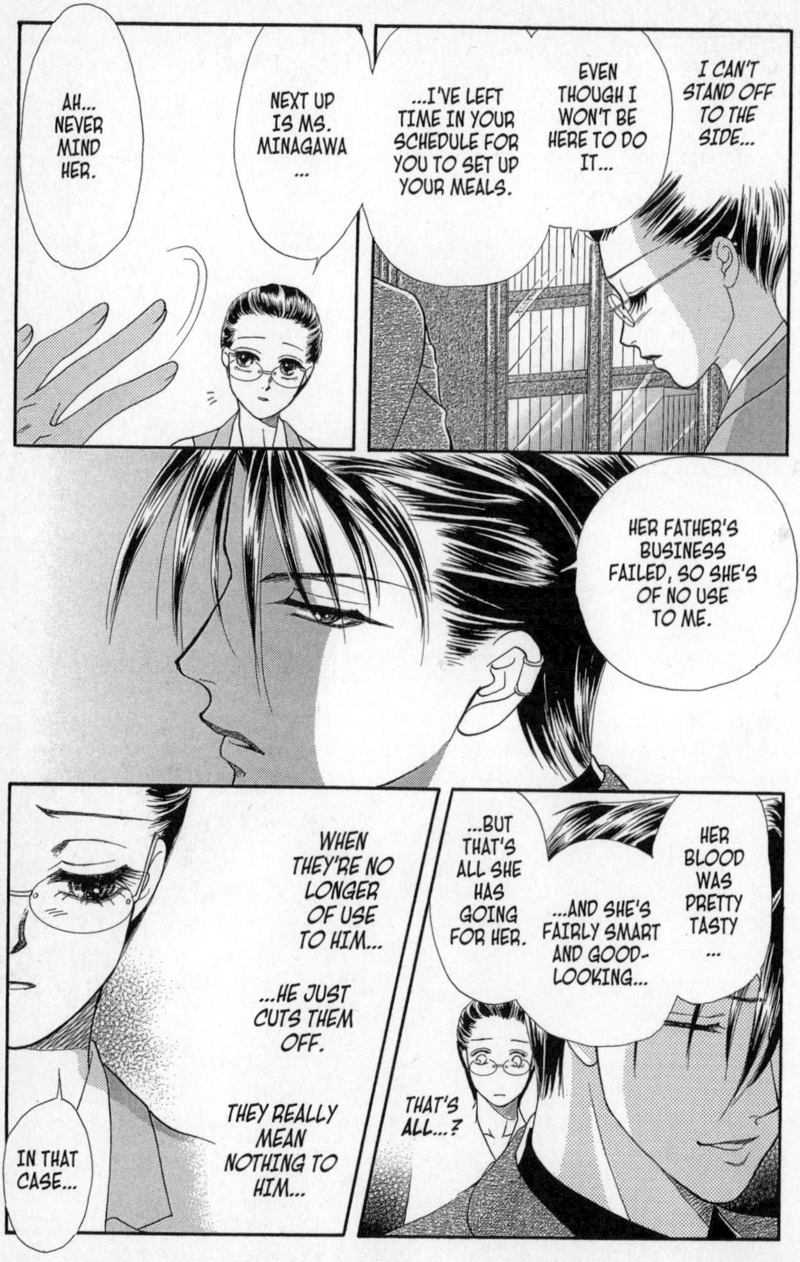
I CAN'T STAND OFF TO THE SIDE...
EVEN THOUGH I WON'T BE HERE TO DO IT...
...I'VE LEFT TIME IN YOUR SCHEDULE FOR YOU TO SET UP YOUR MEALS.
NEXT UP IS MS. MINAGAWA ...
AH... NEVER MIND HER.
HER FATHER'S BUSINESS FAILED, SO SHE'S OF NO USE TO ME.
HER BLOOD WAS PRETTY TASTY ...
...AND SHE'S FAIRLY SMART AND GOOD-LOOKING...
...BUT THAT'S ALL SHE HAS GOING FOR HER.
THAT'S ALL...?
WHEN THEY'RE NO LONGER OF USE TO HIM...
...HE JUST CUTS THEM OFF.
THEY REALLY MEAN NOTHING TO HIM...
IN THAT CASE...

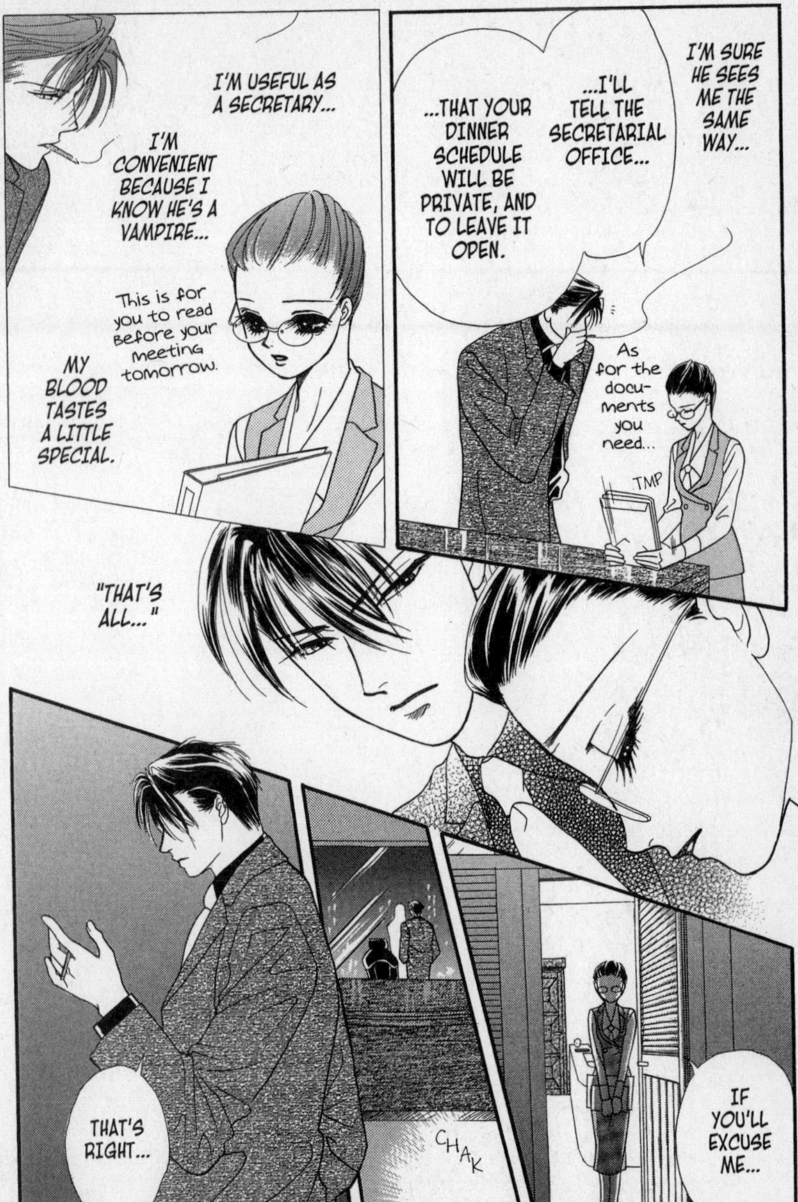
I'M SURE HE SEES ME THE SAME WAY...
...I'LL TELL THE SECRETARIAL OFFICE...
...THAT YOUR DINNER SCHEDULE WILL BE PRIVATE, AND TO LEAVE IT OPEN.
As for the documents you need...
TMP
I'M USEFUL AS A SECRETARY...
I'M CONVENIENT BECAUSE I KNOW HE'S A VAMPIRE...
This is for you to read before your meeting tomorrow.
MY BLOOD TASTES A LITTLE SPECIAL.
"THAT'S ALL..."
IF YOU'LL EXCUSE ME...
CHAK
THAT'S RIGHT...

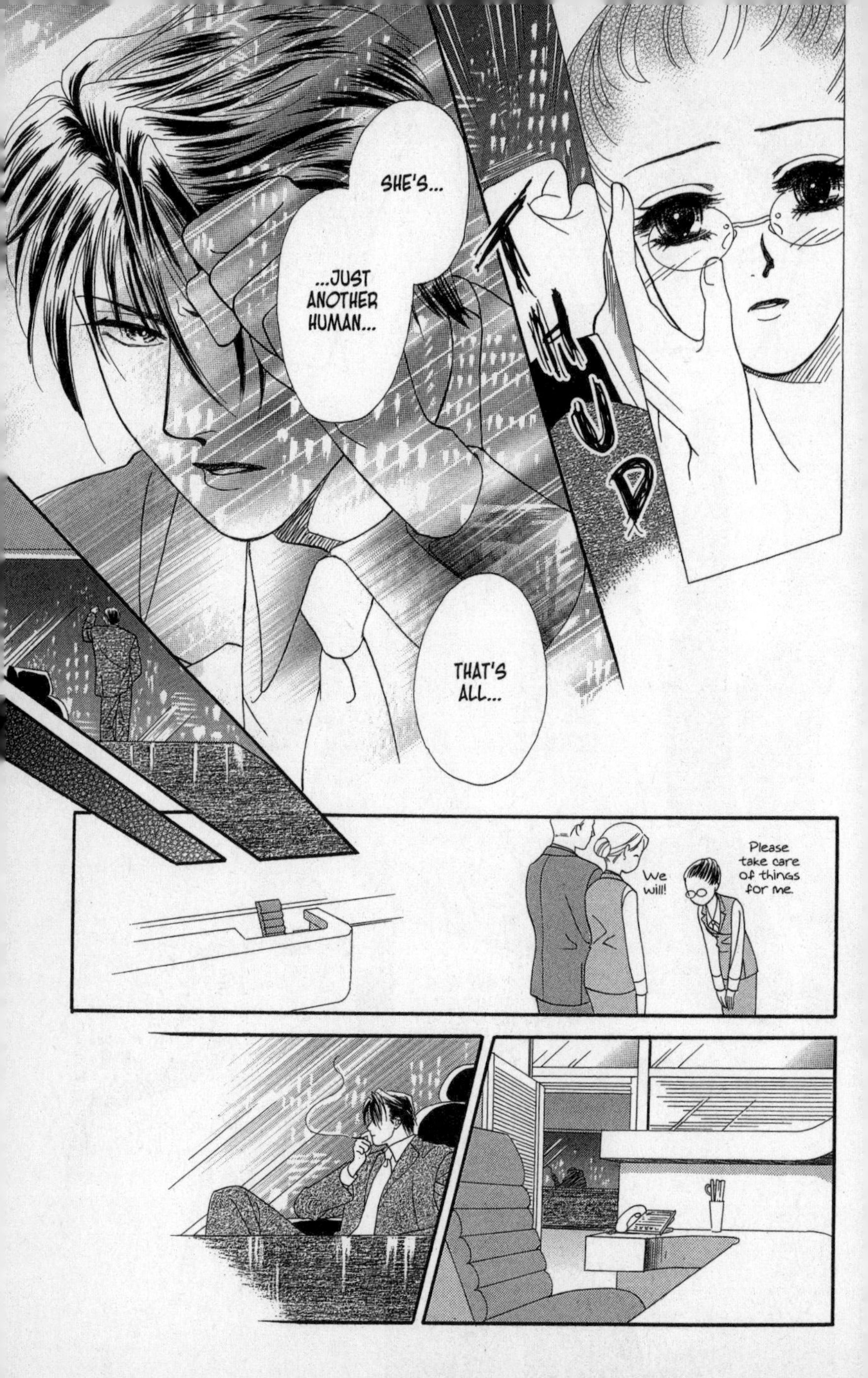
THUD
SHE'S...
...JUST ANOTHER HUMAN...
THAT'S ALL...
Please take care of things for me.
We will!

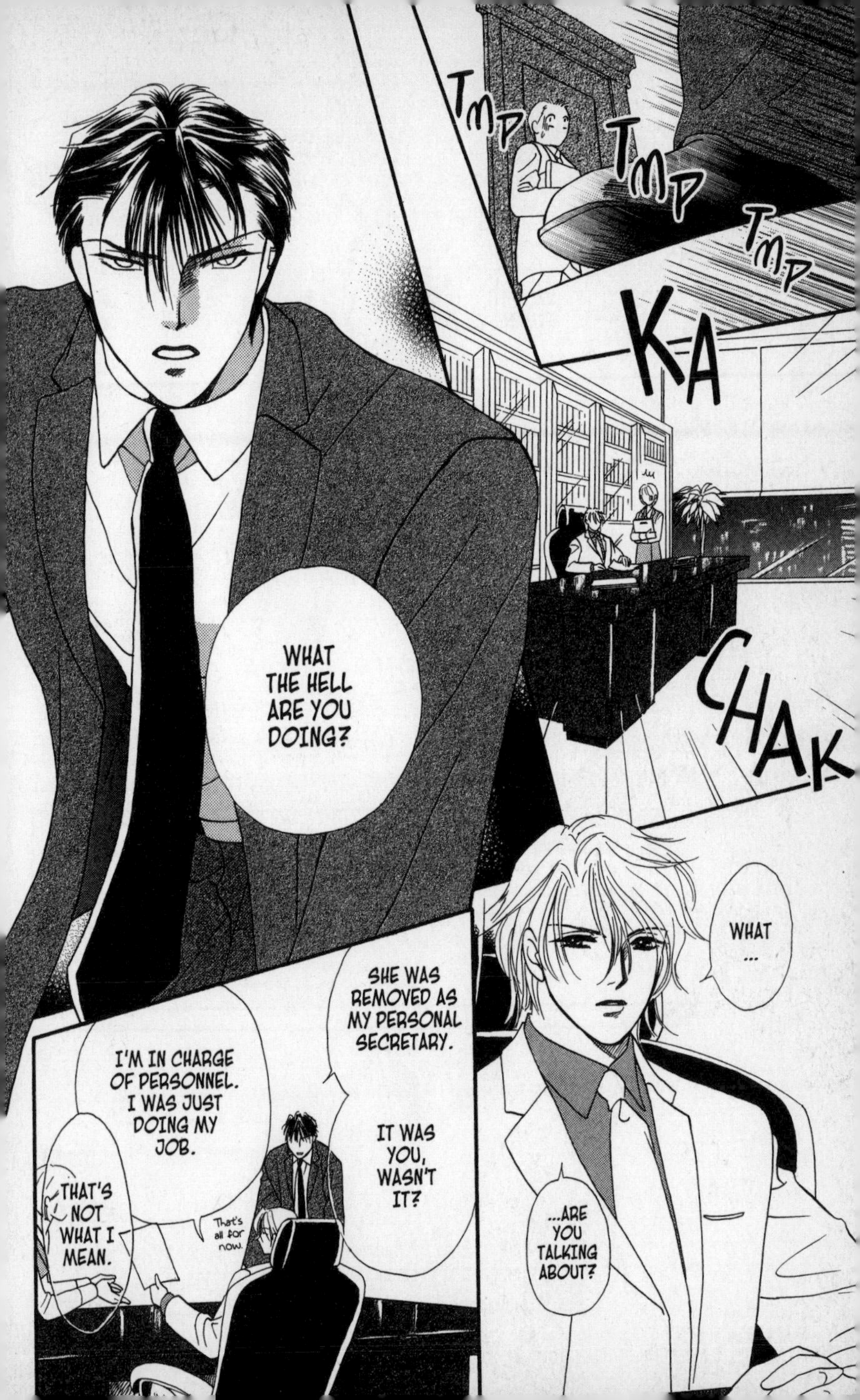
TMP
TMP
TMP
TMP
KA
CHAK
WHAT THE HELL ARE YOU DOING?
WHAT ...
...ARE YOU TALKING ABOUT?
SHE WAS REMOVED AS MY PERSONAL SECRETARY.
IT WAS YOU, WASN'T IT?
That's all for now.
I'M IN CHARGE OF PERSONNEL. I WAS JUST DOING MY JOB.
THAT'S NOT WHAT I MEAN.

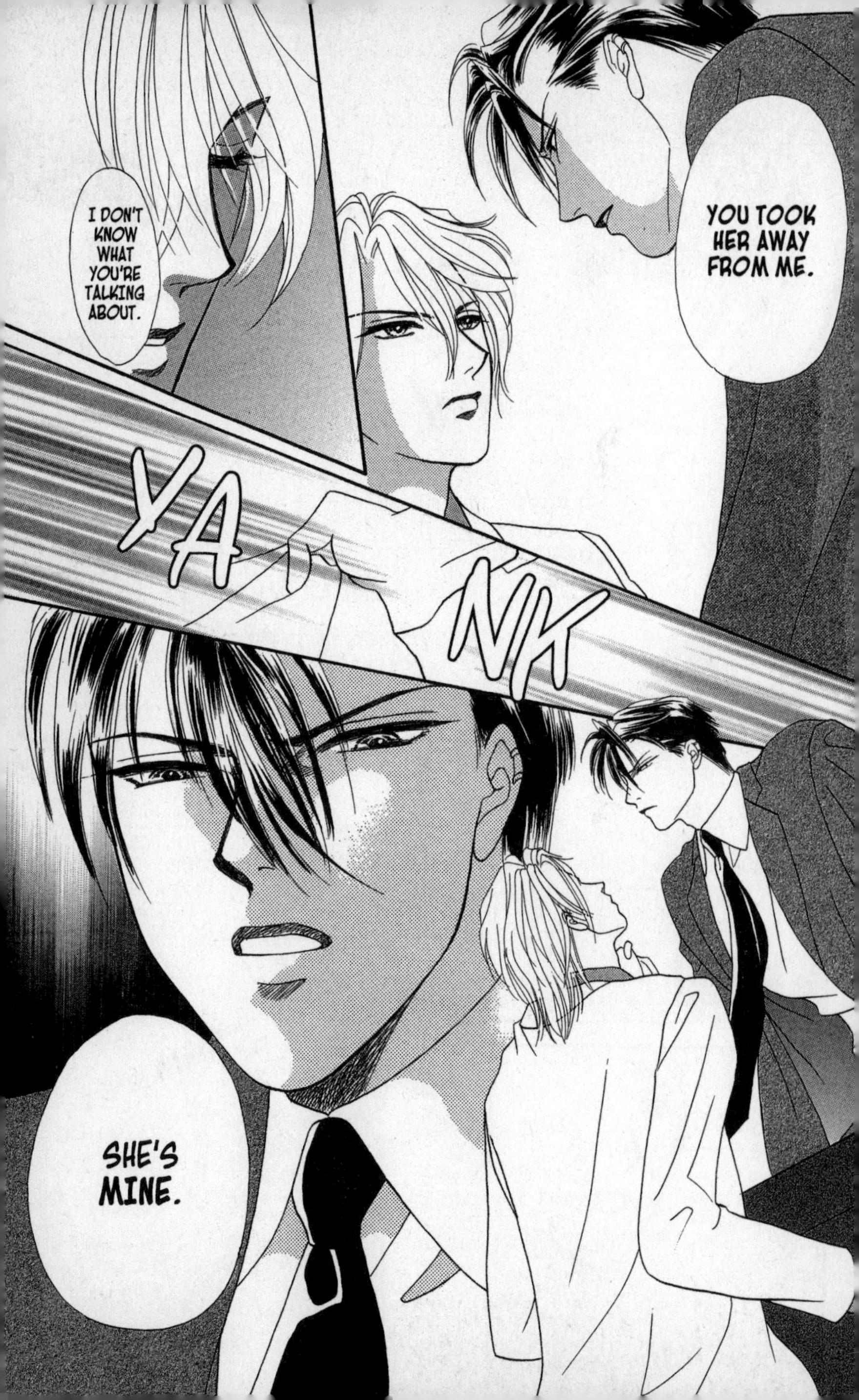
YOU TOOK HER AWAY FROM ME.
I DON'T KNOW WHAT YOU'RE TALKING ABOUT.
YANK
SHE'S MINE.

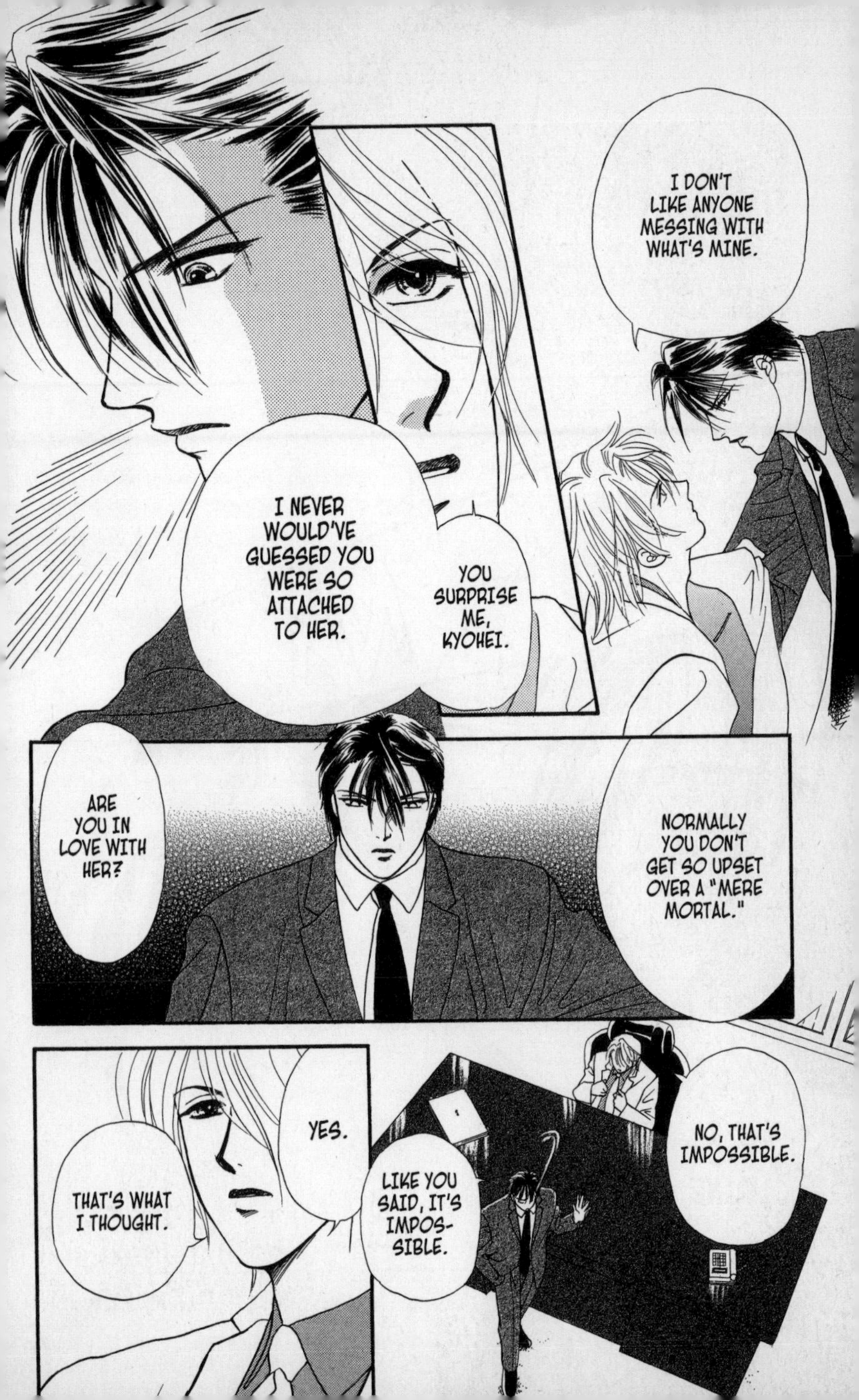

I DON'T LIKE ANYONE MESSING WITH WHAT'S MINE.
YOU SURPRISE ME, KYOHEI.
I NEVER WOULD'VE GUESSED YOU WERE SO ATTACHED TO HER.
NORMALLY YOU DON'T GET SO UPSET OVER A "MERE MORTAL."
ARE YOU IN LOVE WITH HER?
NO, THAT'S IMPOSSIBLE.
YES.
LIKE YOU SAID, IT'S IMPOS-SIBLE.
THAT'S WHAT I THOUGHT.

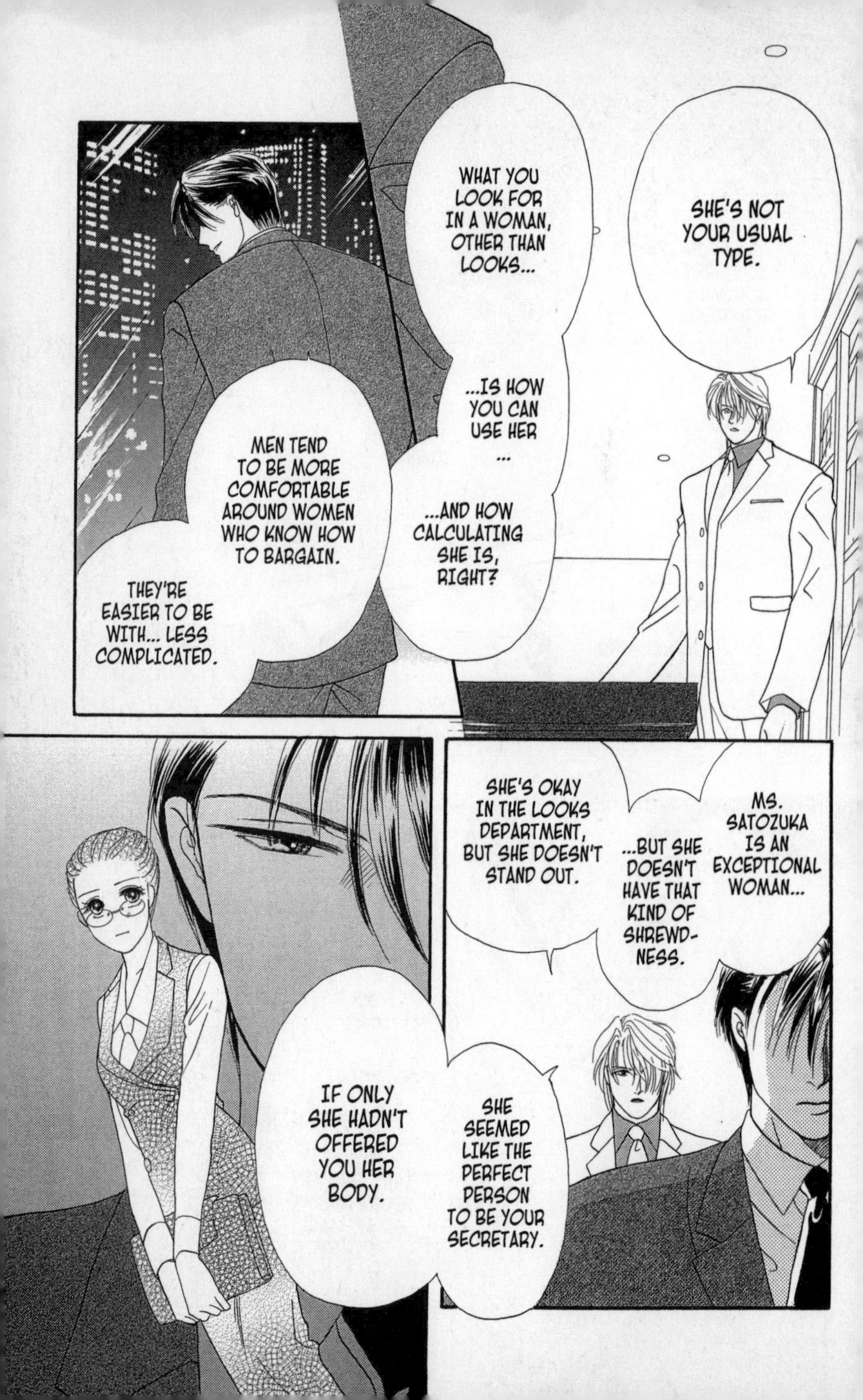
SHE'S NOT YOUR USUAL TYPE.
WHAT YOU LOOK FOR IN A WOMAN, OTHER THAN LOOKS...
...IS HOW YOU CAN USE HER ...
...AND HOW CALCULATING SHE IS, RIGHT?
MEN TEND TO BE MORE COMFORTABLE AROUND WOMEN WHO KNOW HOW TO BARGAIN.
THEY'RE EASIER TO BE WITH... LESS COMPLICATED.
MS. SATOZUKA IS AN EXCEPTIONAL WOMAN...
...BUT SHE DOESN'T HAVE THAT KIND OF SHREWD-NESS.
SHE'S OKAY IN THE LOOKS DEPARTMENT, BUT SHE DOESN'T STAND OUT.
SHE SEEMED LIKE THE PERFECT PERSON TO BE YOUR SECRETARY.
IF ONLY SHE HADN'T OFFERED YOU HER BODY.

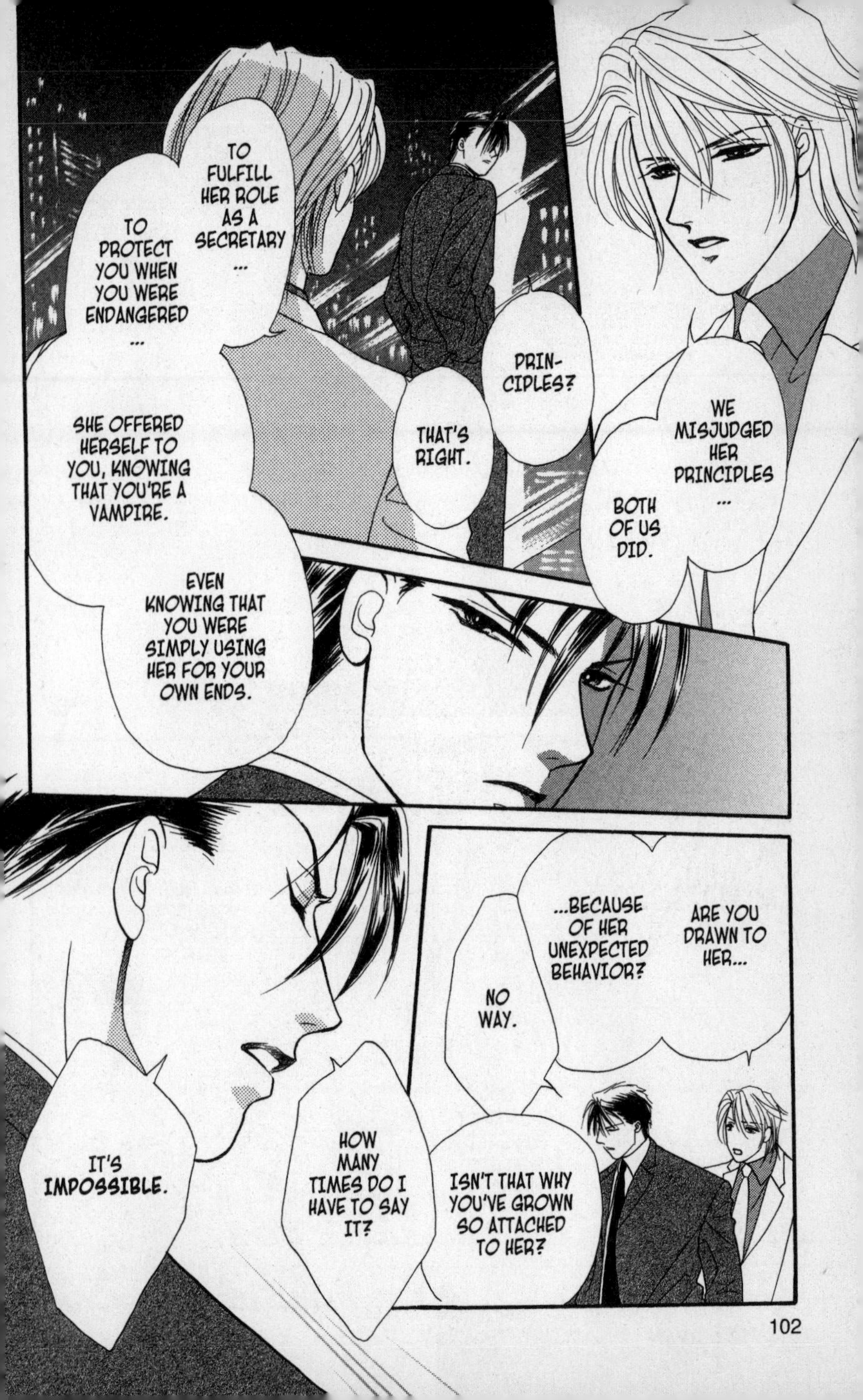
WE MISJUDGED HER PRINCIPLES ...
BOTH OF US DID.
PRIN-CIPLES?
THAT'S RIGHT.
TO FULFILL HER ROLE AS A SECRETARY ...
TO PROTECT YOU WHEN YOU WERE ENDANGERED ...
SHE OFFERED HERSELF TO YOU, KNOWING THAT YOU'RE A VAMPIRE.
EVEN KNOWING THAT YOU WERE SIMPLY USING HER FOR YOUR OWN ENDS.
ARE YOU DRAWN TO HER...
...BECAUSE OF HER UNEXPECTED BEHAVIOR?
NO WAY.
ISN'T THAT WHY YOU'VE GROWN SO ATTACHED TO HER?
HOW MANY TIMES DO I HAVE TO SAY IT?
IT'S IMPOSSIBLE.

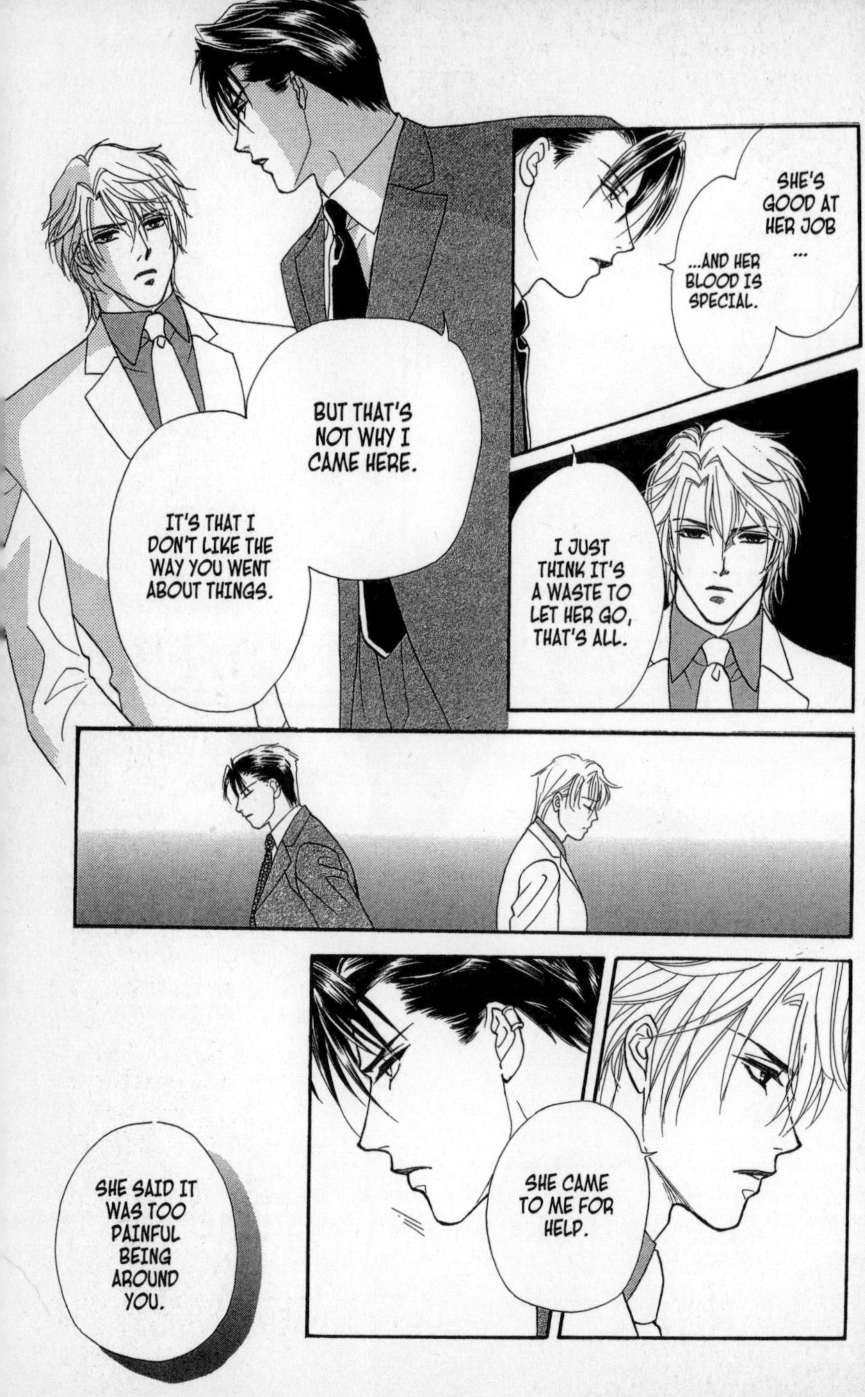
SHE'S GOOD AT HER JOB ...
...AND HER BLOOD IS SPECIAL.
I JUST THINK IT'S A WASTE TO LET HER GO, THAT'S ALL.
BUT THAT'S NOT WHY I CAME HERE.
IT'S THAT I DON'T LIKE THE WAY YOU WENT ABOUT THINGS.
SHE CAME TO ME FOR HELP.
SHE SAID IT WAS TOO PAINFUL BEING AROUND YOU.

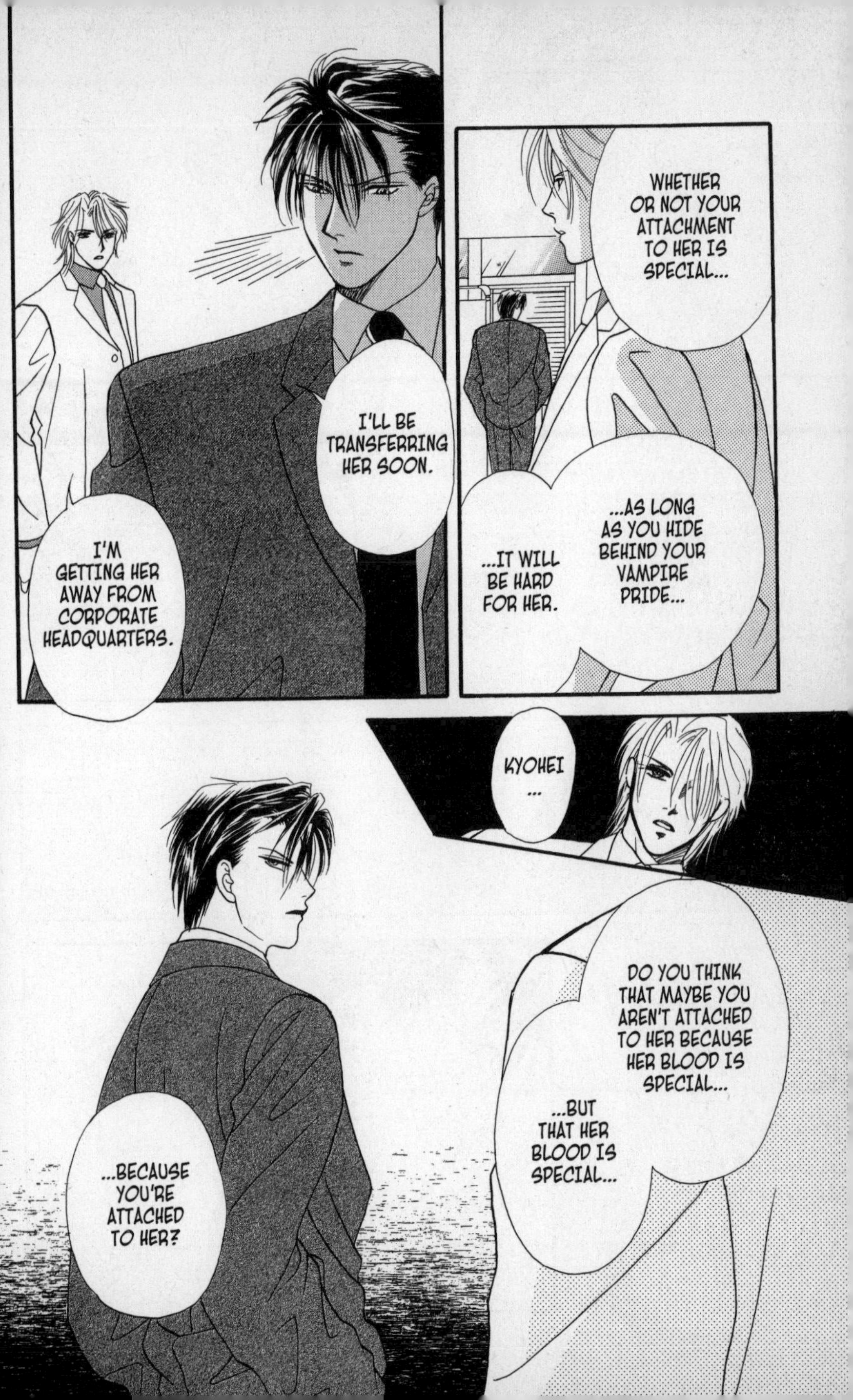
WHETHER OR NOT YOUR ATTACHMENT TO HER IS SPECIAL...
...AS LONG AS YOU HIDE BEHIND YOUR VAMPIRE PRIDE...
...IT WILL BE HARD FOR HER.
I'LL BE TRANSFERRING HER SOON.
I'M GETTING HER AWAY FROM CORPORATE HEADQUARTERS.
KYOHEI ...
DO YOU THINK THAT MAYBE YOU AREN'T ATTACHED TO HER BECAUSE HER BLOOD IS SPECIAL...
...BUT THAT HER BLOOD IS SPECIAL...
...BECAUSE YOU'RE ATTACHED TO HER?

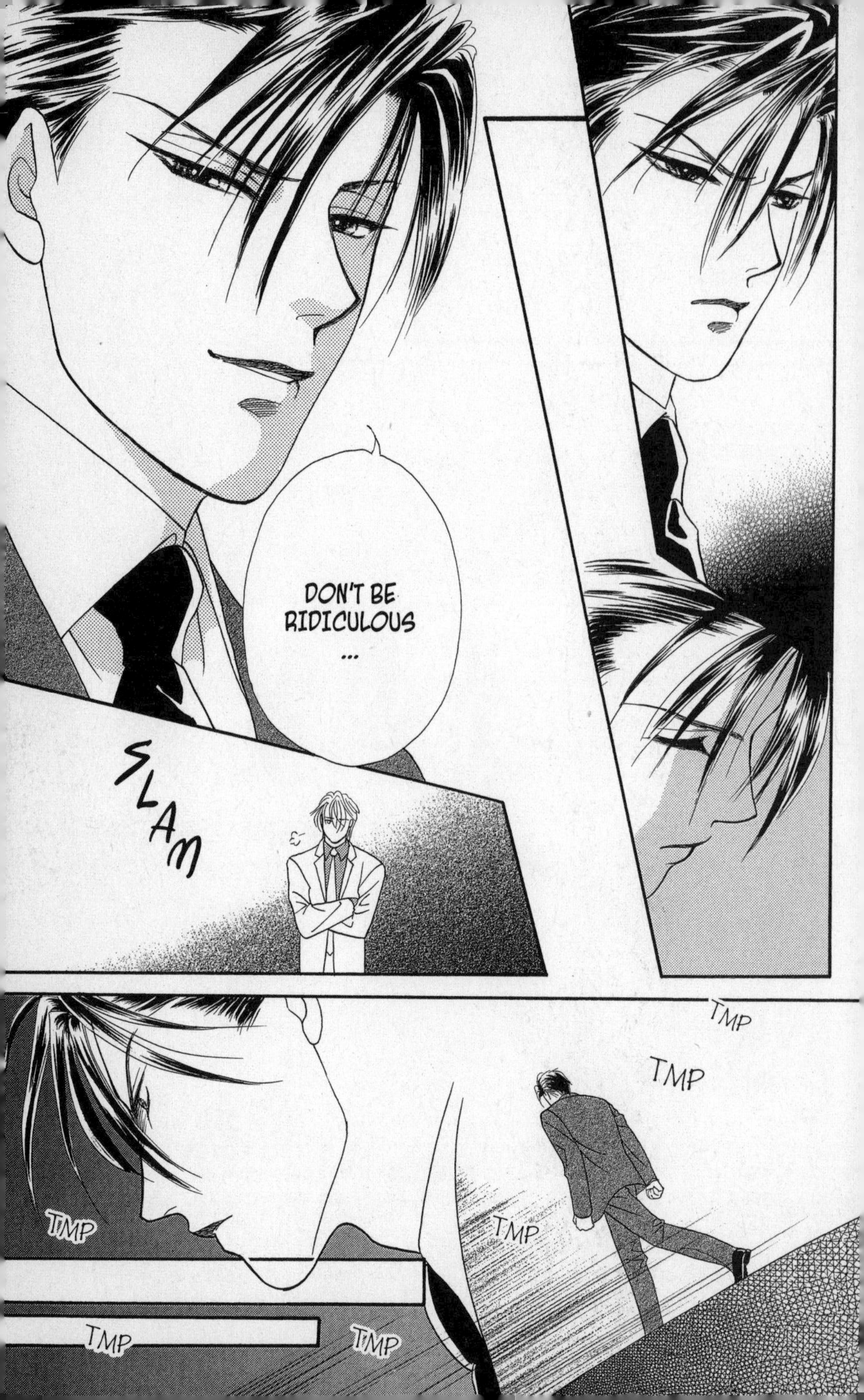
DON'T BE RIDICULOUS ...
SLAM
TMP
TMP
TMP
TMP
TMP
TMP

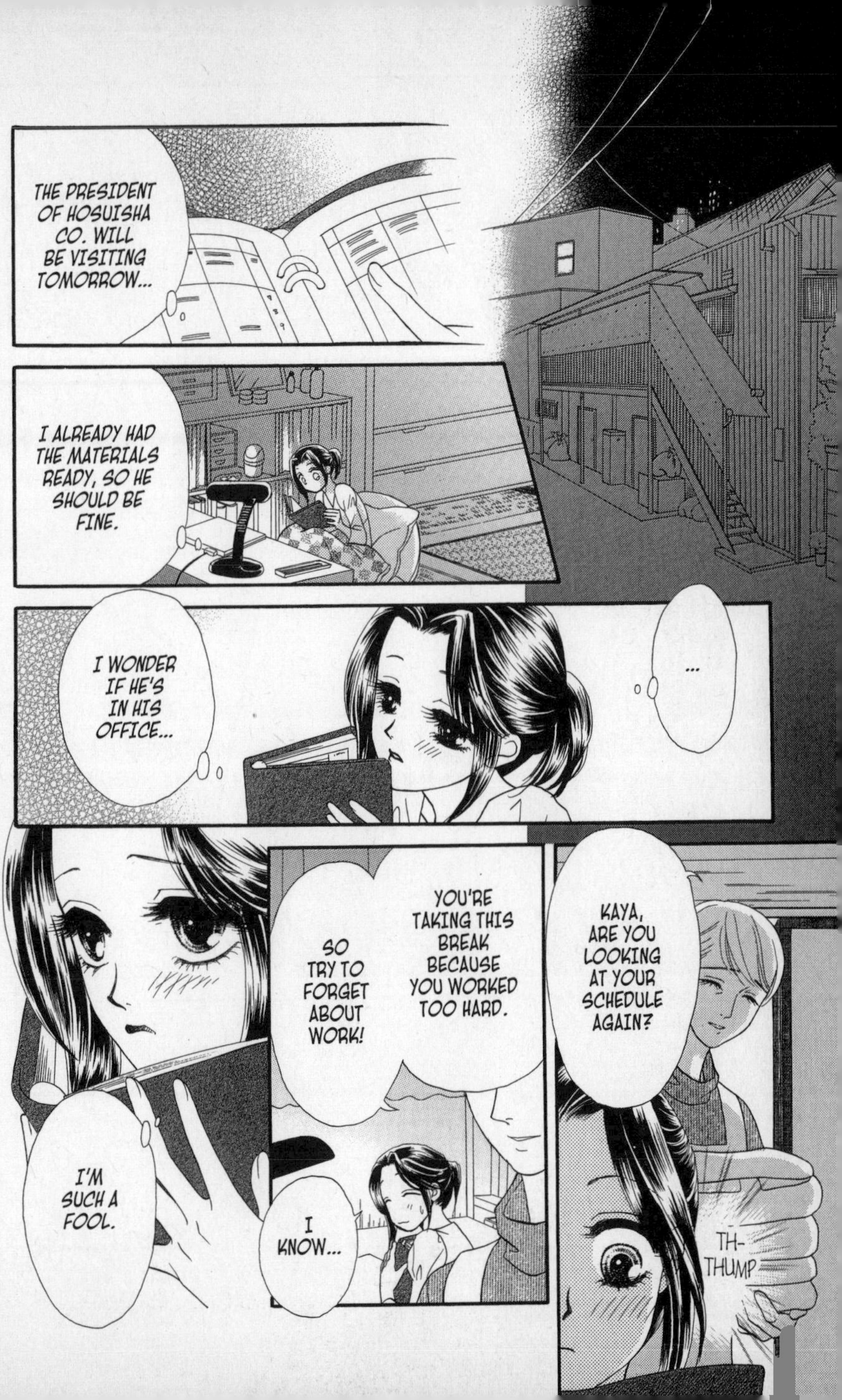
THE PRESIDENT OF HOSUISHA CO. WILL BE VISITING TOMORROW...
I ALREADY HAD THE MATERIALS READY, SO HE SHOULD BE FINE.
I WONDER IF HE'S IN HIS OFFICE...
...
KAYA, ARE YOU LOOKING AT YOUR SCHEDULE AGAIN?
TH-THUMP
YOU'RE TAKING THIS BREAK BECAUSE YOU WORKED TOO HARD.
SO TRY TO FORGET ABOUT WORK!
I KNOW...
I'M SUCH A FOOL.

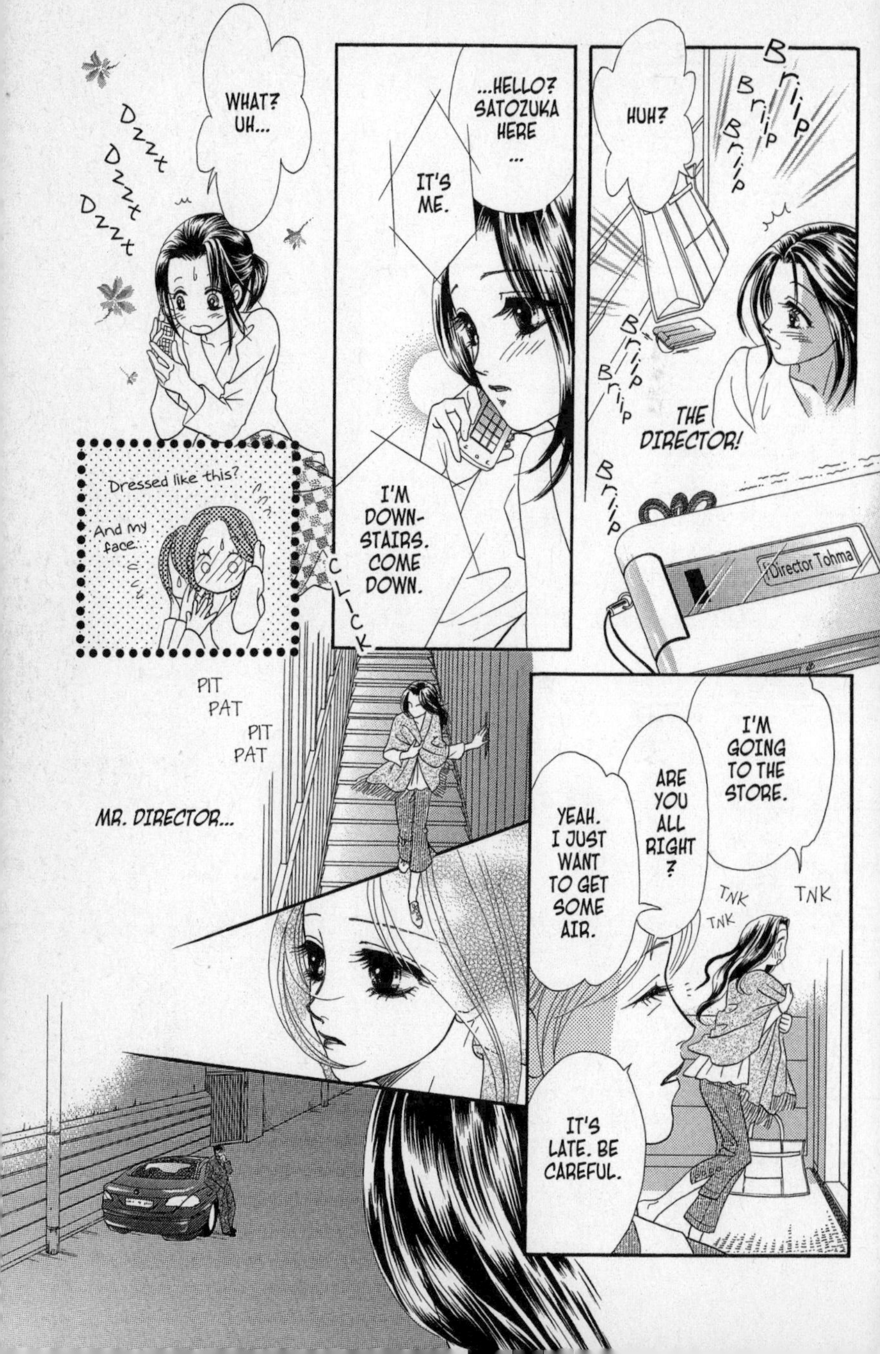
Brrip Brrip Brrip
HUH?
Brrip Brrip Brrip
THE DIRECTOR!
Director Tohma
...HELLO? SATOZUKA HERE ...
IT'S ME.
I'M DOWNSTAIRS. COME DOWN.
CLICK
WHAT? UH...
Dzzt Dzzt Dzzt
Dressed like this?
And my face...
I'M GOING TO THE STORE.
ARE YOU ALL RIGHT?
YEAH. I JUST WANT TO GET SOME AIR.
TNK TNK TNK
IT'S LATE. BE CAREFUL.
PIT PAT PIT PAT
MR. DIRECTOR...

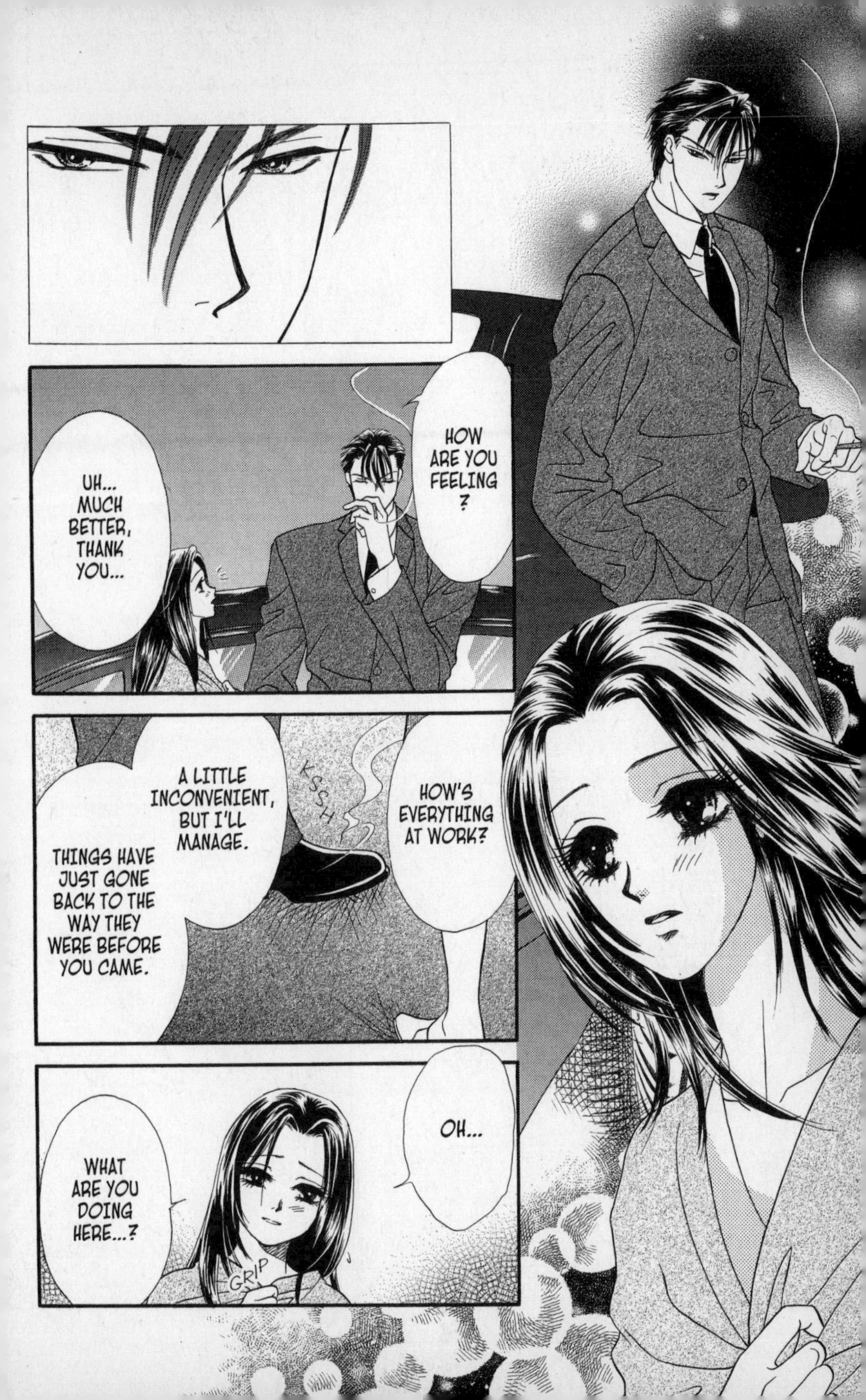
HOW ARE YOU FEELING?
UH... MUCH BETTER, THANK YOU...
HOW'S EVERYTHING AT WORK?
KSSH
A LITTLE INCONVENIENT, BUT I'LL MANAGE.
THINGS HAVE JUST GONE BACK TO THE WAY THEY WERE BEFORE YOU CAME.
OH...
WHAT ARE YOU DOING HERE...?
GRIP

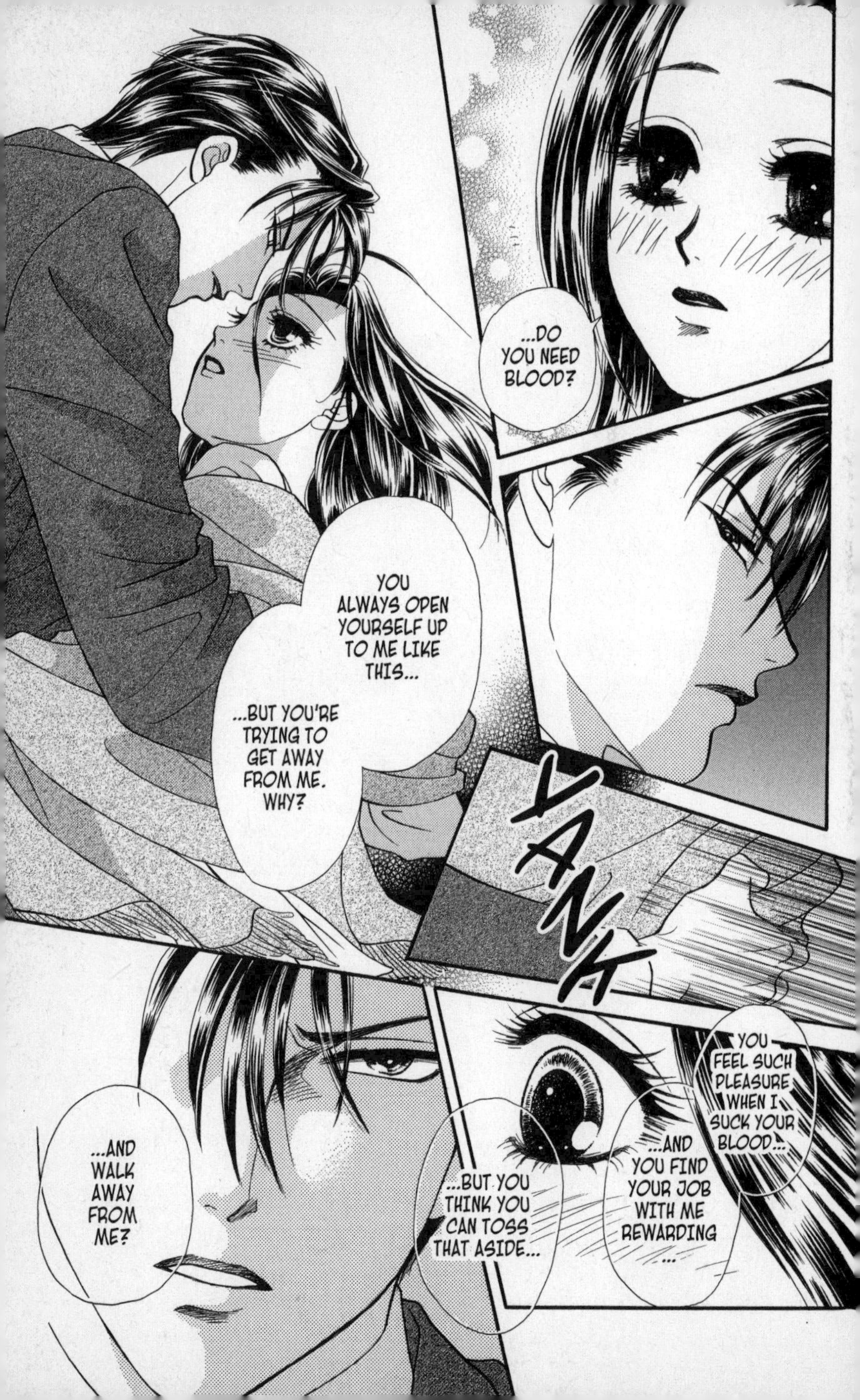
...DO YOU NEED BLOOD?
YANK
YOU ALWAYS OPEN YOURSELF UP TO ME LIKE THIS...
...BUT YOU'RE TRYING TO GET AWAY FROM ME. WHY?
YOU FEEL SUCH PLEASURE WHEN I SUCK YOUR BLOOD...
...AND YOU FIND YOUR JOB WITH ME REWARDING...
...BUT YOU THINK YOU CAN TOSS THAT ASIDE...
...AND WALK AWAY FROM ME?

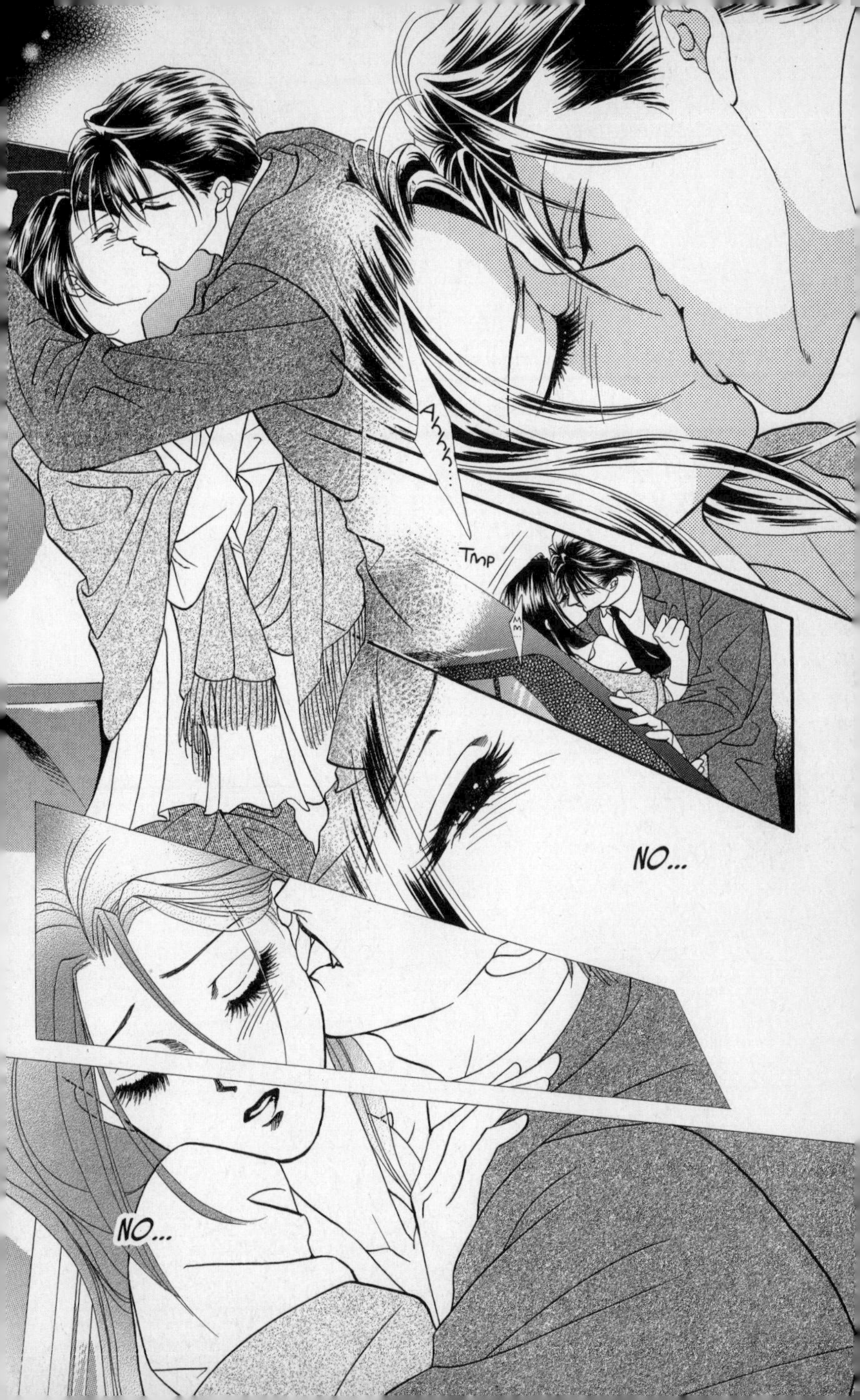
Ahhh...
TMP
MM
NO...
NO...

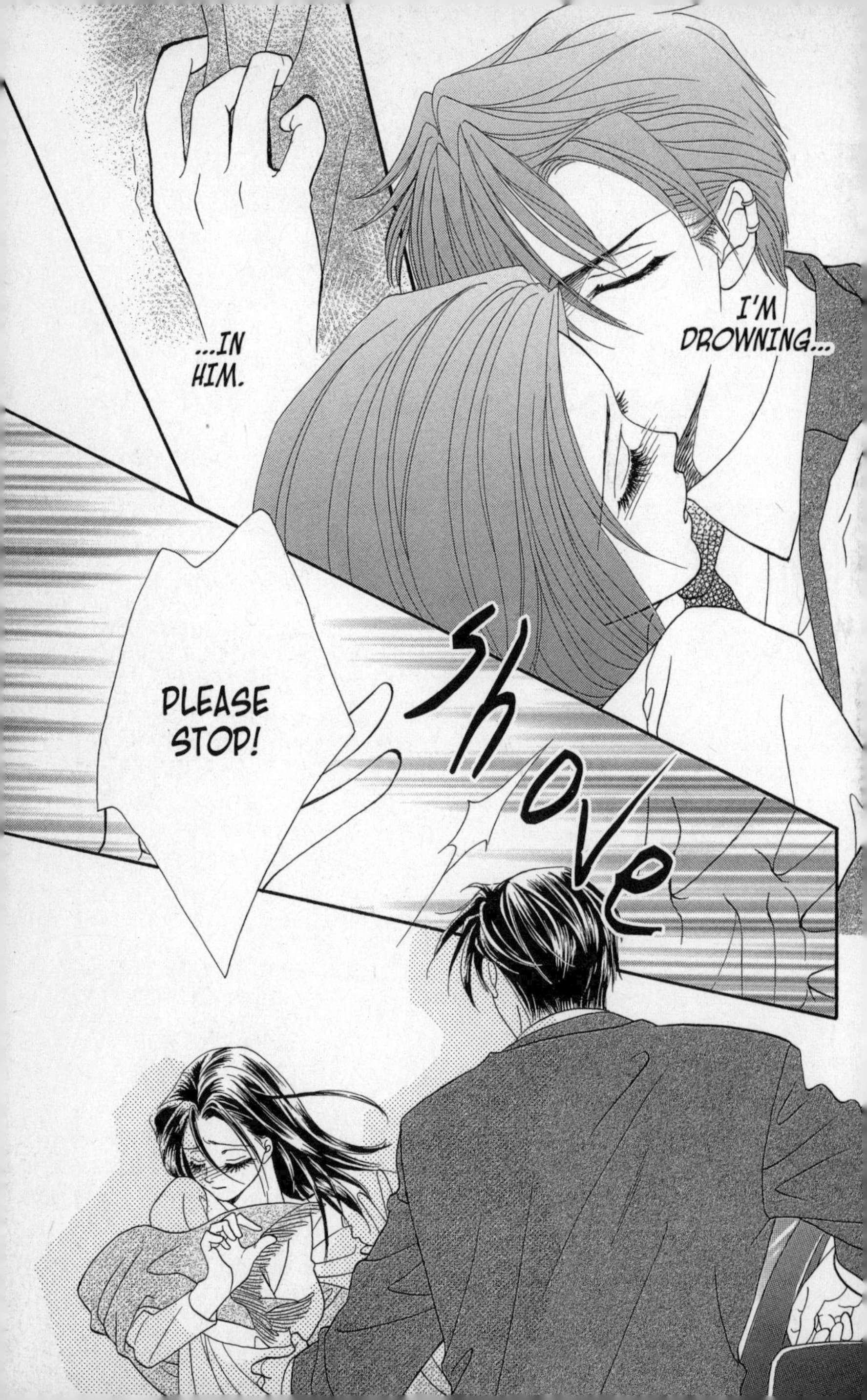
I'M DROWNING...
...IN HIM.
PLEASE STOP!
SHOVE

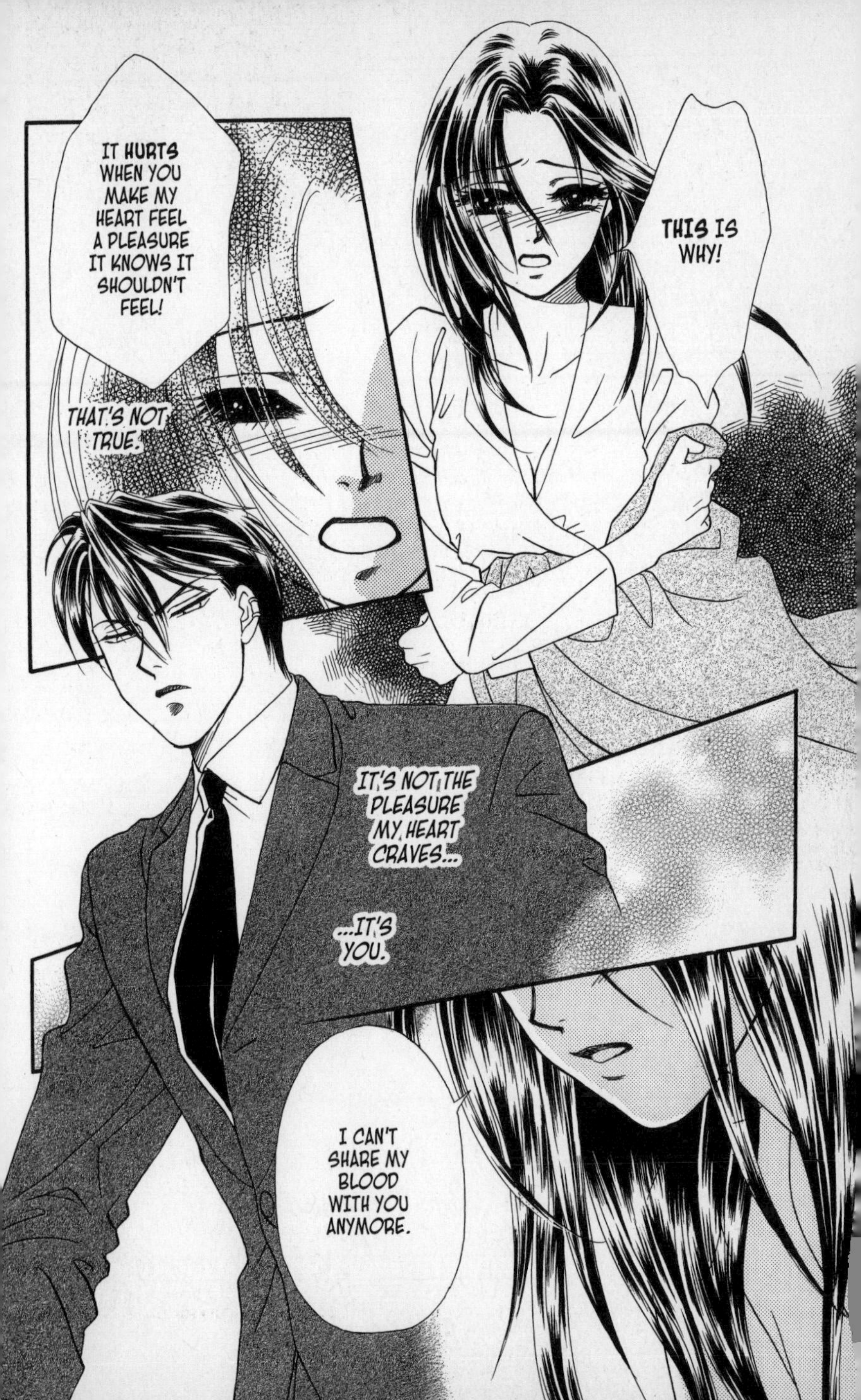
THIS IS WHY!
IT HURTS WHEN YOU MAKE MY HEART FEEL A PLEASURE IT KNOWS IT SHOULDN'T FEEL!
THAT'S NOT TRUE.
IT'S NOT THE PLEASURE MY HEART CRAVES...
...IT'S YOU.
I CAN'T SHARE MY BLOOD WITH YOU ANYMORE.

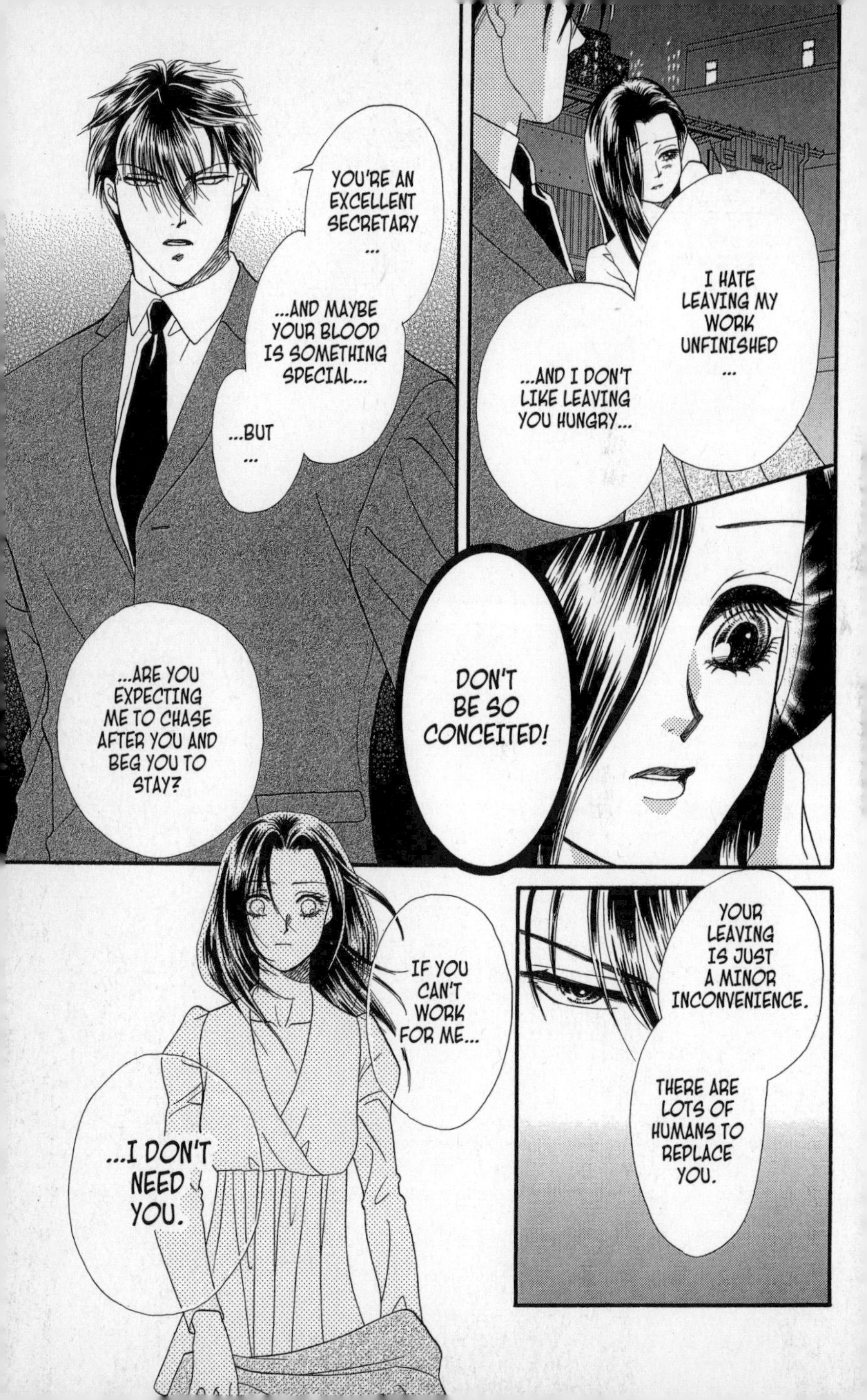
I HATE LEAVING MY WORK UNFINISHED ...
...AND I DON'T LIKE LEAVING YOU HUNGRY...
DON'T BE SO CONCEITED!
YOU'RE AN EXCELLENT SECRETARY ...
...AND MAYBE YOUR BLOOD IS SOMETHING SPECIAL...
...BUT ...
...ARE YOU EXPECTING ME TO CHASE AFTER YOU AND BEG YOU TO STAY?
YOUR LEAVING IS JUST A MINOR INCONVENIENCE.
THERE ARE LOTS OF HUMANS TO REPLACE YOU.
IF YOU CAN'T WORK FOR ME...
...I DON'T NEED YOU.

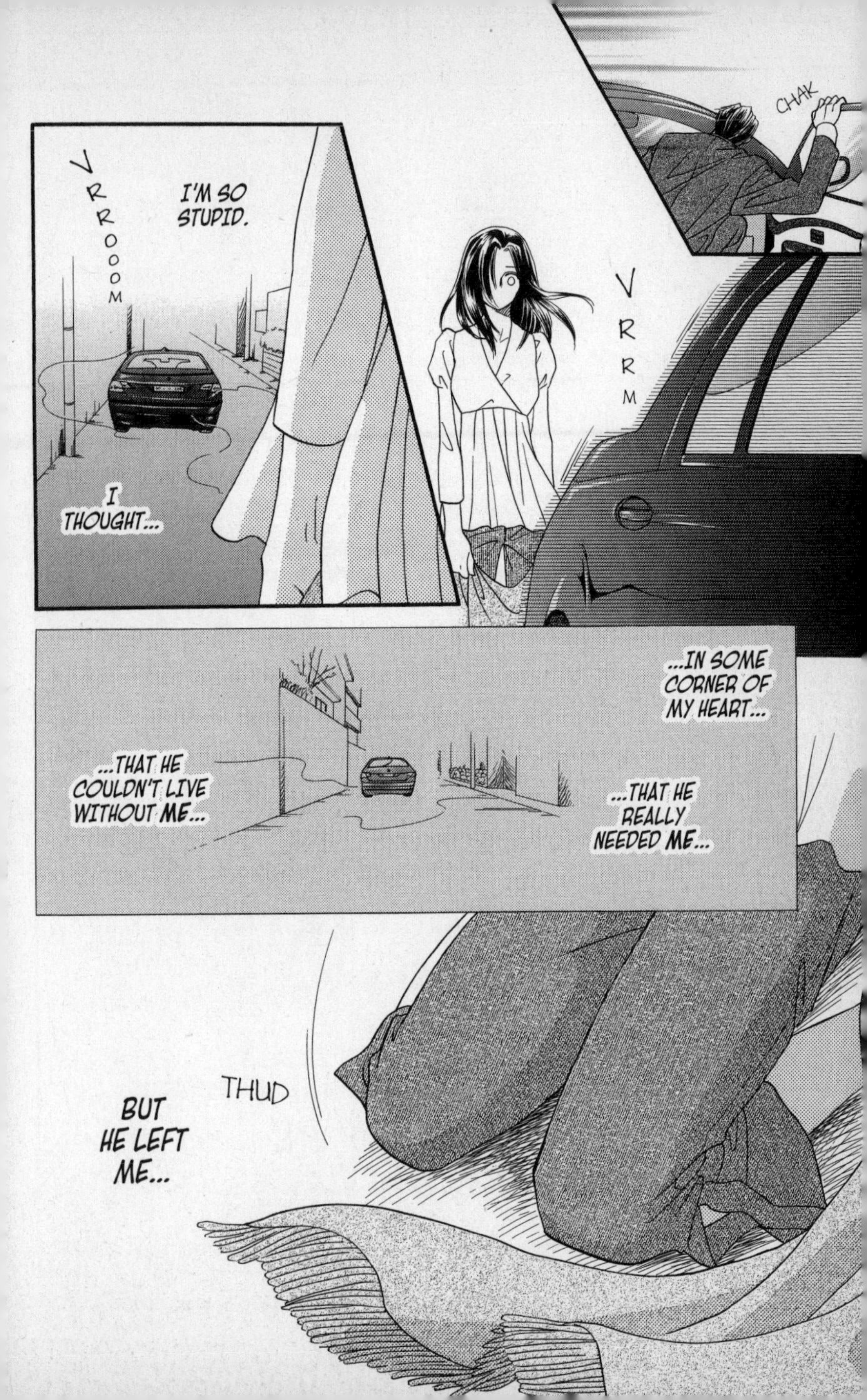

CHAK
VRRM
VRROOOM
I'M SO STUPID.
I THOUGHT...
...IN SOME CORNER OF MY HEART...
...THAT HE REALLY NEEDED ME...
...THAT HE COULDN'T LIVE WITHOUT ME...
THUD
BUT HE LEFT ME...

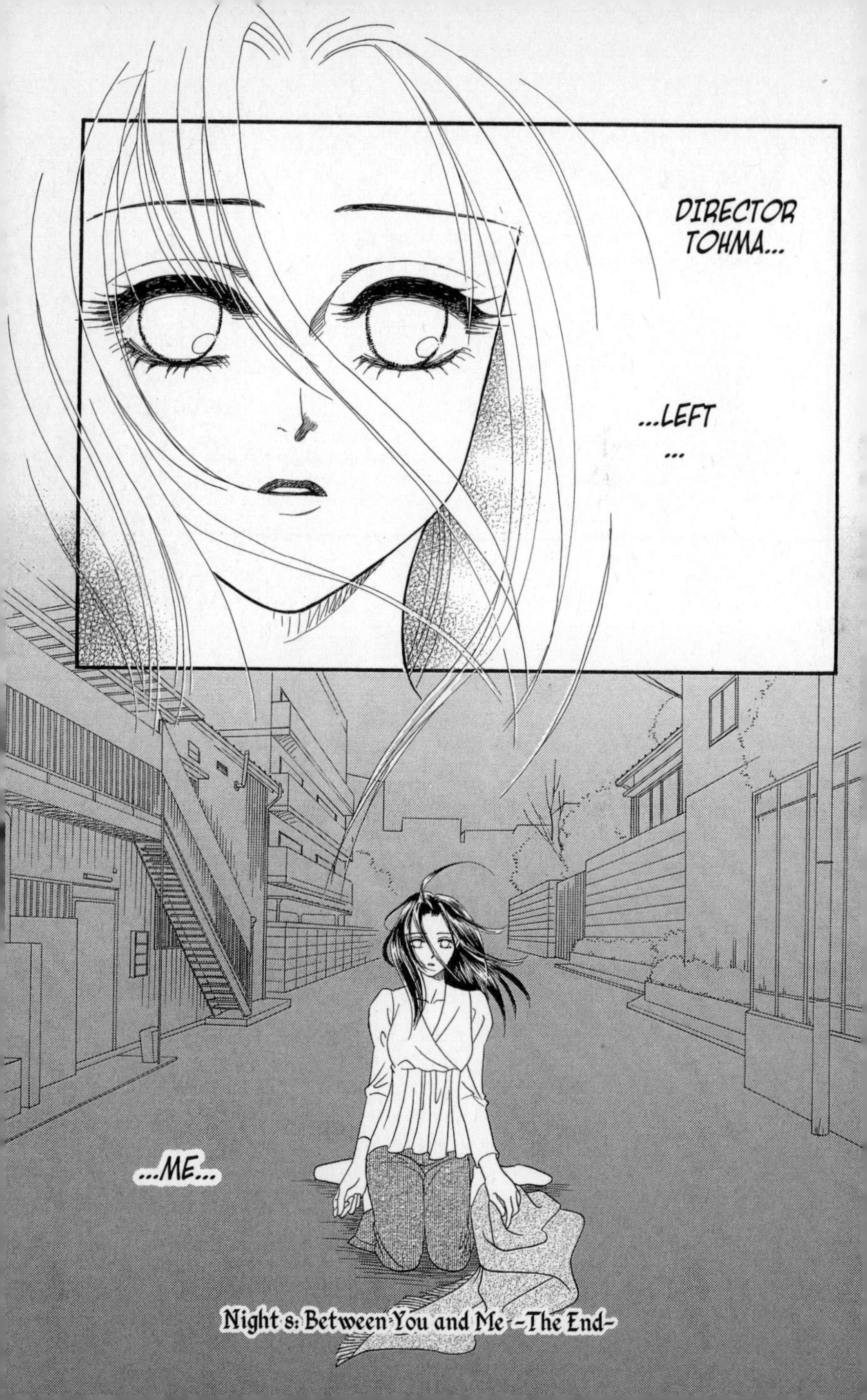
DIRECTOR TOHMA...
...LEFT
...
...ME...

Night 8: Between You and Me –The End–

- Between You and Me -

Kaya has a special ring tone for Director Tohma on her cell phone so that she can tell immediately when he calls. She wanted to use some weird music...

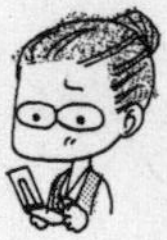
But I can't because there's no telling who will hear it. It's no fun...

- Top Secret -

President Takasu of Erde Co. makes his first appearance. The kanji for his name are kind of a pain to write, but using hiragana makes it harder to convey his image. Whenever I have to make story notes about him, I regret my choice a little.

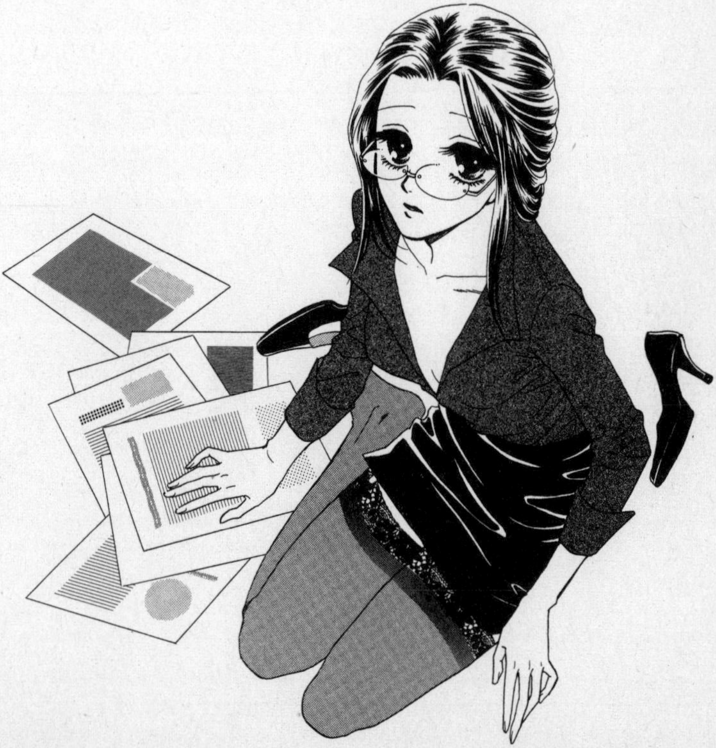

▲ Night 8: Top Secret preview

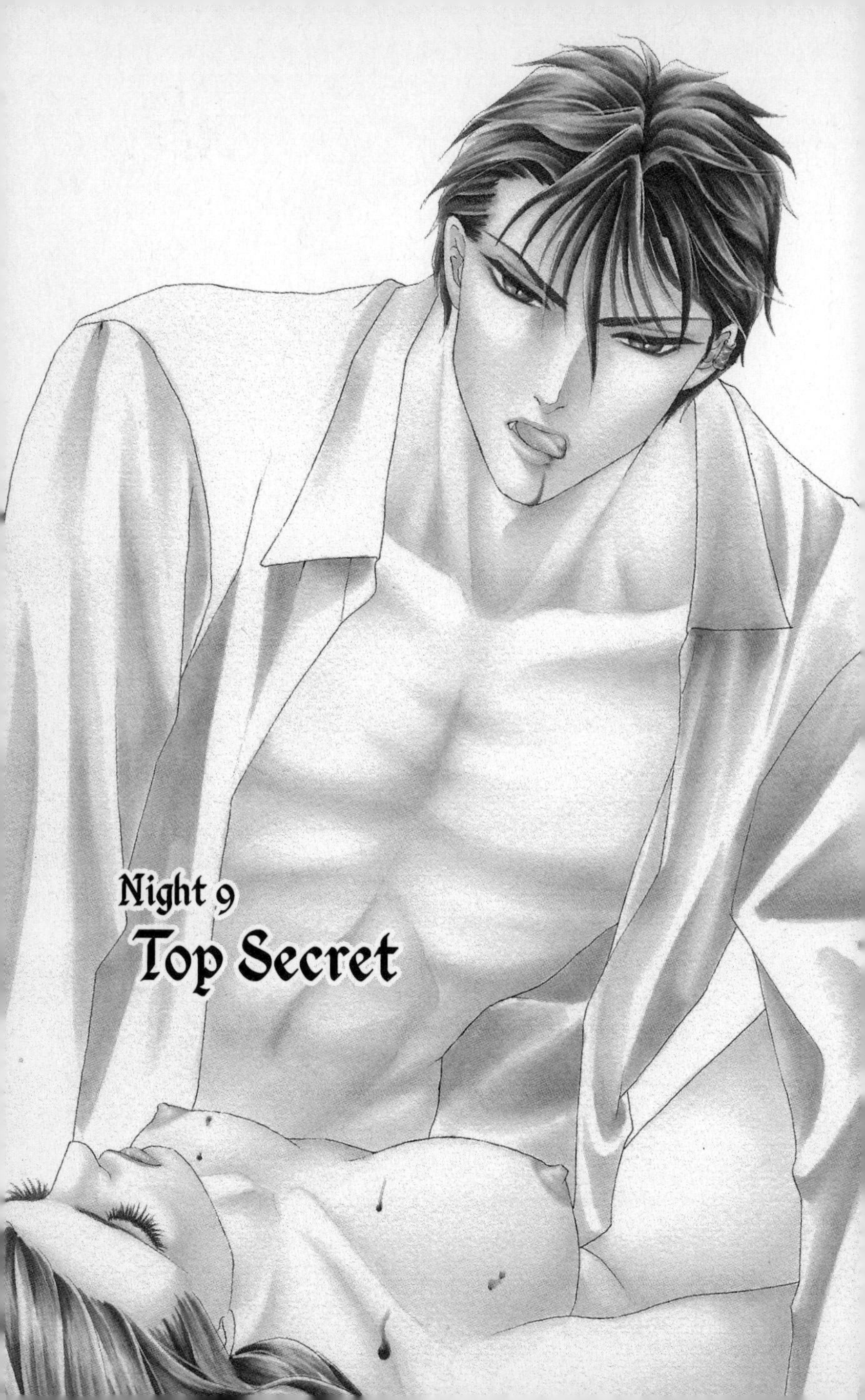
Night 9
Top Secret

▲ Night 10: One Night with You preview

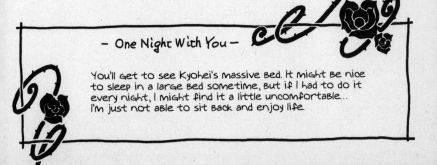

— One Night With You —

You'll get to see Kyohei's massive bed. It might be nice to sleep in a large bed sometime, but if I had to do it every night, I might find it a little uncomfortable... I'm just not able to sit back and enjoy life.

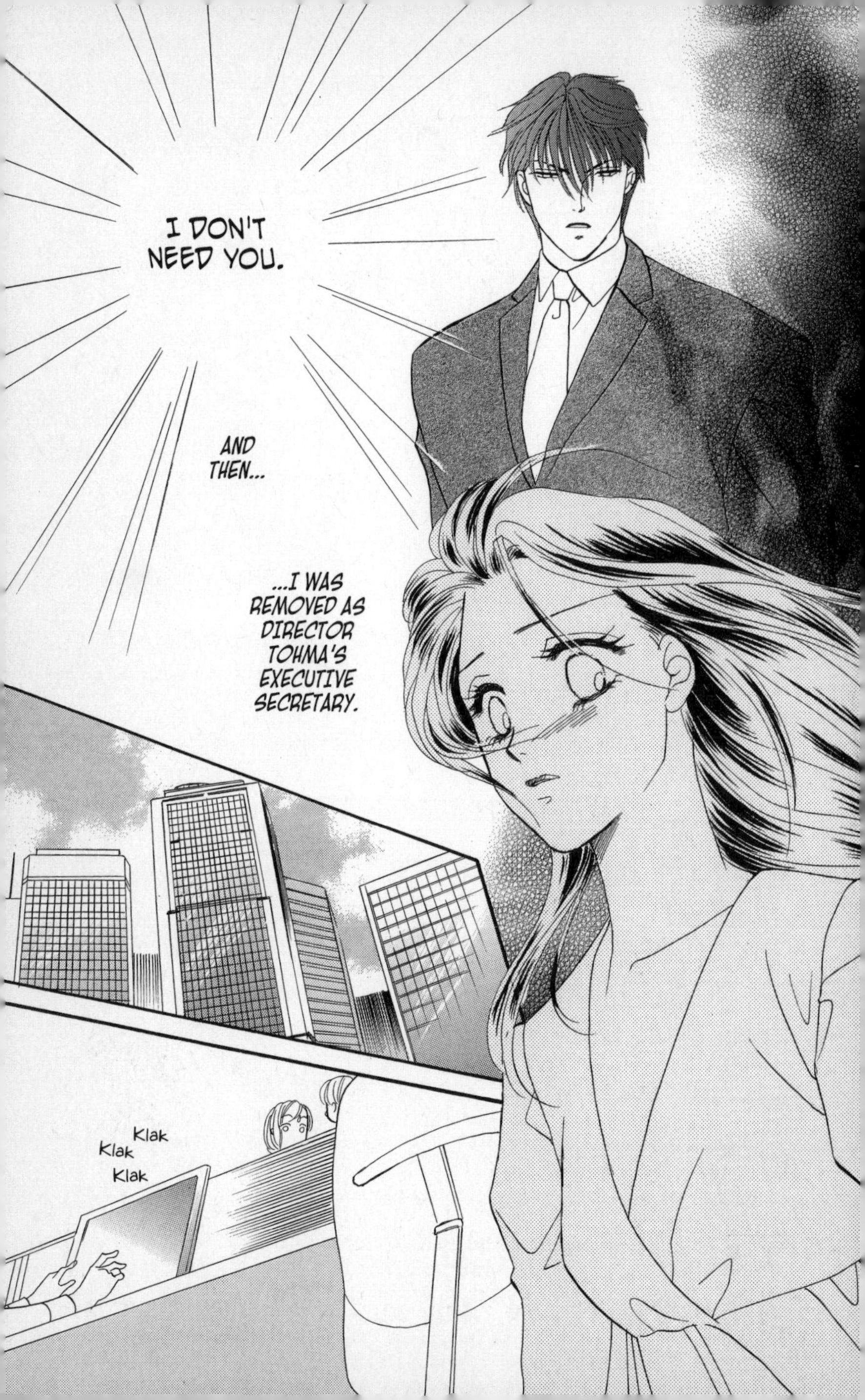
I DON'T NEED YOU.
AND THEN...
...I WAS REMOVED AS DIRECTOR TOHMA'S EXECUTIVE SECRETARY.
Klak
Klak
Klak

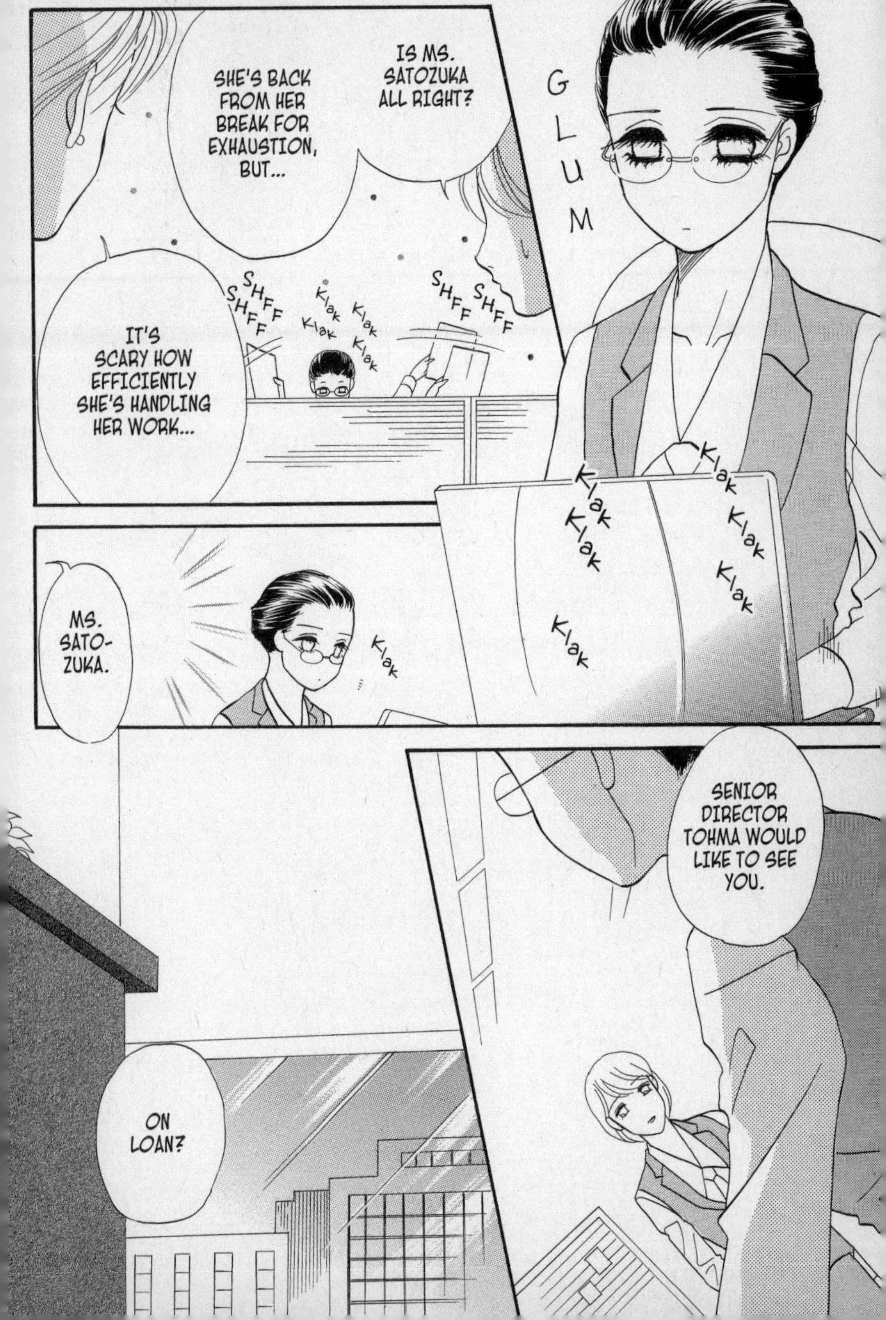

GLUM
Klak Klak Klak Klak Klak
IS MS. SATOZUKA ALL RIGHT?
SHE'S BACK FROM HER BREAK FOR EXHAUSTION, BUT...
SHFF SHFF
Klak Klak Klak Klak
SHFF SHFF
IT'S SCARY HOW EFFICIENTLY SHE'S HANDLING HER WORK...
Klak
MS. SATO-ZUKA.
SENIOR DIRECTOR TOHMA WOULD LIKE TO SEE YOU.
ON LOAN?

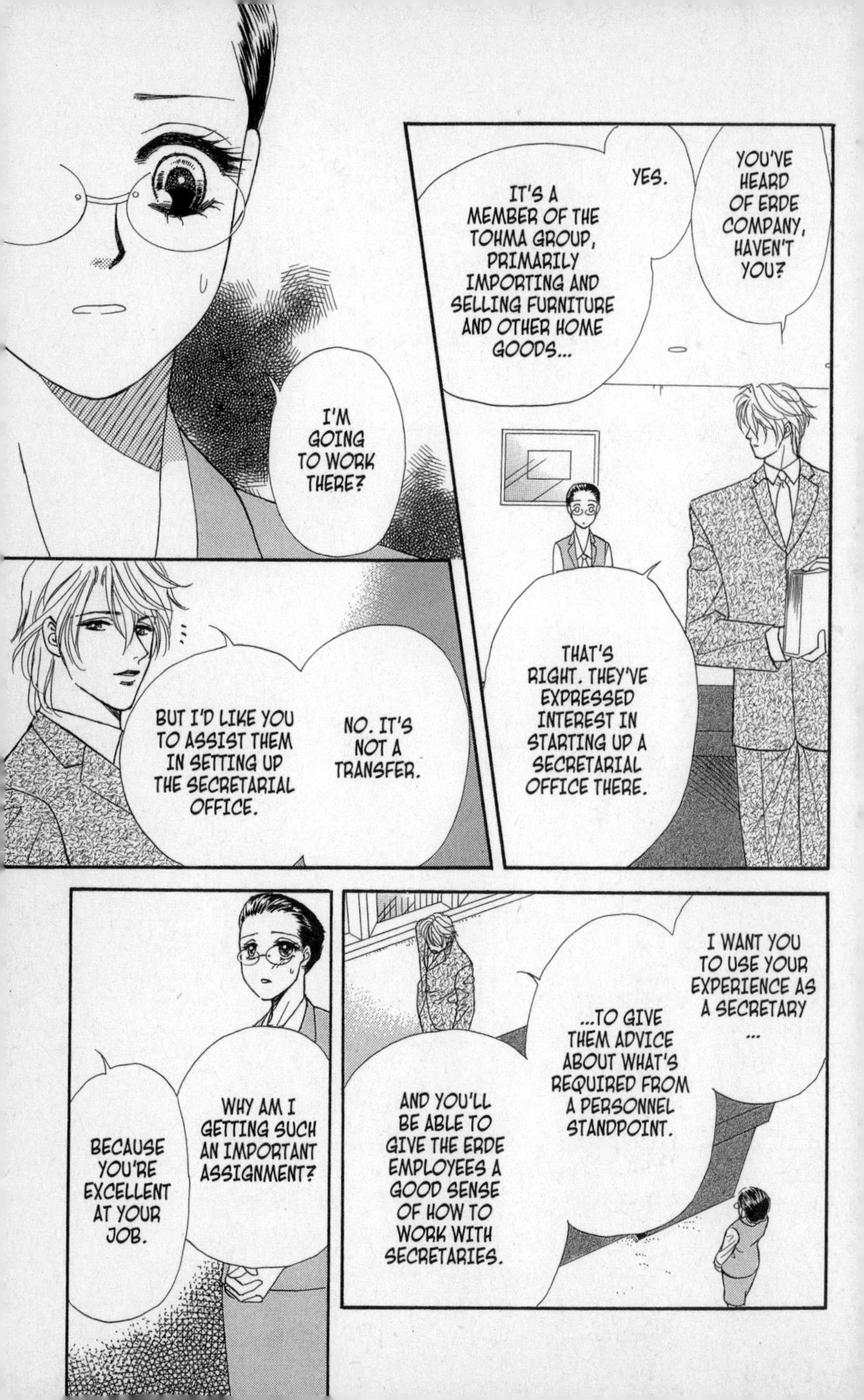
YOU'VE HEARD OF ERDE COMPANY, HAVEN'T YOU?
YES.
IT'S A MEMBER OF THE TOHMA GROUP, PRIMARILY IMPORTING AND SELLING FURNITURE AND OTHER HOME GOODS...
THAT'S RIGHT. THEY'VE EXPRESSED INTEREST IN STARTING UP A SECRETARIAL OFFICE THERE.
I'M GOING TO WORK THERE?
NO. IT'S NOT A TRANSFER.
BUT I'D LIKE YOU TO ASSIST THEM IN SETTING UP THE SECRETARIAL OFFICE.
I WANT YOU TO USE YOUR EXPERIENCE AS A SECRETARY ...
...TO GIVE THEM ADVICE ABOUT WHAT'S REQUIRED FROM A PERSONNEL STANDPOINT.
AND YOU'LL BE ABLE TO GIVE THE ERDE EMPLOYEES A GOOD SENSE OF HOW TO WORK WITH SECRETARIES.
WHY AM I GETTING SUCH AN IMPORTANT ASSIGNMENT?
BECAUSE YOU'RE EXCELLENT AT YOUR JOB.

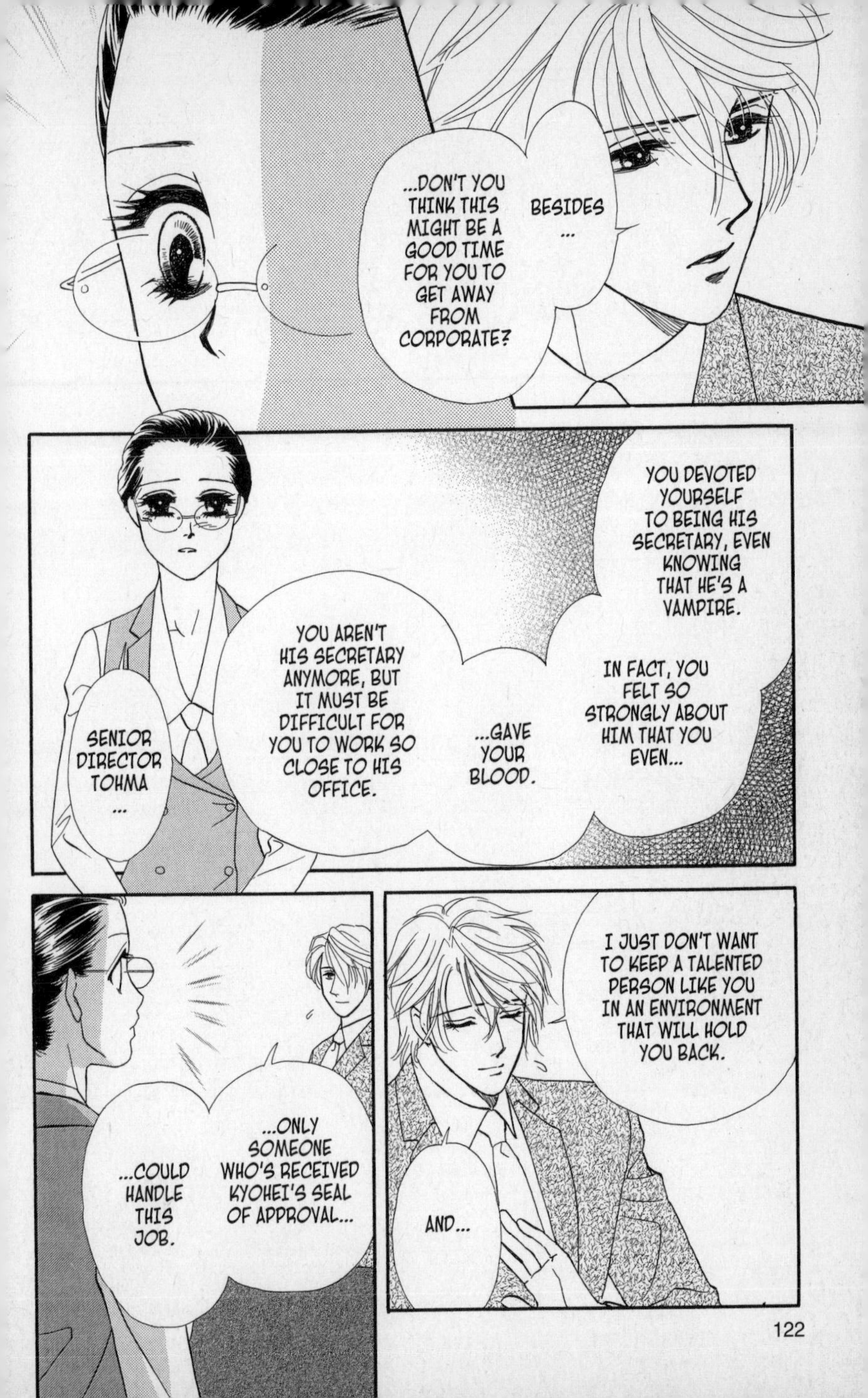
BESIDES ...
...DON'T YOU THINK THIS MIGHT BE A GOOD TIME FOR YOU TO GET AWAY FROM CORPORATE?
YOU DEVOTED YOURSELF TO BEING HIS SECRETARY, EVEN KNOWING THAT HE'S A VAMPIRE.
IN FACT, YOU FELT SO STRONGLY ABOUT HIM THAT YOU EVEN...
...GAVE YOUR BLOOD.
YOU AREN'T HIS SECRETARY ANYMORE, BUT IT MUST BE DIFFICULT FOR YOU TO WORK SO CLOSE TO HIS OFFICE.
SENIOR DIRECTOR TOHMA ...
I JUST DON'T WANT TO KEEP A TALENTED PERSON LIKE YOU IN AN ENVIRONMENT THAT WILL HOLD YOU BACK.
AND...
...ONLY SOMEONE WHO'S RECEIVED KYOHEI'S SEAL OF APPROVAL...
...COULD HANDLE THIS JOB.

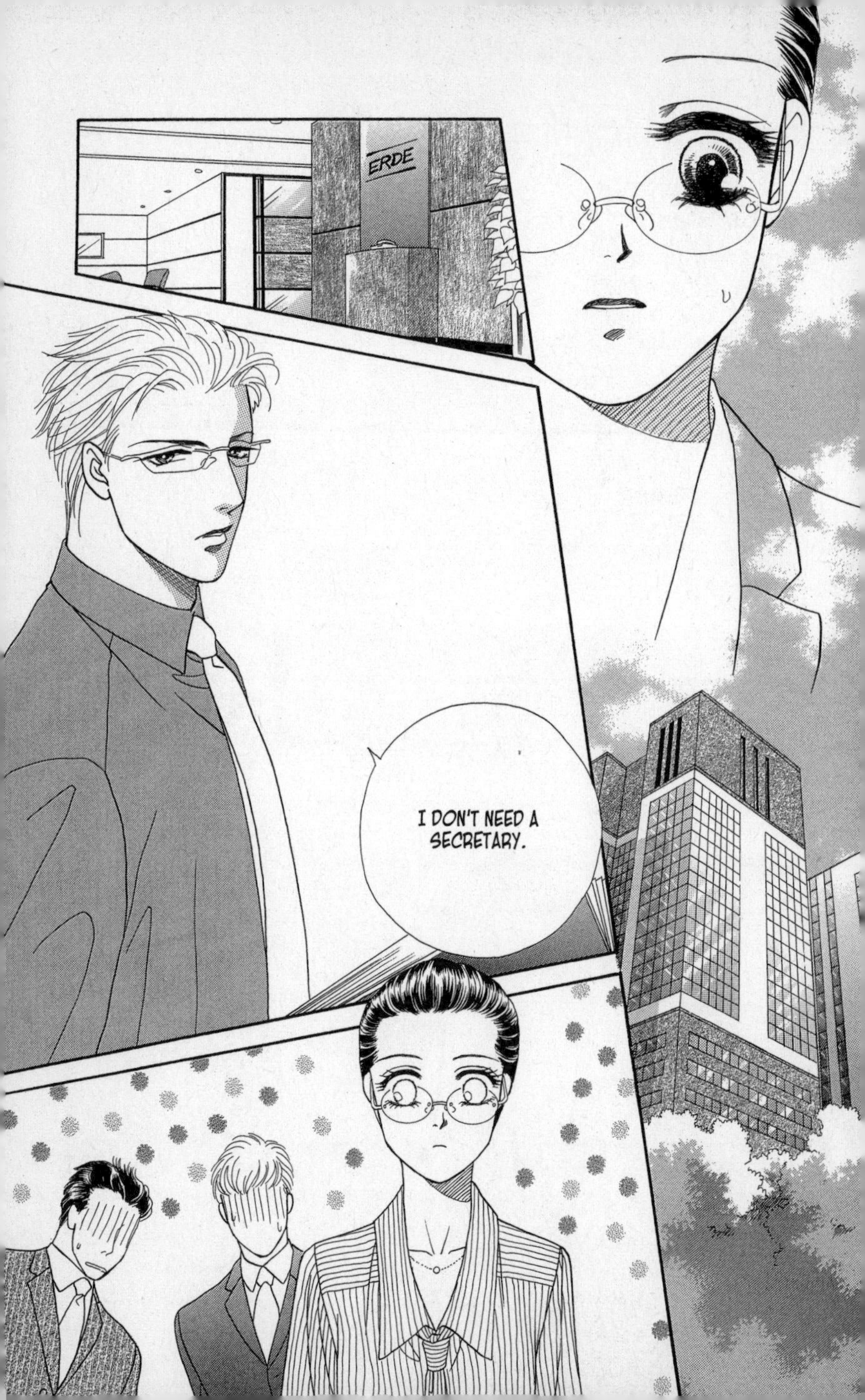
ERDE
I DON'T NEED A SECRETARY.

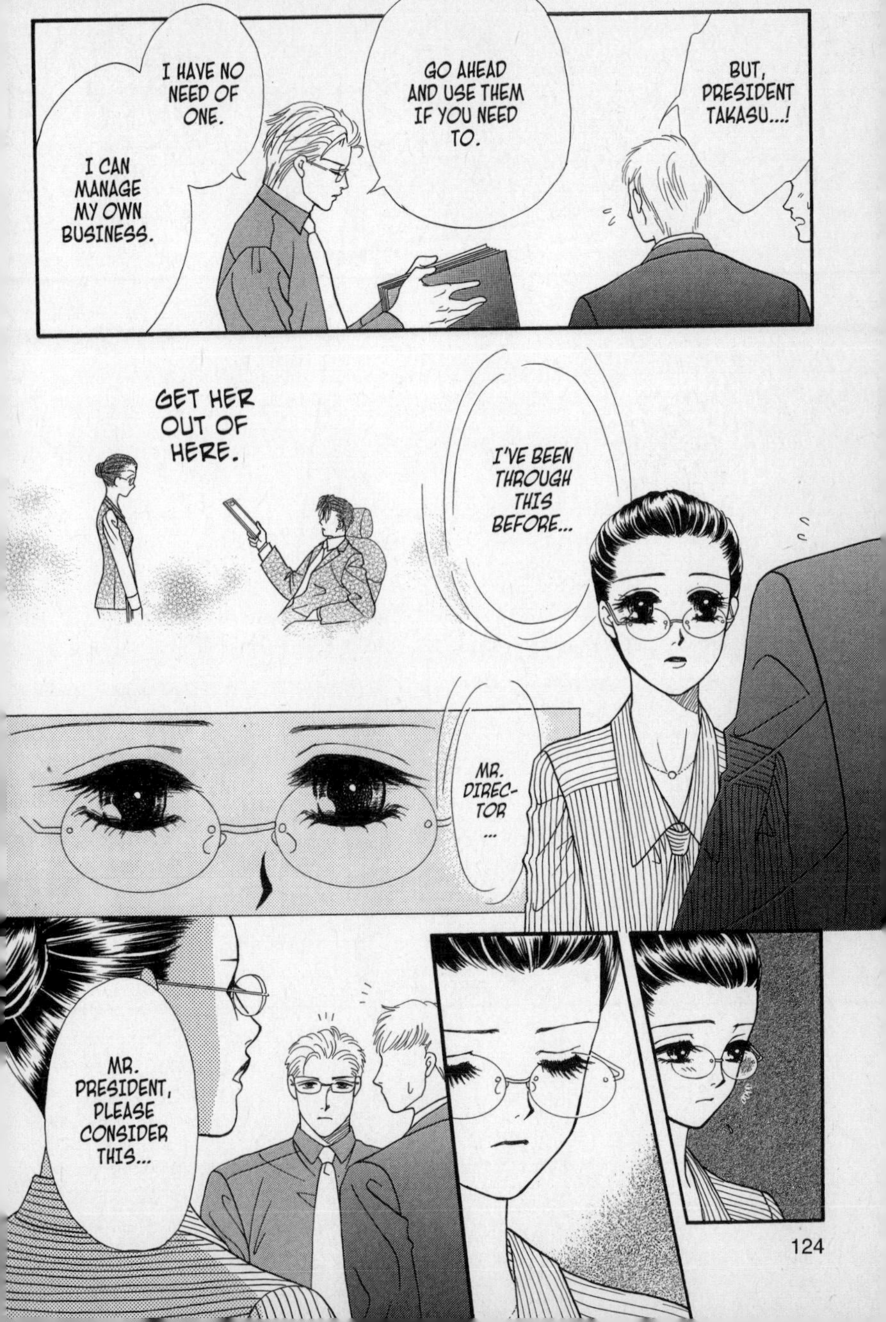
BUT, PRESIDENT TAKASU...!
GO AHEAD AND USE THEM IF YOU NEED TO.
I HAVE NO NEED OF ONE.
I CAN MANAGE MY OWN BUSINESS.
I'VE BEEN THROUGH THIS BEFORE...
GET HER OUT OF HERE.
MR. DIRECTOR...
MR. PRESIDENT, PLEASE CONSIDER THIS...

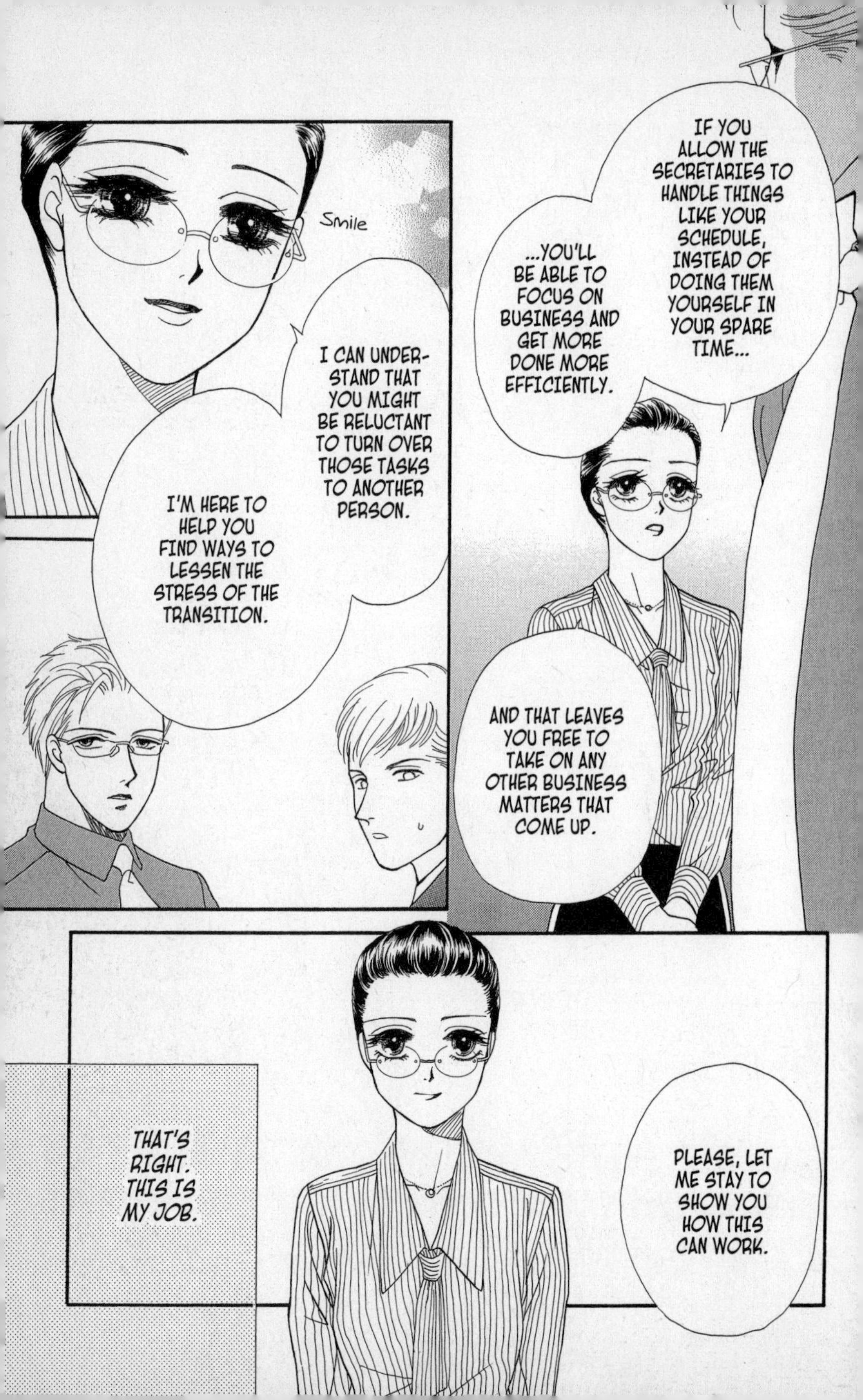
IF YOU ALLOW THE SECRETARIES TO HANDLE THINGS LIKE YOUR SCHEDULE, INSTEAD OF DOING THEM YOURSELF IN YOUR SPARE TIME...
...YOU'LL BE ABLE TO FOCUS ON BUSINESS AND GET MORE DONE MORE EFFICIENTLY.
AND THAT LEAVES YOU FREE TO TAKE ON ANY OTHER BUSINESS MATTERS THAT COME UP.
Smile
I CAN UNDER-STAND THAT YOU MIGHT BE RELUCTANT TO TURN OVER THOSE TASKS TO ANOTHER PERSON.
I'M HERE TO HELP YOU FIND WAYS TO LESSEN THE STRESS OF THE TRANSITION.
PLEASE, LET ME STAY TO SHOW YOU HOW THIS CAN WORK.
THAT'S RIGHT. THIS IS MY JOB.

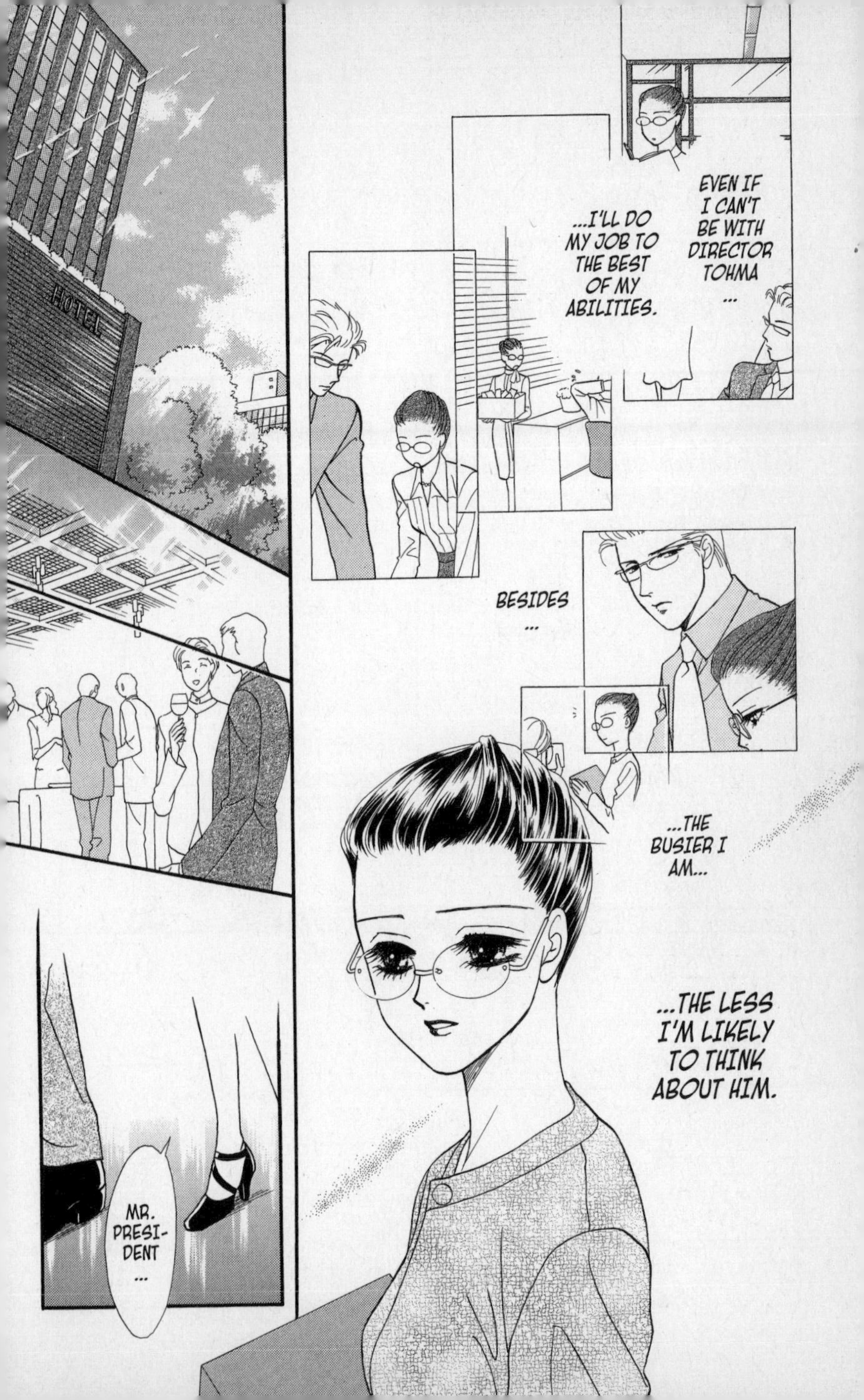
EVEN IF I CAN'T BE WITH DIRECTOR TOHMA...
...I'LL DO MY JOB TO THE BEST OF MY ABILITIES.
BESIDES...
...THE BUSIER I AM...
...THE LESS I'M LIKELY TO THINK ABOUT HIM.
HOTEL
MR. PRESIDENT...

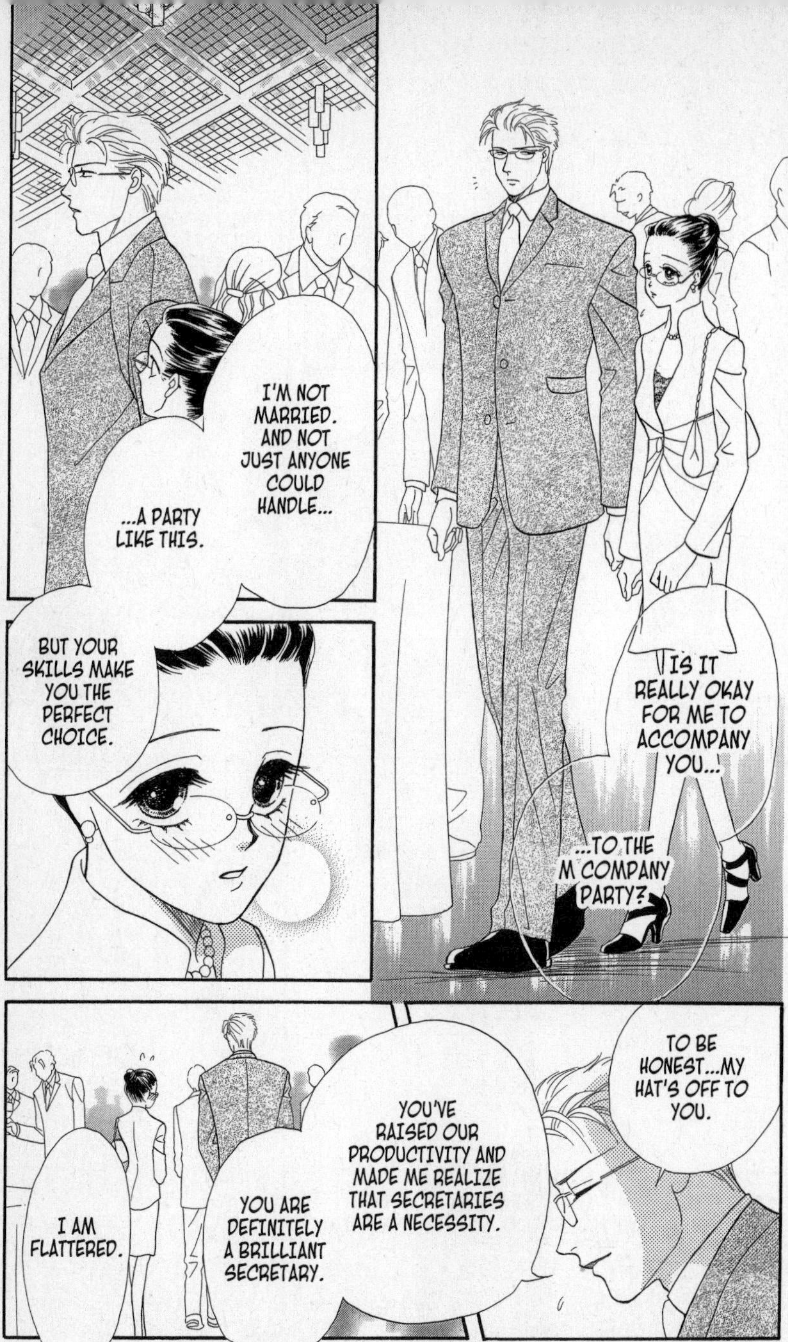
IS IT REALLY OKAY FOR ME TO ACCOMPANY YOU...
...TO THE M COMPANY PARTY?
I'M NOT MARRIED. AND NOT JUST ANYONE COULD HANDLE...
...A PARTY LIKE THIS.
BUT YOUR SKILLS MAKE YOU THE PERFECT CHOICE.
TO BE HONEST...MY HAT'S OFF TO YOU.
YOU'VE RAISED OUR PRODUCTIVITY AND MADE ME REALIZE THAT SECRETARIES ARE A NECESSITY.
YOU ARE DEFINITELY A BRILLIANT SECRETARY.
I AM FLATTERED.

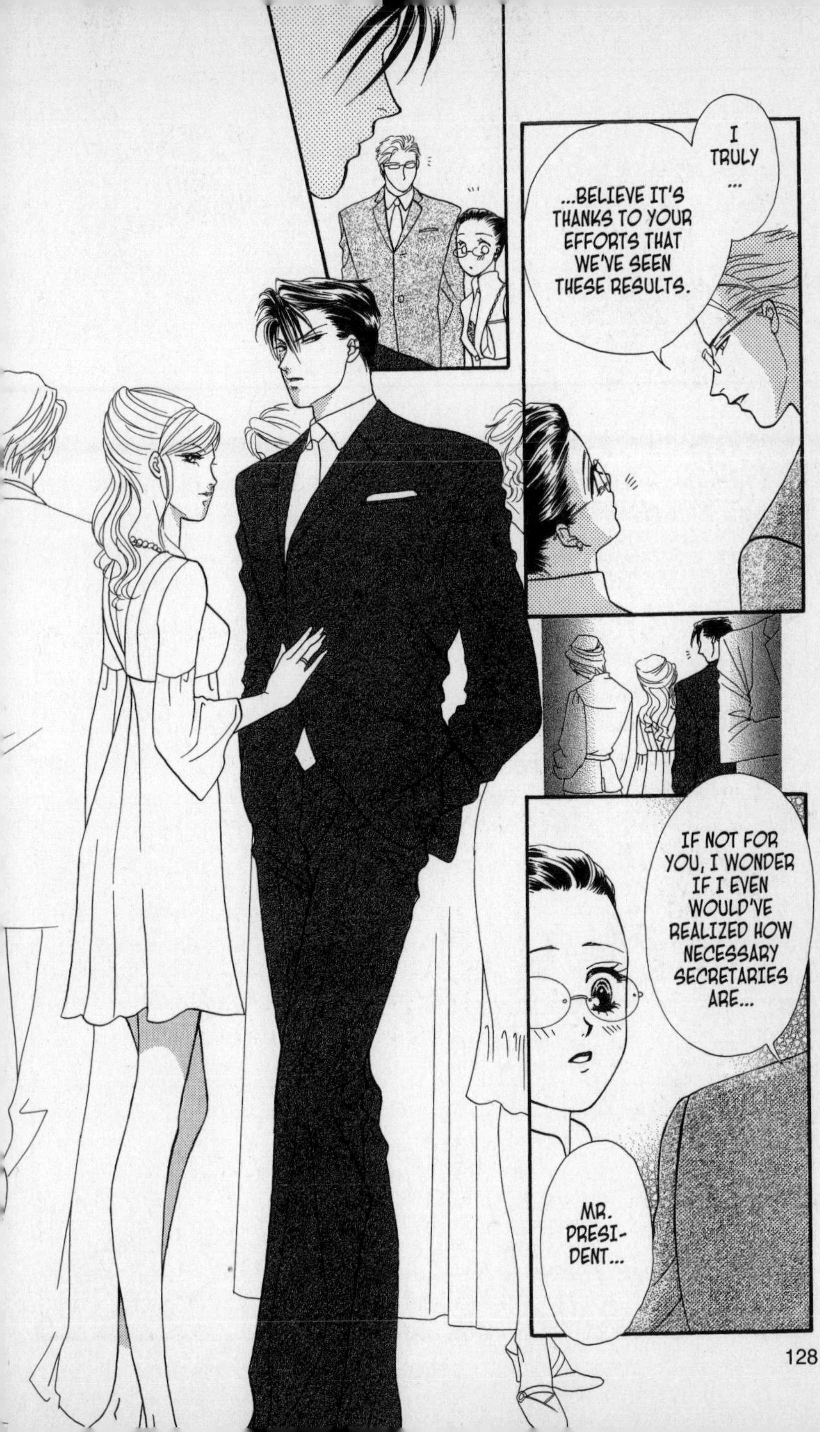
I TRULY ...
...BELIEVE IT'S THANKS TO YOUR EFFORTS THAT WE'VE SEEN THESE RESULTS.
IF NOT FOR YOU, I WONDER IF I EVEN WOULD'VE REALIZED HOW NECESSARY SECRETARIES ARE...
MR. PRESI- DENT...

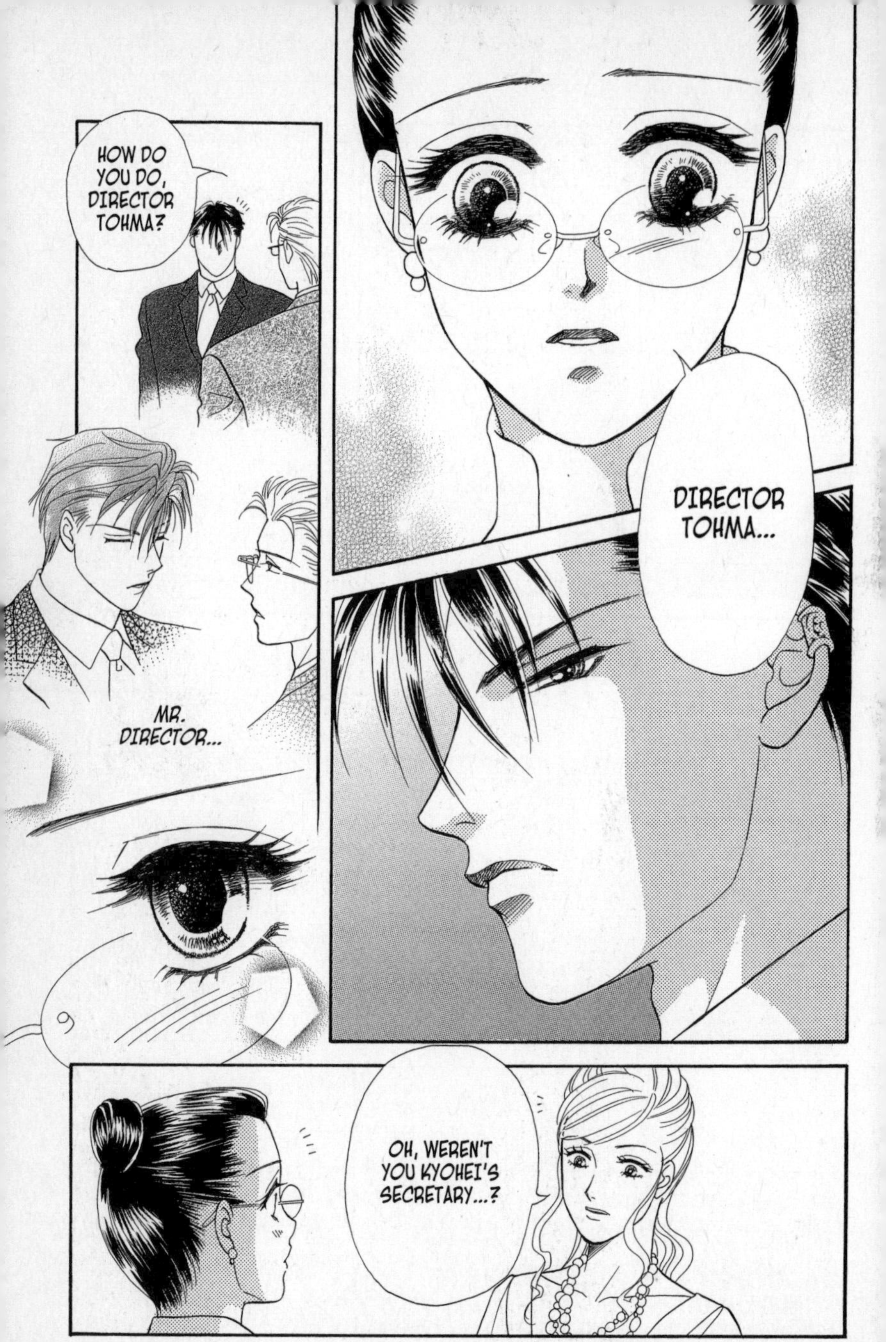
DIRECTOR TOHMA...
HOW DO YOU DO, DIRECTOR TOHMA?
MR. DIRECTOR...
OH, WEREN'T YOU KYOHEI'S SECRETARY...?

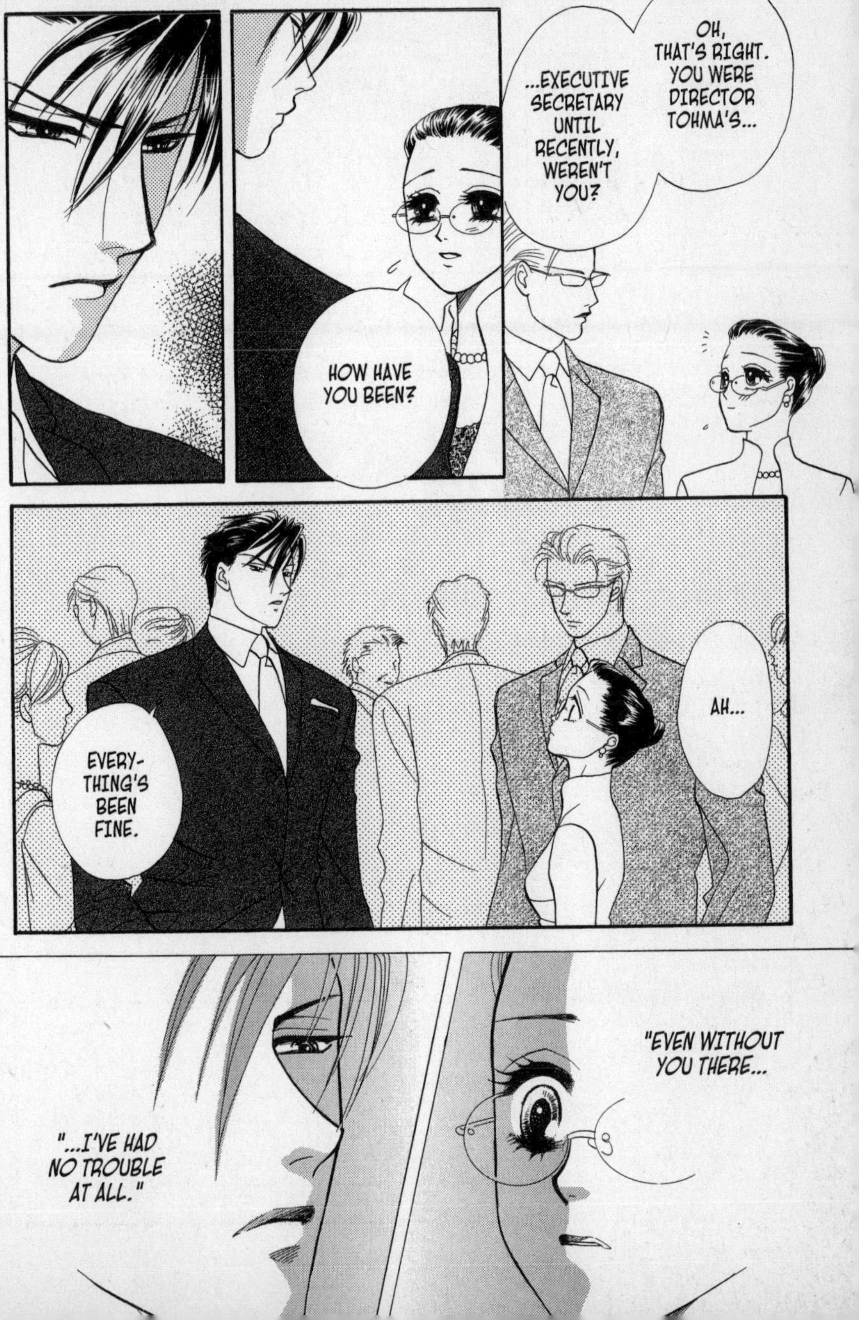
OH, THAT'S RIGHT. YOU WERE DIRECTOR TOHMA'S...
...EXECUTIVE SECRETARY UNTIL RECENTLY, WEREN'T YOU?
HOW HAVE YOU BEEN?
AH...
EVERY-THING'S BEEN FINE.
"EVEN WITHOUT YOU THERE...
"...I'VE HAD NO TROUBLE AT ALL."

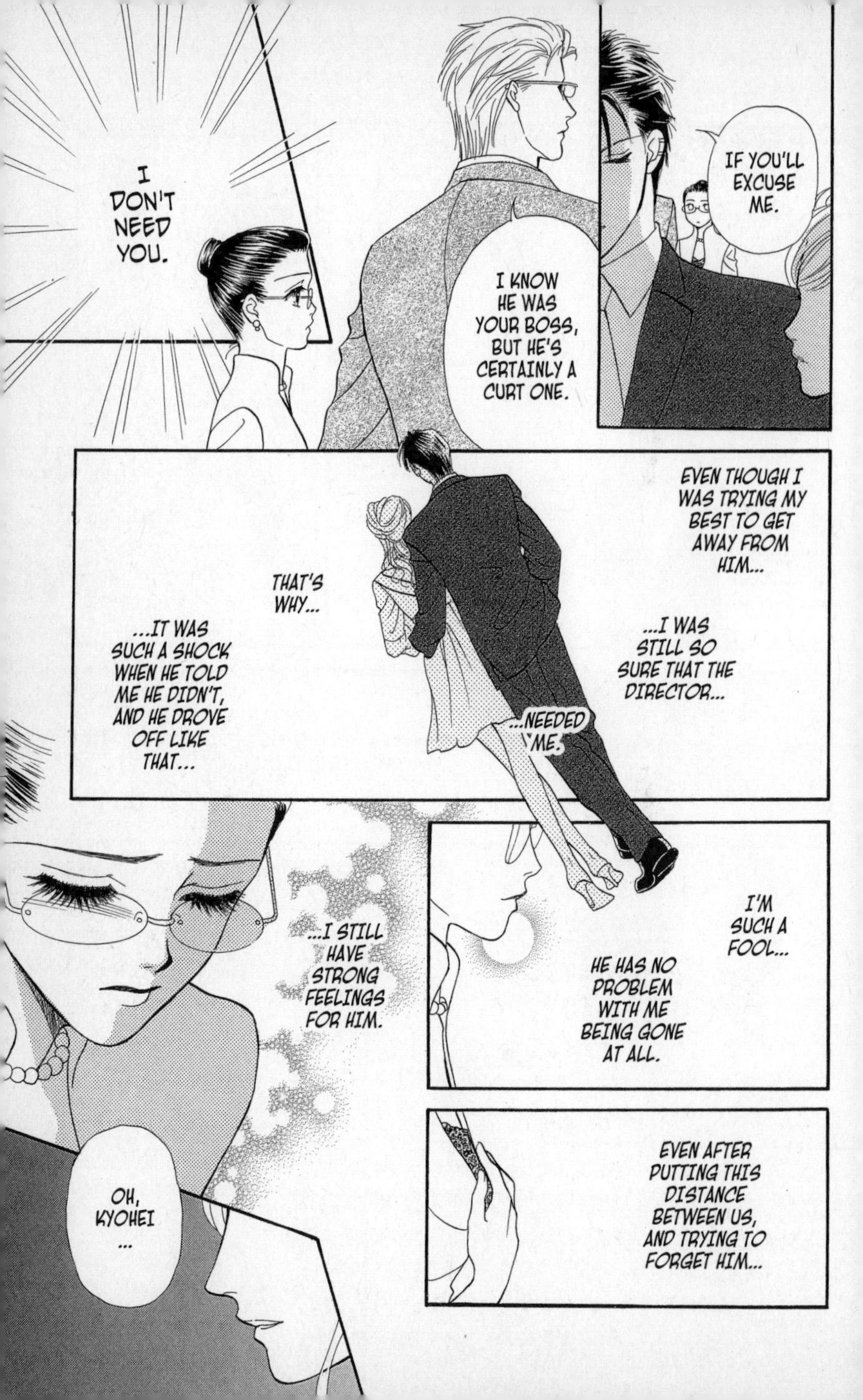
IF YOU'LL EXCUSE ME.
I KNOW HE WAS YOUR BOSS, BUT HE'S CERTAINLY A CURT ONE.
I DON'T NEED YOU.
EVEN THOUGH I WAS TRYING MY BEST TO GET AWAY FROM HIM...
...I WAS STILL SO SURE THAT THE DIRECTOR...
...NEEDED ME.
THAT'S WHY...
...IT WAS SUCH A SHOCK WHEN HE TOLD ME HE DIDN'T, AND HE DROVE OFF LIKE THAT...
I'M SUCH A FOOL...
HE HAS NO PROBLEM WITH ME BEING GONE AT ALL.
EVEN AFTER PUTTING THIS DISTANCE BETWEEN US, AND TRYING TO FORGET HIM...
...I STILL HAVE STRONG FEELINGS FOR HIM.
OH, KYOHEI ...

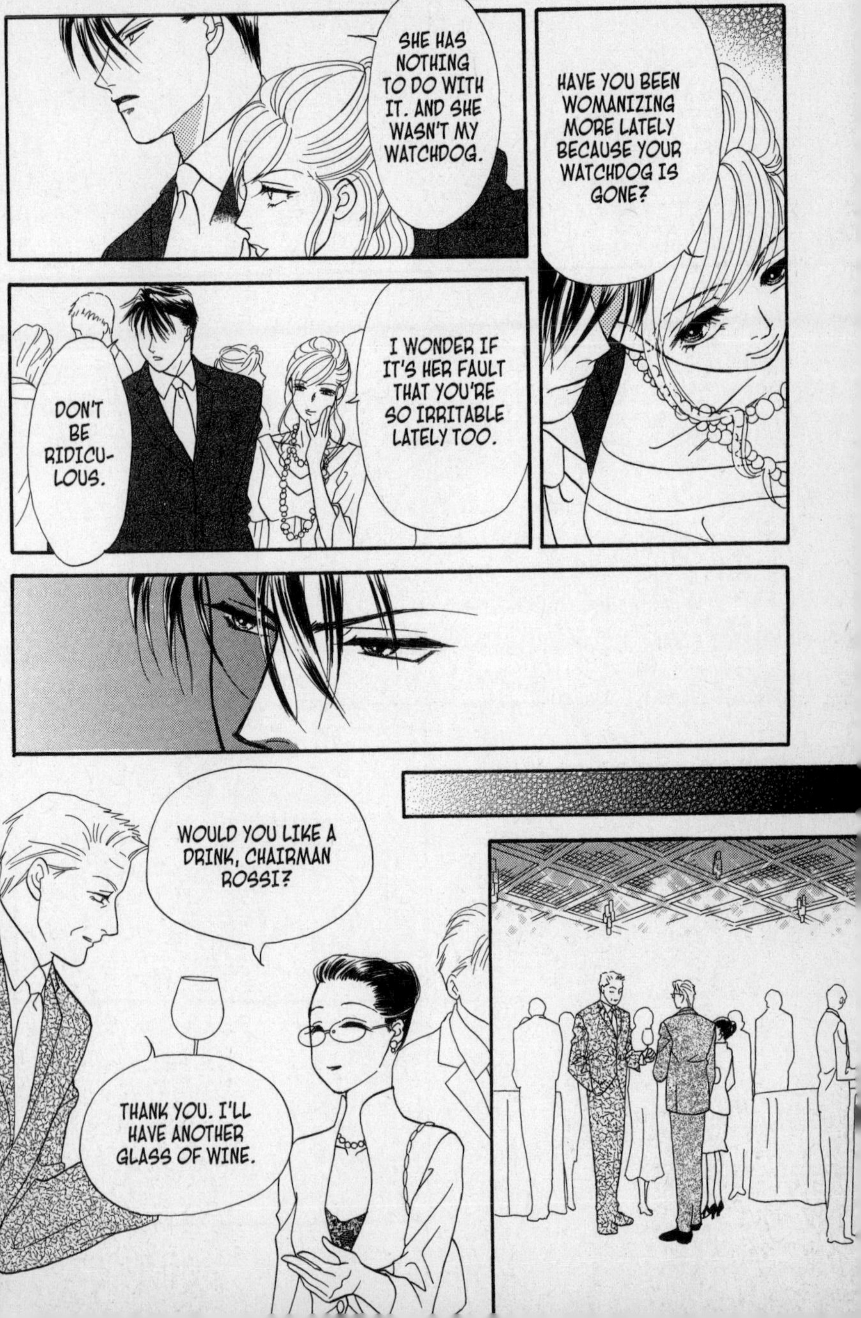
HAVE YOU BEEN WOMANIZING MORE LATELY BECAUSE YOUR WATCHDOG IS GONE?
SHE HAS NOTHING TO DO WITH IT. AND SHE WASN'T MY WATCHDOG.
I WONDER IF IT'S HER FAULT THAT YOU'RE SO IRRITABLE LATELY TOO.
DON'T BE RIDICU-LOUS.
WOULD YOU LIKE A DRINK, CHAIRMAN ROSSI?
THANK YOU. I'LL HAVE ANOTHER GLASS OF WINE.

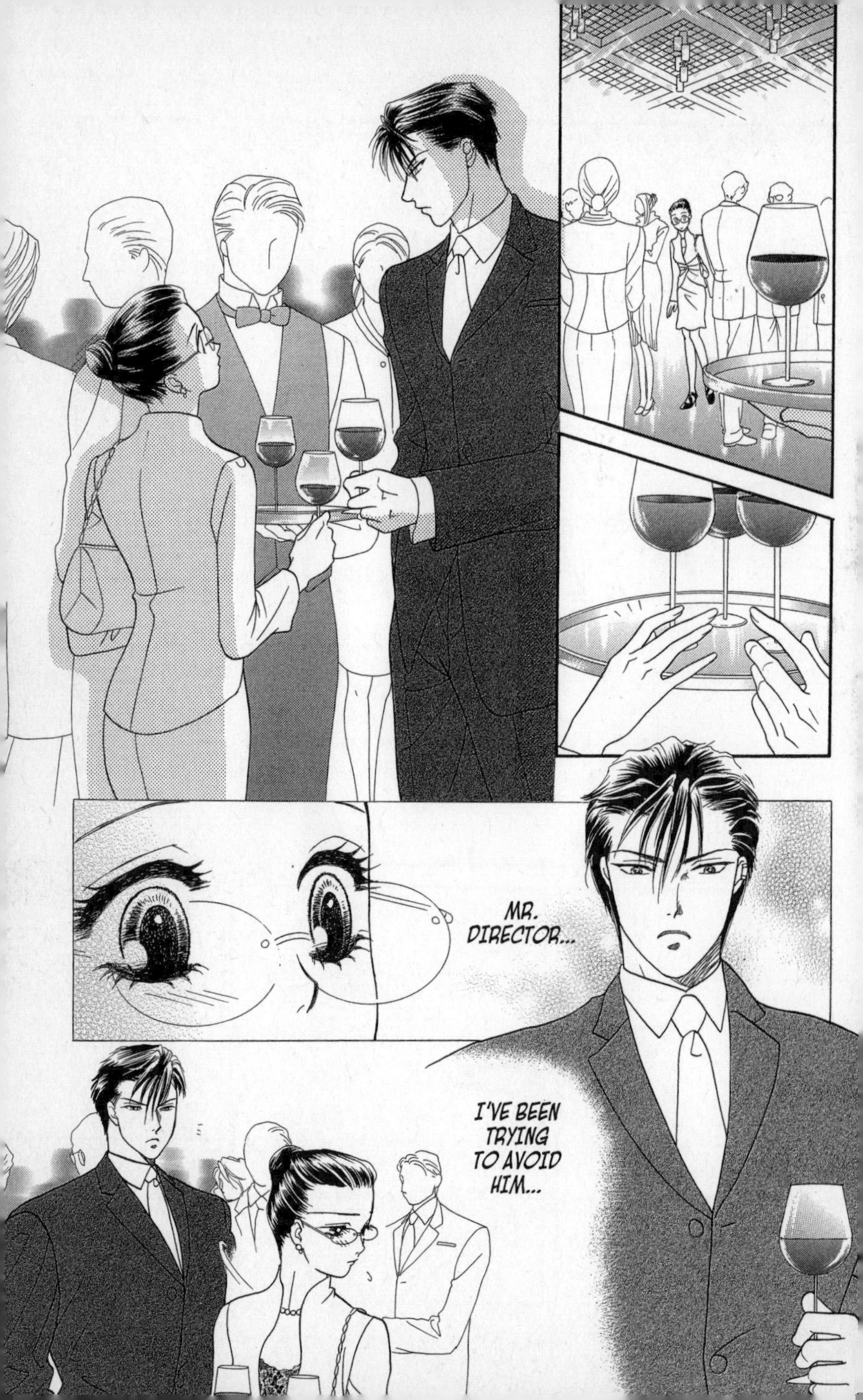
MR. DIRECTOR...
I'VE BEEN TRYING TO AVOID HIM...

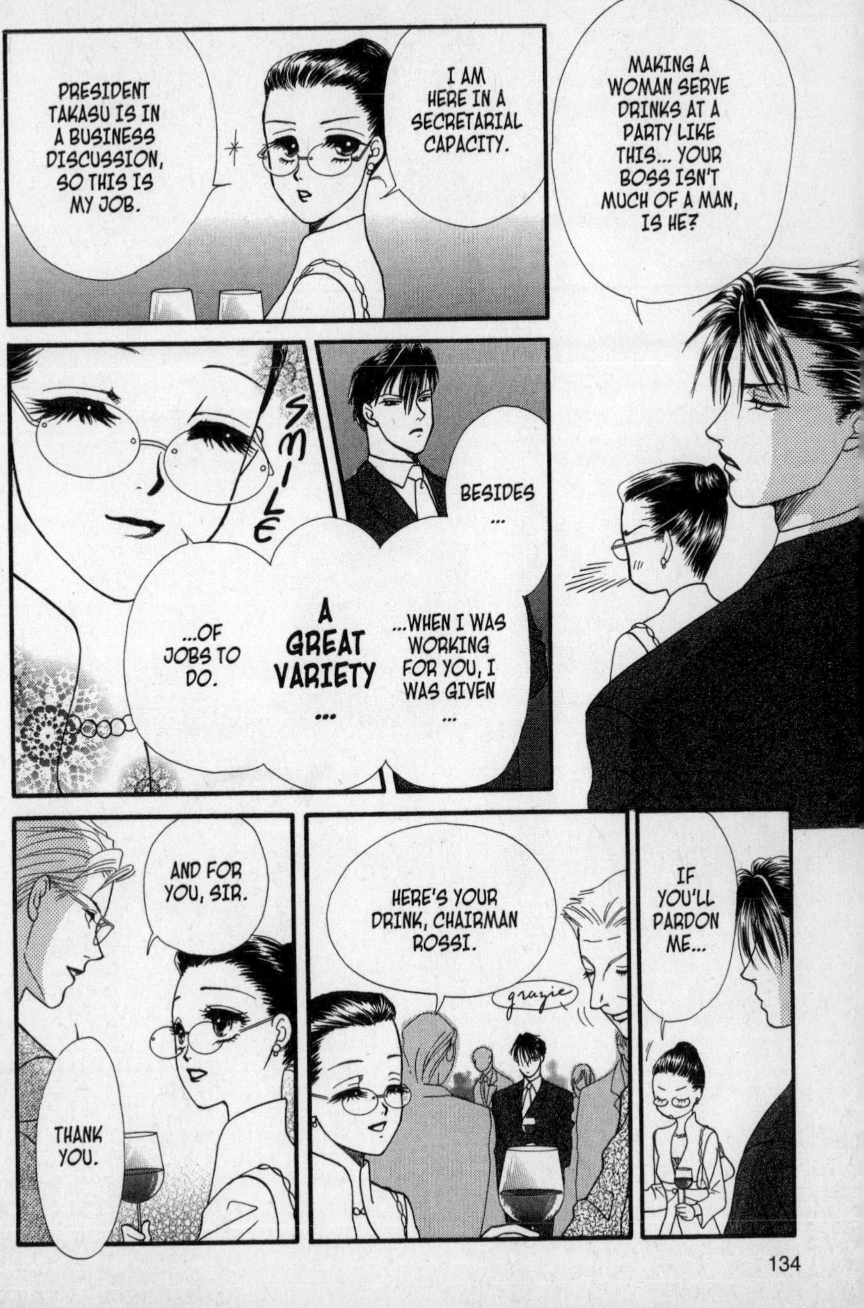
MAKING A WOMAN SERVE DRINKS AT A PARTY LIKE THIS... YOUR BOSS ISN'T MUCH OF A MAN, IS HE?
I AM HERE IN A SECRETARIAL CAPACITY.
PRESIDENT TAKASU IS IN A BUSINESS DISCUSSION, SO THIS IS MY JOB.
BESIDES...
...WHEN I WAS WORKING FOR YOU, I WAS GIVEN...
A GREAT VARIETY...
...OF JOBS TO DO.
SMILE
IF YOU'LL PARDON ME...
HERE'S YOUR DRINK, CHAIRMAN ROSSI.
grazie
AND FOR YOU, SIR.
THANK YOU.

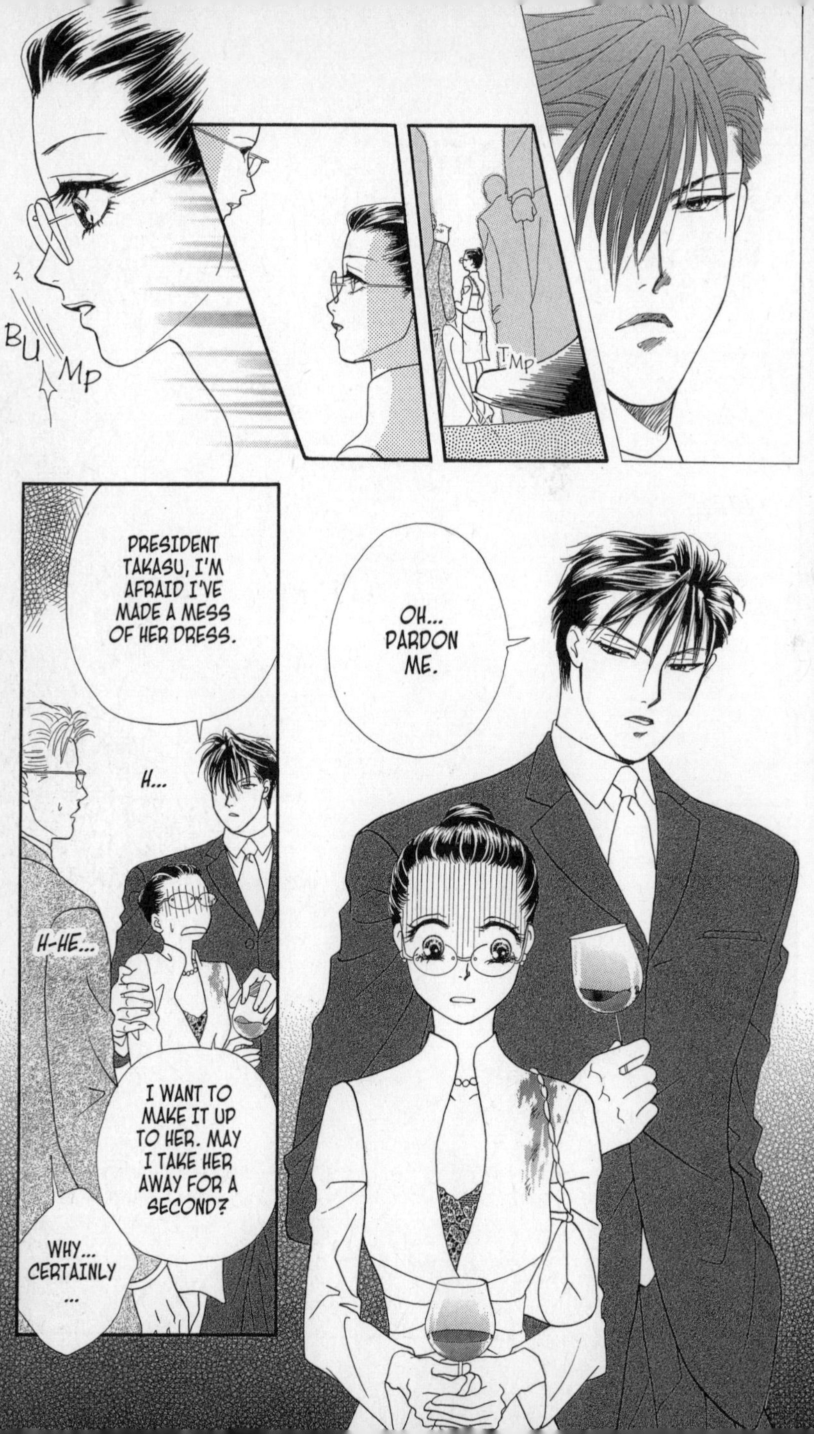
TMP
BUMP
OH... PARDON ME.
PRESIDENT TAKASU, I'M AFRAID I'VE MADE A MESS OF HER DRESS.
H...
H-HE...
I WANT TO MAKE IT UP TO HER. MAY I TAKE HER AWAY FOR A SECOND?
WHY... CERTAINLY ...

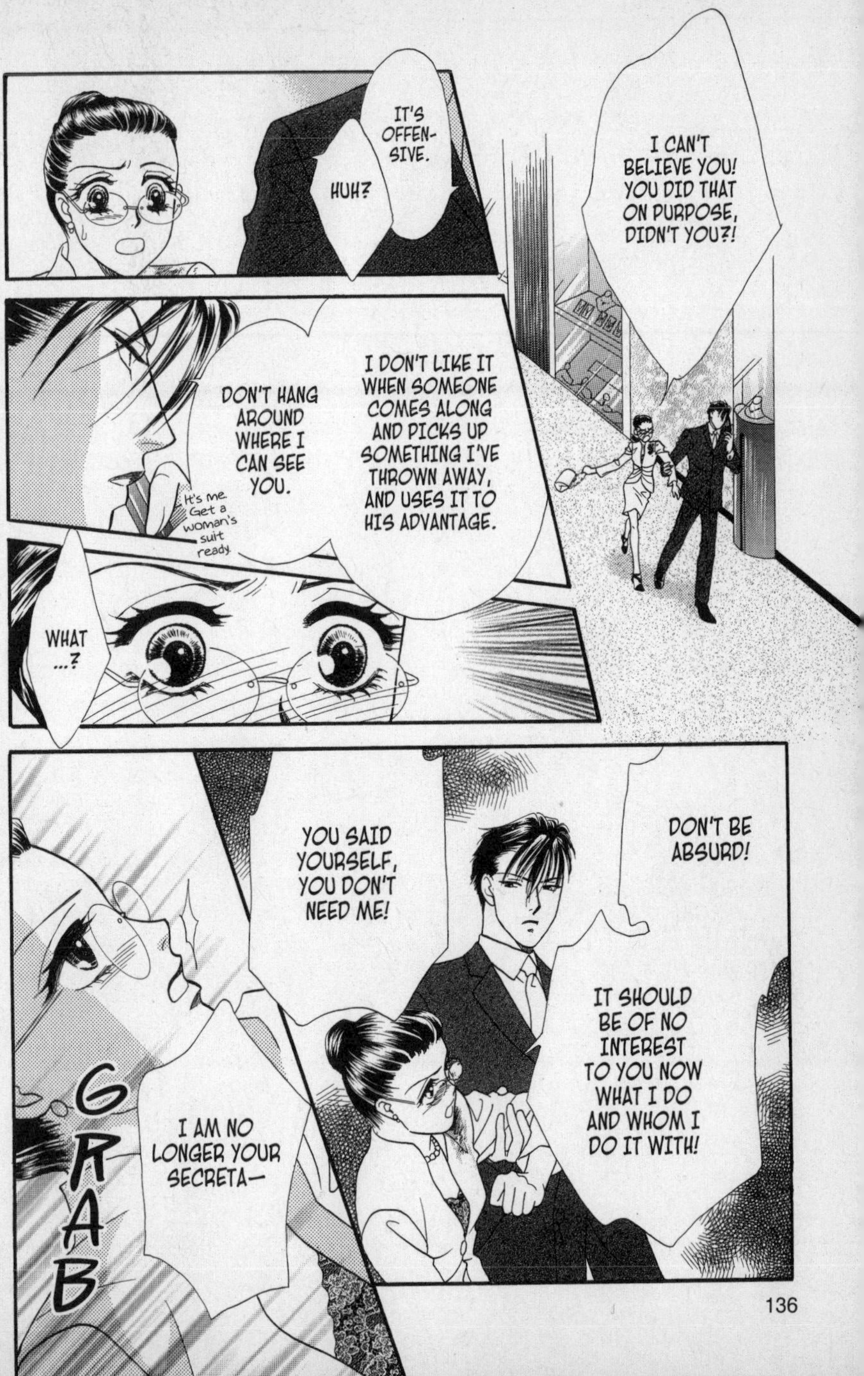
I CAN'T BELIEVE YOU! YOU DID THAT ON PURPOSE, DIDN'T YOU?!
IT'S OFFEN-SIVE.
HUH?
I DON'T LIKE IT WHEN SOMEONE COMES ALONG AND PICKS UP SOMETHING I'VE THROWN AWAY, AND USES IT TO HIS ADVANTAGE.
DON'T HANG AROUND WHERE I CAN SEE YOU.
It's me. Get a woman's suit ready.
WHAT ...?
DON'T BE ABSURD!
IT SHOULD BE OF NO INTEREST TO YOU NOW WHAT I DO AND WHOM I DO IT WITH!
YOU SAID YOURSELF, YOU DON'T NEED ME!
I AM NO LONGER YOUR SECRETA—
GRAB

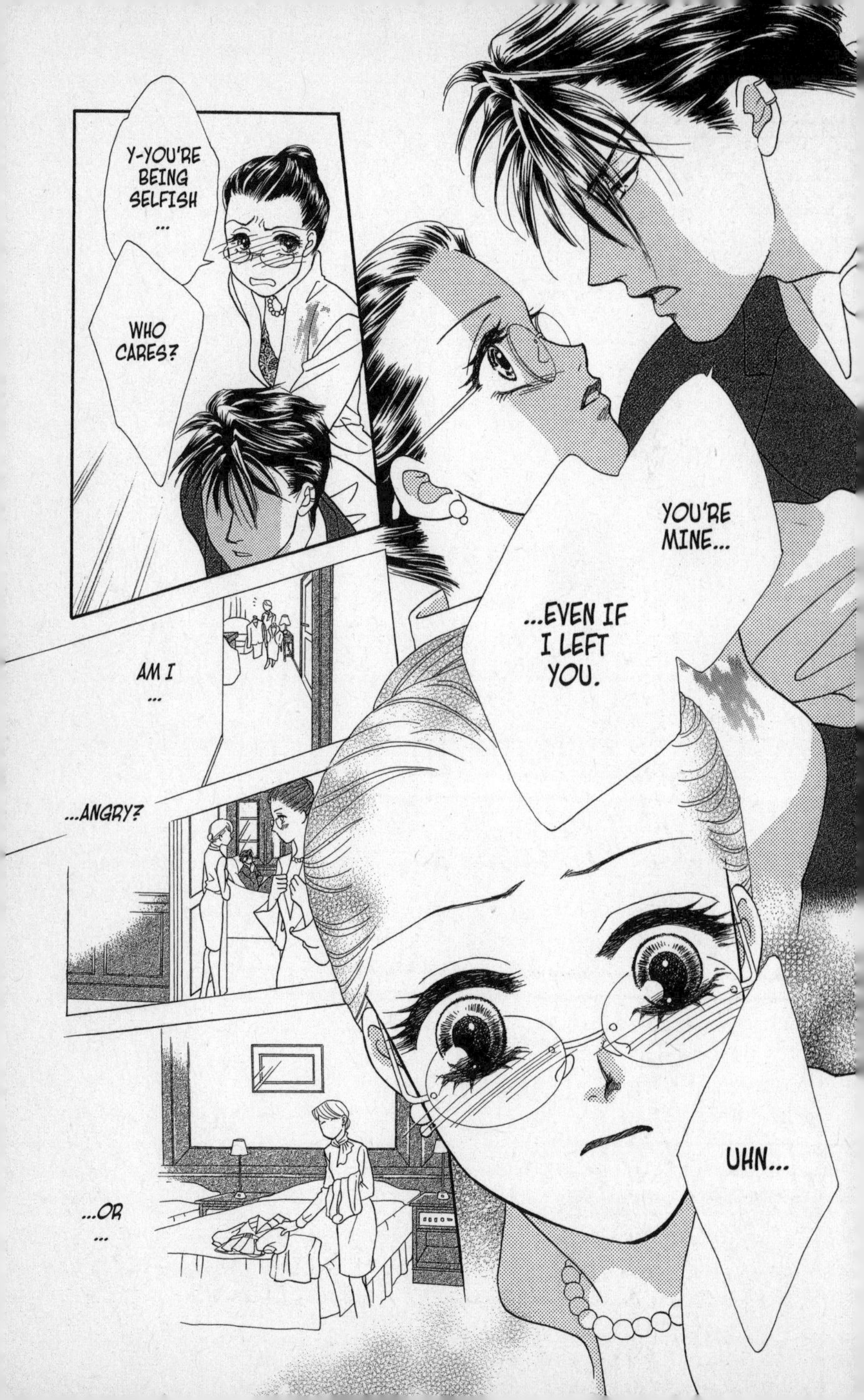
YOU'RE MINE...
...EVEN IF I LEFT YOU.
UHN...
Y-YOU'RE BEING SELFISH ...
WHO CARES?
AM I ...
...ANGRY?
...OR ...

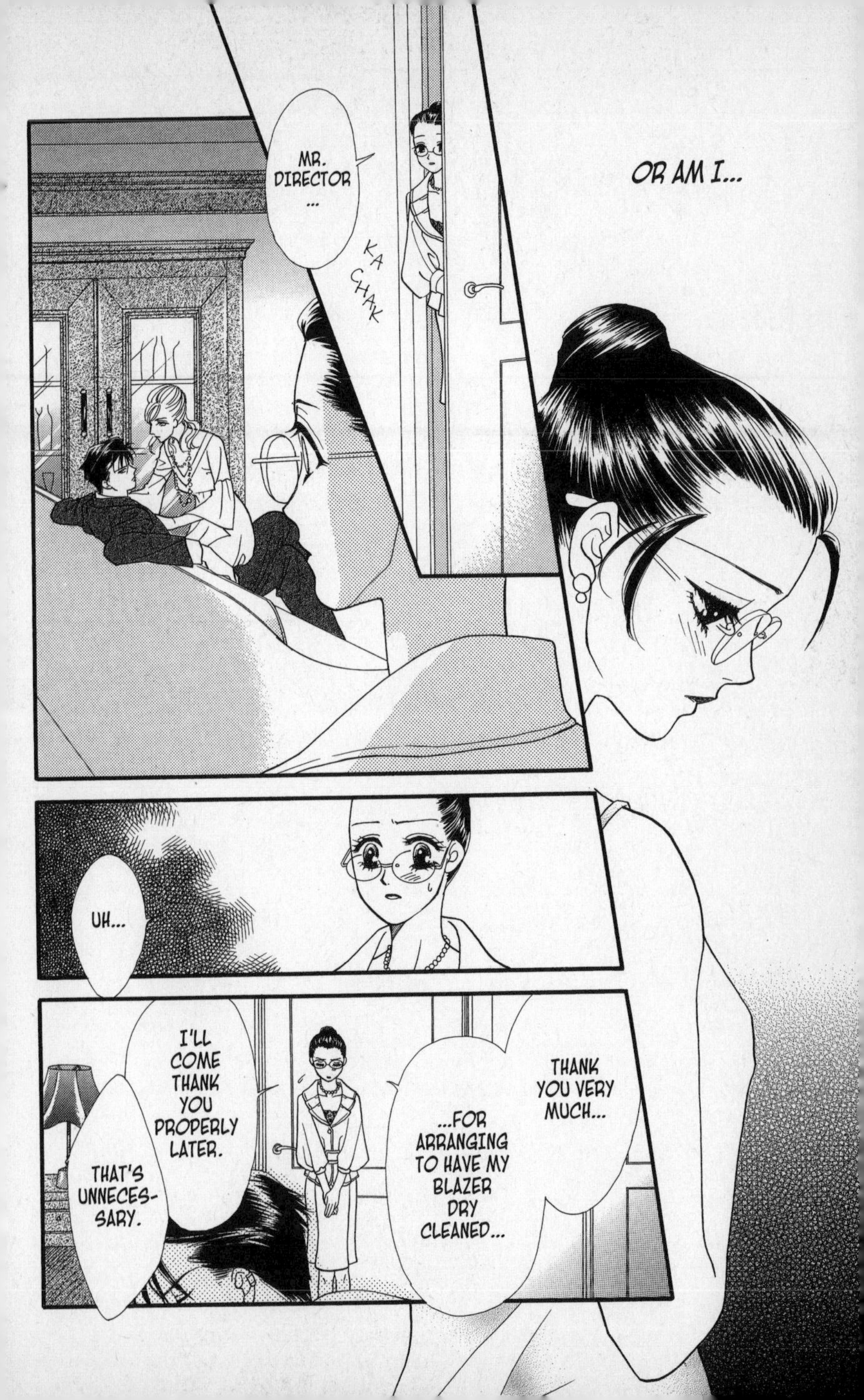
OR AM I...
MR. DIRECTOR ...
KA CHAK
UH...
THANK YOU VERY MUCH...
...FOR ARRANGING TO HAVE MY BLAZER DRY CLEANED...
I'LL COME THANK YOU PROPERLY LATER.
THAT'S UNNECES-SARY.

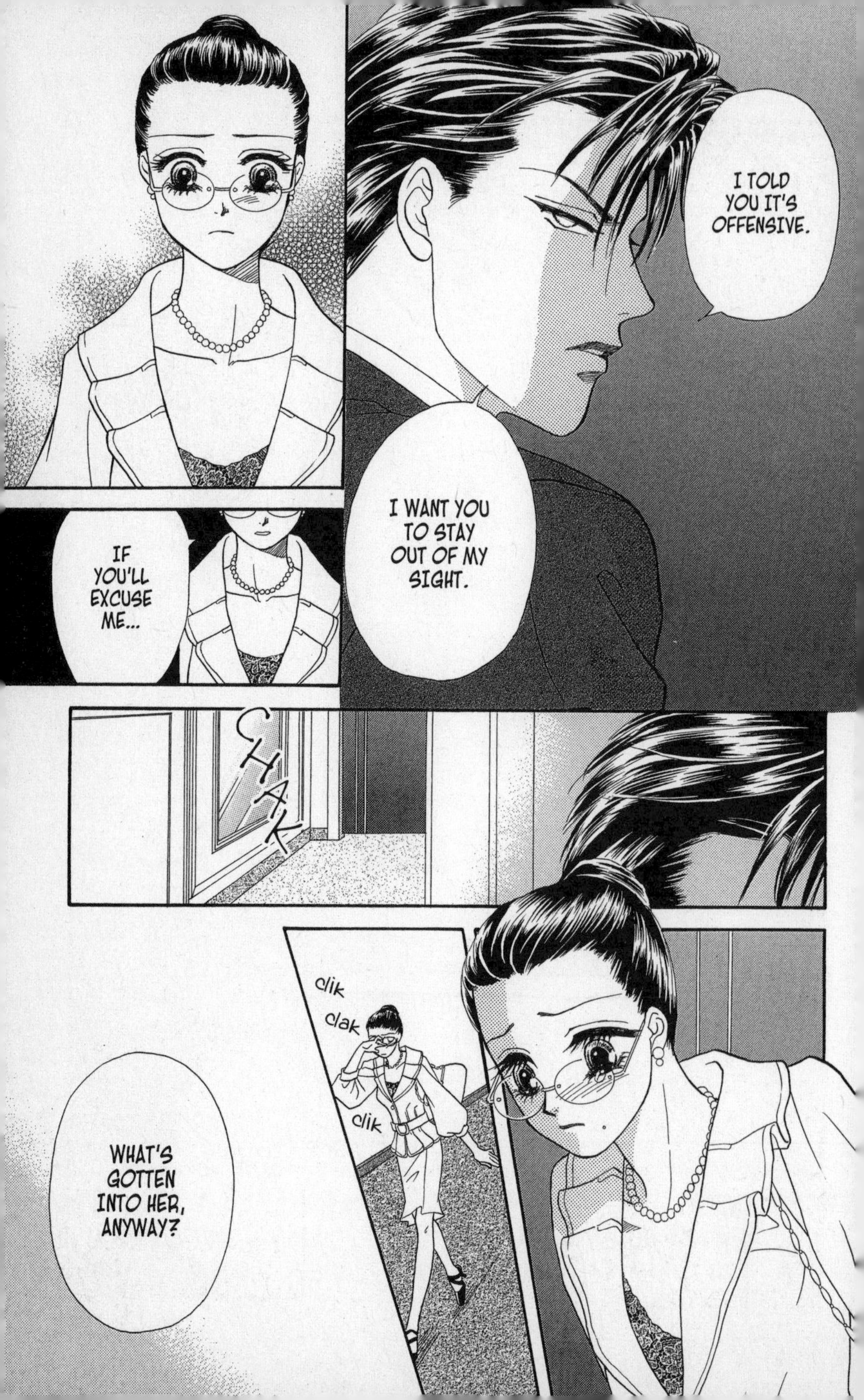
I TOLD YOU IT'S OFFENSIVE.
I WANT YOU TO STAY OUT OF MY SIGHT.
IF YOU'LL EXCUSE ME...
CHAK
clik
clak
clik
WHAT'S GOTTEN INTO HER, ANYWAY?

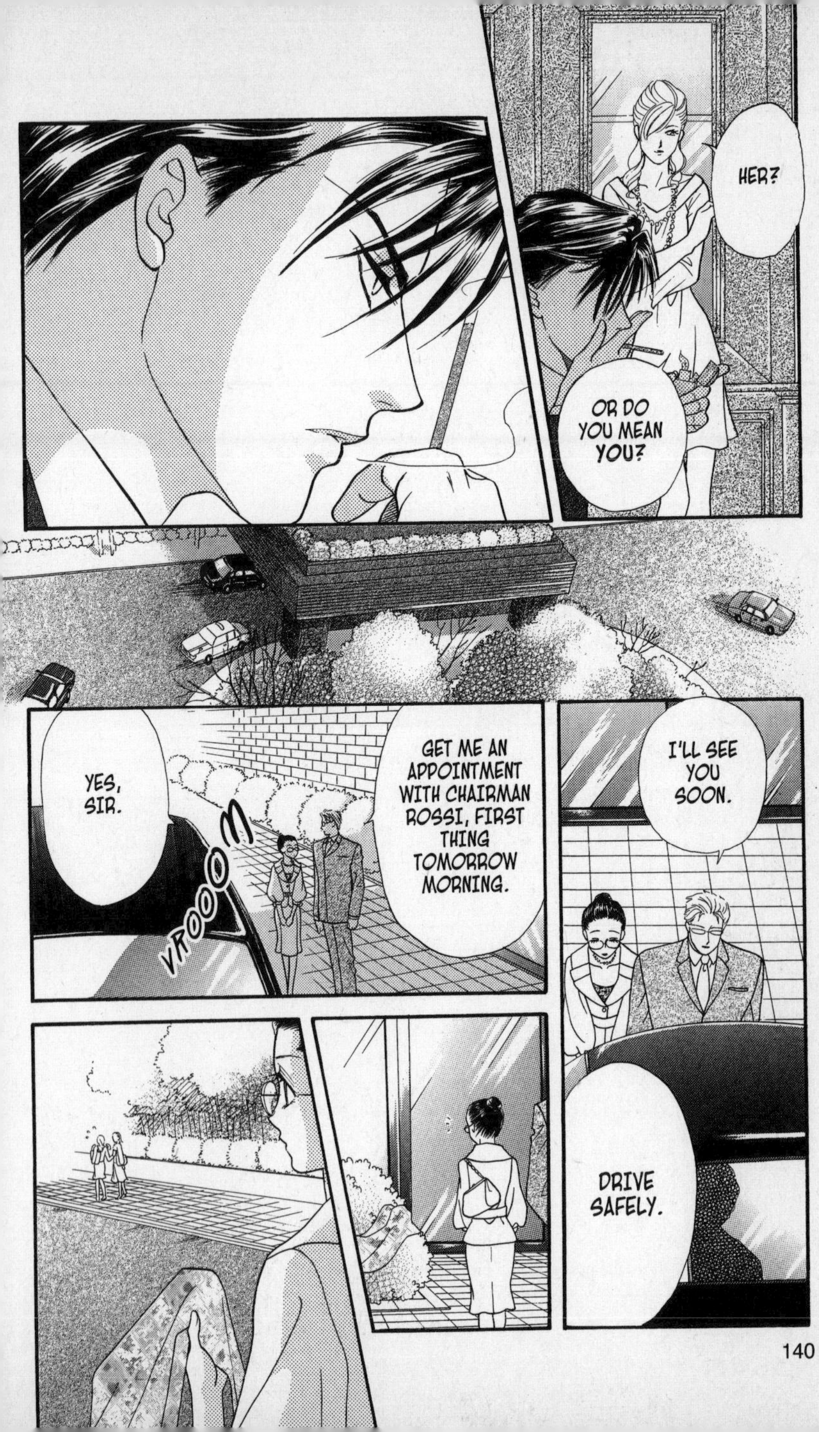
HER?
OR DO YOU MEAN YOU?
I'LL SEE YOU SOON.
DRIVE SAFELY.
GET ME AN APPOINTMENT WITH CHAIRMAN ROSSI, FIRST THING TOMORROW MORNING.
YES, SIR.
VROOOM

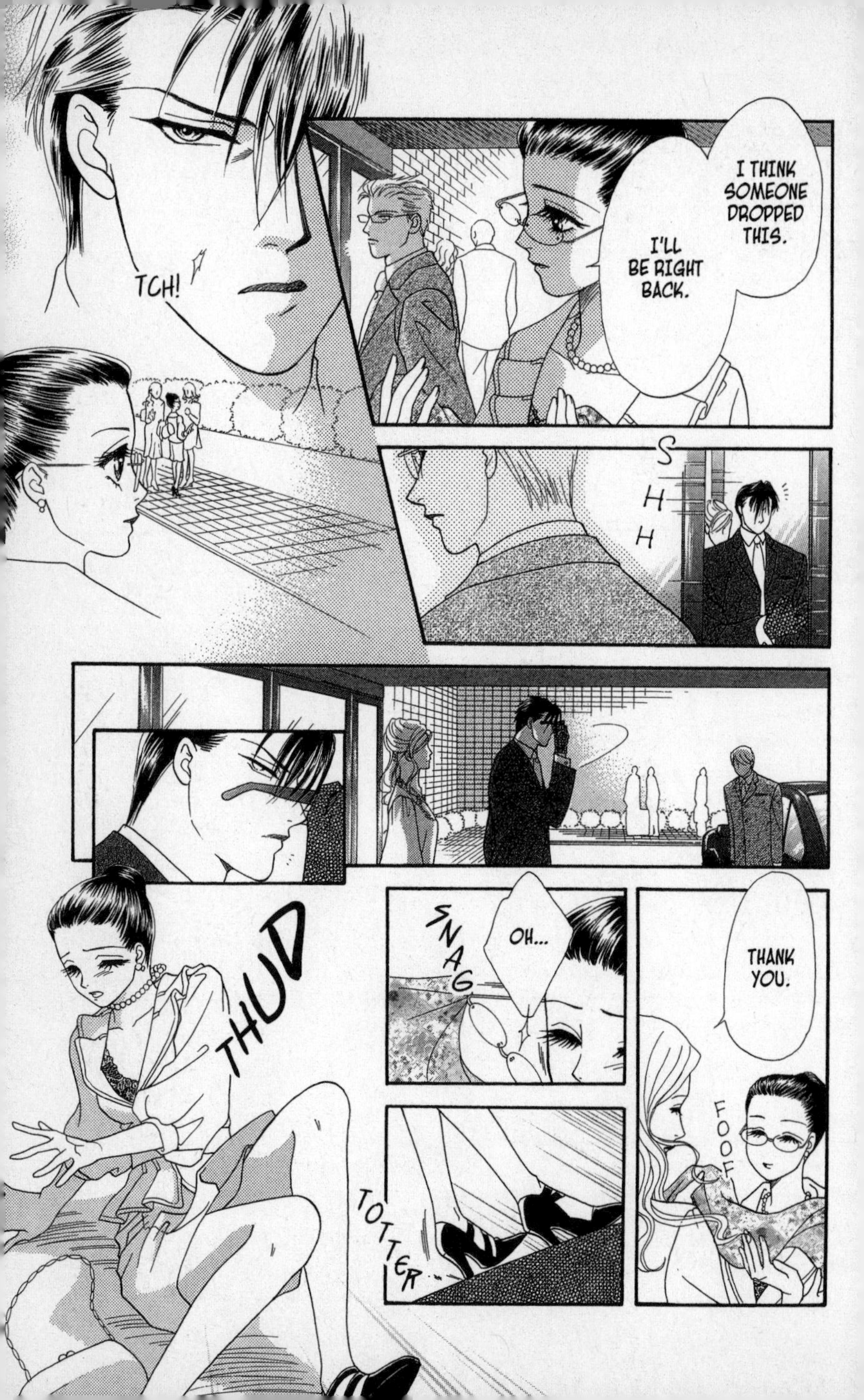
I THINK SOMEONE DROPPED THIS.
I'LL BE RIGHT BACK.
SHH
TCH!
THANK YOU.
FOOF
OH...
SNAG
TOTTER...
THUD

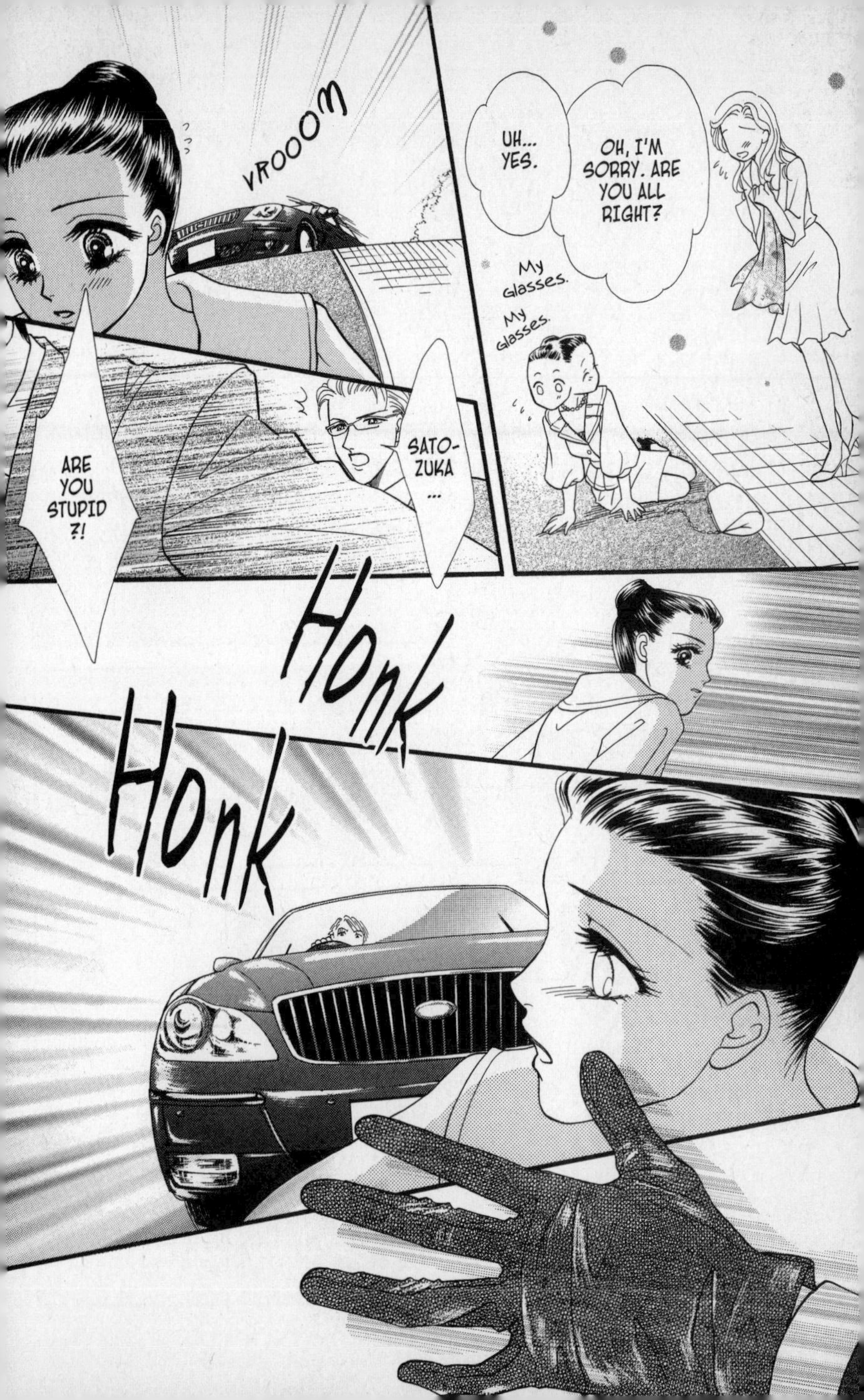
OH, I'M SORRY. ARE YOU ALL RIGHT?
UH... YES.
My Glasses.
My Glasses.
VROOOM
SATO-ZUKA ...
ARE YOU STUPID ?!
Honk
Honk

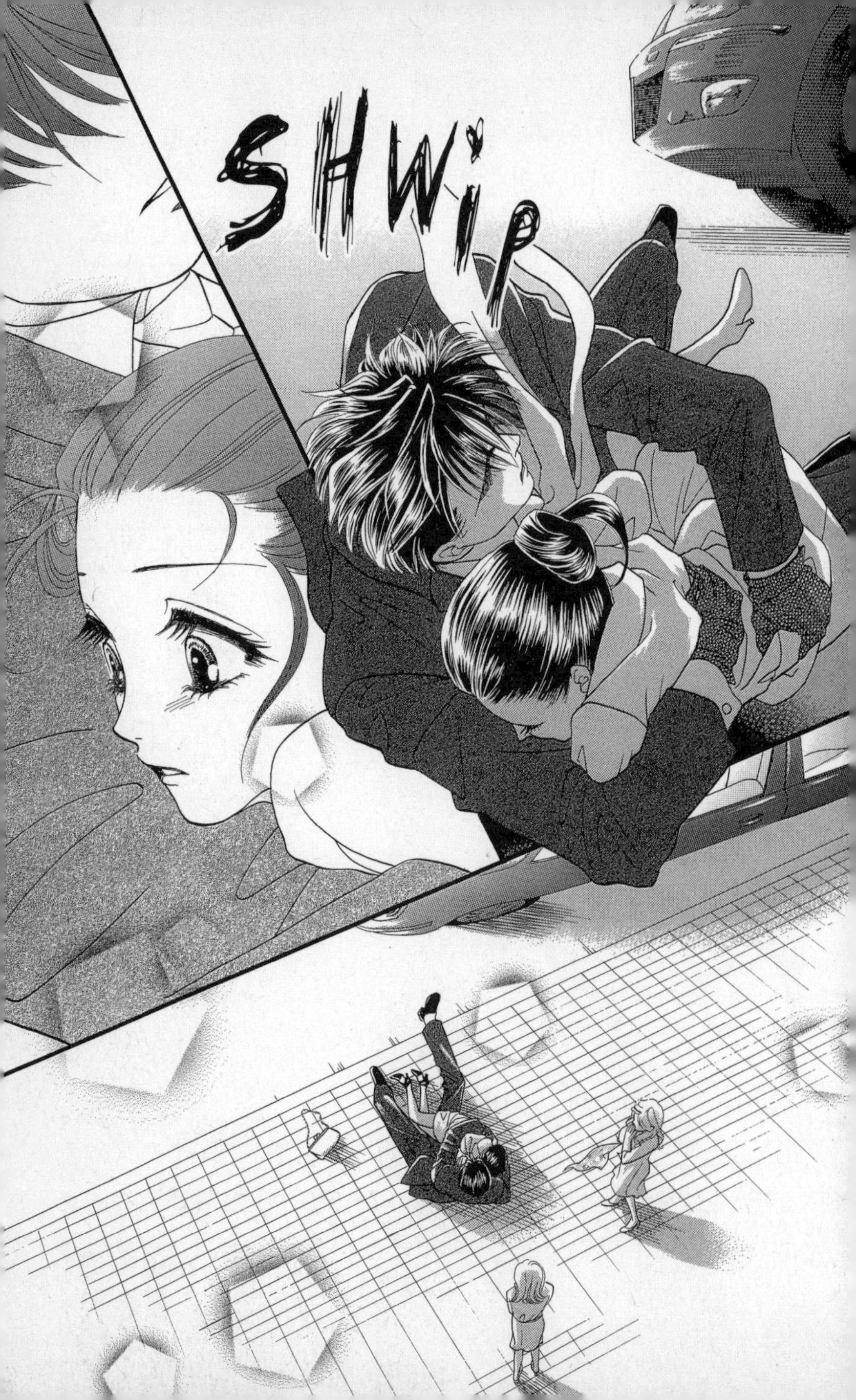
SHWIP

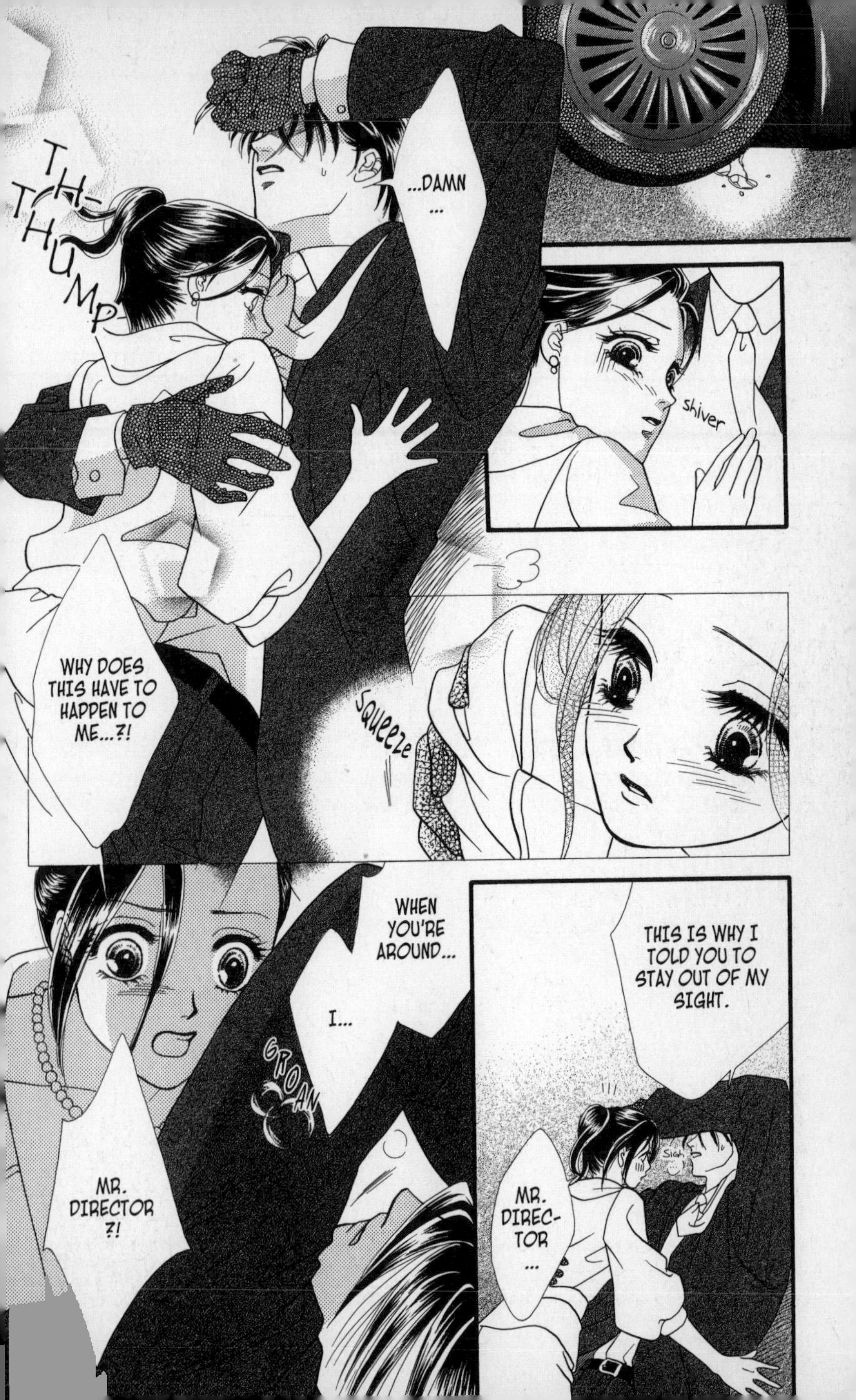

...DAMN ...
TH-THUMP
shiver
Squeeze
WHY DOES THIS HAVE TO HAPPEN TO ME...?!
THIS IS WHY I TOLD YOU TO STAY OUT OF MY SIGHT.
Sigh
MR. DIREC-TOR ...
WHEN YOU'RE AROUND...
I...
GROAN
MR. DIRECTOR ?!

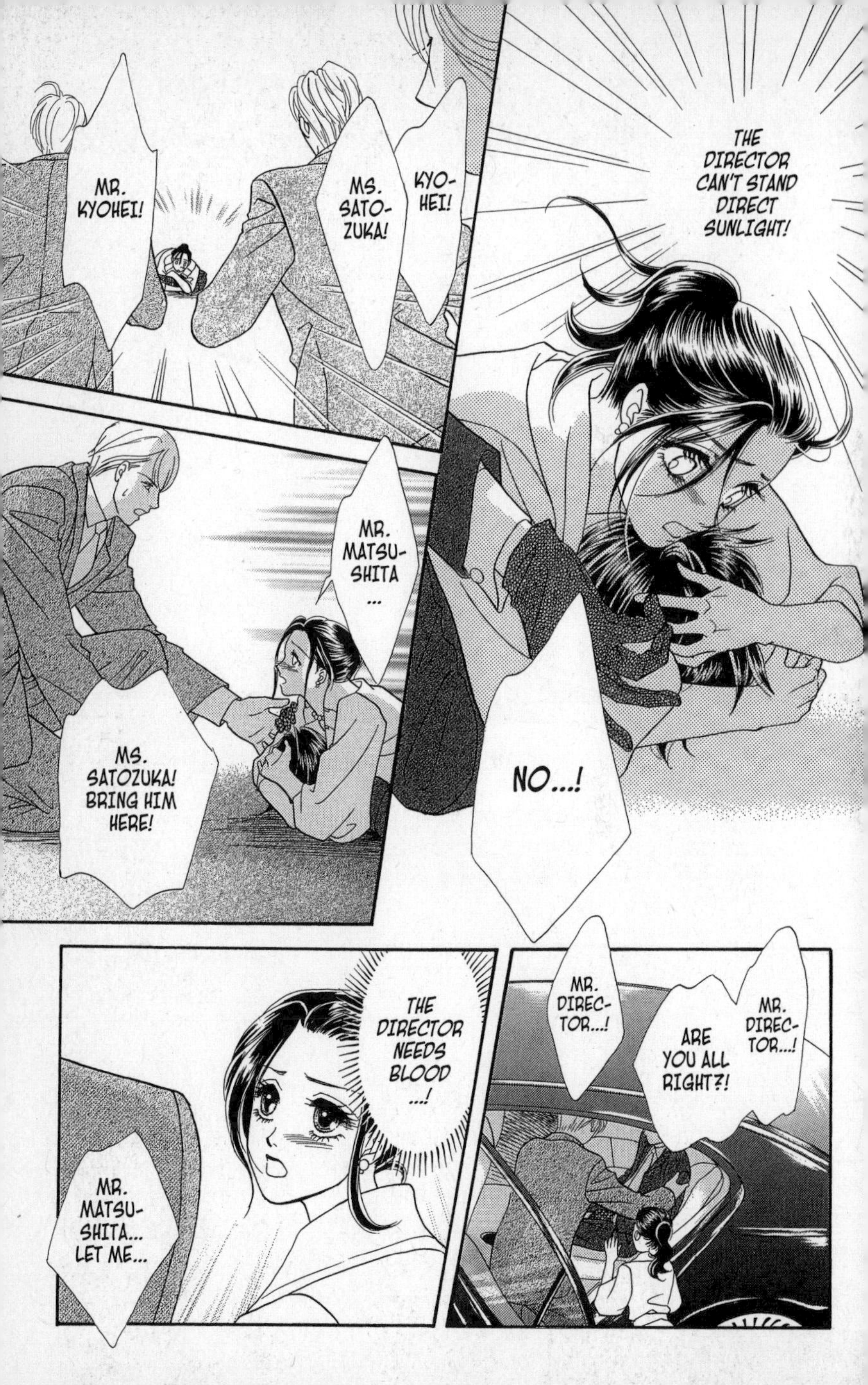
THE DIRECTOR CAN'T STAND DIRECT SUNLIGHT!
NO...!
KYO-HEI!
MS. SATO-ZUKA!
MR. KYOHEI!
MR. MATSU-SHITA ...
MS. SATOZUKA! BRING HIM HERE!
MR. DIREC-TOR...!
ARE YOU ALL RIGHT?!
MR. DIRECTOR...!
THE DIRECTOR NEEDS BLOOD ...!
MR. MATSU-SHITA... LET ME...

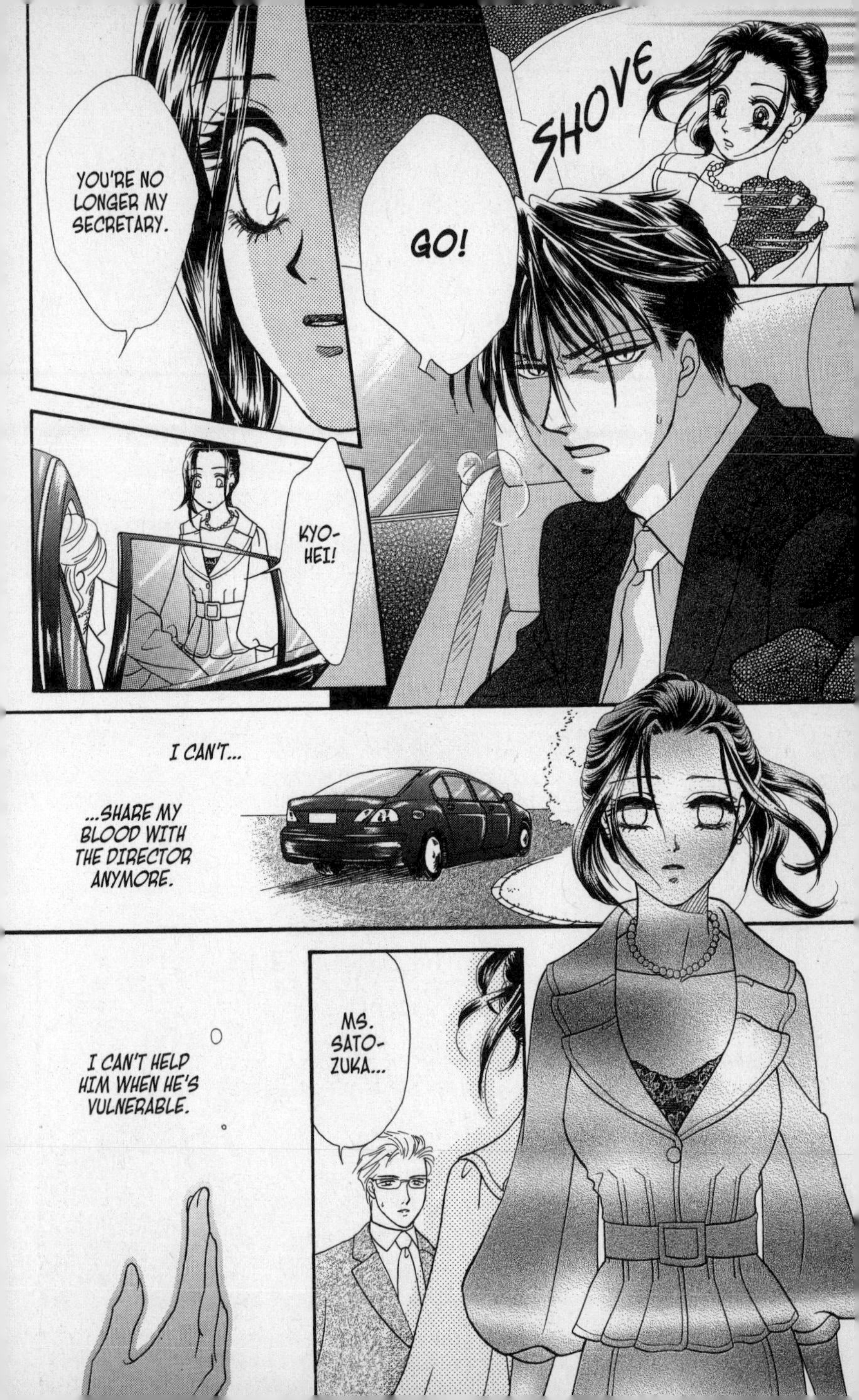
SHOVE
GO!
YOU'RE NO LONGER MY SECRETARY.
KYO-HEI!
I CAN'T...
...SHARE MY BLOOD WITH THE DIRECTOR ANYMORE.
MS. SATO-ZUKA...
I CAN'T HELP HIM WHEN HE'S VULNERABLE.

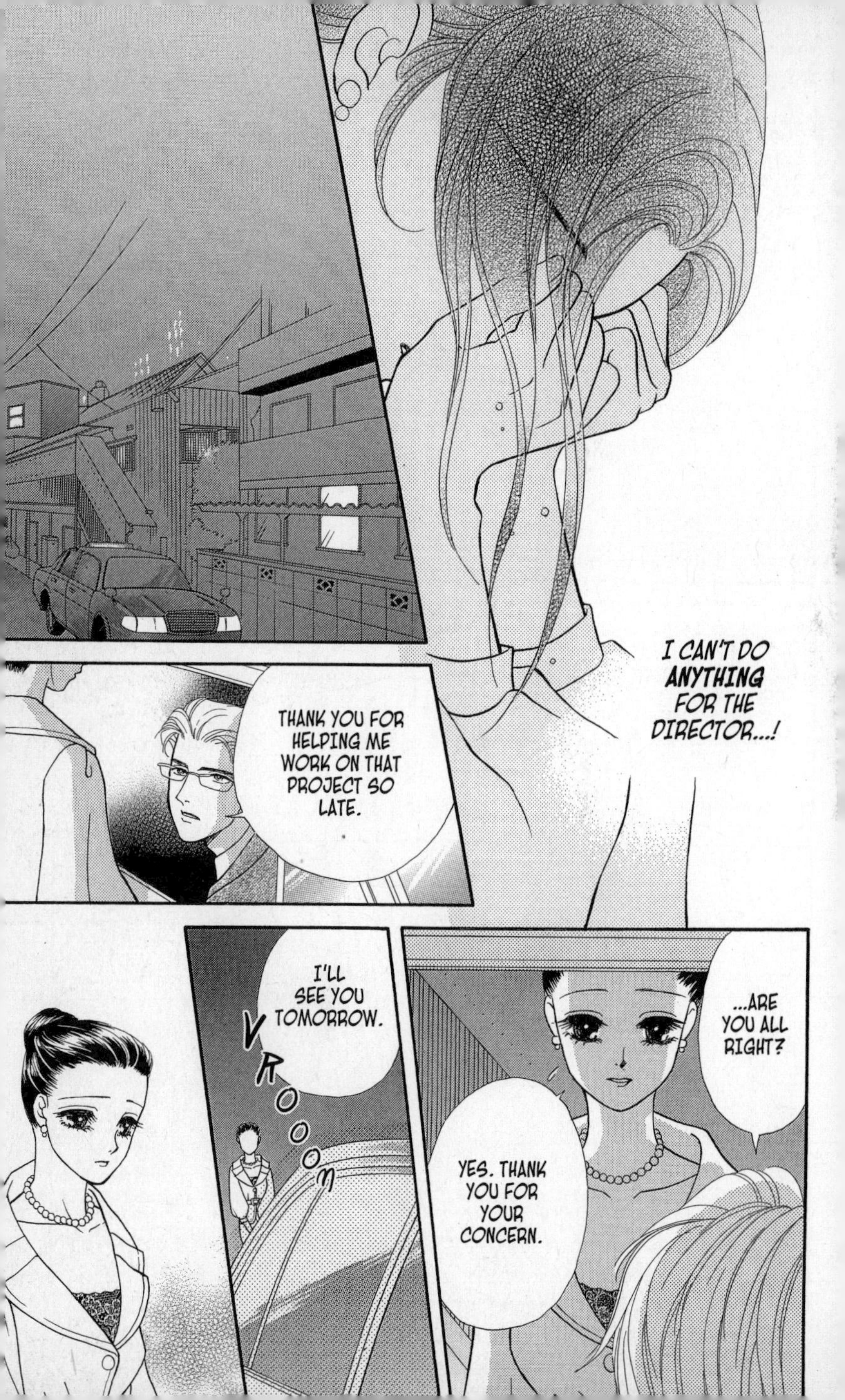
I CAN'T DO **ANYTHING** FOR THE DIRECTOR...!
THANK YOU FOR HELPING ME WORK ON THAT PROJECT SO LATE.
...ARE YOU ALL RIGHT?
YES. THANK YOU FOR YOUR CONCERN.
I'LL SEE YOU TOMORROW.
VROOOOM

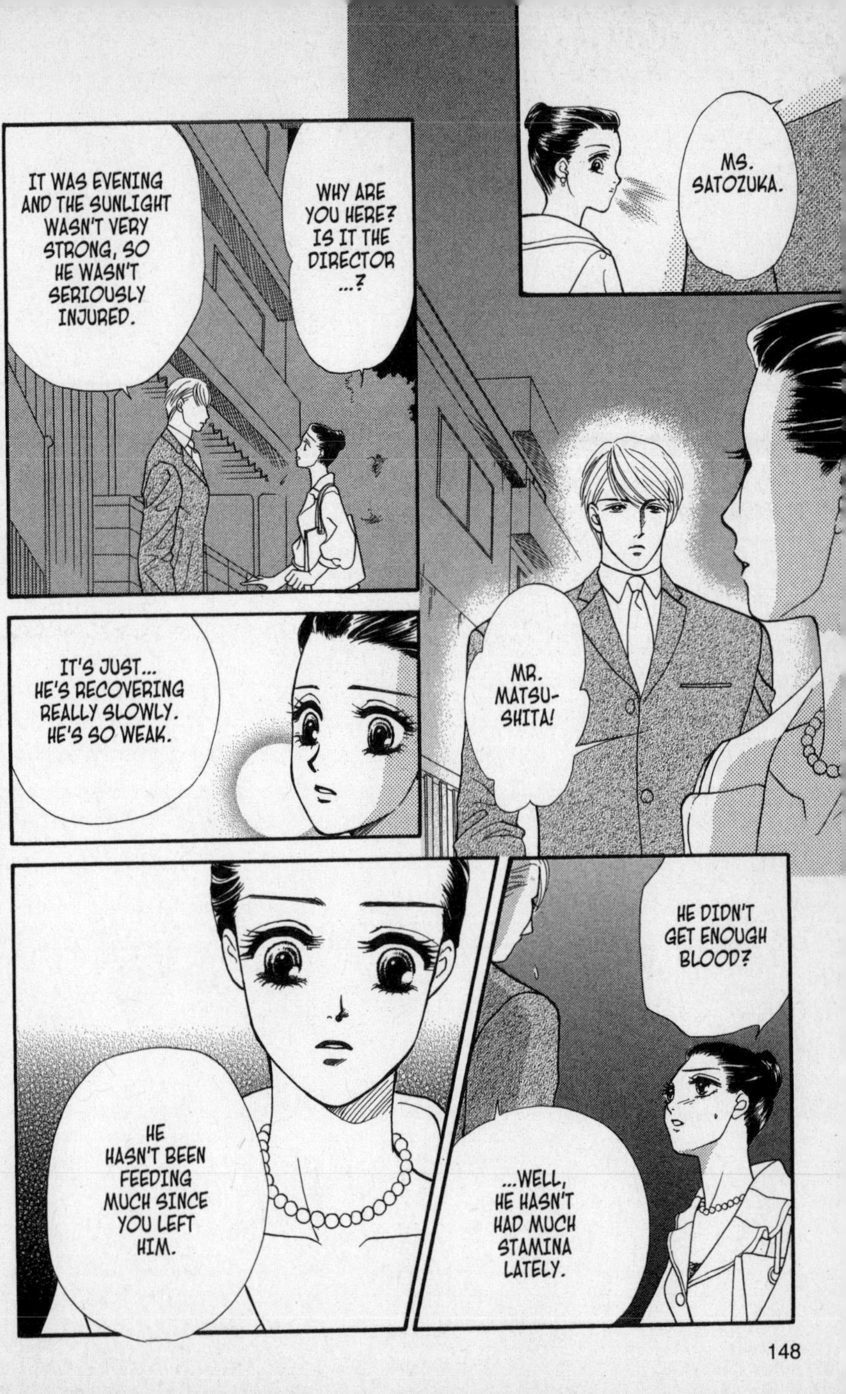
MS. SATOZUKA.
MR. MATSU-SHITA!
WHY ARE YOU HERE? IS IT THE DIRECTOR ...?
IT WAS EVENING AND THE SUNLIGHT WASN'T VERY STRONG, SO HE WASN'T SERIOUSLY INJURED.
IT'S JUST... HE'S RECOVERING REALLY SLOWLY. HE'S SO WEAK.
HE DIDN'T GET ENOUGH BLOOD?
...WELL, HE HASN'T HAD MUCH STAMINA LATELY.
HE HASN'T BEEN FEEDING MUCH SINCE YOU LEFT HIM.

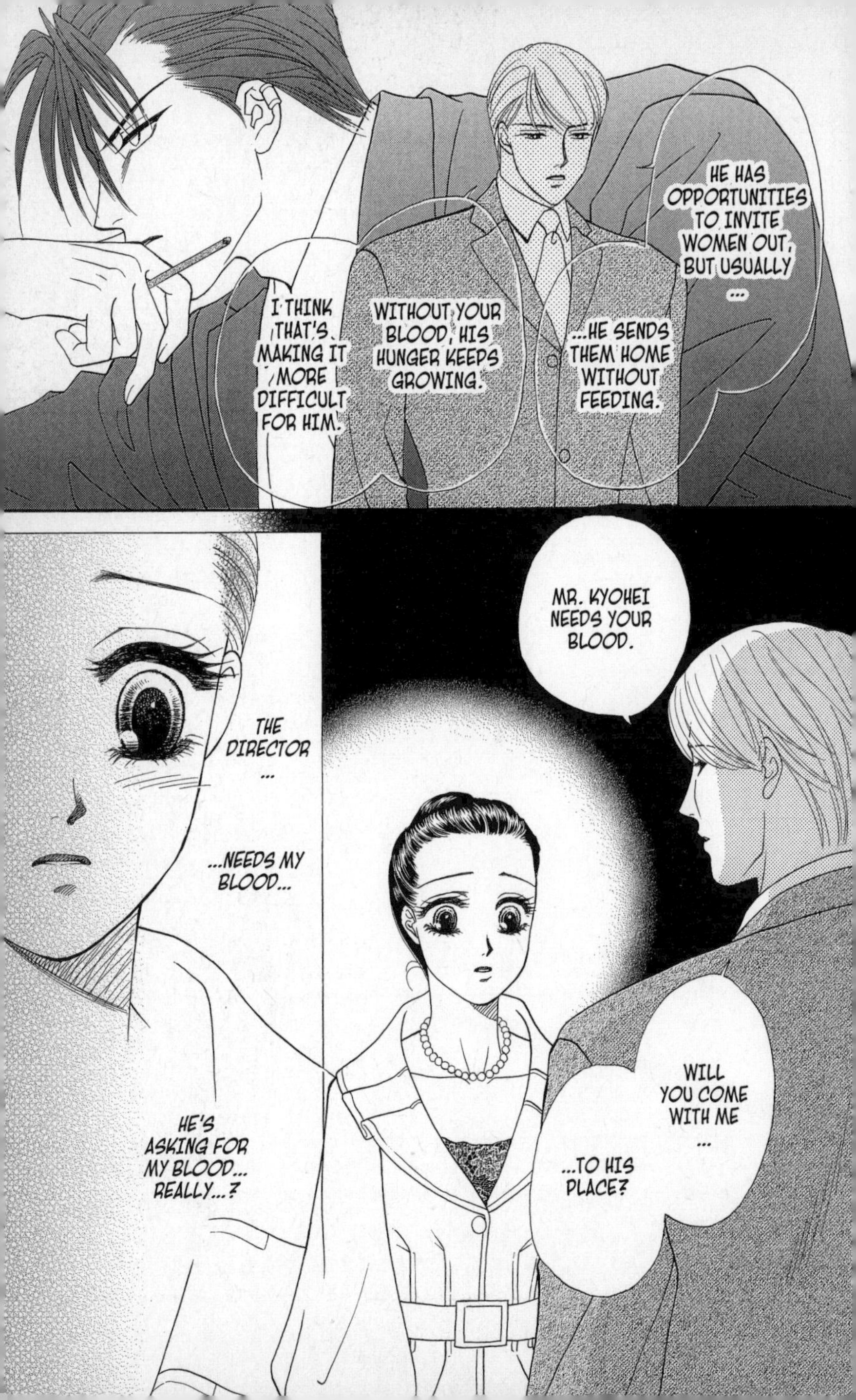
HE HAS OPPORTUNITIES TO INVITE WOMEN OUT, BUT USUALLY ...
...HE SENDS THEM HOME WITHOUT FEEDING.
WITHOUT YOUR BLOOD, HIS HUNGER KEEPS GROWING.
I THINK THAT'S MAKING IT MORE DIFFICULT FOR HIM.
MR. KYOHEI NEEDS YOUR BLOOD.
WILL YOU COME WITH ME ...
...TO HIS PLACE?
THE DIRECTOR ...
...NEEDS MY BLOOD...
HE'S ASKING FOR MY BLOOD... REALLY...?

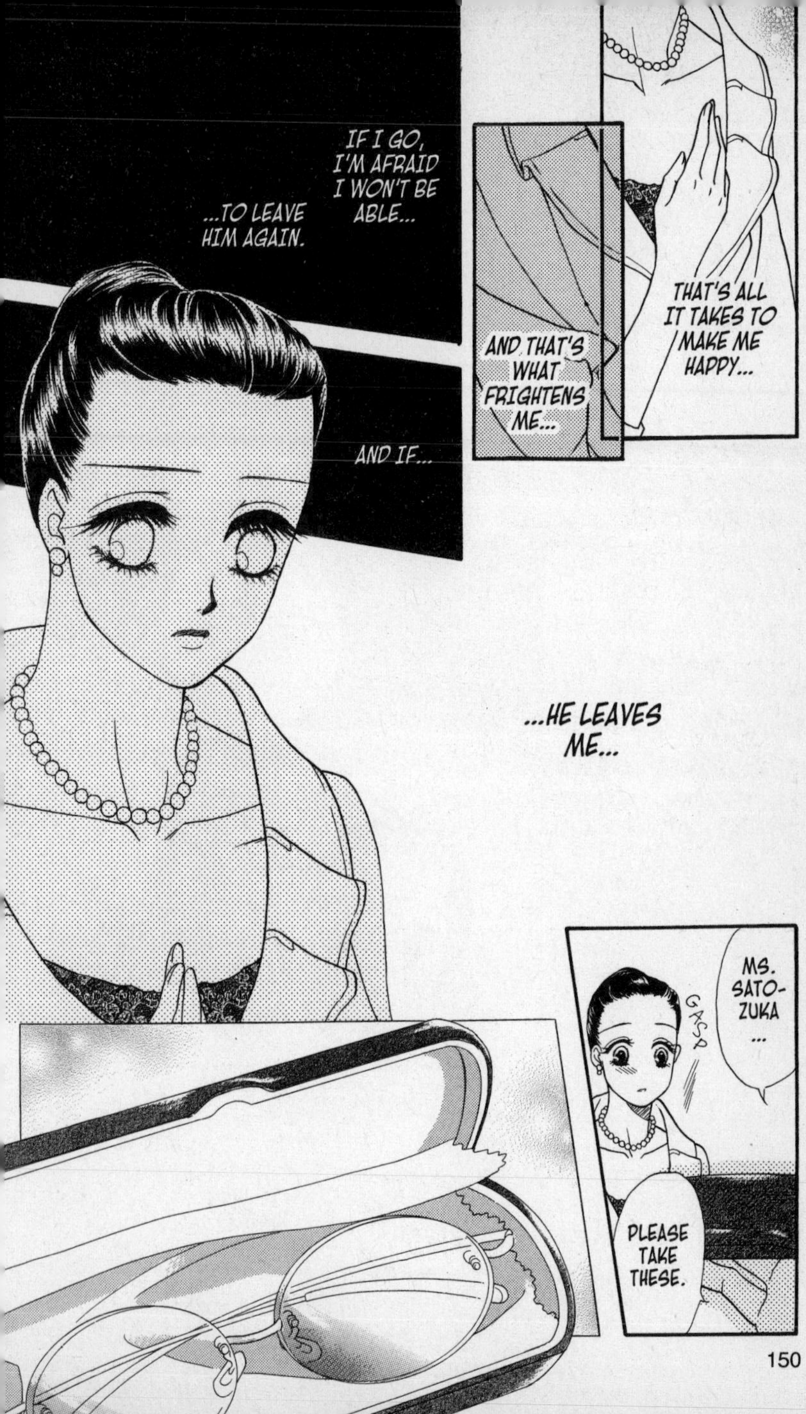
THAT'S ALL IT TAKES TO MAKE ME HAPPY...
AND THAT'S WHAT FRIGHTENS ME...
IF I GO, I'M AFRAID I WON'T BE ABLE...
...TO LEAVE HIM AGAIN.
AND IF...
...HE LEAVES ME...
MS. SATO-ZUKA ...
GASA
PLEASE TAKE THESE.

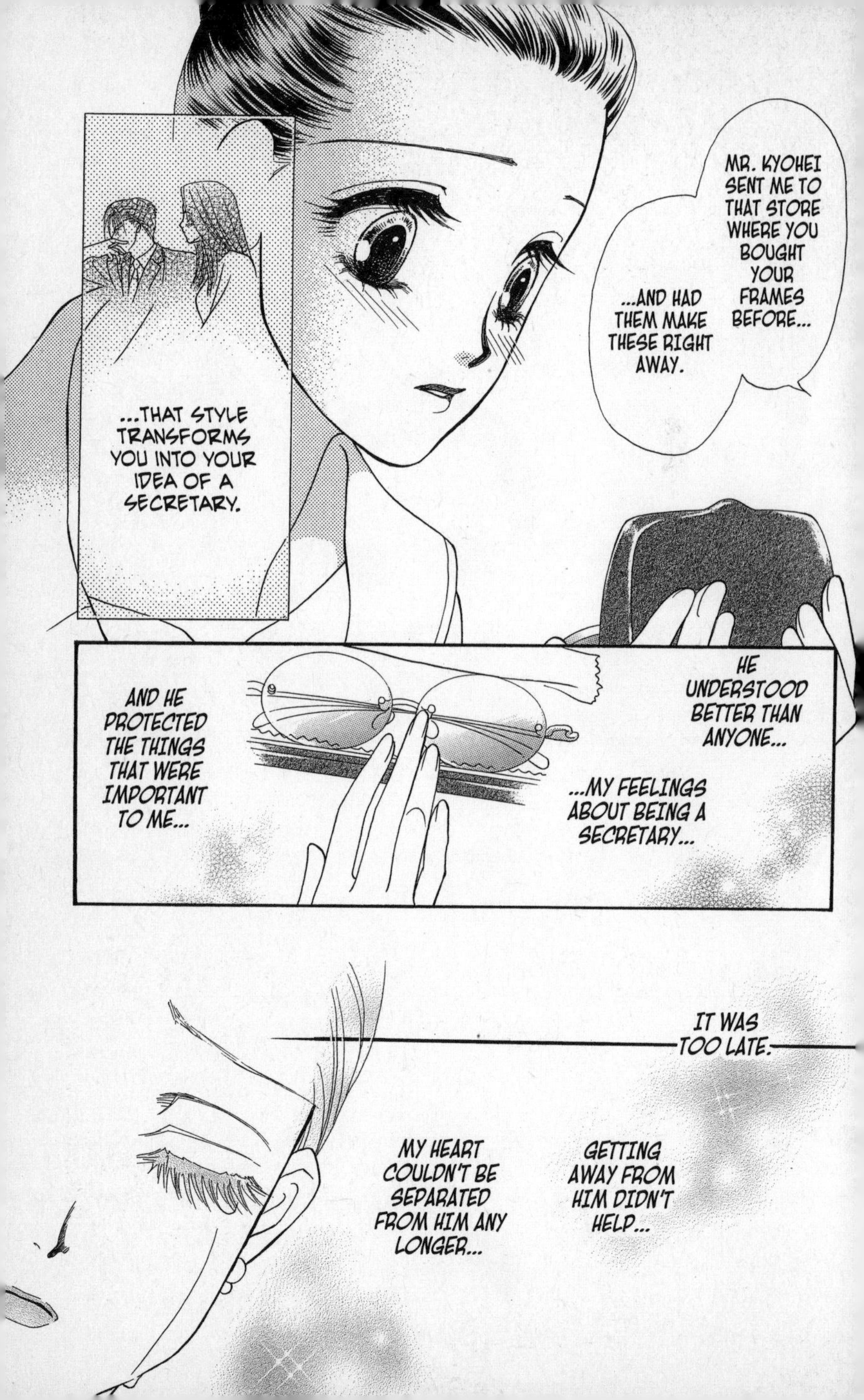
MR. KYOHEI SENT ME TO THAT STORE WHERE YOU BOUGHT YOUR FRAMES BEFORE...
...AND HAD THEM MAKE THESE RIGHT AWAY.
...THAT STYLE TRANSFORMS YOU INTO YOUR IDEA OF A SECRETARY.
HE UNDERSTOOD BETTER THAN ANYONE...
...MY FEELINGS ABOUT BEING A SECRETARY...
AND HE PROTECTED THE THINGS THAT WERE IMPORTANT TO ME...
IT WAS TOO LATE.
GETTING AWAY FROM HIM DIDN'T HELP...
MY HEART COULDN'T BE SEPARATED FROM HIM ANY LONGER...

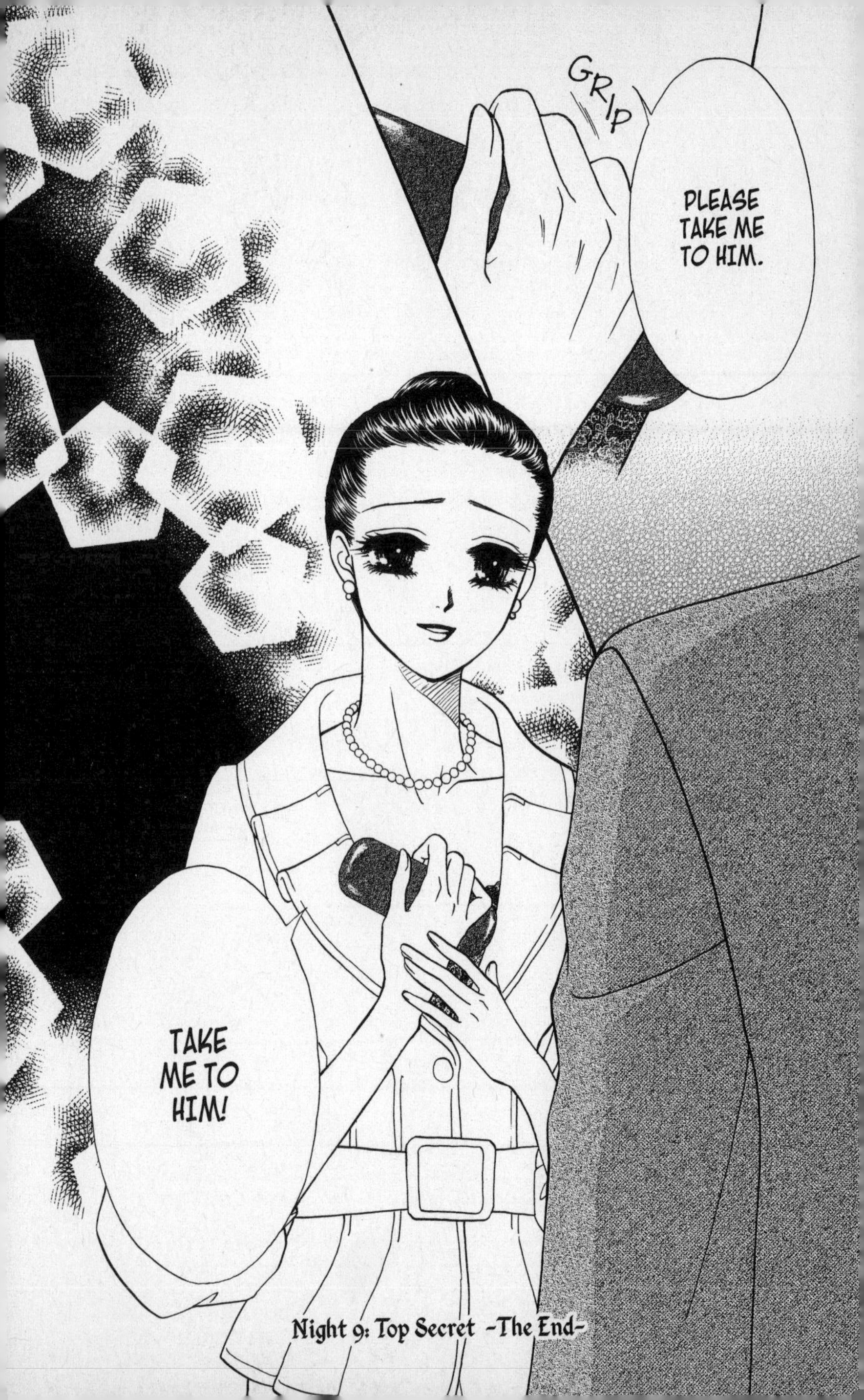
GRIP
PLEASE TAKE ME TO HIM.
TAKE ME TO HIM!

Night 9: Top Secret -The End-

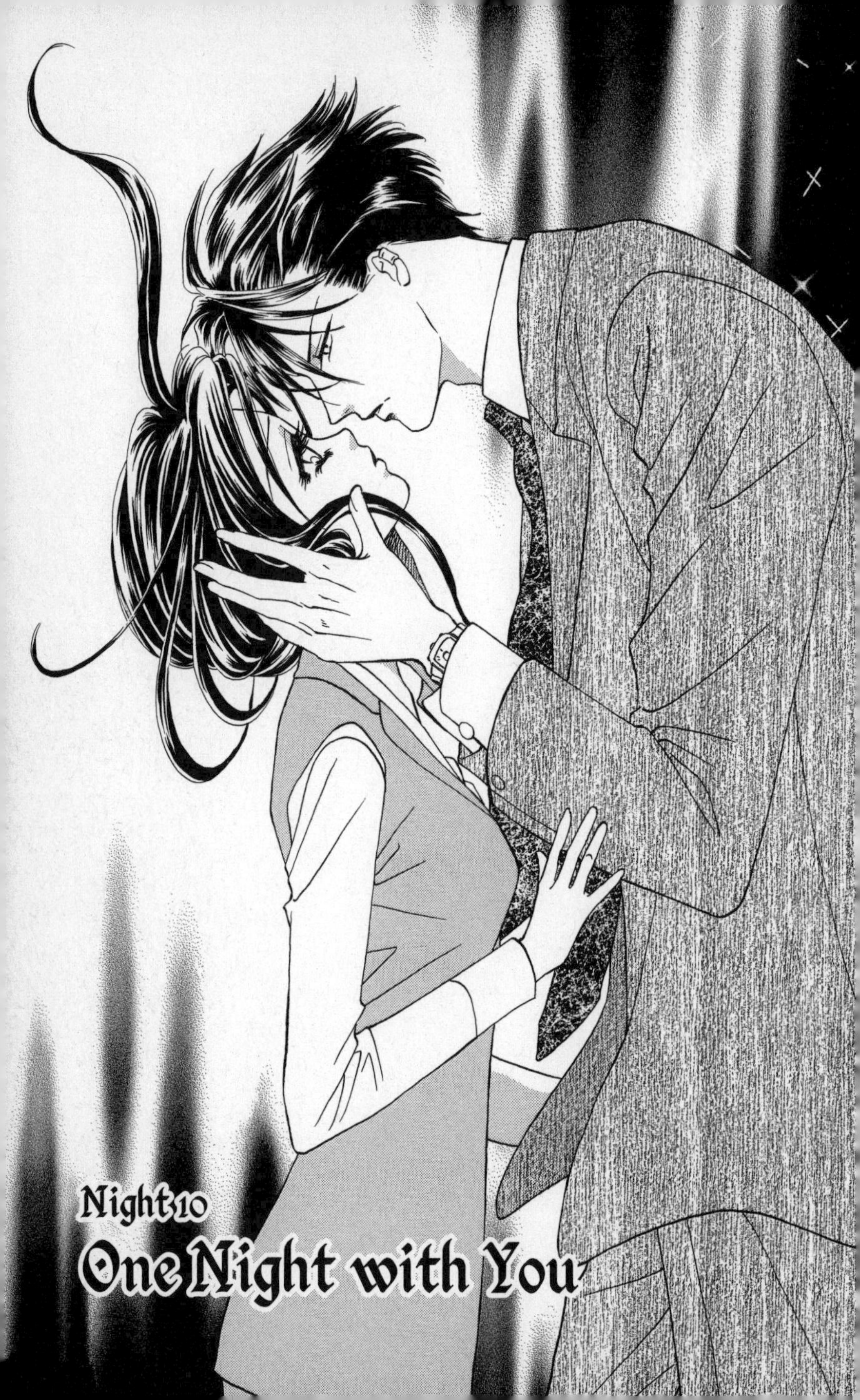

Night 10
One Night with You

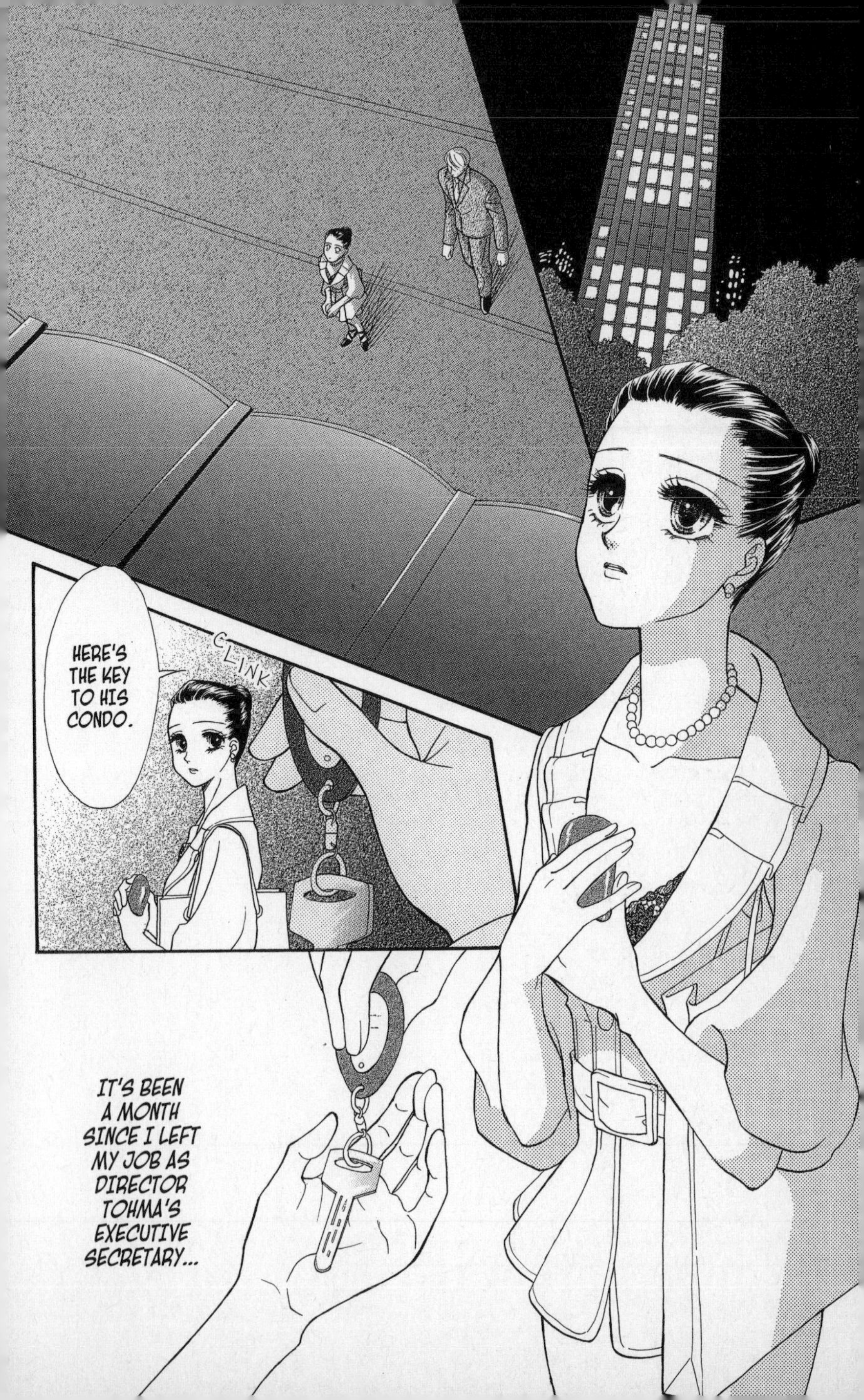
HERE'S THE KEY TO HIS CONDO.
CLINK
IT'S BEEN A MONTH SINCE I LEFT MY JOB AS DIRECTOR TOHMA'S EXECUTIVE SECRETARY...

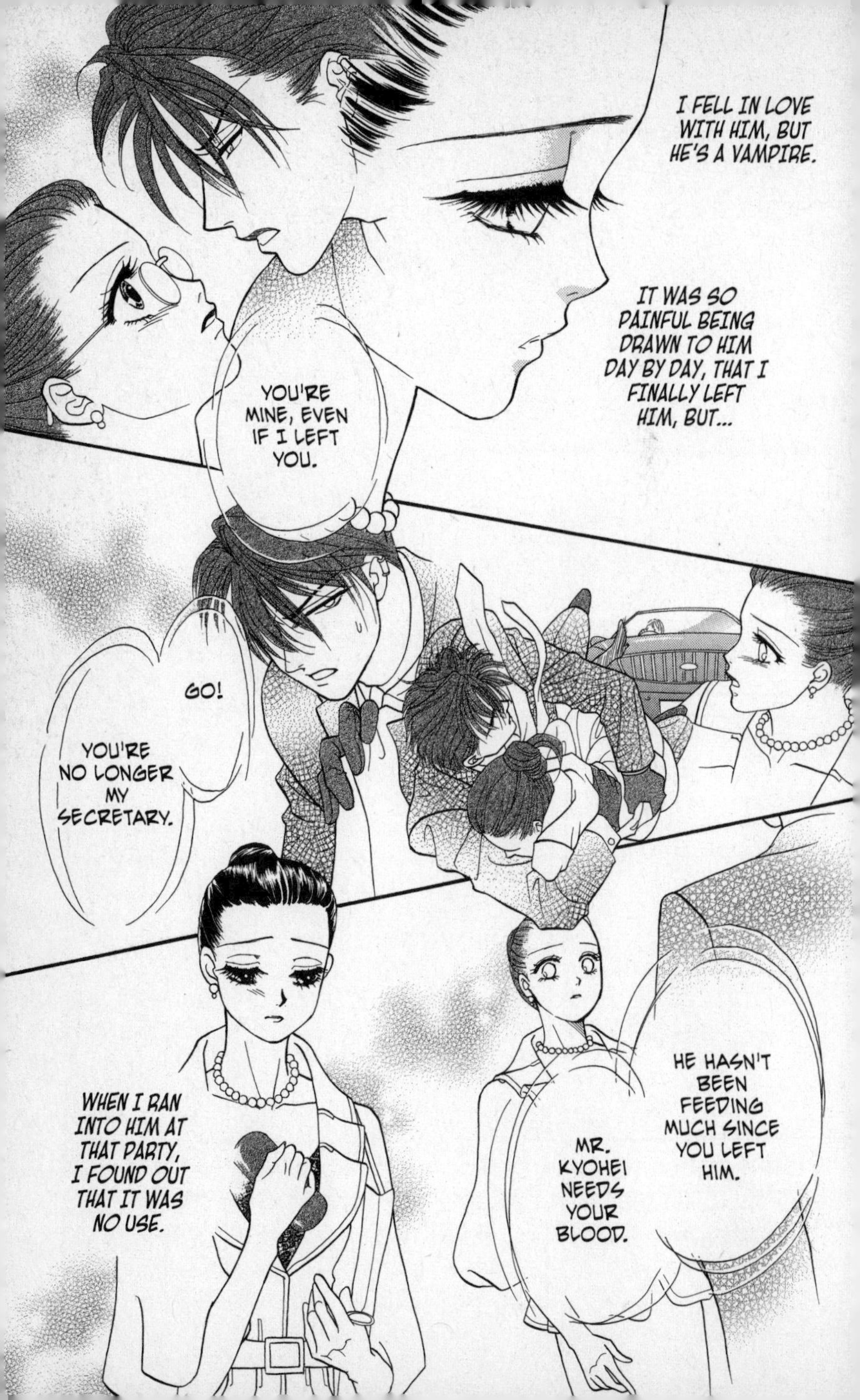

I FELL IN LOVE WITH HIM, BUT HE'S A VAMPIRE.
IT WAS SO PAINFUL BEING DRAWN TO HIM DAY BY DAY, THAT I FINALLY LEFT HIM, BUT...
YOU'RE MINE, EVEN IF I LEFT YOU.
GO!
YOU'RE NO LONGER MY SECRETARY.
HE HASN'T BEEN FEEDING MUCH SINCE YOU LEFT HIM.
MR. KYOHEI NEEDS YOUR BLOOD.
WHEN I RAN INTO HIM AT THAT PARTY, I FOUND OUT THAT IT WAS NO USE.

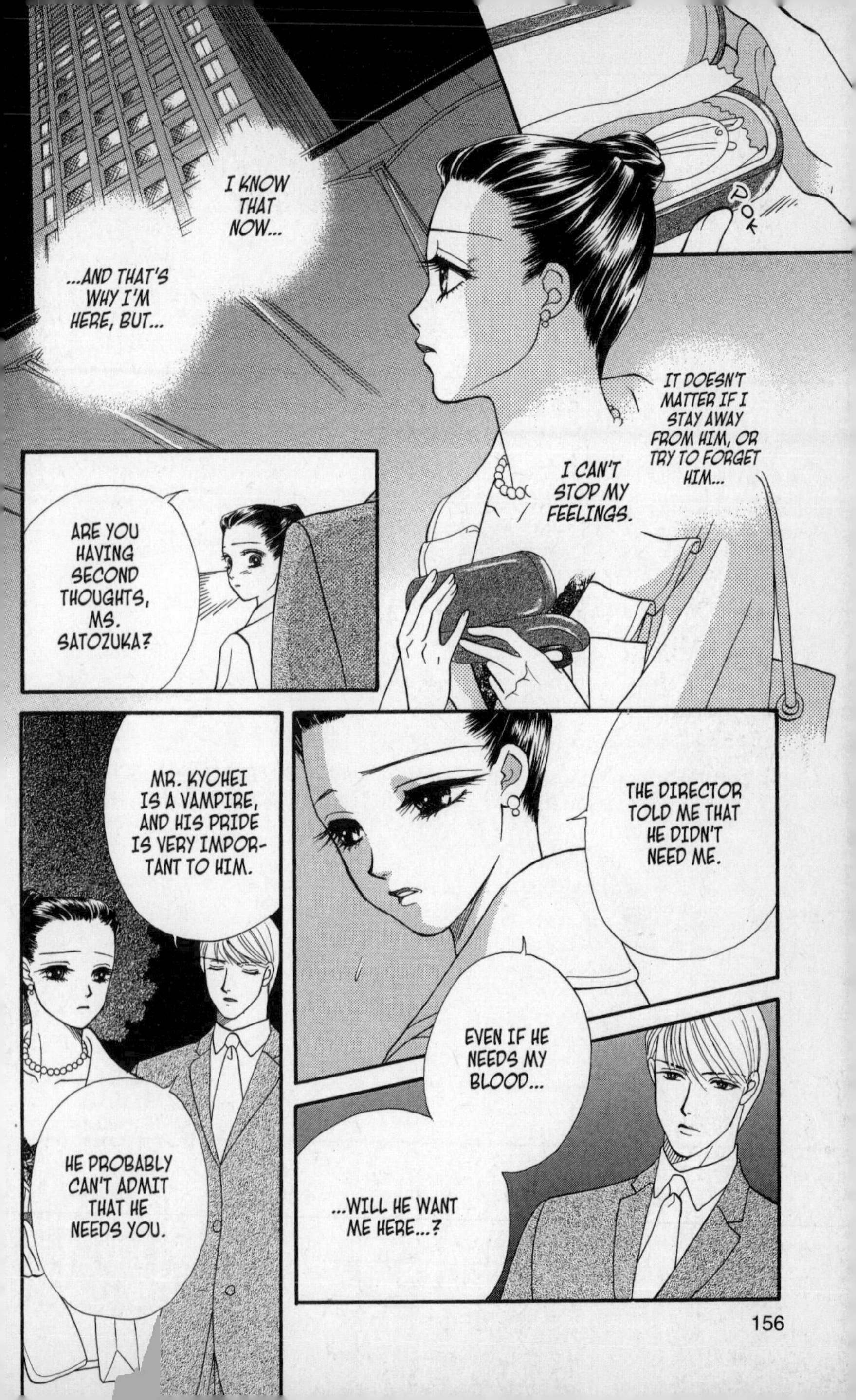
POK
I KNOW THAT NOW...
...AND THAT'S WHY I'M HERE, BUT...
IT DOESN'T MATTER IF I STAY AWAY FROM HIM, OR TRY TO FORGET HIM...
I CAN'T STOP MY FEELINGS.
ARE YOU HAVING SECOND THOUGHTS, MS. SATOZUKA?
THE DIRECTOR TOLD ME THAT HE DIDN'T NEED ME.
EVEN IF HE NEEDS MY BLOOD...
...WILL HE WANT ME HERE...?
MR. KYOHEI IS A VAMPIRE, AND HIS PRIDE IS VERY IMPOR-TANT TO HIM.
HE PROBABLY CAN'T ADMIT THAT HE NEEDS YOU.

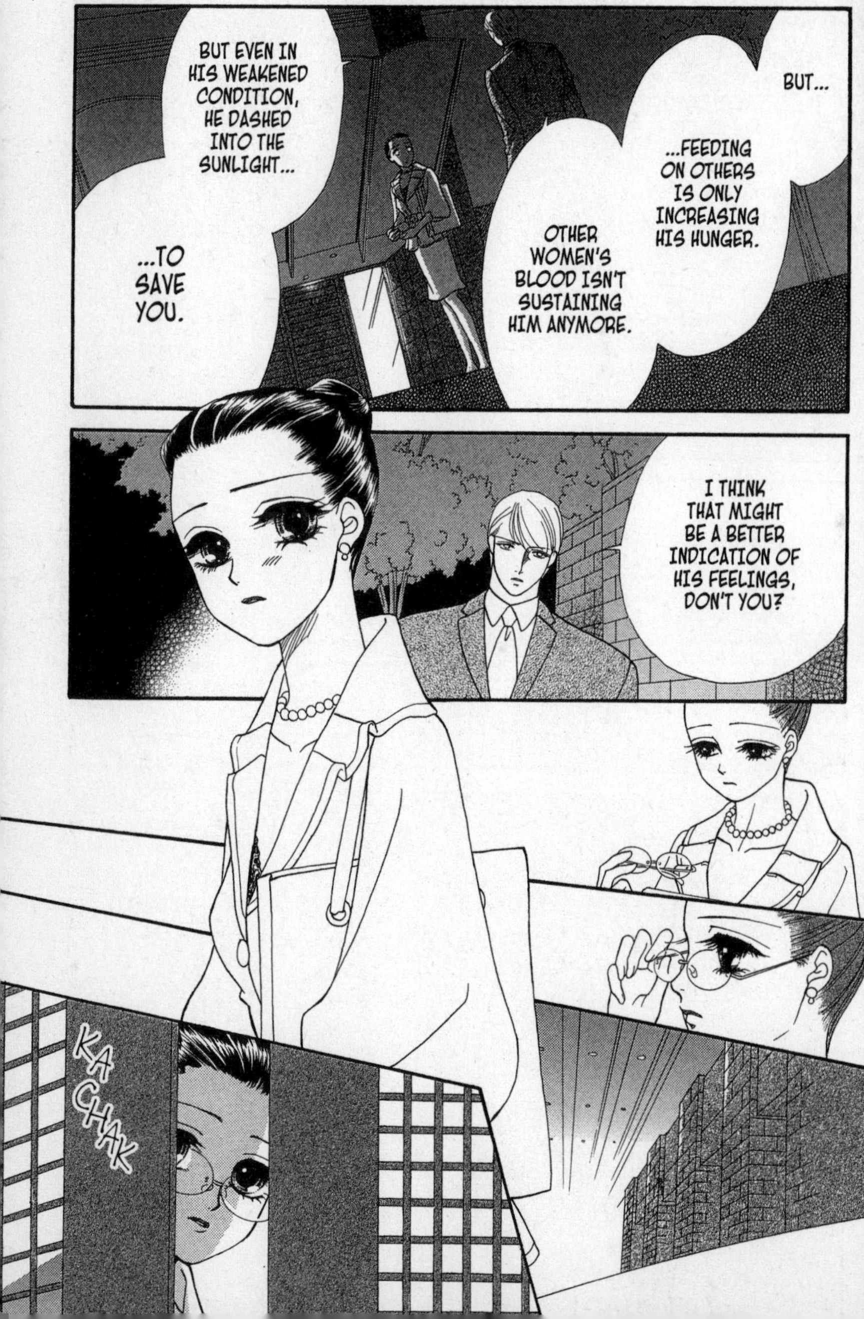
BUT...
...FEEDING ON OTHERS IS ONLY INCREASING HIS HUNGER.
OTHER WOMEN'S BLOOD ISN'T SUSTAINING HIM ANYMORE.
BUT EVEN IN HIS WEAKENED CONDITION, HE DASHED INTO THE SUNLIGHT...
...TO SAVE YOU.
I THINK THAT MIGHT BE A BETTER INDICATION OF HIS FEELINGS, DON'T YOU?
KA CHAK

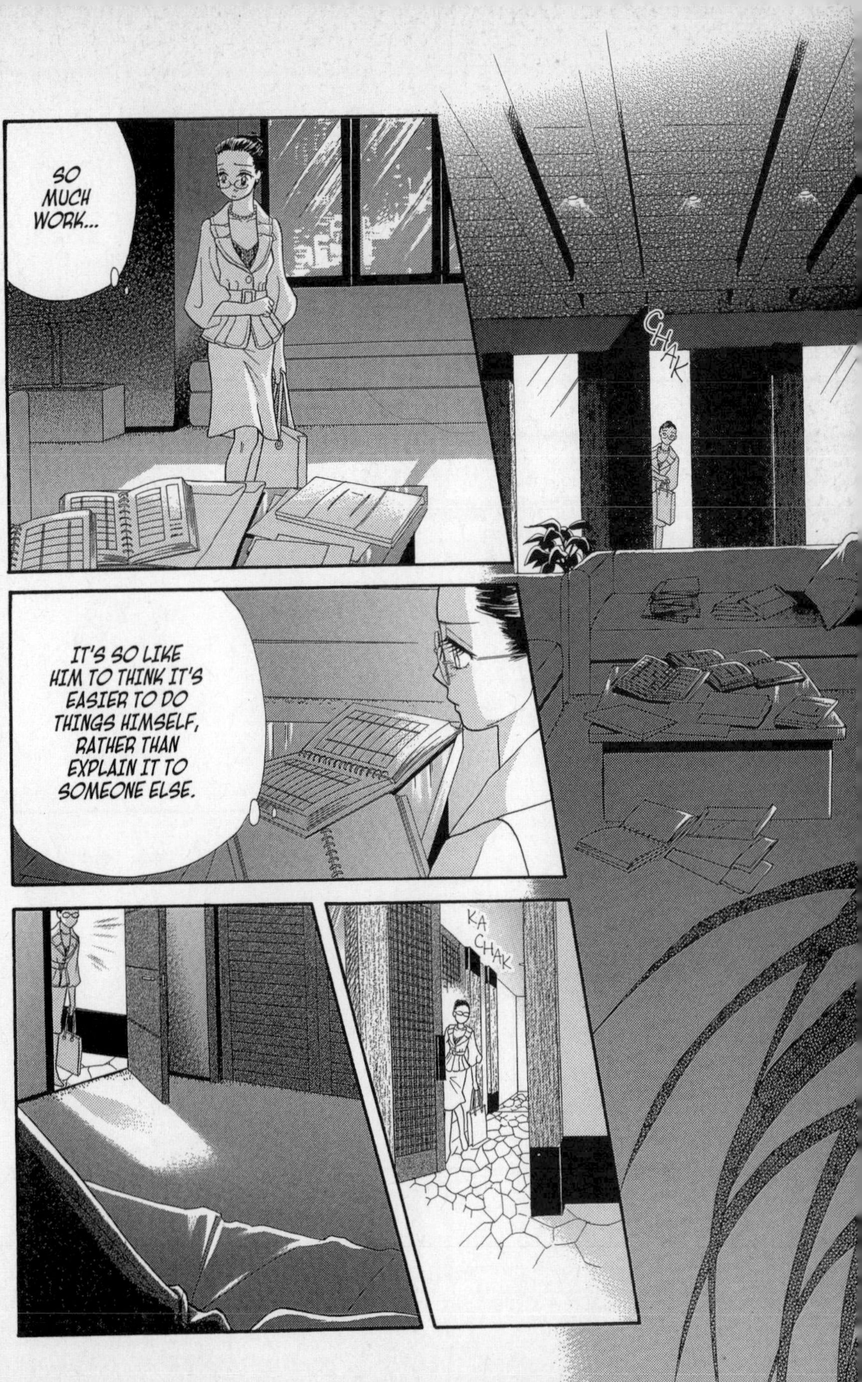
CHAK
SO MUCH WORK...
IT'S SO LIKE HIM TO THINK IT'S EASIER TO DO THINGS HIMSELF, RATHER THAN EXPLAIN IT TO SOMEONE ELSE.
KA CHAK

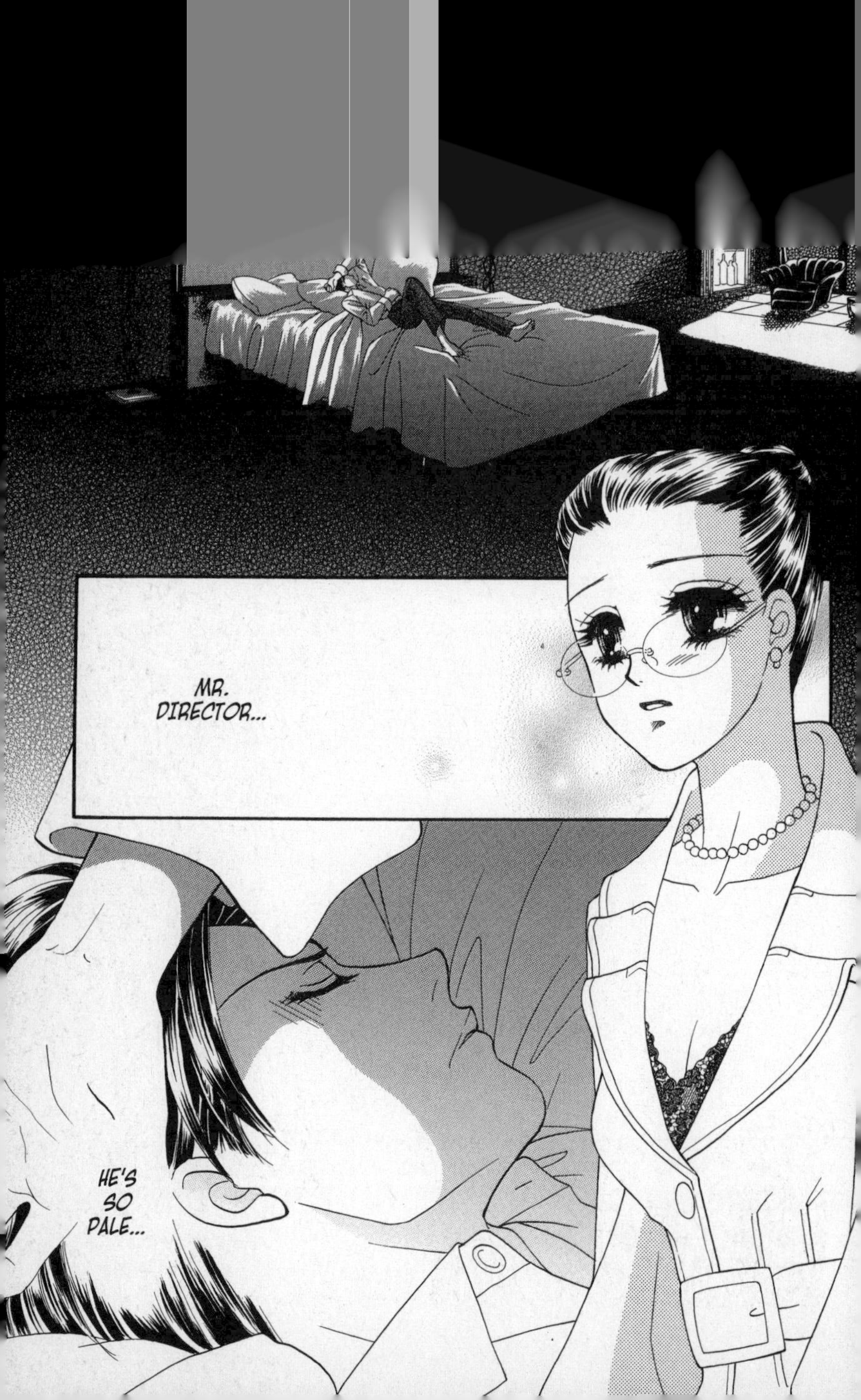
MR. DIRECTOR...
HE'S SO PALE...

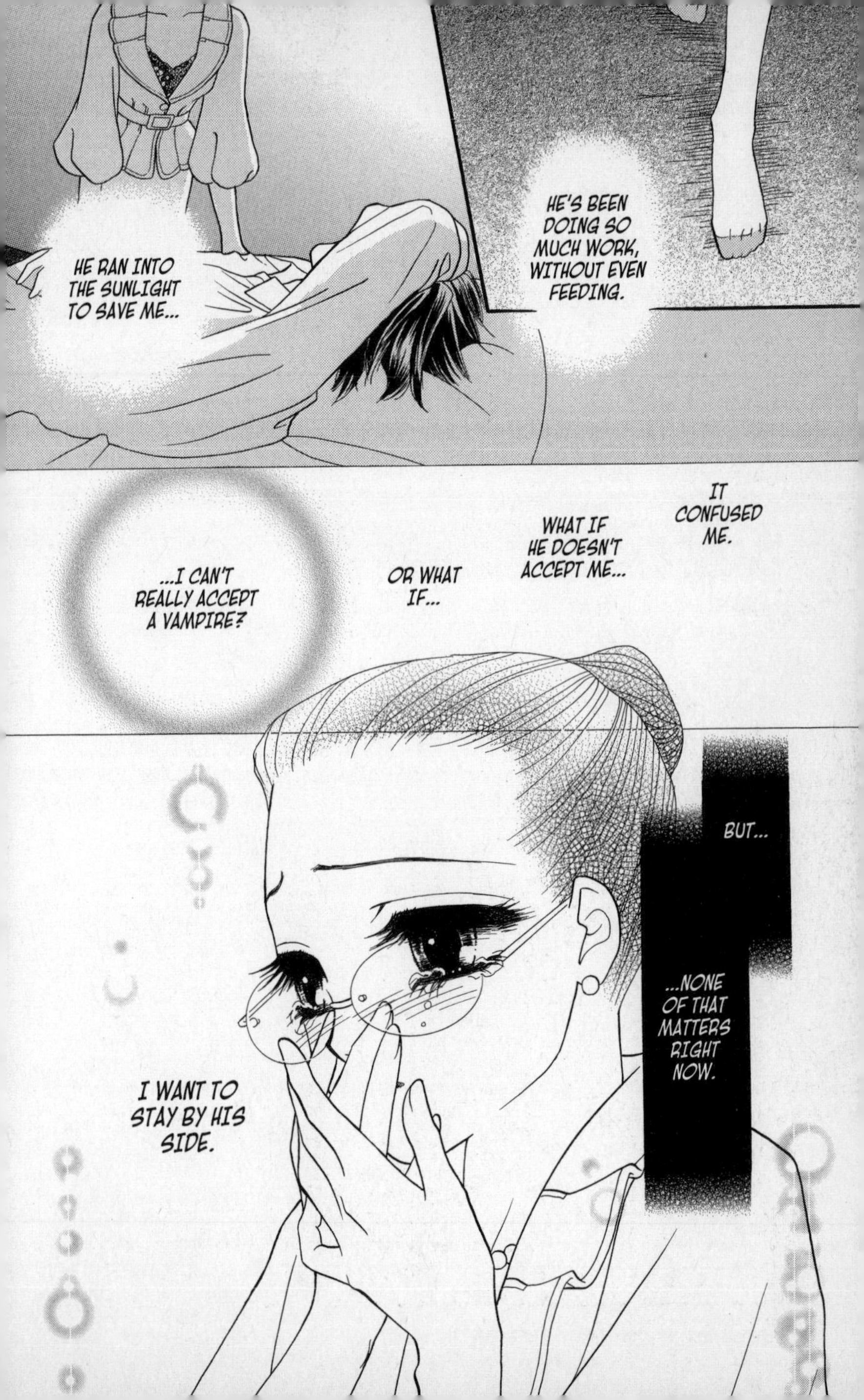
HE'S BEEN DOING SO MUCH WORK, WITHOUT EVEN FEEDING.
HE RAN INTO THE SUNLIGHT TO SAVE ME...
IT CONFUSED ME.
WHAT IF HE DOESN'T ACCEPT ME...
OR WHAT IF...
...I CAN'T REALLY ACCEPT A VAMPIRE?
BUT...
...NONE OF THAT MATTERS RIGHT NOW.
I WANT TO STAY BY HIS SIDE.

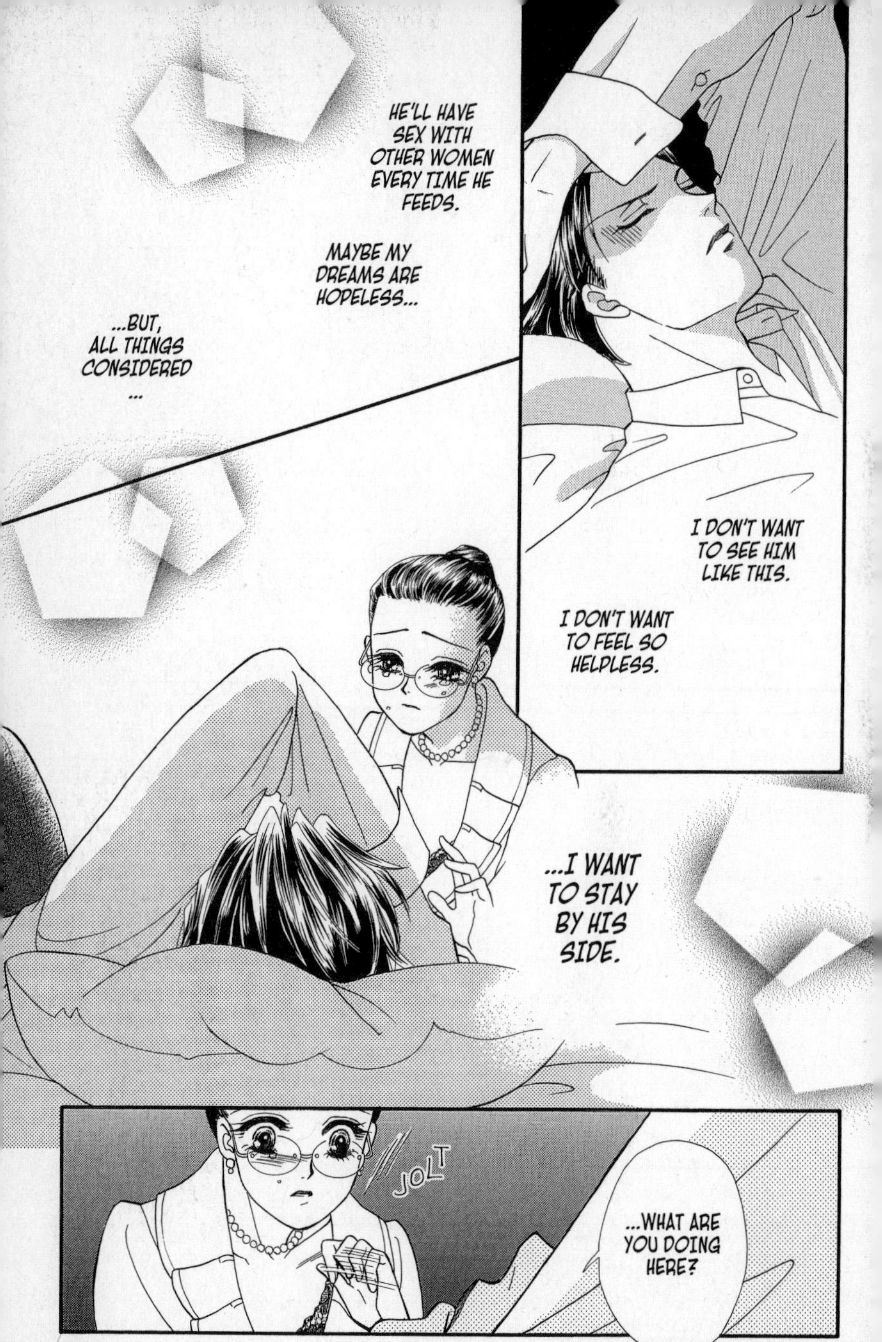
I DON'T WANT TO SEE HIM LIKE THIS.
I DON'T WANT TO FEEL SO HELPLESS.
HE'LL HAVE SEX WITH OTHER WOMEN EVERY TIME HE FEEDS.
MAYBE MY DREAMS ARE HOPELESS...
...BUT, ALL THINGS CONSIDERED ...
...I WANT TO STAY BY HIS SIDE.
JOLT
...WHAT ARE YOU DOING HERE?

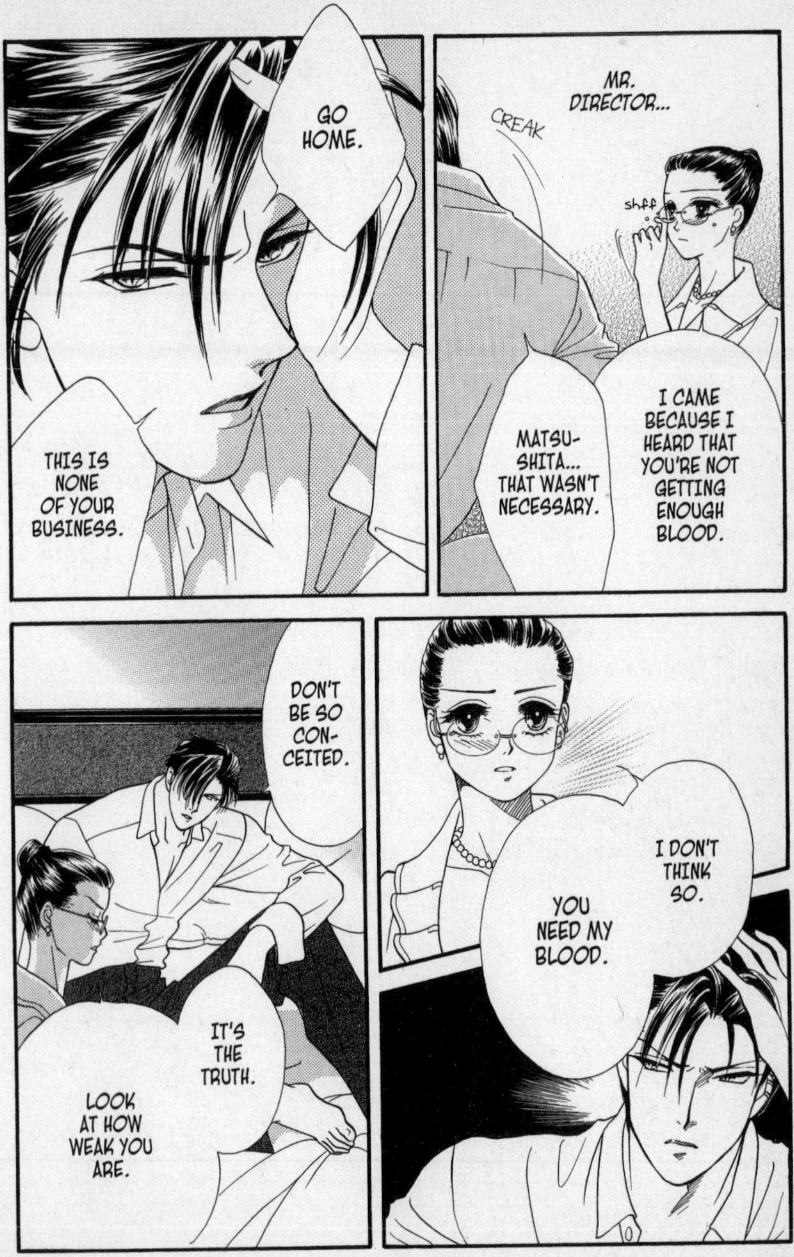
MR. DIRECTOR...
CREAK
shff
I CAME BECAUSE I HEARD THAT YOU'RE NOT GETTING ENOUGH BLOOD.
MATSU-SHITA... THAT WASN'T NECESSARY.
GO HOME.
THIS IS NONE OF YOUR BUSINESS.
I DON'T THINK SO.
YOU NEED MY BLOOD.
DON'T BE SO CON-CEITED.
IT'S THE TRUTH.
LOOK AT HOW WEAK YOU ARE.

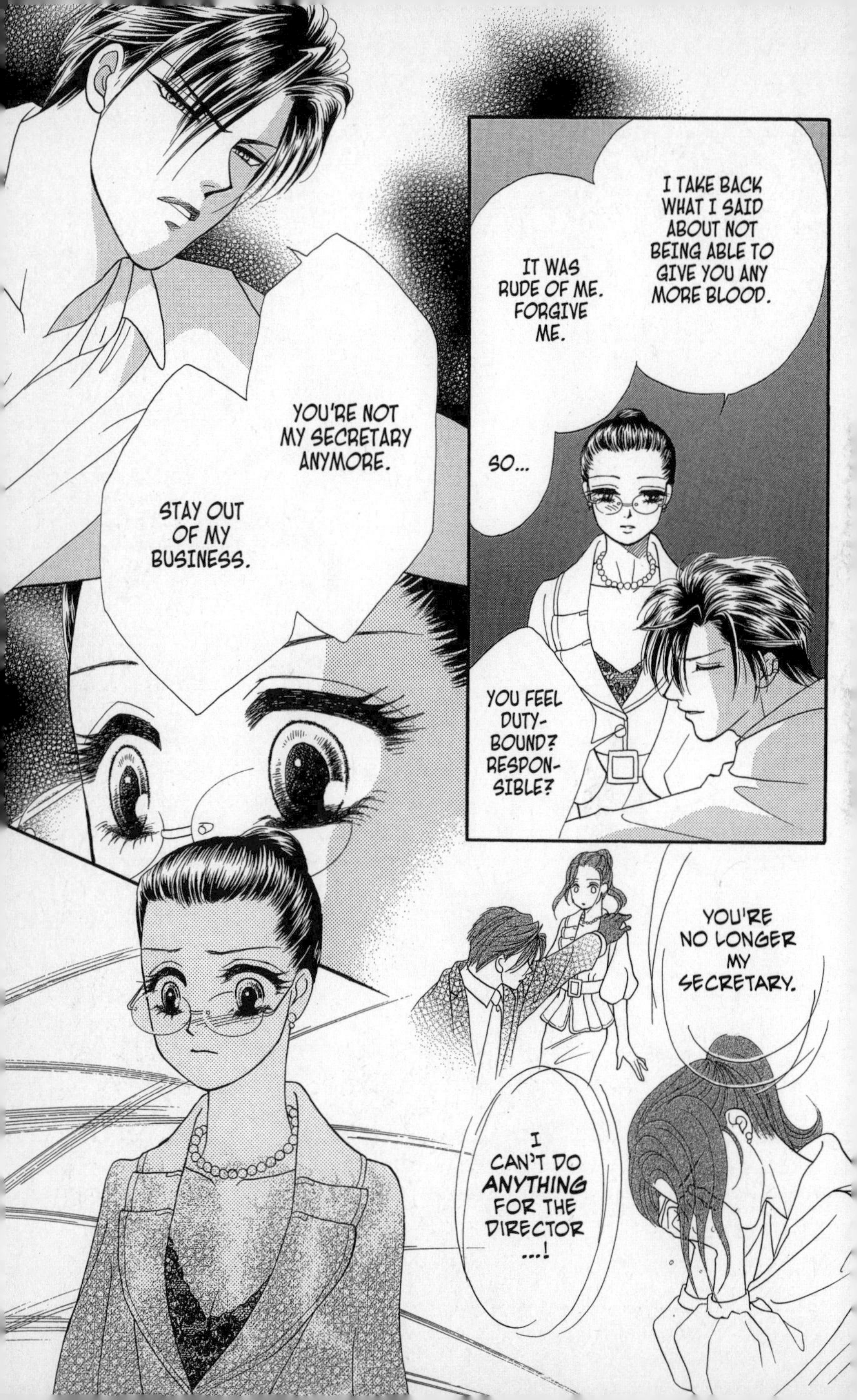
I TAKE BACK WHAT I SAID ABOUT NOT BEING ABLE TO GIVE YOU ANY MORE BLOOD.
IT WAS RUDE OF ME. FORGIVE ME.
SO...
YOU FEEL DUTY-BOUND? RESPONSIBLE?
YOU'RE NOT MY SECRETARY ANYMORE.
STAY OUT OF MY BUSINESS.
YOU'RE NO LONGER MY SECRETARY.
I CAN'T DO **ANYTHING** FOR THE DIRECTOR ...!

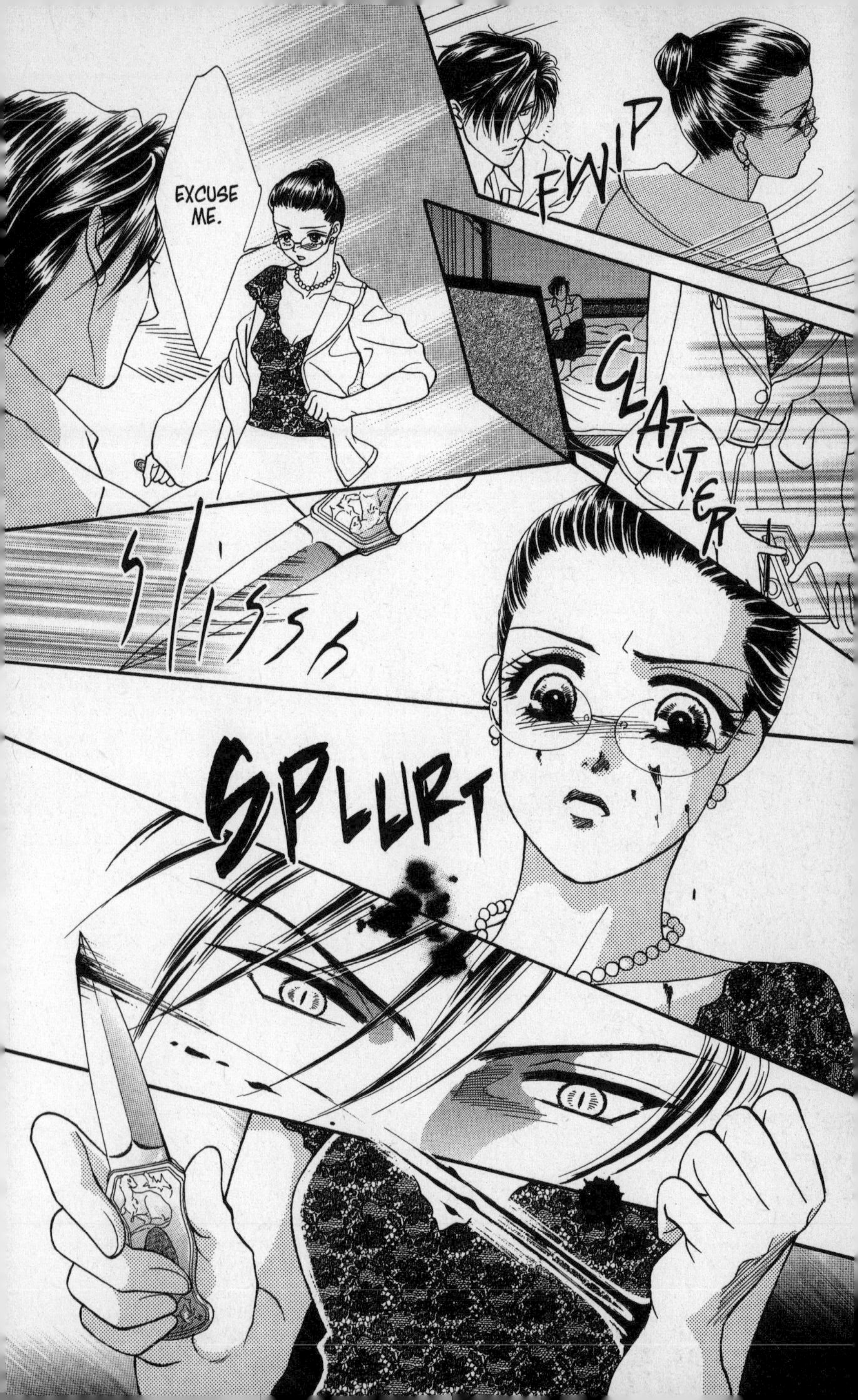
FWIP
CLATTER
EXCUSE ME.
SLISSH
SPLURT

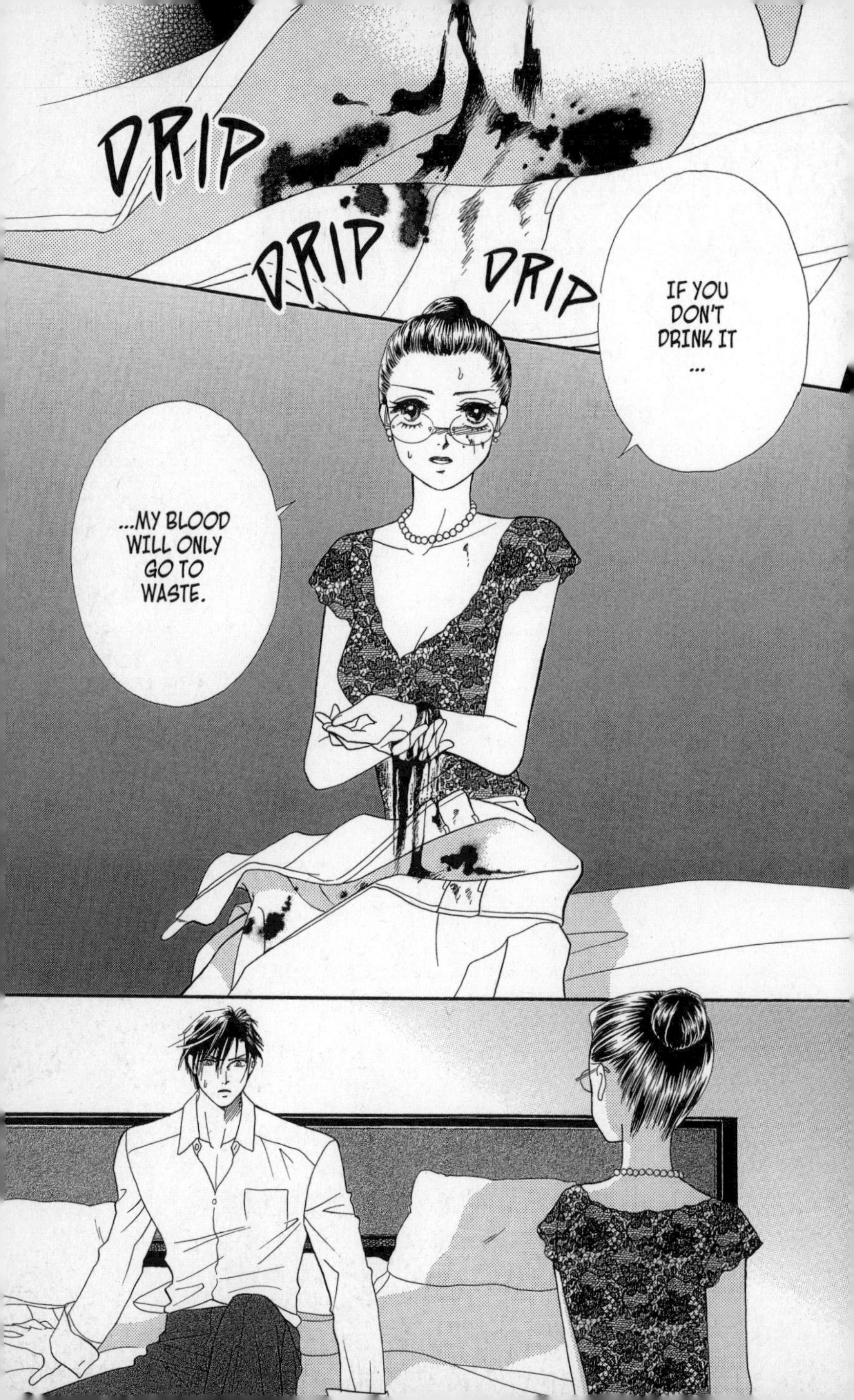
DRIP
DRIP
DRIP
IF YOU DON'T DRINK IT ...
...MY BLOOD WILL ONLY GO TO WASTE.

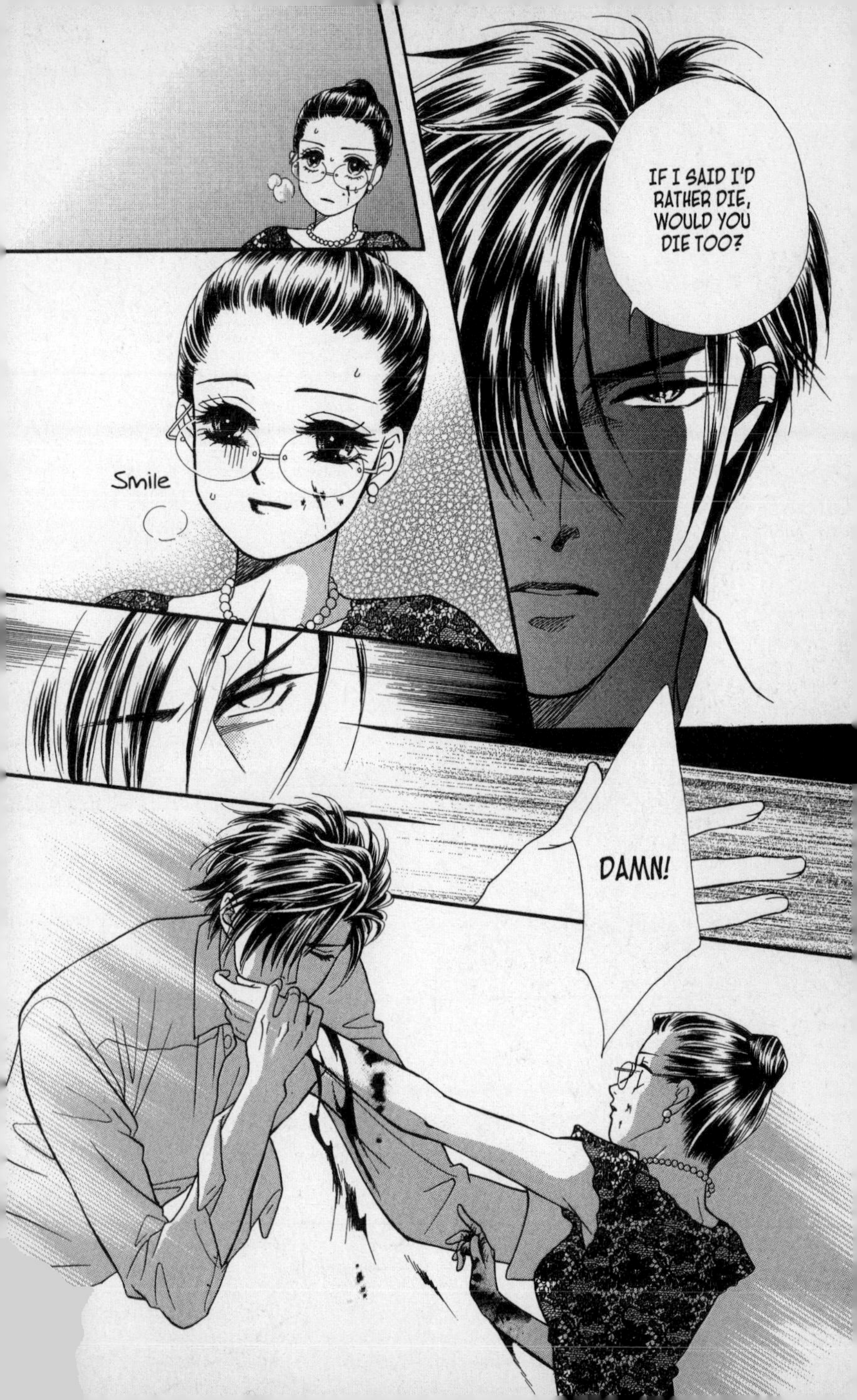
IF I SAID I'D RATHER DIE, WOULD YOU DIE TOO?
Smile
DAMN!

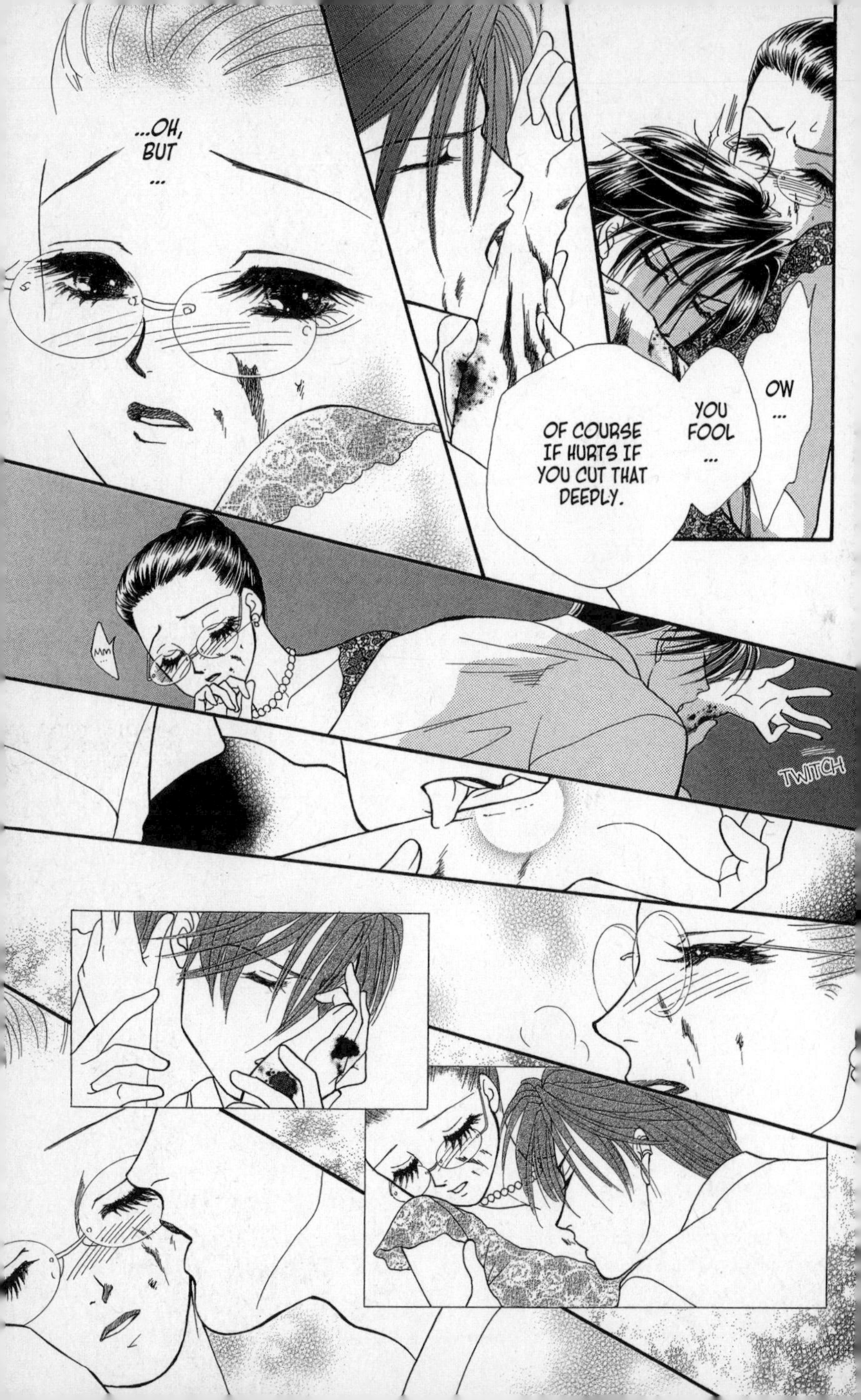
OW ...
YOU FOOL ...
OF COURSE IF HURTS IF YOU CUT THAT DEEPLY.
...OH, BUT ...
MM ...
TWITCH

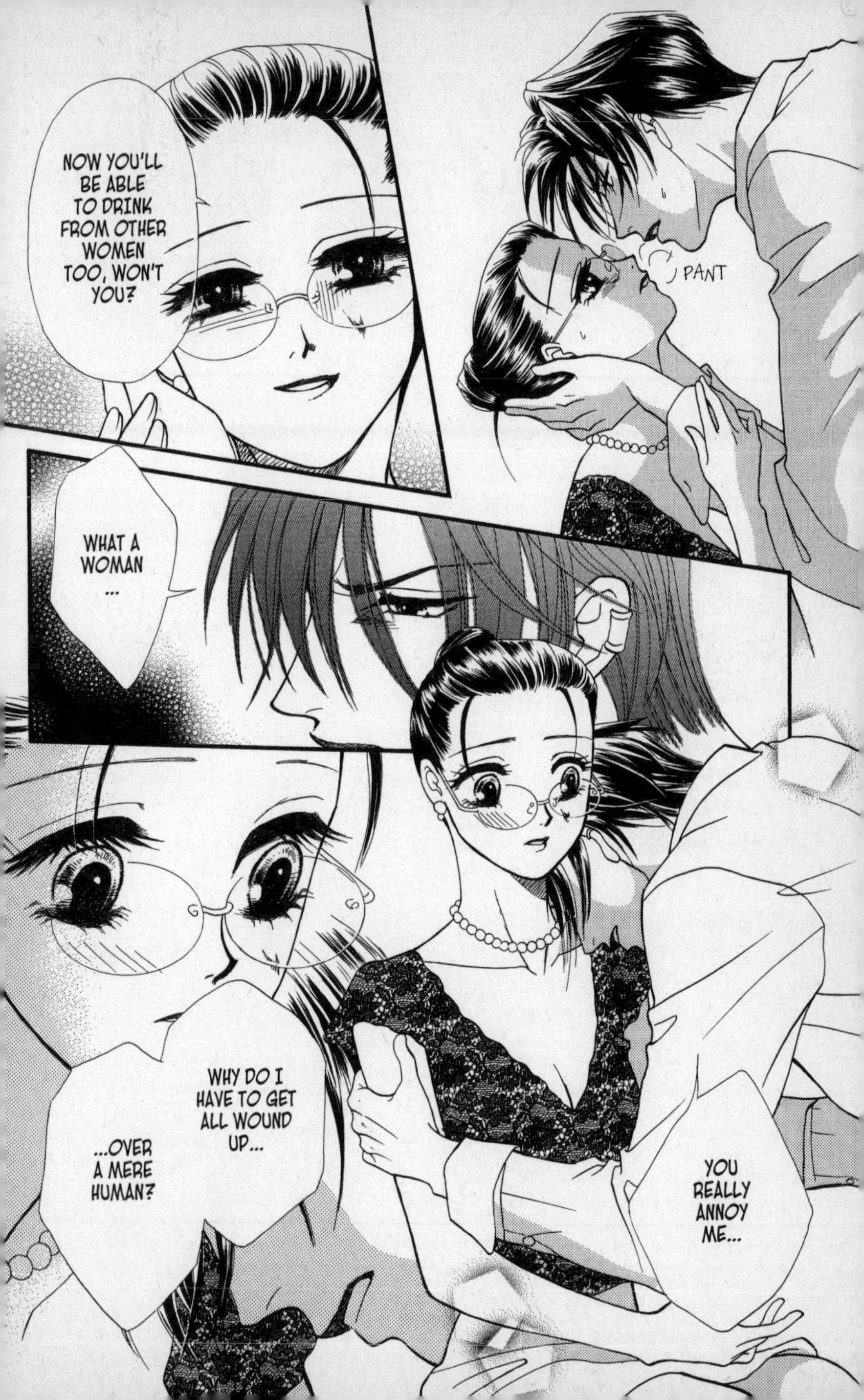
PANT
NOW YOU'LL BE ABLE TO DRINK FROM OTHER WOMEN TOO, WON'T YOU?
WHAT A WOMAN ...
YOU REALLY ANNOY ME...
WHY DO I HAVE TO GET ALL WOUND UP...
...OVER A MERE HUMAN?

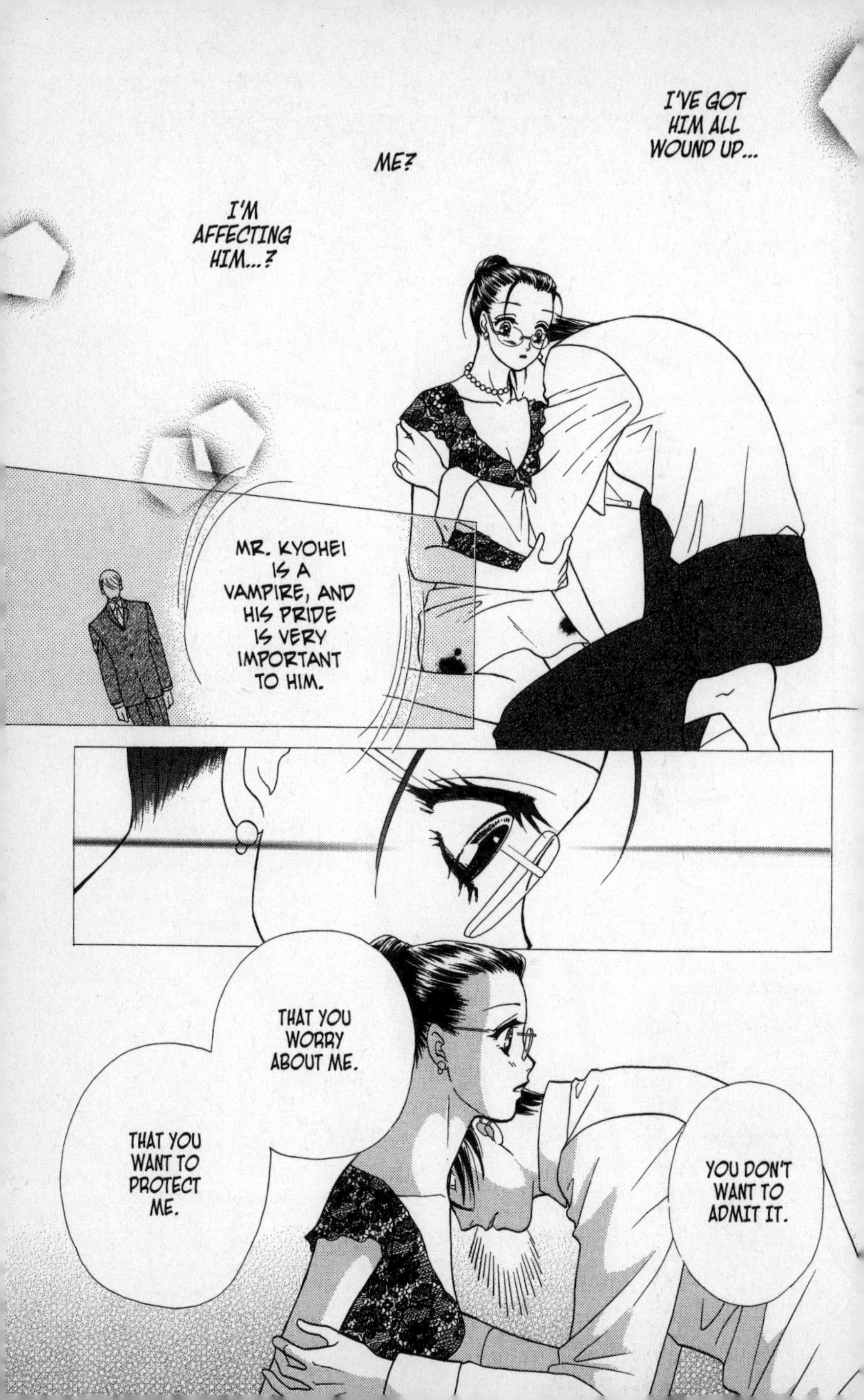
I'VE GOT HIM ALL WOUND UP...
ME?
I'M AFFECTING HIM...?
MR. KYOHEI IS A VAMPIRE, AND HIS PRIDE IS VERY IMPORTANT TO HIM.
YOU DON'T WANT TO ADMIT IT.
THAT YOU WORRY ABOUT ME.
THAT YOU WANT TO PROTECT ME.

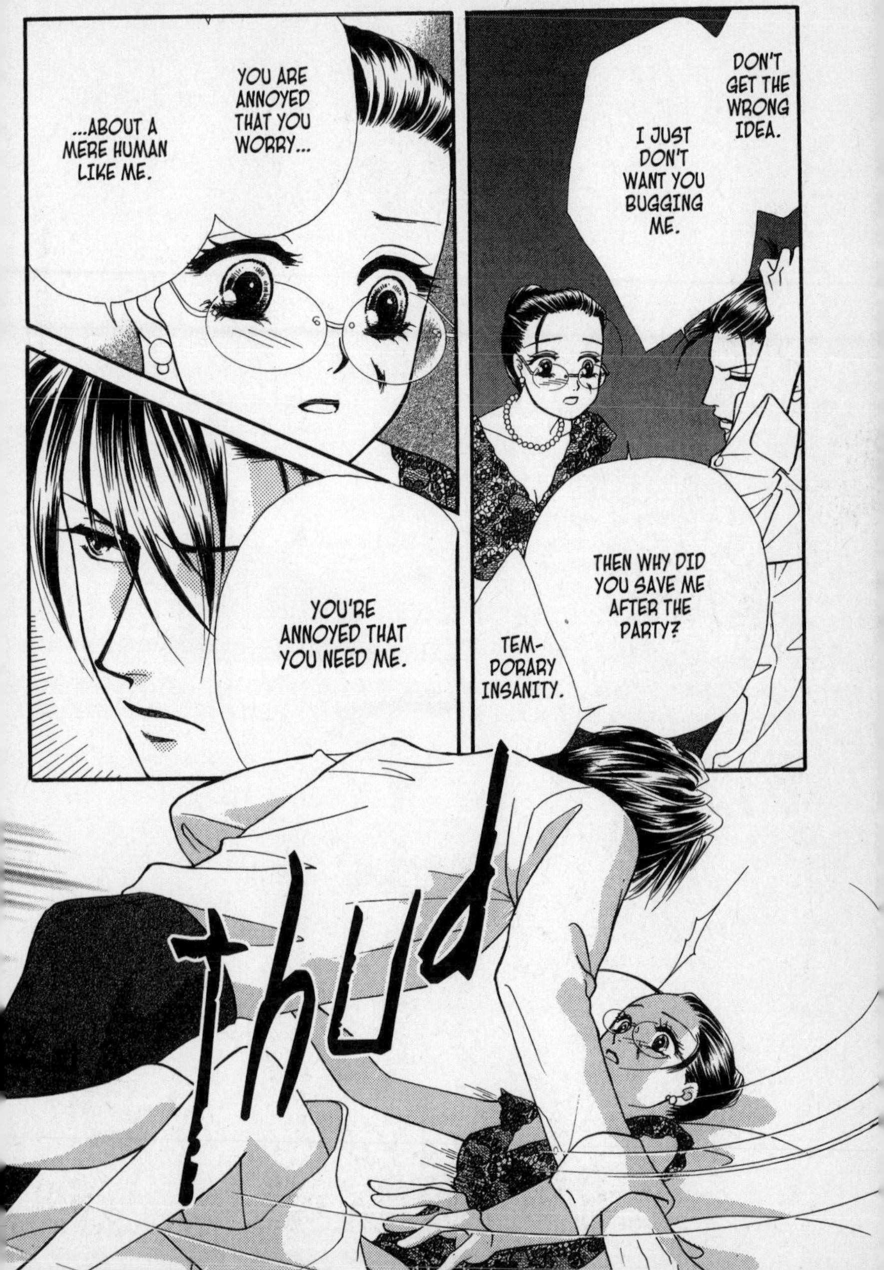
DON'T GET THE WRONG IDEA.
I JUST DON'T WANT YOU BUGGING ME.
THEN WHY DID YOU SAVE ME AFTER THE PARTY?
TEM-PORARY INSANITY.
YOU ARE ANNOYED THAT YOU WORRY...
...ABOUT A MERE HUMAN LIKE ME.
YOU'RE ANNOYED THAT YOU NEED ME.
thud

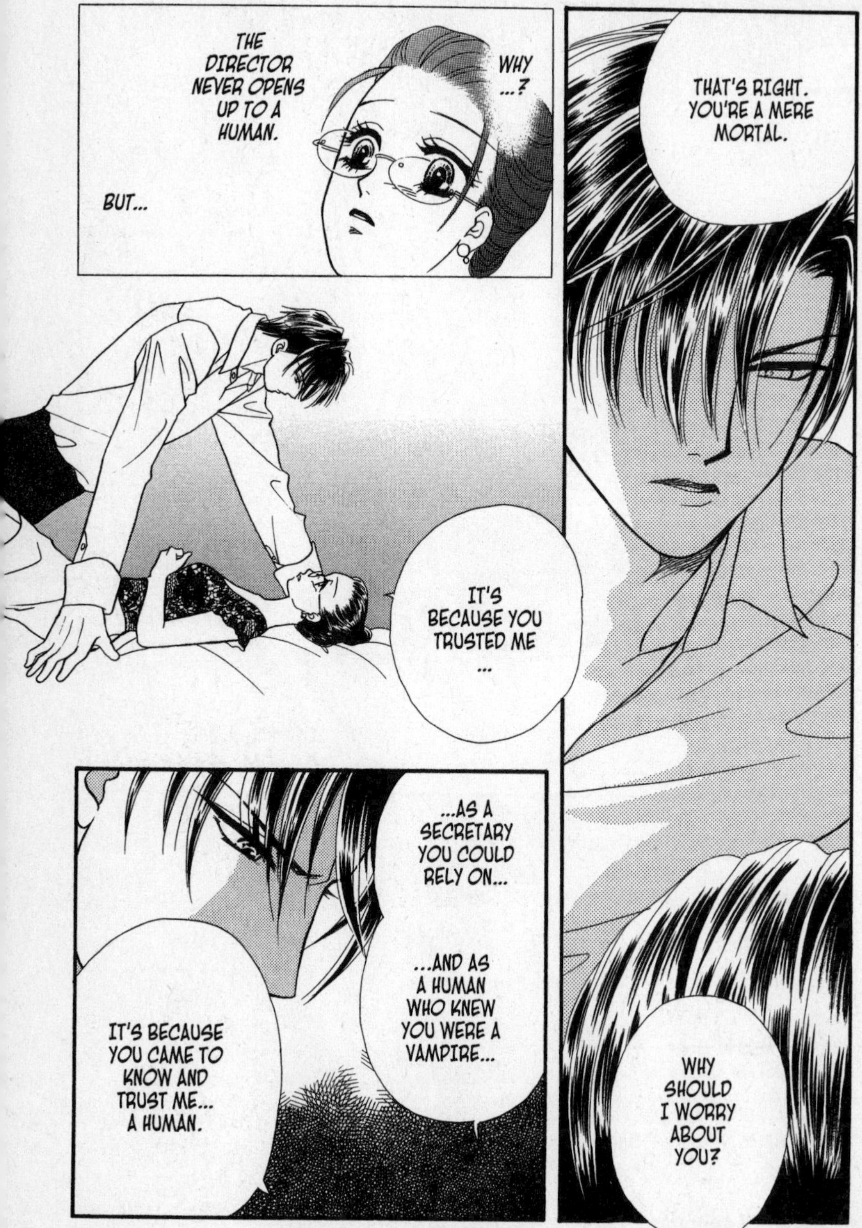
THAT'S RIGHT. YOU'RE A MERE MORTAL.
WHY SHOULD I WORRY ABOUT YOU?
WHY ...?
THE DIRECTOR NEVER OPENS UP TO A HUMAN.
BUT...
IT'S BECAUSE YOU TRUSTED ME ...
...AS A SECRETARY YOU COULD RELY ON...
...AND AS A HUMAN WHO KNEW YOU WERE A VAMPIRE...
IT'S BECAUSE YOU CAME TO KNOW AND TRUST ME... A HUMAN.

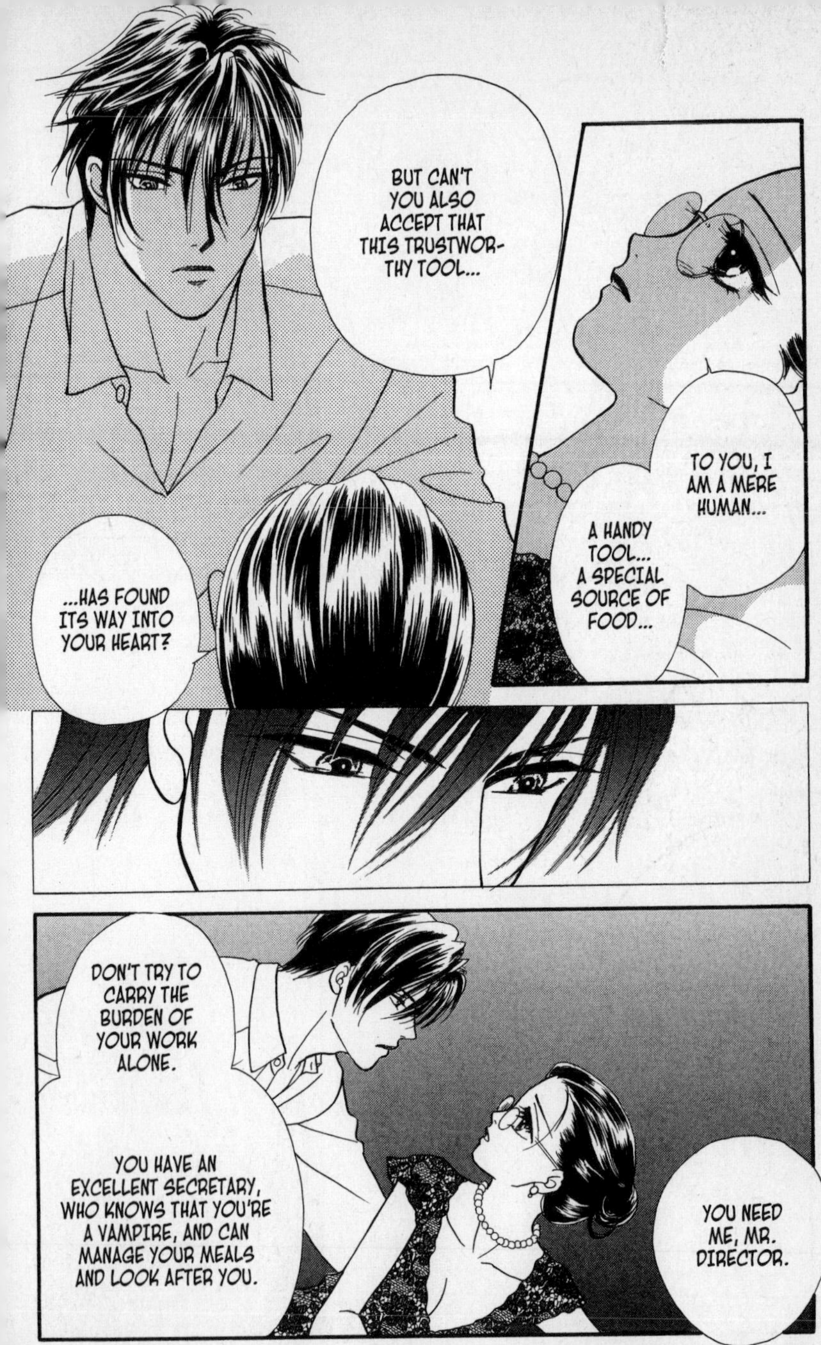
TO YOU, I AM A MERE HUMAN...
A HANDY TOOL... A SPECIAL SOURCE OF FOOD...
BUT CAN'T YOU ALSO ACCEPT THAT THIS TRUSTWORTHY TOOL...
...HAS FOUND ITS WAY INTO YOUR HEART?
DON'T TRY TO CARRY THE BURDEN OF YOUR WORK ALONE.
YOU HAVE AN EXCELLENT SECRETARY, WHO KNOWS THAT YOU'RE A VAMPIRE, AND CAN MANAGE YOUR MEALS AND LOOK AFTER YOU.
YOU NEED ME, MR. DIRECTOR.

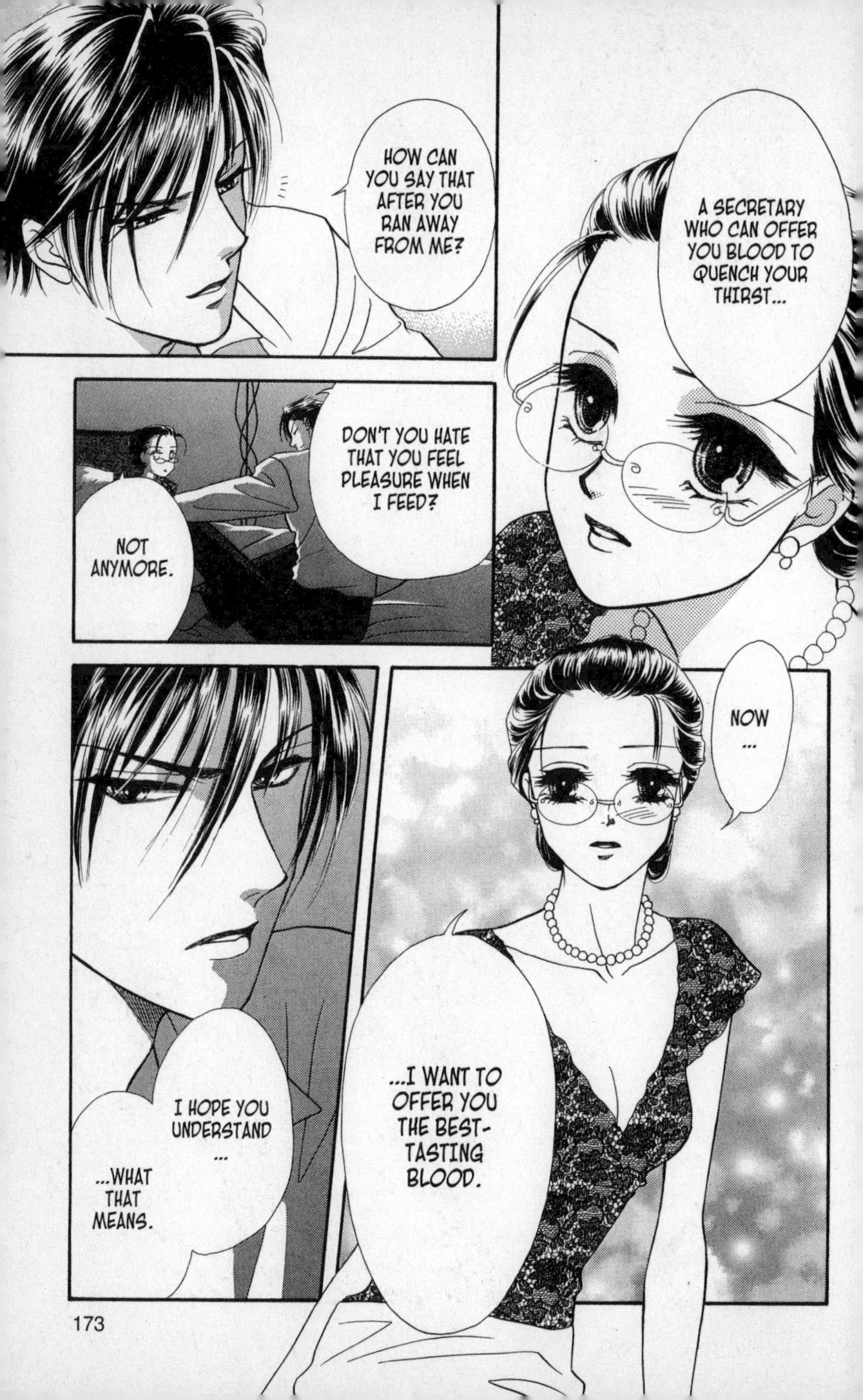
A SECRETARY WHO CAN OFFER YOU BLOOD TO QUENCH YOUR THIRST...
HOW CAN YOU SAY THAT AFTER YOU RAN AWAY FROM ME?
DON'T YOU HATE THAT YOU FEEL PLEASURE WHEN I FEED?
NOT ANYMORE.
NOW ...
...I WANT TO OFFER YOU THE BEST-TASTING BLOOD.
I HOPE YOU UNDERSTAND ...
...WHAT THAT MEANS.

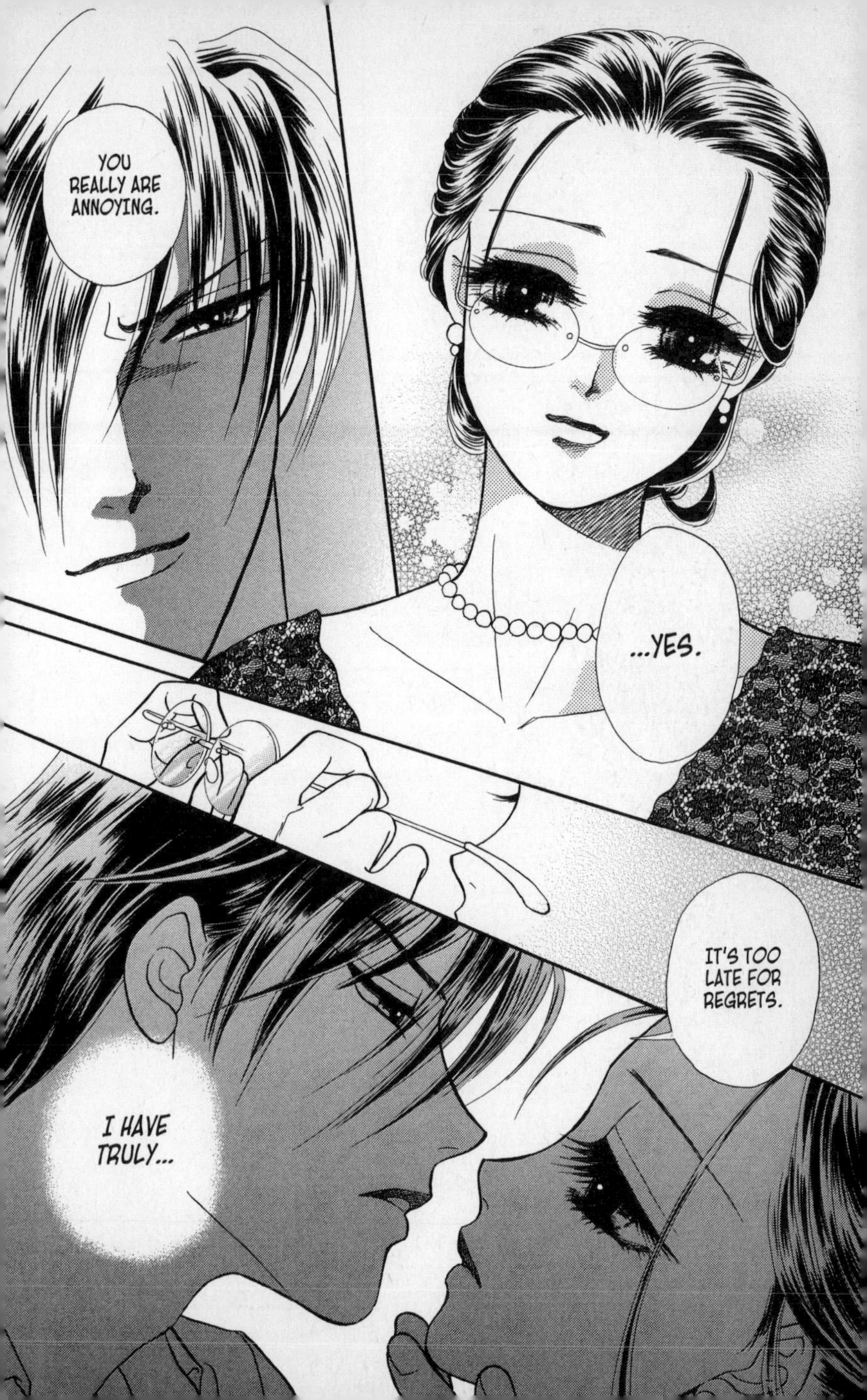
YOU REALLY ARE ANNOYING.
...YES.
IT'S TOO LATE FOR REGRETS.
I HAVE TRULY...

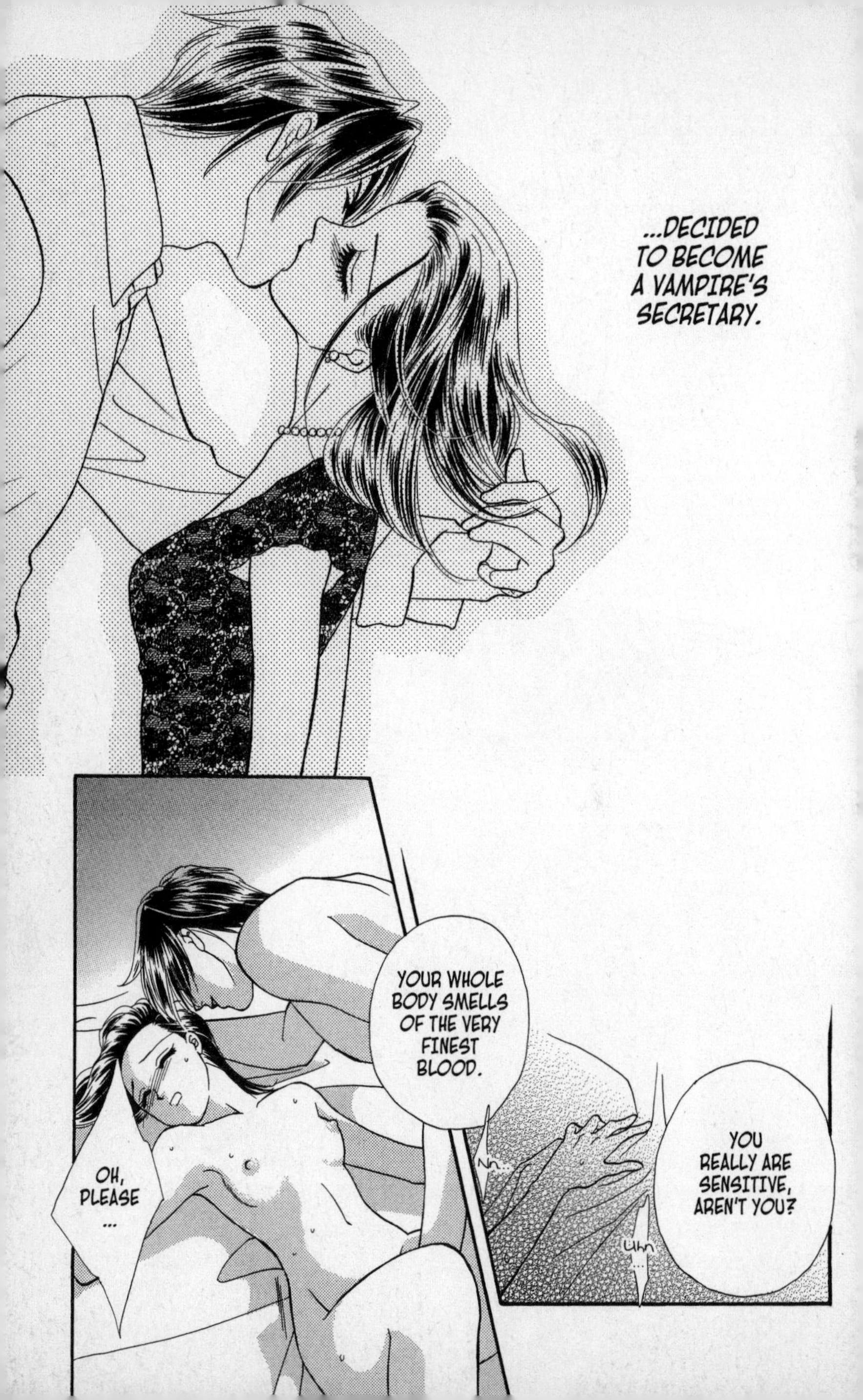
...DECIDED TO BECOME A VAMPIRE'S SECRETARY.
YOU REALLY ARE SENSITIVE, AREN'T YOU?
Nn...
Uhn...
YOUR WHOLE BODY SMELLS OF THE VERY FINEST BLOOD.
OH, PLEASE...

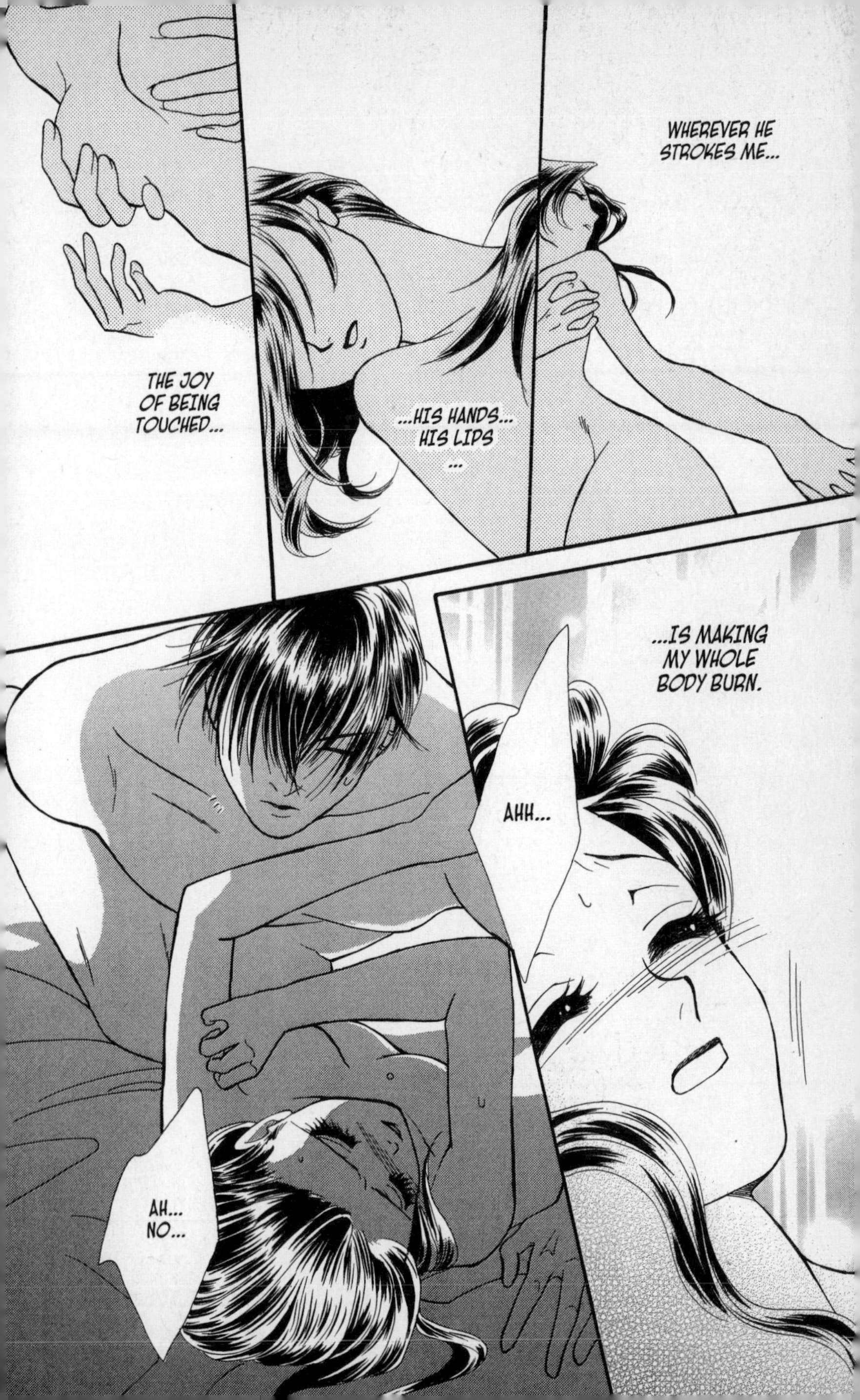
WHEREVER HE STROKES ME...
...HIS HANDS... HIS LIPS ...
THE JOY OF BEING TOUCHED...
...IS MAKING MY WHOLE BODY BURN.
AHH...
AH... NO...

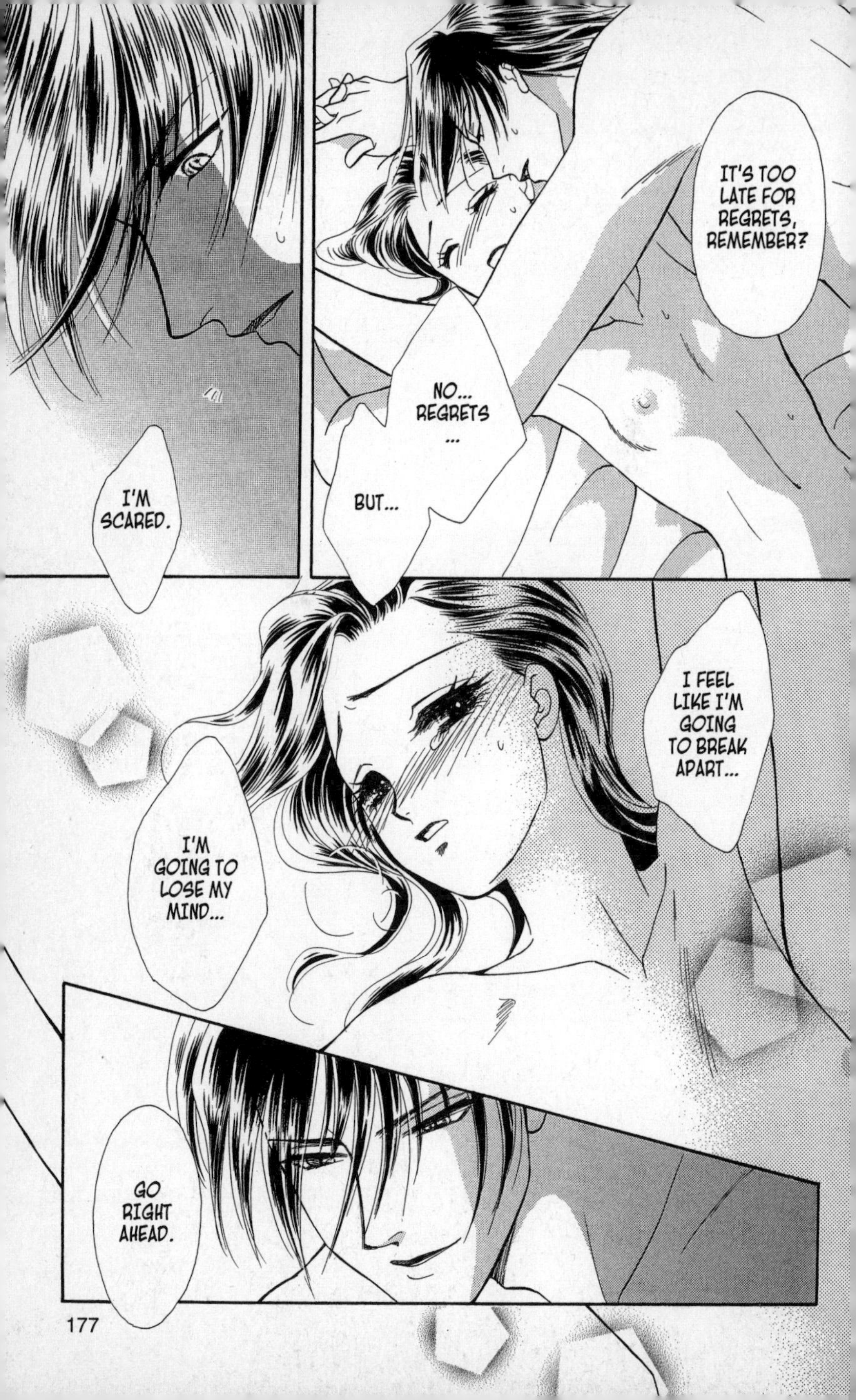
IT'S TOO LATE FOR REGRETS, REMEMBER?
NO... REGRETS ...
BUT...
I'M SCARED.
I FEEL LIKE I'M GOING TO BREAK APART...
I'M GOING TO LOSE MY MIND...
GO RIGHT AHEAD.

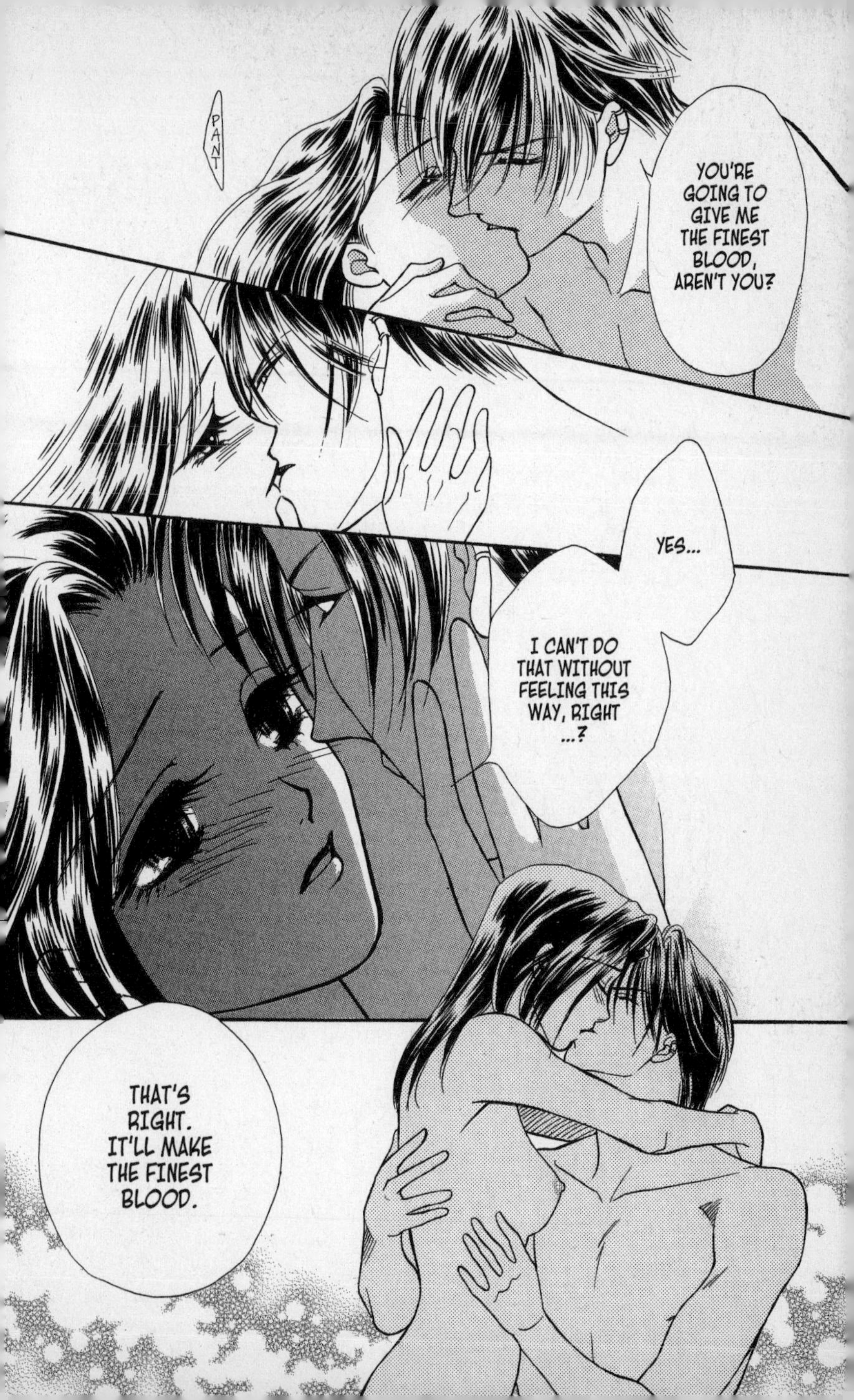
YOU'RE GOING TO GIVE ME THE FINEST BLOOD, AREN'T YOU?
PANT
YES...
I CAN'T DO THAT WITHOUT FEELING THIS WAY, RIGHT ...?
THAT'S RIGHT. IT'LL MAKE THE FINEST BLOOD.

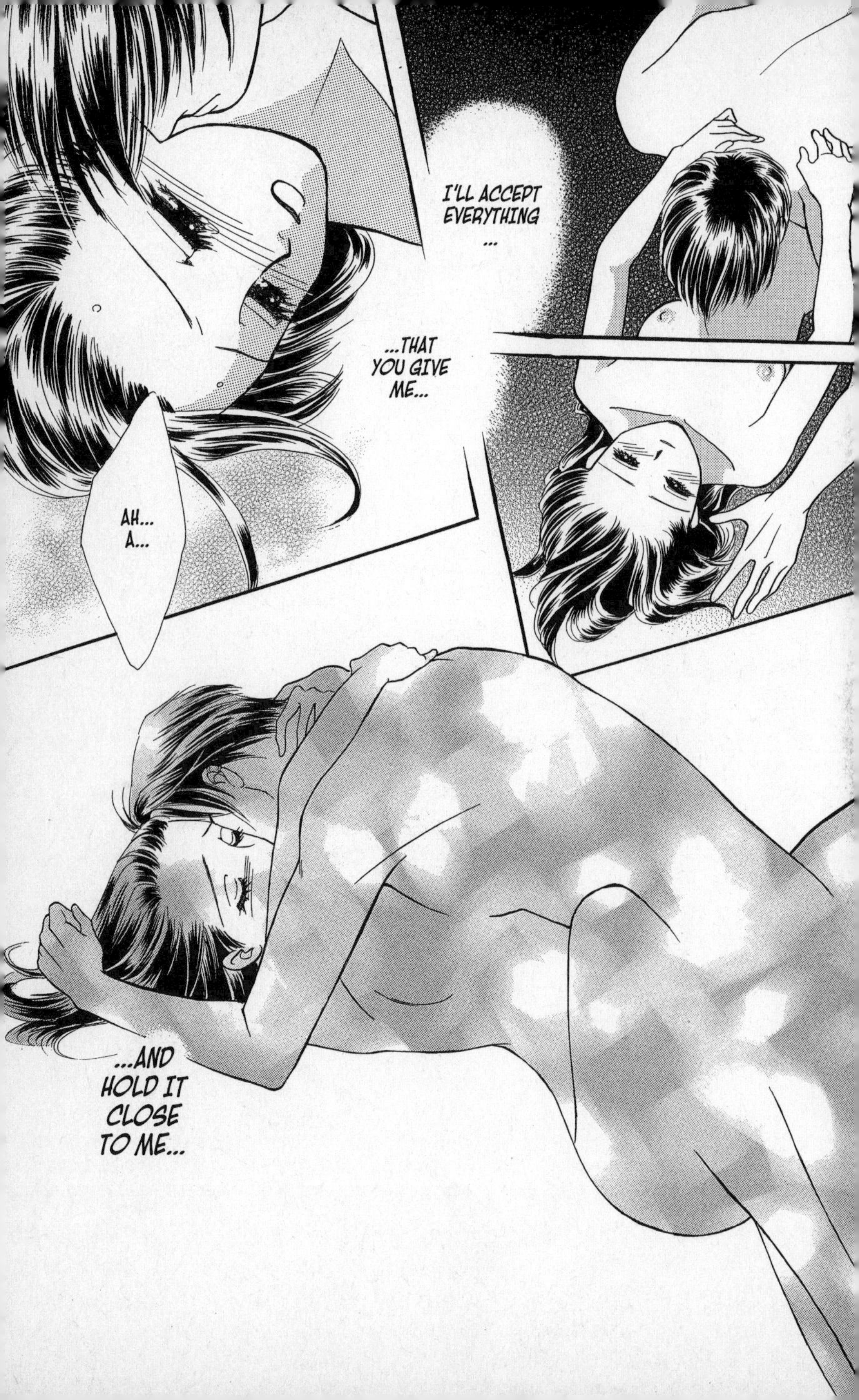
I'LL ACCEPT EVERYTHING ...
...THAT YOU GIVE ME...
AH... A...
...AND HOLD IT CLOSE TO ME...

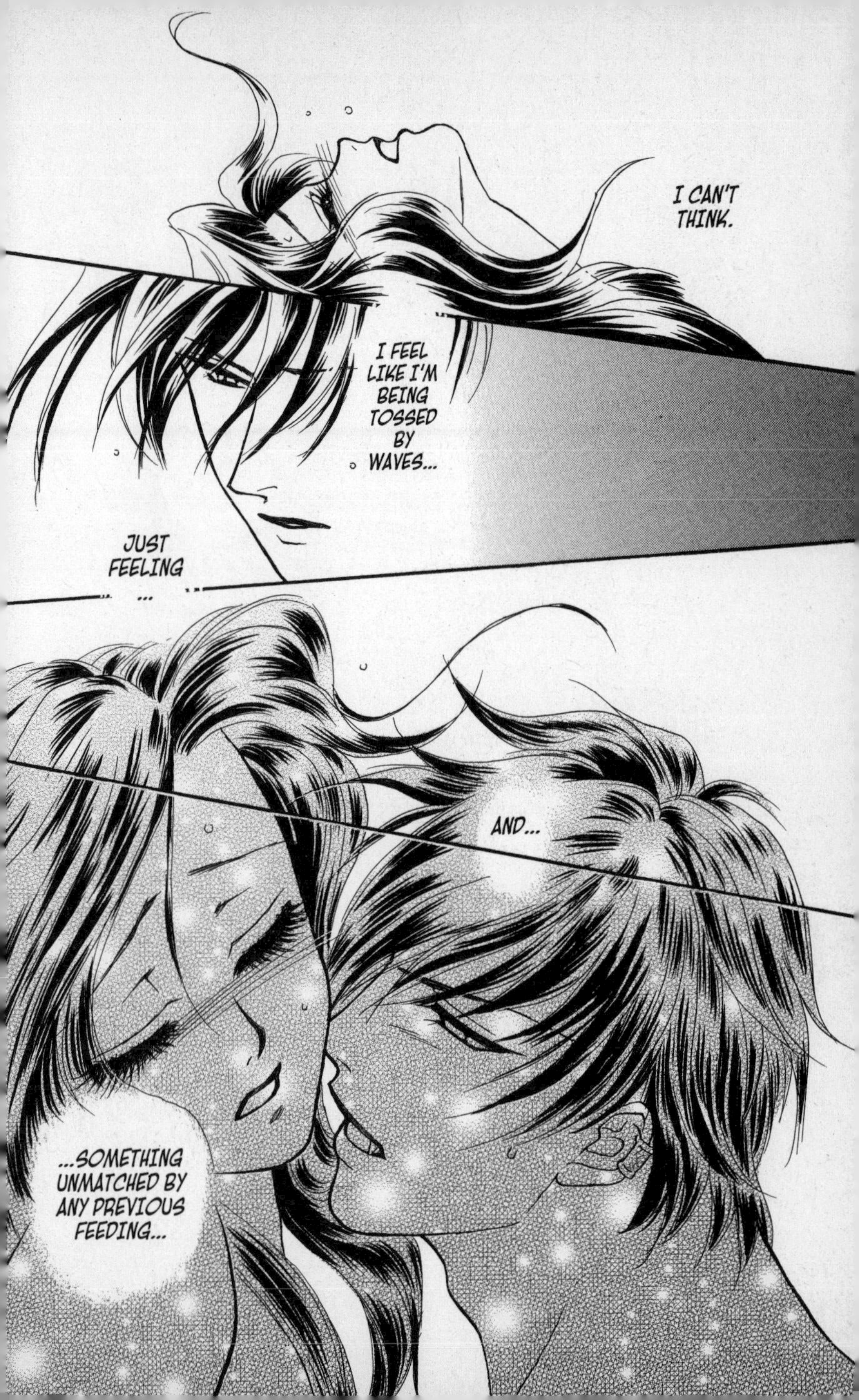
I CAN'T THINK.
I FEEL LIKE I'M BEING TOSSED BY WAVES...
JUST FEELING ...
AND...
...SOMETHING UNMATCHED BY ANY PREVIOUS FEEDING...

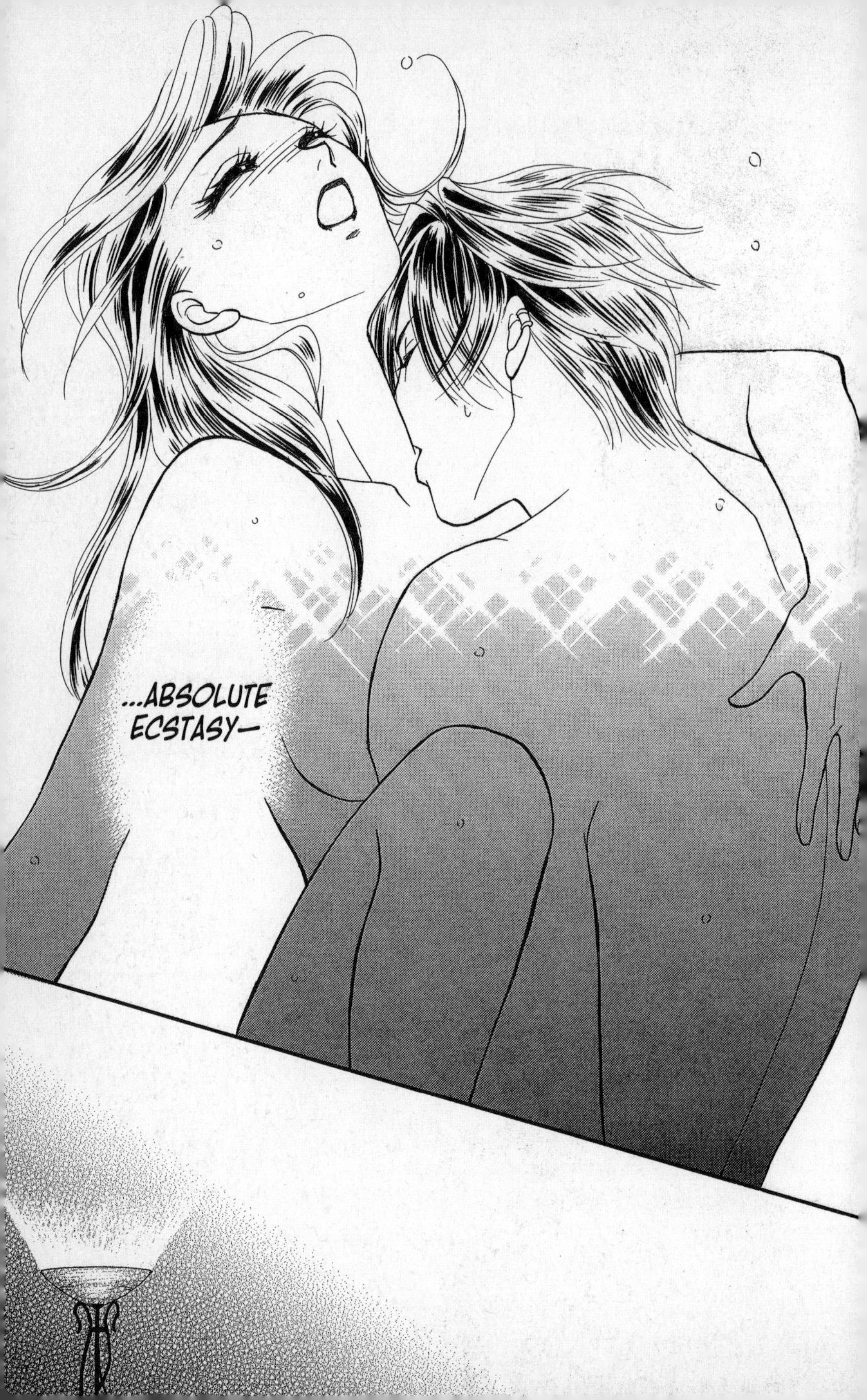
...ABSOLUTE ECSTASY—

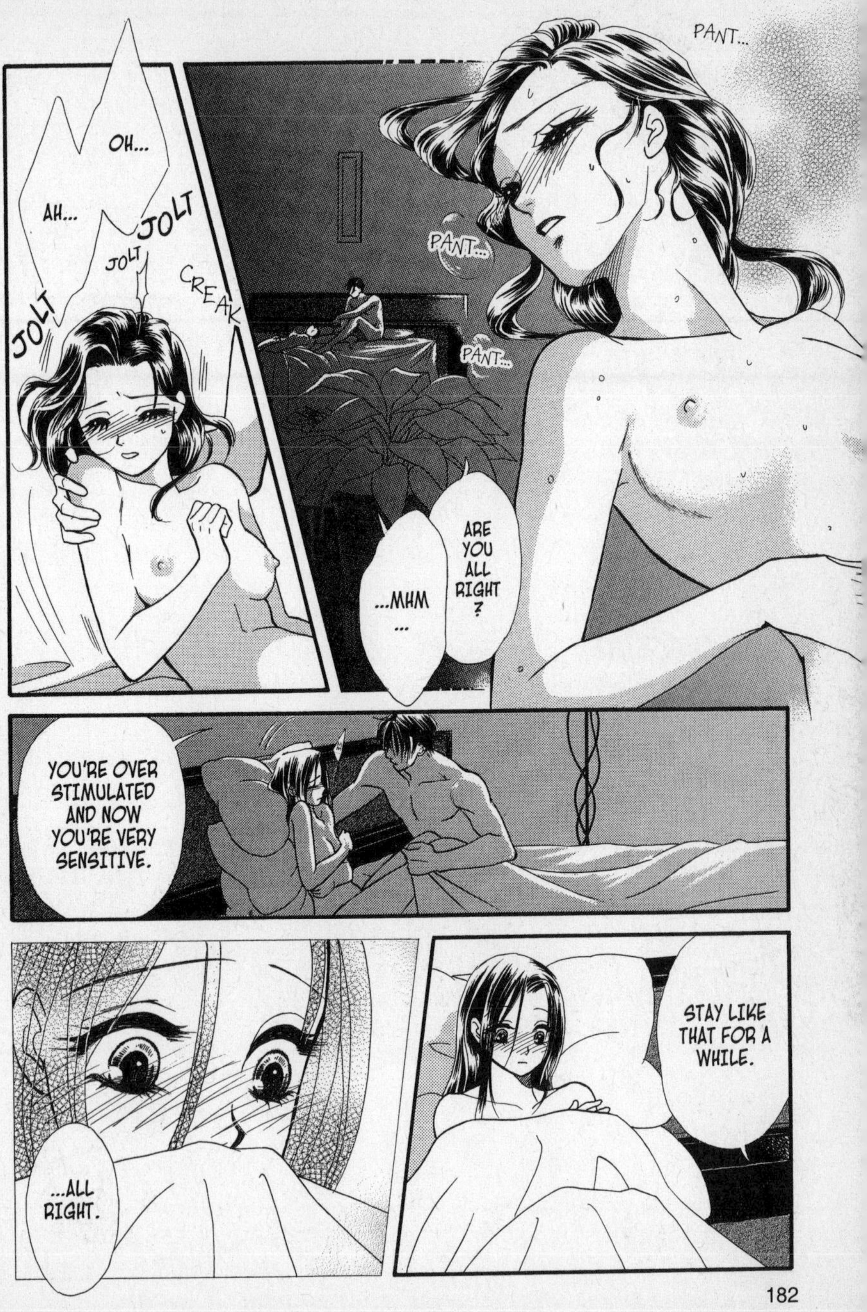
PANT...
PANT...
PANT...
ARE YOU ALL RIGHT?
...MHM ...
OH...
AH...
JOLT
JOLT
JOLT
CREAK
YOU'RE OVER STIMULATED AND NOW YOU'RE VERY SENSITIVE.
STAY LIKE THAT FOR A WHILE.
...ALL RIGHT.

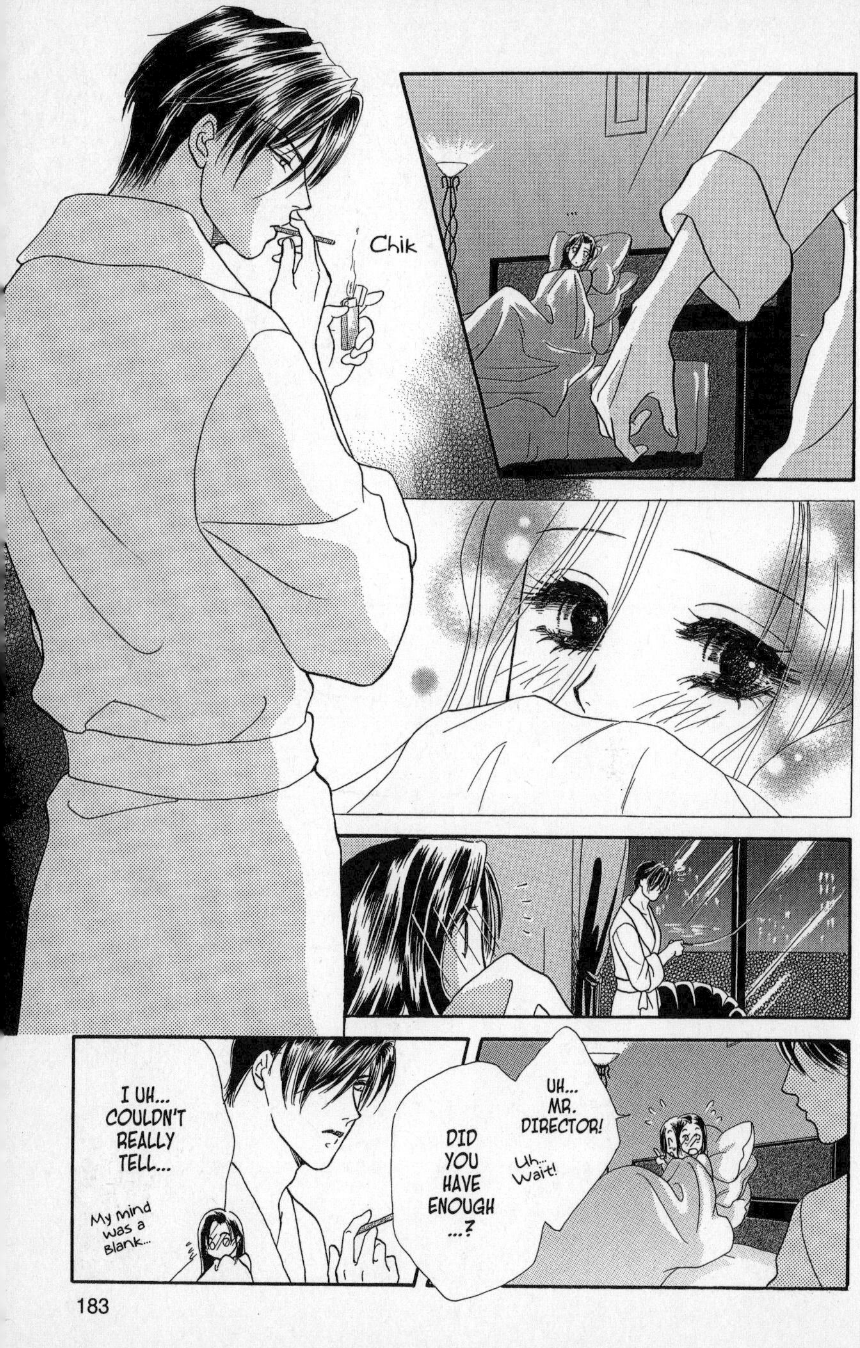
...
Chik
UH... MR. DIRECTOR!
Uh... Wait!
DID YOU HAVE ENOUGH ...?
I UH... COULDN'T REALLY TELL...
My mind was a Blank...

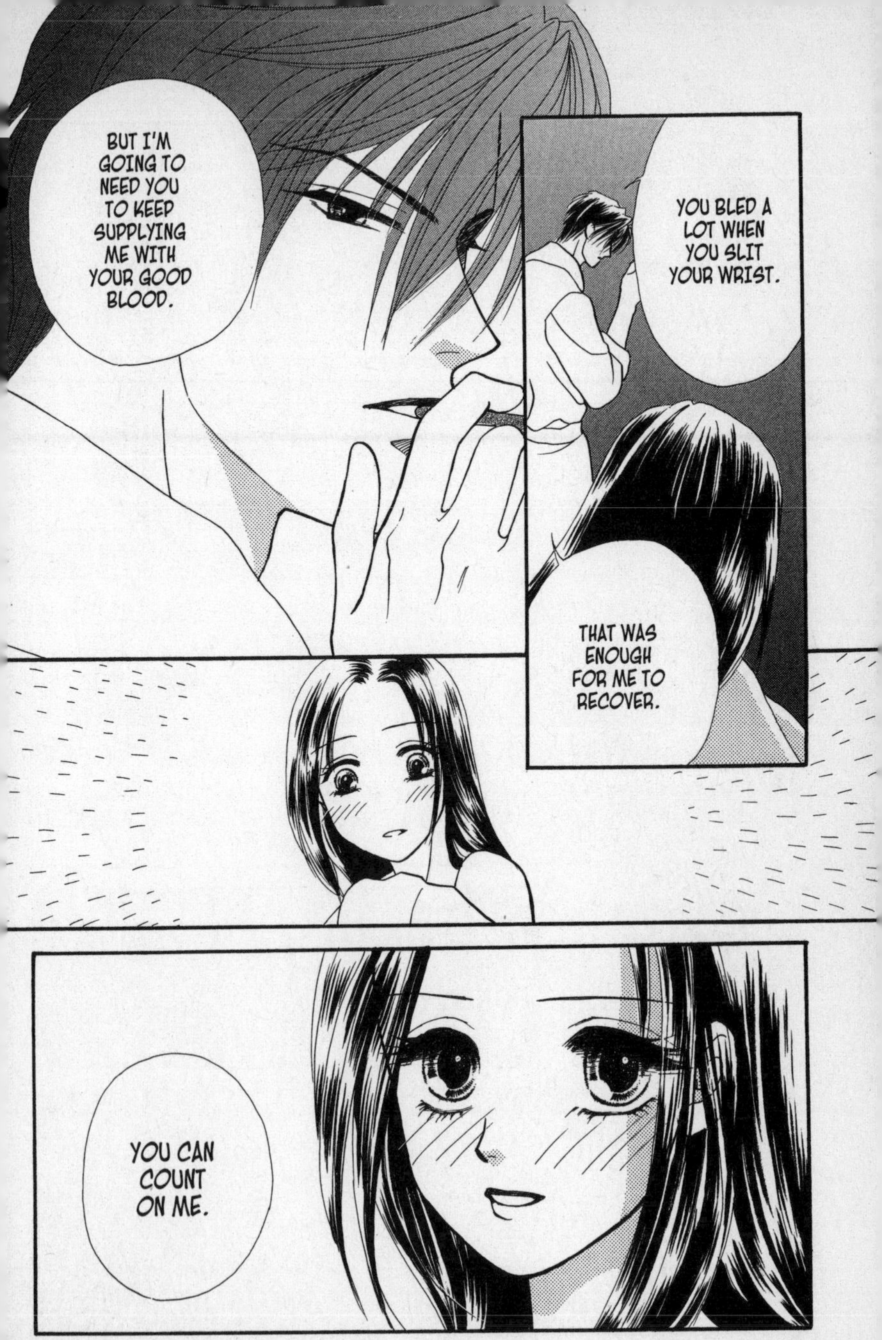
YOU BLED A LOT WHEN YOU SLIT YOUR WRIST.
THAT WAS ENOUGH FOR ME TO RECOVER.
BUT I'M GOING TO NEED YOU TO KEEP SUPPLYING ME WITH YOUR GOOD BLOOD.
YOU CAN COUNT ON ME.

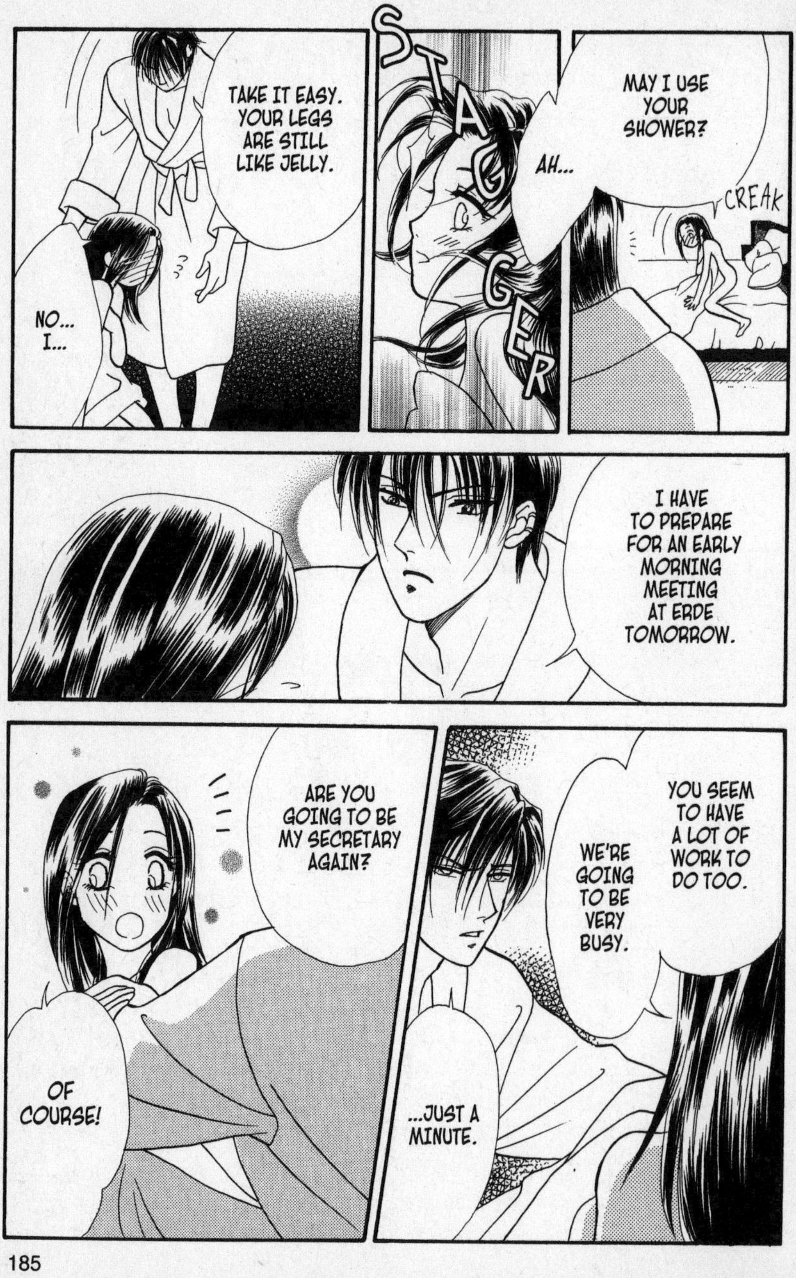
MAY I USE YOUR SHOWER?
AH...
CREAK
STAGGER
TAKE IT EASY. YOUR LEGS ARE STILL LIKE JELLY.
NO... I...
I HAVE TO PREPARE FOR AN EARLY MORNING MEETING AT ERDE TOMORROW.
YOU SEEM TO HAVE A LOT OF WORK TO DO TOO.
WE'RE GOING TO BE VERY BUSY.
...JUST A MINUTE.
ARE YOU GOING TO BE MY SECRETARY AGAIN?
OF COURSE!

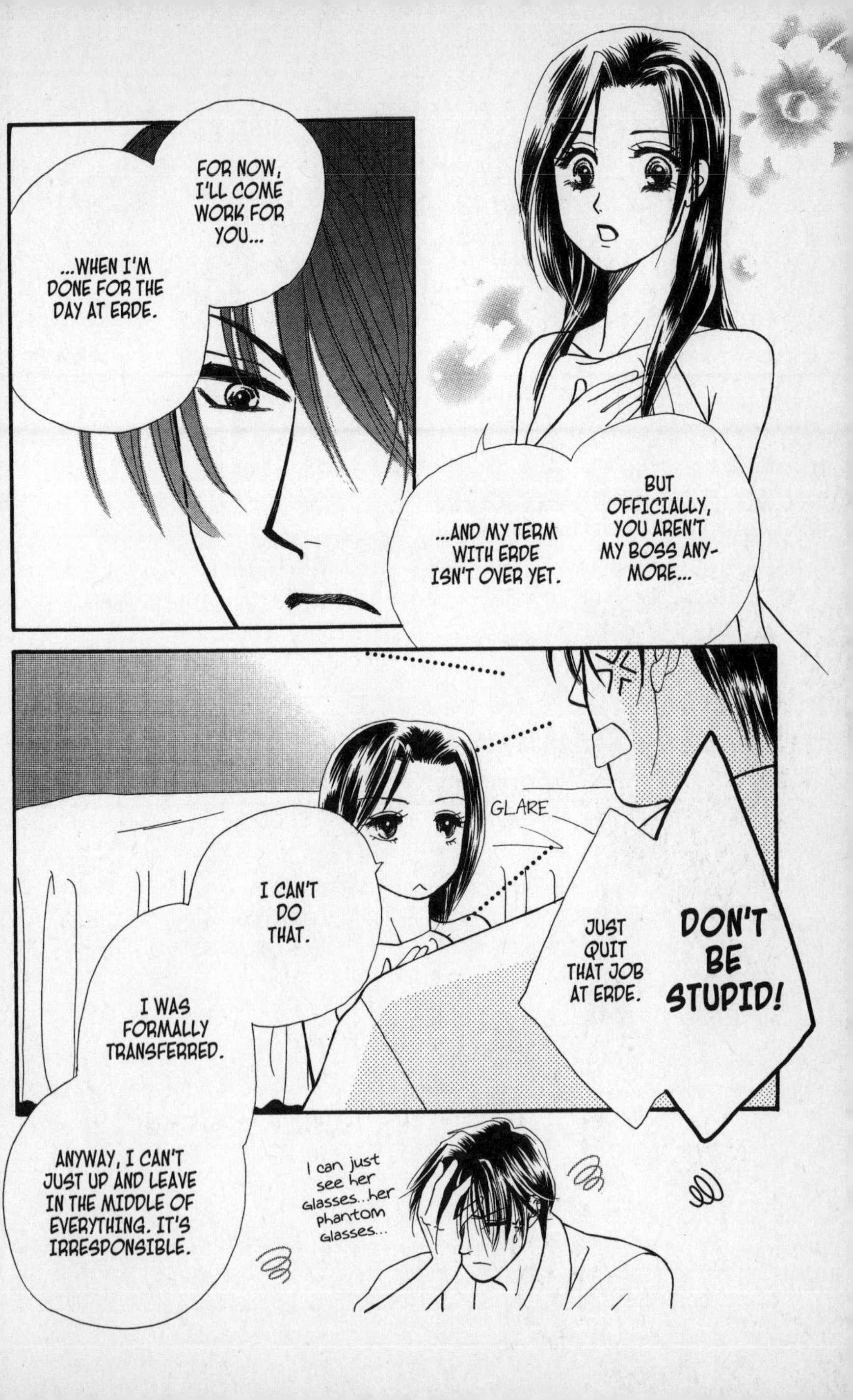

FOR NOW, I'LL COME WORK FOR YOU...
...WHEN I'M DONE FOR THE DAY AT ERDE.
BUT OFFICIALLY, YOU AREN'T MY BOSS ANY-MORE...
...AND MY TERM WITH ERDE ISN'T OVER YET.
DON'T BE STUPID!
JUST QUIT THAT JOB AT ERDE.
GLARE
I CAN'T DO THAT.
I WAS FORMALLY TRANSFERRED.
ANYWAY, I CAN'T JUST UP AND LEAVE IN THE MIDDLE OF EVERYTHING. IT'S IRRESPONSIBLE.
I can just see her glasses...her phantom glasses...

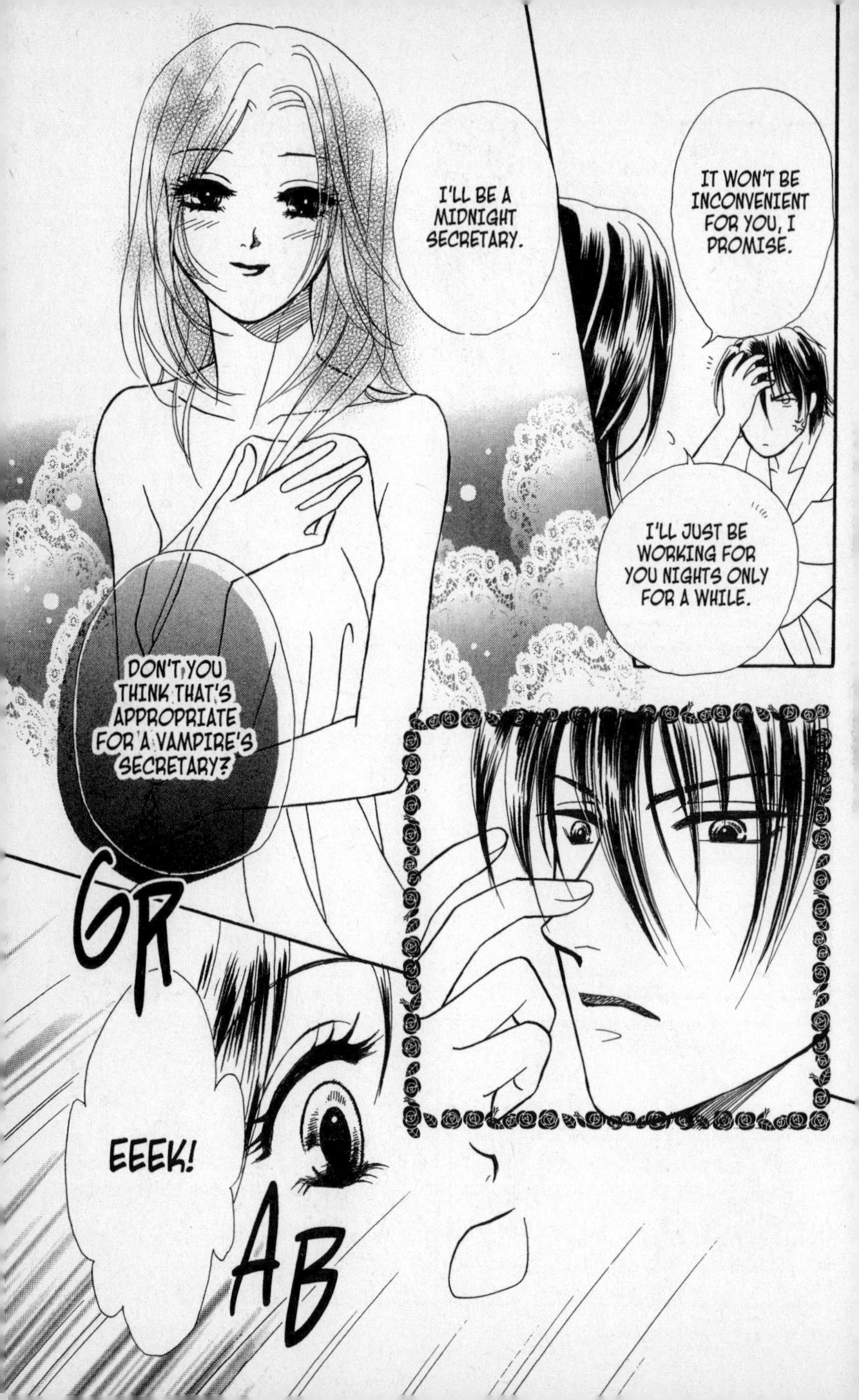
I'LL BE A MIDNIGHT SECRETARY.
IT WON'T BE INCONVENIENT FOR YOU, I PROMISE.
I'LL JUST BE WORKING FOR YOU NIGHTS ONLY FOR A WHILE.
DON'T YOU THINK THAT'S APPROPRIATE FOR A VAMPIRE'S SECRETARY?
GR
AB
EEEK!

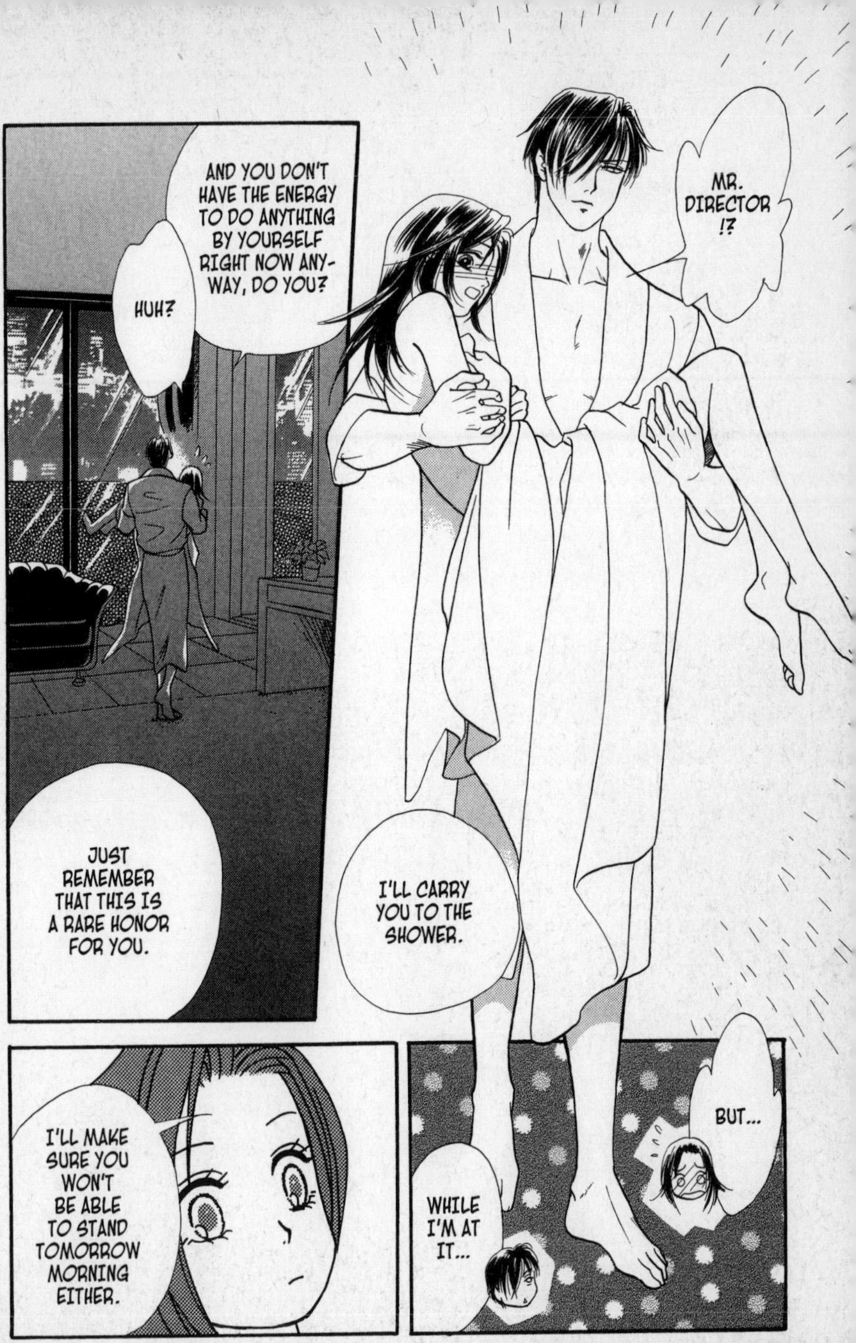
MR. DIRECTOR !?
I'LL CARRY YOU TO THE SHOWER.
AND YOU DON'T HAVE THE ENERGY TO DO ANYTHING BY YOURSELF RIGHT NOW ANY-WAY, DO YOU?
HUH?
JUST REMEMBER THAT THIS IS A RARE HONOR FOR YOU.
BUT...
WHILE I'M AT IT...
I'LL MAKE SURE YOU WON'T BE ABLE TO STAND TOMORROW MORNING EITHER.

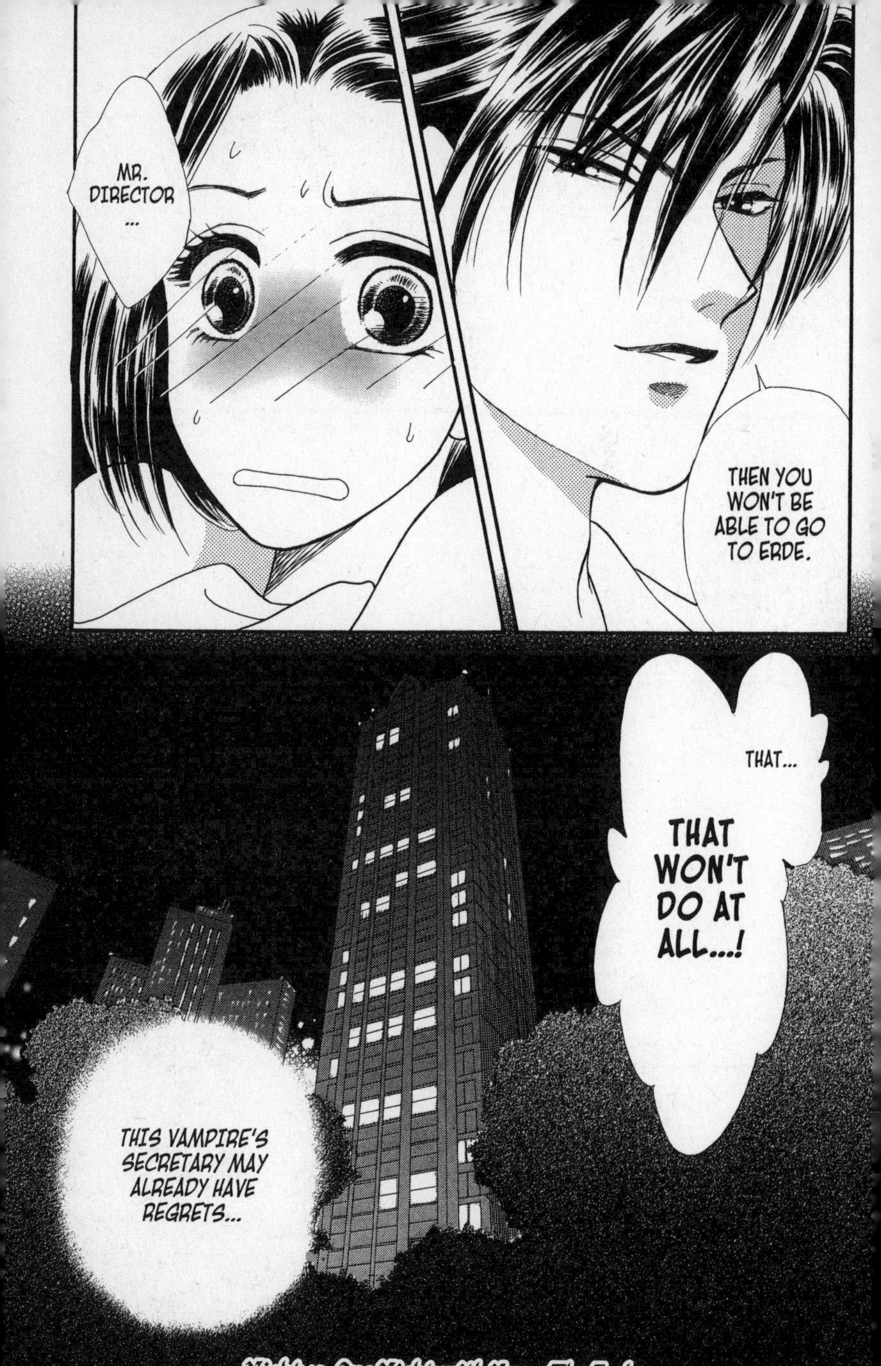
THEN YOU WON'T BE ABLE TO GO TO ERDE.
MR. DIRECTOR ...
THAT...
THAT WON'T DO AT ALL...!
THIS VAMPIRE'S SECRETARY MAY ALREADY HAVE REGRETS...

Night 10: One Night with You ~The End~

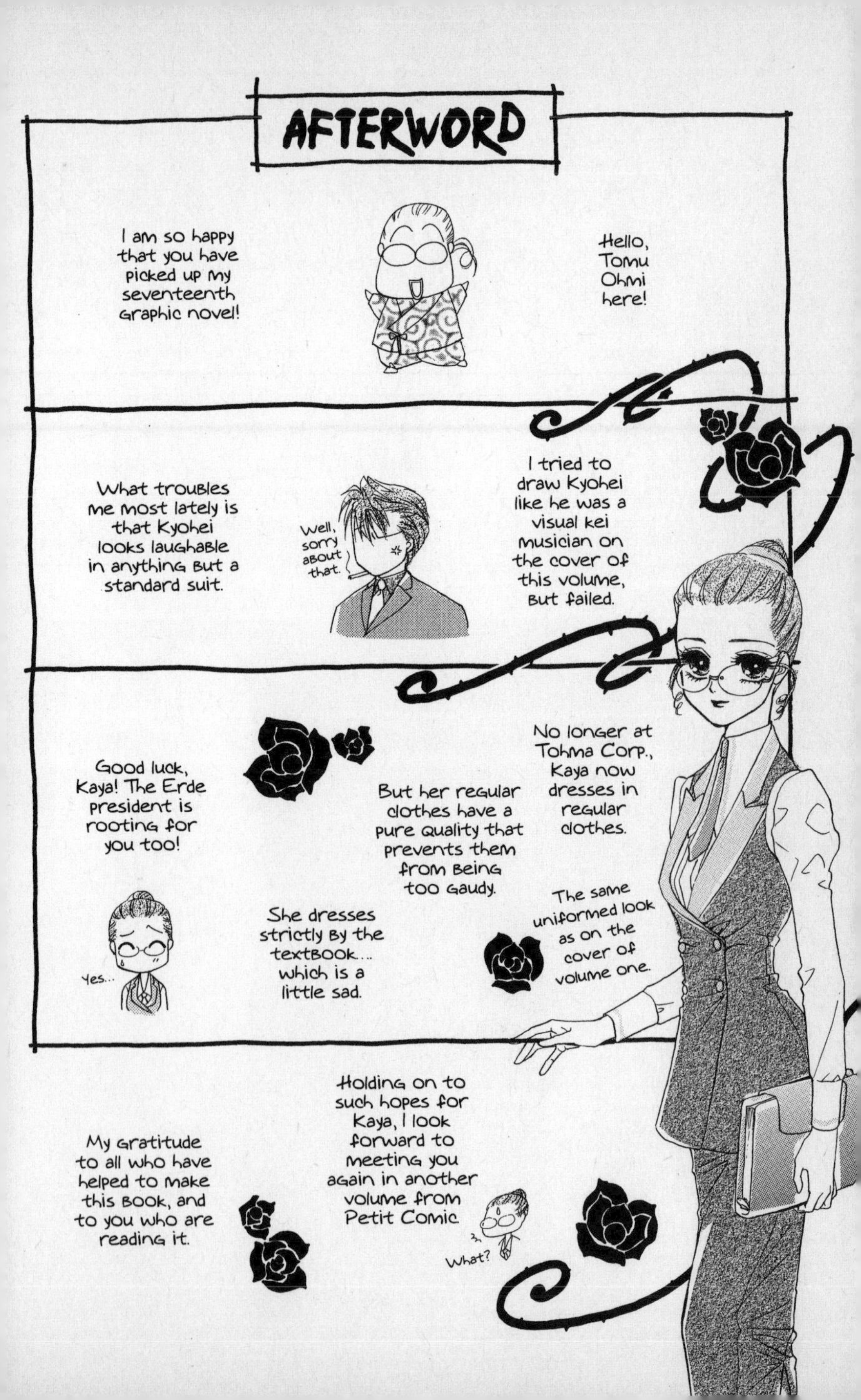
AFTERWORD
Hello, Tomu Ohmi here!
I am so happy that you have picked up my seventeenth graphic novel!
I tried to draw Kyohei like he was a visual kei musician on the cover of this volume, but failed.
Well, sorry about that.
What troubles me most lately is that Kyohei looks laughable in anything but a standard suit.
No longer at Tohma Corp., Kaya now dresses in regular clothes.
But her regular clothes have a pure quality that prevents them from being too gaudy.
The same uniformed look as on the cover of volume one.
She dresses strictly by the textbook... which is a little sad.
Good luck, Kaya! The Erde president is rooting for you too!
Yes...
Holding on to such hopes for Kaya, I look forward to meeting you again in another volume from Petit Comic.
What?
My gratitude to all who have helped to make this book, and to you who are reading it.

There are no Bats...
...in this story!

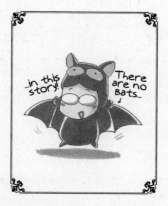

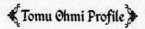

Tomu Ohmi Profile

Hurray! It's my 17th manga volume! Thank you for purchasing this copy! When I was asked to do a color illustration for this series, I chose purple as the main color to convey "the deep of night." Hence the purple in the cover for volume 1. I'm using red for volume 2 to convey "blood." I think it suits Kyohei perfectly.

-Tomu Ohmi

Midnight Secretary
Volume 2
Shojo Beat Edition

STORY AND ART BY
Tomu Ohmi

MIDNIGHT SECRETARY Vol. 2
by Tomu OHMI
© 2007 Tomu OHMI
All rights reserved.
Original Japanese edition published by SHOGAKUKAN.
English translation rights in the United States of America, Canada,
the United Kingdom and Ireland arranged with SHOGAKUKAN.

English Translation & Adaptation/JN Productions
Touch-up Art & Lettering/Joanna Estep
Design/Izumi Evers
Editor/Pancha Diaz

Printed in the U.S.A.

Published by VIZ Media, LLC
P.O. Box 77010
San Francisco, CA 94107

10 9 8 7 6 5 4 3 2 1
First printing, November 2013

www.viz.com   www.shojobeat.com

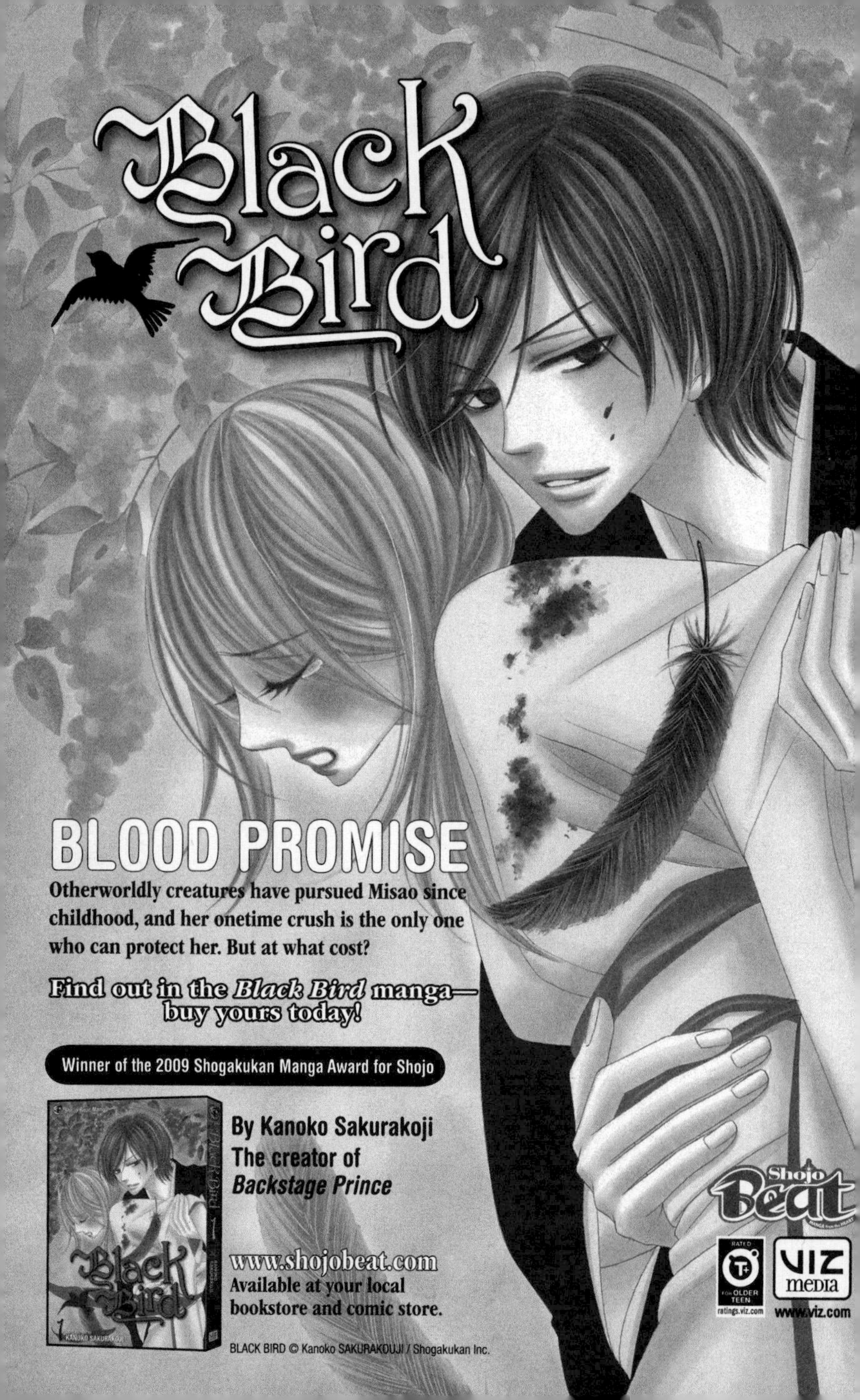
Black Bird
BLOOD PROMISE
Otherworldly creatures have pursued Misao since childhood, and her onetime crush is the only one who can protect her. But at what cost?
Find out in the Black Bird manga—buy yours today!
Winner of the 2009 Shogakukan Manga Award for Shojo
Black Bird
KANOKO SAKURAKOJI
By Kanoko Sakurakoji
The creator of
Backstage Prince
www.shojobeat.com
Available at your local bookstore and comic store.
BLACK BIRD © Kanoko SAKURAKOUJI / Shogakukan Inc.
Shojo Beat
RATED T+ FOR OLDER TEEN
ratings.viz.com
VIZ media
www.viz.com

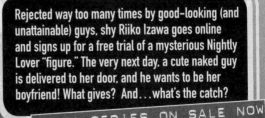

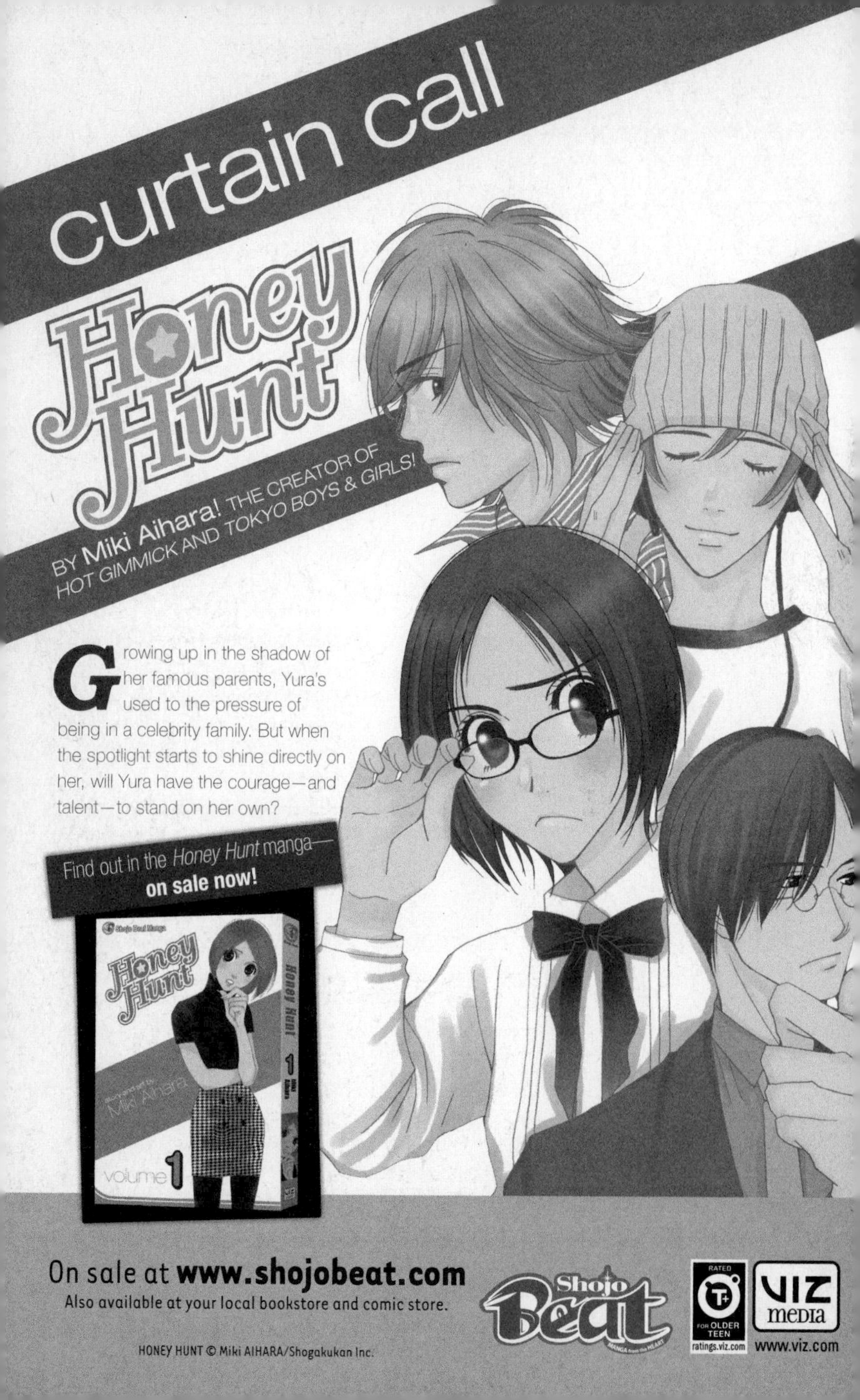
curtain call
Honey Hunt
BY Miki Aihara! THE CREATOR OF HOT GIMMICK AND TOKYO BOYS & GIRLS!
Growing up in the shadow of her famous parents, Yura's used to the pressure of being in a celebrity family. But when the spotlight starts to shine directly on her, will Yura have the courage—and talent—to stand on her own?
Find out in the Honey Hunt manga— on sale now!
Shojo Beat Manga
Honey Hunt
Story and art by Miki Aihara
volume 1
On sale at www.shojobeat.com
Also available at your local bookstore and comic store.
HONEY HUNT © Miki AIHARA/Shogakukan Inc.
Shojo Beat
RATED T+ FOR OLDER TEEN
ratings.viz.com
VIZ media
www.viz.com

Five Leaves

Complete Series Premium Edition

This beautiful box set features the complete two-volume, twelve-episode DVD set of the acclaimed anime series and features the original Japanese audio with English subtitles, as well as a sturdy slipcase and full-color hardcover art book.

House of Five Leaves Complete Series Premium Edition comes with a hardcover art book (full-color, 30+ pages), featuring character information, episode guides, artwork, behind-the-scenes storyboards, draft designs, concept art, and even a glossary of terms for insight on the culture of feudal Japan.

For more information, visit
NISAmerica.com

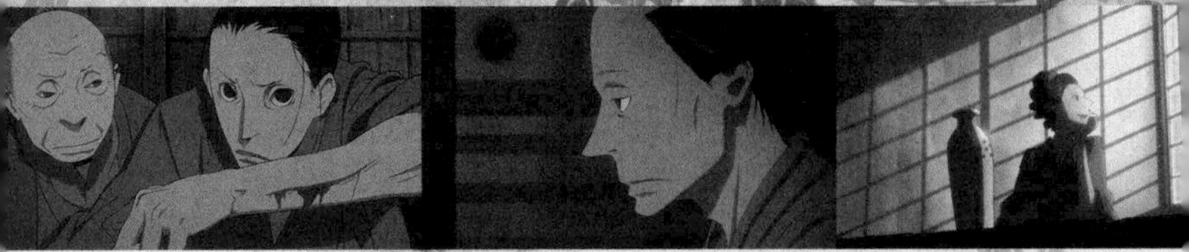

House of

from groundbreaking manga creator

Natsume Ono!

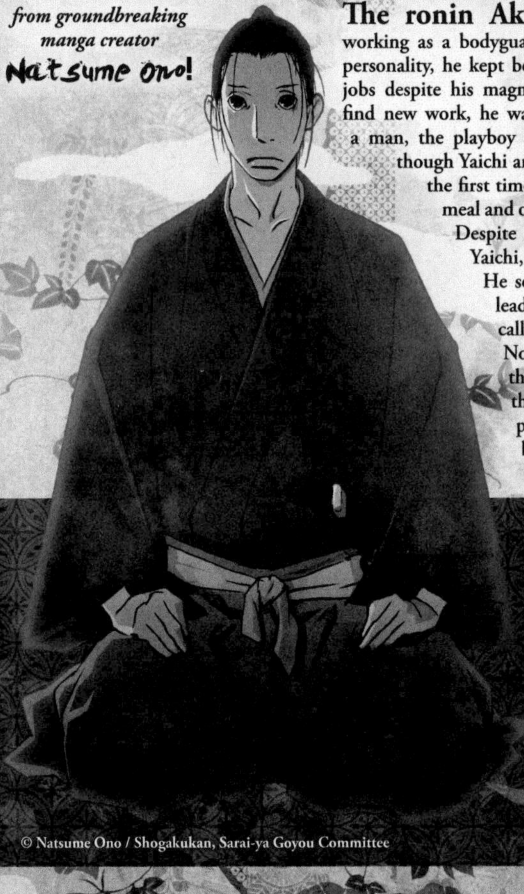

The ronin Akitsu Masanosuke was working as a bodyguard in Edo, but due to his shy personality, he kept being let go from his bodyguard jobs despite his magnificent sword skills. Unable to find new work, he wanders around town and meets a man, the playboy who calls himself Yaichi. Even though Yaichi and Masanosuke had just met for the first time, Yaichi treats Masanosuke to a meal and offers to hire him as a bodyguard. Despite the mysteries that surround Yaichi, Masanosuke takes the job. He soon finds out that Yaichi is the leader of a group of kidnappers who call themselves the "Five Leaves." Now Masanosuke is faced with the dilemma of whether to join the Five Leaves and share in the profits of kidnapping, or to resist becoming a criminal.

This is the last page.

In keeping with the original Japanese comic format, this book reads from right to left—so action, sound effects, and word-balloons are completely reversed. This preserves the orientation of the original artwork—plus, it's fun! Check out the diagram shown here to get the hang of things, and then turn to the other side of the book to get started!

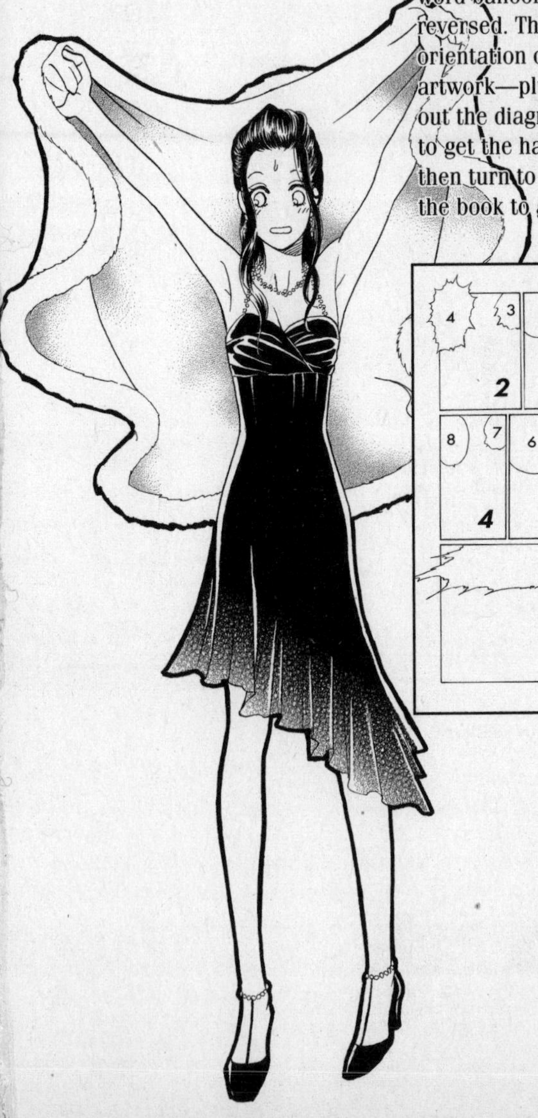

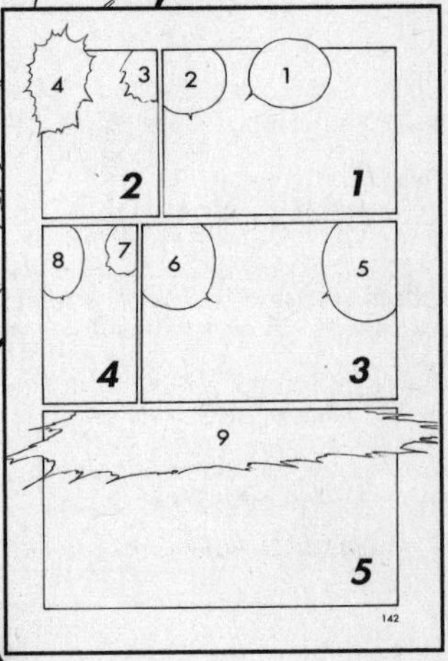
1
2
1
3
4
2
5
6
3
7
8
4
9
5
142